The Claire Macdonald Cookbook

Also by Claire Macdonald

Seasonal Cooking

Sweet Things

The Harrods Book of Entertaining

Delicious Fish

More Seasonal Cooking

Celebrations

Suppers

The Best of Food and Drink in Scotland

Lunches

The **Claire** **Macdonald**
COOKBOOK

BANTAM PRESS

LONDON · NEW YORK · TORONTO · SYDNEY · AUCKLAND

TRANSWORLD PUBLISHERS
61–63 Uxbridge Road, London W5 5SA
A division of the Random House Group Ltd

RANDOM HOUSE AUSTRALIA PTY LTD
20 Alfred Street, Milsons Point, NSW 2061, Australia

RANDOM HOUSE NEW ZEALAND
18 Poland Road, Glenfield, Auckland, New Zealand

RANDOM HOUSE SOUTH AFRICA (PTY) LTD
Endulini, 5a Jubilee Road, Parktown 2193, South Africa

Reprinted 1997, 1999, 2000

Copyright © Claire Macdonald 1997

Photography © Tim Hill 1997
Line Drawings © Fred van Deelen 1997
Home economy: Louise Burbidge/Stephen Wheeler
Styling: Zoë Hill

A catalogue record for this book is available
from the British Library.
ISBN 0593 042689

Typeset by Falcon Oast Graphic Art
Printed in Great Britain
by Mackays of Chatham, Chatham, Kent

For Gog, and Alexandra, Isabella, Meriel and Hugo too

Contents

Acknowledgements

I am indebted to several people for their invaluable help with this book. Top of the list must be my dearest friends Minty and Gavin Dallmeyer, and Rachel MacKinnon, our secretary here at Kinloch, who tries to keep Godfrey and me in order.

I am so very lucky in that Carol Smith is not only my agent but also a great friend and ally in fun. In fact, I so enjoy working with all with whom I come into contact at Transworld that I consider myself very lucky, too, in my publishers. Sally Gaminara is just terrific. Katrina Whone is clear-sighted and skilful and I am so grateful to her, and to Cathy Hopkins. I could go on mentioning endless names at Transworld, but suffice to say that I feel real affection as well as gratitude for and to all.

Here at home Godfrey, Alexandra, Isabella, Meriel and Hugo are both patient when I get into a flap and honest with experiments in recipes. As Godfrey said recently on a television programme, 'Claire doesn't often produce something really disgusting . . .' Peter Macpherson, with whom I have cooked now for more years than it would be prudent to calculate, and, too, Kath Stephenson, Claire Hanna, and Sharon MacInnes are all keen and enthusiastic when I have ideas, and also in keeping the show on the road here at Kinloch when I have to be away from home. Such peace of mind is without price.

Introduction

A surname like mine, Macdonald, can be a distinct drawback in any food-related work. Scottish history appears not to be taught at all south of the border, and instead of instant recognition and association with the greatest of the highland clans, the name is far more readily associated with the hamburger chain. I am not only called Macdonald, but I'm married to Godfrey, who is the High Chief of Clan Donald. Our home, here on the Isle of Skye, is also a small hotel. We live on a sea loch, at the foot of a small mountain at the end of a bumpy forestry track and our main road, over a mile away, is single track. So our lifestyle is a far cry from the more usual British existence.

I have written about food for seventeen years, both books – this is my thirteenth – and regular writing work for the *Herald* newspaper and the *Press and Journal*, and also for the *Field* magazine, as well as all sorts of other freelance work that comes my way. I am sure I couldn't write about food the way I do if I didn't cook. I have never been trained or done any kind of cookery course, but I have cooked here at the hotel ever since we began, twenty-four years ago. I have always thought that if you can read and are keen enough on eating, you will be able to cook.

When I was a child my family lived a fairly peripatetic life, moving every two years according to where my father, who was in the Navy, was posted. The period we spent living in Rome, when my father was Naval Attaché, was the most important time as far as my life is concerned. I was at a most impressionable age, thirteen to fifteen, and those years were to mark the beginning of my love of Italy. When I am asked about how I would describe my cooking style, I can only answer that I have always been geared to the seasons, and also to combining Italian foods and styles of cooking with Scottish.

It is only recently that people outside Scotland have come to realize, sometimes grudgingly, the excellence of Scottish foods. Quite simply, they are the best in the world. If you think I am over-reaching myself, stop for a moment and think of meat: the best beef in the world comes from our five main breeds, Aberdeen Angus, Highland, Galloway, Longhorn and Shorthorn. Lamb in Scotland tastes as it should, when you consider the food the sheep eat. Scottish game is the best in the world and is sought after by game dealers throughout Europe. Fish and shellfish are second to none. Scotland is surrounded by and crisscrossed with clean waters, whether sea or fresh. The huge refrigerated lorries bearing 'our' fish and shellfish to London and mainland Europe bear witness to this statement. In addition, Scottish cheeses made from cows', sheep's and goats' milks are of a consistently high standard, in some cases surpassing those made in France. And Scottish soft fruits taste better than those grown anywhere else – it must be our climate!

Getting hold of foods hasn't always been easy on Skye. Many's the time I have gnashed my teeth in rage on reading some cooking articles written by food writers who appear to forget that there are those, like me, who don't live within a stone's throw of Soho and don't have access to unusual or specialist ingredients. Anyone who follows my recipes will realize very quickly that I cook only with ingredients that are readily available. If I can buy something here in Skye then it must be available anywhere in the most rural areas of the British Isles! We are now very well provided for by my local food mecca, the Co-op in Broadford, our local town. But twenty-five years ago you couldn't buy a tomato in a tin in the Co-op. These days I can buy not only lemons but limes, fresh root ginger, three colours of pepper (I only ever eat two, red and yellow – I find green peppers awfully indigestible and so do most other people) and even mangoes. This reflects how our eating habits have changed, and my dear Co-op is only supplying demand.

Nowadays we are far more adventurous in what we eat, and far more aware of the importance to our health of what we eat. Over the years my recipes have changed, reflecting this change of eating style. And yet there are still occasions when traditional dishes are exactly what is right, when a steak and kidney pie or a steamed lemon and blackberry pudding, for instance, are the most comforting foods. And I feel that we should be aware of, and wary of, our guilt with eating, which tends to pervade our attitudes towards food. The word is moderation – a word I am so good at using, whether in speech at my many cooking demonstrations up and down the country, or in print, but which I am not so good at putting into practice!

This book contains many new recipes, and also my choice of recipes from my other books that I am always being asked to put between two covers. It has given me a chance to reassess what I have written over the years, adjusting recipes in certain cases. There is, as always, a definite seasonal bias in this book. I fear that there is a generation growing up today who are unaware that strawberries, for example, have a natural season in Britain because they can be bought twelve months of the year. Eating long-anticipated foods in season is a treat – like strawberries, or the first asparagus or rhubarb – and we are losing this. Just about everything can be imported from all over the world outside its natural growing season here in Britain, and I think this is appalling. And when it comes to nutrition, it stands to reason that food which has been picked halfway across the world and flown to our shops can't contain the nutrients of those fruits grown as close as possible to where they are eaten. As you can see, this is one of my hobby horses when it comes to food.

Another is pretension. I can't bear it when food is elevated out of all proportion to its importance – what I call worshipping at the shrine of gastronomy. The vital components for a good meal, whether lunch or dinner, are the very best ingredients, the right company, and a total lack of any desire to impress. Better by far a simple one-course meal with friends than the finest five-course repast in surroundings in which you feel uncomfortable, or where you are under pressure to 'enjoy' and analyse each sacred mouthful.

Mercifully, the days are just about gone when chefs denied salt and pepper to their guests. Taste is an individual and personal thing, and I make a point of saying, at demonstrations, that seasonings should be adjusted to suit the individual taste of the person making the dish. I deplore being told how and what I should like to eat. Only three days ago we had a French couple as guests in our hotel who openly sneered at other guests who were eating cheese following their pud, instead of before. We put out our cheeses and fruit on the sideboard each evening for our guests to help themselves when they like, before or after pud, because tastes are not the same, and there is no reason why they should be. We felt hotly indignant on behalf of those that evening who like their cheese last!

So my philosophy of food and eating is that when at all possible it should be made from foods in season; that you should cook it according to how *you* like to eat it; that it should be uncomplicated – and those of you who are familiar with my recipes will find every recipe in this book is easy to follow (I always maintain that if I can make up a recipe, anyone can); and also that anyone, anywhere, should be able to find all the ingredients listed. What I hope above all is that you will find the recipes in this book tempting, that you will feel you want to cook them, and, most importantly, that you enjoy the results!

A Note on Ingredients

CREAM. You will see that I use double cream in many of the recipes in this book. This is because its high fat content makes it more stable for all methods of cooking than creams containing less fat (double cream contains 48% fat, whipping 35% and single 18%). Double cream thickens as it bubbles, with no risk of splitting or curdling. I wouldn't recommend that you substitute yoghurt, fromage frais or crème fraîche where these are not already specified in the recipe. They are unlikely to give the dish the desired consistency, and the level of acidity is often unsuitable for the overall effect and taste of the recipe.

Cream freezes very well when whipped or incorporated in a dish, but it does not freeze well in the carton.

FLOUR. Throughout the book I have specified when a recipe requires self-raising flour. If the recipe states only 'flour' you can assume that no raising agent is needed and that you can use plain flour.

I am sure that breadmakers will know the importance of using *strong* plain flour for bread and rolls; strong plain flour has a higher gluten content than plain flour, and this gives bread a much better texture. But there is one better still: Double O, referred to on the packet as OO, which contains an even higher gluten content than strong plain. I buy this from my invaluable Italian delicatessens and great friends Yalvona and Crolla, in Edinburgh.

GELATINE. I usually give quantities of gelatine in terms of the powdered version, which comes in ½ oz/14 g packets, but if you prefer to use leaf gelatine you can substitute four leaves for ½ oz/14 g. This quantity is sufficient to set 1 pint of liquid.

A word of warning: if the weather is particularly warm, and if you are going to turn out what you have made, I advise you to increase the gelatine content. In hot weather a gelatine-set mousse or jelly very quickly 'relaxes' – or melts. Equally, left for any length of time in the fridge, gelatine toughens. It is as well to take a mousse out of the fridge and into room temperature for half an hour before serving it.

A vegetarian equivalent – made from caragheen, a seaweed – is to be found in all health food shops. It gives a slightly different set, rather thicker than the non-vegetarian version.

HERBS. Now that fresh herbs are so widely available in greengrocers and supermarkets (that is if you don't grow your own), I use them almost all of the time, and the quantities stated in this book are for the fresh variety. Dried herbs taste like old lawn cuttings – I think that the only herbs that dry satisfactorily are the woody ones, thyme and rosemary. The fleshy ones don't dry at all well.

PASTRY. The only kind of pastry I make is shortcrust. I once made puff pastry, following the recipe to the letter, but it was a disaster and I've never tried again because I can buy extremely good ready-made puff pastry fresh (I use Bell's, made in Scotland). It is also possible to buy ready-rolled puff pastry.

I don't even think about making filo pastry because the bought kind is so good. The Jus Rol version comes in smaller sheets than other makes and is easier to handle, but my favourite brand is King James.

STOCK CUBES. Although I would rather use home-made stock than bought cubes, I would be a liar if I said that I don't keep stock cubes. Of course I do – but I buy those that contain no additives. The chief additive to avoid is monosodium glutamate, which lends an identical taste to the different kinds of stock cube, whatever its flavour is meant to be, and gives the stock a syrupy texture. You can find additive-free stock cubes in health food shops and delicatessens, and some supermarkets.

First Courses

The first course of a meal, whether lunch or dinner, sets the tone for what is to follow. It is vital to plan a menu with several points in mind, and probably the most important of these is the balance of richness in the various courses. For the gastric comfort of your family and/or friends, it really does matter not to include cream in each course, but to balance out the three (or four) courses by having a fairly light first course if you plan a rich and creamy pud. On the other hand, you can have a rich first course if your pud is to consist of a light and fruity dish.

Egg- and cheese-based first courses may be safe food when you are uncertain whether all your guests eat meat, for example, but they are usually fairly filling eating. Deep-fried Cheese Beignets, for instance, while being utterly delicious, need a light main course and a fruity pud to follow. And a soufflé, wonderful food that all soufflés are (and convenient – see the recipes!), is filling too.

As well as the balance between the richness of each course, it is necessary to consider their colour and texture contrasts. For example, it wouldn't be ideal, far from it, to choose a tomato and basil mousse for a first course and then to have a fruity mousse, such as a lemon mousse, for a pud. They are too similar in texture. But you could choose a salady first course, either something cold such as the Quails' Eggs, Artichoke Hearts and Smoked Salmon Salad on page 66 or, if the weather is very cold, the Warm Chicken Liver Salad on page 61. There are many other salads suitable for a first course in the main Salads chapter. And the added bonus of a salad-based first course is that it is supposed to get the digestive juices working!

The weather is another important point to consider when planning a menu. In cold weather it is very comforting to have a hot first course, for which there are plenty of ideas in this chapter, especially in the soups section. But conversely, on a warm evening a light and refreshing chilled soup can be just the thing.

Although you will find my main suggestions for first courses in this chapter, their accompaniments are often listed in later chapters. For instance, any of the breads, or the Fresh Herb Scones, are good with soups and salads, and very often a sauce can complement the main item in a first course. In the Sauces chapter there are a large number of savoury sauces to tempt by both taste and appearance. To go back to the Cheese Beignets, I always serve a tomatoey sauce with them. It tastes good with the beignets, its colour enhances their pale gold, and its smoothness contrasts well with their crispness.

Despite the fact that this chapter is entitled 'First Courses', many of the recipes can easily be adapted as a light main course for lunch or supper. And there are many potential first courses to be found in other chapters throughout this book. Be guided by inclination, as well as the season, the weather and the balance – these are all things I try to consider when planning daily menus for our guests here at Kinloch! But then, my role is easier than yours. We always have two first courses on the menu here, one fish-based, the other non-fishy. And soup is a separate course, so I can indulge myself daily when choosing what follows.

I think the hardest thing of all is to make a decision, and it seems to be more difficult to plan what to put on a menu than to choose what to eat off it!

Soups

Asparagus Soup

Avocado Soup with Prawns and Yoghurt

Beetroot Soup with Crème Fraîche

Carrot, Leek and Lentil Soup

Celery and Apple Soup

Chicken and Prune Soup

Chilled Courgette and Rosemary Soup

Chilled Lime and Watercress Soup

Chunky Root Vegetable Soup

Courgette and Fennel Soup

Courgette and Mint Soup

Creamy Roast Red Pepper Soup

Cucumber and Dill Soup

Fish and Vegetable Chowder

Game Soup

Ham and Bean Soup

Jerusalem Artichoke Soup

Julienne of Root Vegetables Soup

Leek and Bacon Soup

Leek, Mushroom and Madeira Soup

Leek and Potato Soup

Leek and Smoked Haddock Chowder

Leek and Tomato Soup

Mint, Pea and Lettuce Soup

Parsnip, Lemon and Ginger Soup

Pea, Apple and Mint Soup

Pheasant and Mushroom Soup

Red Onion Soup with Balsamic Vinegar and Goats' Cheese Croûtons

Smoked Haddock Soup

Spicy Tomato Soup with Avocado Cream

Spinach, Tomato and Garlic Soup

Asparagus Soup

I love to take advantage of asparagus when it comes into the shops, and luckily the season appears to lengthen each year. As with all soups, its strength rests entirely on the stock from which it is made. I like to chop off the heads of the asparagus and steam them, then serve them in the soup – somehow it seems such a waste to cook and liquidize them along with the rest of the soup.

Serves 8

2 oz/56 g butter

2 medium onions, skinned and chopped

1 lb/450 g asparagus, heads removed and set aside, stalks chopped

2 pints/1.1 litre good chicken stock

Salt and freshly ground black pepper

A squeeze of lemon juice (optional)

Melt the butter and add the chopped onions to the butter in a saucepan. Cook for about 5 minutes, stirring occasionally. Then add the chopped asparagus stalks, and cook for a further few minutes before pouring on the stock. Half-cover the pan with a lid, and simmer gently until the pieces of stalk are tender when you stick the point of a knife in one. Meanwhile, steam the heads of the asparagus. Cool the soup a bit, then liquidize it and pour it into a bowl if you intend to keep it in the fridge, or into a clean saucepan if it is for reheating.

Serve the soup with the steamed asparagus heads stirred through it and seasoned to your taste with salt and pepper. Add a squeeze of lemon juice if you like.

Avocado Soup with Prawns and Yoghurt

This is a pretty looking and delicious tasting summer soup. The chopped prawn garnish is optional – substitute chopped chives if you prefer. I suggest using yoghurt or sour cream to swirl on top of the soup; the more figure conscious can do as I do and use yoghurt.

Serves 6–8

2 oz/56 g butter

1 onion, skinned and chopped

½ green pepper, de-seeded and chopped

1½ pints/850 ml chicken stock

2 avocados

Juice of half a lemon

Salt and freshly ground black pepper

5 fl oz/140 ml natural yoghurt

4 oz/112 g cooked shelled prawns, chopped, or a handful of chopped chives

Melt the butter in a saucepan. Add the chopped onion and pepper and cook over a gentle heat for about 10 minutes, until the onion is transparent and both the onion and pepper are soft. Pour on the chicken stock, bring to the boil, then draw the saucepan off the heat, and leave to cool.

Skin the avocados, remove the stones, and chop half the flesh into a blender. Pour on half the onion, pepper and chicken stock and blend until smooth. Pour into a bowl. Then blend the remaining avocado flesh and chicken stock mixture, and pour into the bowl. Stir in the lemon juice, and salt and black pepper to taste. Put the bowl into the refrigerator to chill the soup until you are ready to serve.

Divide the soup between chilled soup plates, and on top of each plateful put a dessertspoon of yoghurt, with a few chopped prawns in the middle of the yoghurt. Or instead of the prawns, add some chopped chives to the yoghurt.

Beetroot Soup with Crème Fraîche

We don't eat nearly enough beetroot. Such a delicious root vegetable deserves far more attention than it gets. This is such a simple soup, yet spectacular in its appearance. Raw beetroot is as good as cooked.

Serves 6

5 beetroots – each about the size of a cricket ball

1 tub of full fat crème fraîche (10.6 oz/300 g)

2 oz/56 g butter

1 fairly large or 2 smaller onions, skinned and chopped

½ teaspoon good horseradish – that made by Moniack is the best

1½ pints/850 ml good chicken stock

Salt and freshly ground black pepper

Juice of ½ lemon

Peel all the beetroots and chop four of them. Grate the remaining beetroot, not too coarsely, and mix it into the crème fraîche. Set on one side – this is for the garnish, which is, at the same time, an integral part of the soup.

Melt the butter in a saucepan and sauté the chopped onion in the butter for several

minutes, until it is soft and just beginning to turn transparent and golden at the edges. Stir in the chopped beetroot and cook for a minute or two in the butter. Stir in the horseradish and stock, and bring the liquid to simmering point. Simmer gently, the pan half covered with its lid, till the pieces of beetroot are soft when you stick a fork into one. Cool the soup a bit, then liquidize till smooth. Taste, and season with salt, pepper and lemon juice.

Reheat gently, and ladle into soup plates. Spoon a generous teaspoon of the grated beetroot and crème fraîche into the centre of each.

Carrot, Leek and Lentil Soup

This is one of my favourite soups. It is very substantial, and it is ideal for a chilly evening. Again, it is only as good as the stock it is made with.

Serves 8

2 oz/56 g butter or 3 tbsp oil (I use sunflower)

2 medium onions, skinned and chopped

2 carrots, peeled and chopped

3 leeks, washed, trimmed and sliced

4 oz/112 g orange lentils

2 pints/1.1 litres good chicken stock

Salt and freshly ground black pepper

2 tbsp finely chopped parsley

Melt the butter in a saucepan. Add the chopped onions and, over a moderate heat, cook for about 5 minutes, stirring occasionally, then add the chopped carrots and sliced leeks. Cook for a further 5 minutes or so, then stir in the lentils and the chicken stock. Season, then half-cover the pan with a lid and simmer the soup for 35–40 minutes. Liquidize, and sieve into a clean saucepan.

When ready to eat reheat the soup, stirring the chopped parsley through just before serving, to prevent the herb losing its bright fresh green colour.

Celery and Apple Soup

The flavours of celery and apple combine well. The curry is optional. The soup has the advantage of being thickened only by the apples and so it is good but satisfying for those who, if not exactly slimming, are trying to economize here and there on their calorie intake.

Serves 8

2 oz/56 g butter or margarine

2 large onions, skinned and chopped

3 medium to large cooking apples, peeled, cored and chopped

3 eating apples, cored and chopped, but with the skin left on

6 sticks of celery, chopped into 1-inch/2.5-cm pieces

1–2 garlic cloves, skinned and chopped

3 rounded tsp curry powder (optional), or more if you love curry

2½ pints/1.4 litres chicken or vegetable stock

1 tbsp lemon juice

Salt and freshly ground black pepper

1 rounded tsp sugar (optional)

Melt the butter or margarine in a large saucepan and add the chopped onions. Cook gently until the onions are soft and transparent. Add the chopped apples and celery, garlic and curry powder and cook for a further few minutes, stirring from time to time.

Pour in the stock and the lemon juice. Cover with a tightly fitting lid, and simmer very gently for about 45 minutes. Remove from the heat and cool. Purée in a blender and sieve to remove the stringy bits from the celery. Season to taste with salt, pepper and sugar if you wish (saccharine if you seriously are calorie counting), and either freeze, or reheat to serve.

Chicken and Prune Soup

To anyone familiar with the traditional Scots soup Cock a' Leekie, this soup won't sound at all strange with its combination of chicken and prunes. I love it, and it's one of those soups which come into the meal-in-one-soup category. It's very filling and substantial, yet not calorie-laden – the rare and perfect dish! It has to be made a day before it is to be eaten.

Serves 6–8

1 chicken weighing approximately 3½ lb/1.6 kg

6 leeks (more if they are particularly small)

3 medium onions, skinned and thinly sliced

2 celery sticks, thinly sliced

6 carrots, peeled and thinly sliced

18 large prunes

2 pints/1.1 litres chicken stock

3 oz/84 g rice

Salt and freshly ground black pepper

Chopped parsley (optional)

Put the chicken in a large saucepan or a casserole which has a lid. Pack the vegetables and prunes all round the chicken and pour the chicken stock over. Cover and cook in a moderate oven – 350°F/180°C/Gas Mark 4 – for 1–1½ hours, or until the juices from a chicken thigh run clear when pierced with the point of a sharp knife. If you prefer, the cooking can be done on top of the stove, with the stock gently simmering. Remove the pan or casserole from the heat. Leave to cool completely.

Take the chicken out of the vegetables and stock, and separate all the flesh from the carcass. Cut the chicken into smallish (½-inch/1-cm) pieces and put on one side. You can stone the prunes at this point if you wish – I do. Skim any fat off the top of the cold stock, add the rice to the vegetables in the stock, and reheat. Cover the saucepan and cook until the rice is tender. Return the chicken meat to the soup and allow to reheat.

Taste and season before serving. Sprinkle each plateful with chopped parsley if you like, and tell your guests to beware of the stones in the prunes unless you have already removed them. Use the carcass to make more delicious chicken stock for the future.

Chilled Courgette and Rosemary Soup

If you have a glut of courgettes, which can happen if you grow your own, this is a quick and simple soup flavoured with rosemary which will use some up. I usually serve it cold, but if the weather should happen to be foul it is equally good served hot.

Serves 6–8

2 oz/56 g butter

2 medium onions, skinned and chopped

1½ lb/675 g courgettes, wiped, with their ends trimmed off and sliced

1 garlic clove, skinned and chopped (optional)

2 tsp fresh rosemary leaves

2 pints/1.1 litres chicken stock

Salt and freshly ground black pepper

5 fl oz/140 ml natural yoghurt, to garnish

2 tbsp chopped chives, to garnish

Melt the butter in a saucepan and add the chopped onions, sauté for about 5 minutes, stirring occasionally, then add the sliced courgettes. Cook for a further 5 minutes, then add the garlic (if you are using it), rosemary, chicken stock, salt and pepper. Simmer for about 25 minutes. Allow to cool a little. Liquidize and, for an extra smooth soup, sieve the liquidized soup into a bowl.

Chill thoroughly in the refrigerator for several hours. Swirl a spoonful of yoghurt into each plateful, sprinkle some chopped chives over the yoghurt and serve. This soup is a boon to calorie counters (of whom I'm one) – it really is very low in the dreaded calories.

Chilled Lime and Watercress Soup

Although this is just a variation of the more usual lemon and watercress soup, the end result is quite different because limes have such a distinctive flavour. If you are serving it on a cold evening, just heat it up – it loses nothing by being served hot rather than chilled, and your guests will prefer a warming dish if the weather does turn inclement! On a proper fine summer's day, this is a convenient first course for a dinner or lunch party, which can be made a day or two ahead and kept in the refrigerator. As with all soups, it will only be as good as the stock it is made with – sorry to sound so schoolmarmy, but it is so true.

Serves 6–8

2 oz/56 g butter
2 medium onions, skinned and chopped
2 medium potatoes, peeled and chopped
2 pints/1.1 litres chicken or vegetable stock
Finely pared rind of 1 lime
Salt and freshly ground black pepper
Freshly grated nutmeg
3 good handfuls of watercress
Juice of 2 limes
1 lime, thinly sliced, for garnish

Melt the butter in a saucepan and add the onions. Sauté for 5 minutes or so, stirring occasionally, until the onion is soft and transparent. Add the potatoes, and cook for a further 5 minutes, stirring occasionally to prevent them sticking. Pour in the stock, add the pared lime rind and season with salt, pepper and nutmeg. Cover the pan and simmer the soup very gently for 20 minutes, or until the potato pieces are soft. Draw the pan off the heat, and allow to cool. Liquidize the soup together with the watercress, and pour into a bowl. Stir in the lime juice and put the bowl into the refrigerator to chill the soup thoroughly.

Float a slice of lime in each plateful to serve. The watercress gives the soup a beautiful bright green colour because it hasn't been cooked. If you do heat the soup to serve it, the green colour will dull a little but it will still taste very good.

Chunky Root Vegetable Soup

This soup is actually even nicer if made a day ahead and reheated.

Serves 8

4 medium beetroots (3 if one's a whopper)
2 carrots
2 parsnips
2 medium potatoes
4 tbsp oil (I use sunflower)
2 medium onions, skinned and sliced thinly
2 pints/1.1 litres good chicken or vegetable stock
Salt and freshly ground black pepper
Chopped parsley, for garnish (optional)

Peel the beetroots and slice them into thick short strips – about 1 inch/2.5 cm in size. Peel the carrots, parsnips and potatoes, and cut them in roughly the same sized pieces as the beetroot.

Heat the oil in a large saucepan and add the onions. Cook for about 5 minutes, stirring occasionally to prevent them from burning, then add the rest of the vegetables to the saucepan. Cook for a further 5 minutes, then pour in the stock – and remember, any soup will only be as good as the stock it is made from. (I have a personal crusade against stock cubes!) Season to taste with salt and freshly ground black pepper.

Simmer gently, with the pan half-covered with a lid, for 40–45 minutes, till the vegetables are tender when you stick a knife into one – try the carrot, as it will need more cooking than any of the others. Take the pan off the heat, cool the soup completely, pour it into a bowl and keep it in a cool place till the next day.

Reheat to serve, and, if you like, sprinkle some chopped parsley over the surface of each serving. Serve this hearty soup with warm brown rolls or bread, and cheese and fruit to follow, for a simple lunch.

Courgette and Fennel Soup

This is another soup which is equally good served hot or chilled. I find the slightly aniseed flavour from the fennel combines well with the courgettes. I love warm bread with this soup, particularly the Granary Bread on page 368.

Serves 8

2 oz/ 56 g butter

2 medium onions, skinned and chopped

1 lb/450 g courgettes, trimmed and cut in

1-inch/2.5-cm chunks

2 heads of fennel, chopped

2 pints/1.1 litres good chicken stock (do try and use the Real Thing; water and a stock cube just doesn't give the same result at all)

Salt and freshly ground black pepper

Lemon juice

Melt the butter and add the chopped onions. Cook for about 5 minutes, till the onions are soft and transparent looking. Add the chopped courgettes and the fennel, and pour on the stock. Half-cover the pan with a lid, and simmer for about 30 minutes. Then liquidize and sieve the soup.

Season with salt and pepper, and lemon juice to your taste, and either reheat to serve, or serve chilled.

Courgette and Mint Soup

This soup is equally good served hot or cold. Courgettes are so useful as a soup base – and the mint in this recipe enhances their flavour. This is delicious with the Fresh Herb Scones on page 373.

Serves 6

2 oz/56 g butter

2 medium onions, skinned and chopped

2 lb/900 g courgettes, with the ends cut off, chopped in chunks

2 pints/1.1 litres chicken stock

2 handfuls of mint leaves, preferably applemint

Salt and freshly ground black pepper

Melt the butter in a saucepan and add the chopped onions. Cook over a gentle heat for about 10 minutes, until the onions are soft and transparent. Add the chopped courgettes and cook for another 5 minutes. Then pour on the chicken stock and add a handful of mint leaves. Cover the saucepan, and simmer for 30 minutes. Cool. Then purée the contents of the pan in a blender together with the remaining handful of mint leaves.

Taste and season with a little salt and black pepper before serving.

Creamy Roast Red Pepper Soup

This soup is delicious served hot or chilled. It isn't a very thick soup – I loathe using flour to thicken a soup – but it is intense in its flavour. Roasting vegetables gives such a depth of taste, and how I love it! The colour of this soup is particularly attractive. Black Olive, Sun-Dried Tomato and Garlic Bread (see page 368) is ideal as an accompaniment for this soup.

Serves 6

3 tbsp olive oil

2 onions, skinned and chopped

6 red peppers

2 garlic cloves, skinned and chopped

2 tbsp olive oil – for roasting the peppers and garlic

1½–2 pints/850 ml–1.1 litres good chicken or vegetable stock

Salt and freshly ground black pepper

A squeeze of lemon juice

2 tbsp crème fraîche, to garnish

Heat the oil in a saucepan and cook the chopped onions for 5–7 minutes, stirring from time to time, till they are beginning to turn golden at the edges. Meanwhile, heat a grill to red-hot and put the peppers under it, turning them, till they char with great black blisters. Put them into a polythene bag for 10 minutes. Their skins will then slip off. Cut each in half and remove their stalks and seeds. Chop the flesh roughly.

Put the chopped peppers and garlic together on a roasting tray, and mix well with the olive oil. Roast in a hot oven, 425°F/220°C/Gas Mark 7 for 10 minutes. Take them out of the oven, and stir them into the onions in the saucepan. Stir in the stock, and season with salt, pepper and a squeeze of lemon juice. Simmer all the ingredients together, very gently, for 10 minutes. Cool, and liquidize the soup to a velvety smooth texture.

Either chill in a bowl in the fridge, or reheat gently, to serve. Whether you serve the soup hot or cold, put a teaspoonful of crème fraîche in each serving.

Cucumber and Dill Soup

Cucumber has such an elegant, cool, distinctive summery taste, and this makes a perfect first course for a summer evening. It is convenient, too, in that it can be made entirely in the morning. I like to leave the skin on the cucumber before liquidizing it, because I love the tiny flecks of dark green. We need never fear a bitter cucumber these days – all possible bitterness has been bred out of commercially grown cucumbers. By scooping out the seeds, all potential indigestibility is removed, and any wateriness as well.

Serves 6

2 cucumbers
1 oz/28 g butter + 1 tbsp sunflower oil
1 onion, skinned and finely chopped
1 pint/570 ml chicken stock
2 large handfuls of dill weed, chopped – remove any stalks
1 pint/570 ml creamy fromage frais
Salt and freshly ground black pepper

Cut each cucumber in chunks, then each chunk in half lengthways, and scoop away the seeds.

Melt the butter and heat the oil in a saucepan and add the chopped onion. Cook for 2 or 3 minutes, then pour in the stock. Simmer gently for 10 minutes. Cool, then liquidize this with the chunks of cucumber, the dill weed and the fromage frais. Taste, and add salt and pepper to your liking.

Keep in a covered bowl in the fridge till you are ready to ladle it into soup plates or bowls. It looks so pretty I think it needs no garnishing.

Fish and Vegetable Chowder

This is a most sustaining soup, full of the lovely flavours of fish, shellfish, vegetables and saffron. It is much the best made then eaten straight away – if you make it in advance, I advise you not to add the tomato, fish, or shellfish till you are going to reheat the soup. It is quite filling. The fish will cook in the soup if simmered gently for 5 minutes before serving.

Serves 6

3 tbsp olive oil
1 onion, skinned and finely chopped
2 sticks of celery, trimmed and very finely sliced
1 blade of fennel, trimmed and chopped very small
1 carrot, peeled and sliced into fine matchsticks
2 potatoes, peeled and chopped into small dice
1½ pints/850 ml fish stock
Salt and freshly ground black pepper
A good pinch of saffron strands (rather than powder)
1½ lb/675 g mixed white fish, bones and skin removed, and flesh cut into 1-inch/2.5-cm chunks
8 oz/225 g shellfish, e.g. cooked mussels, prawns, squid sliced in circles
2 tomatoes, skinned, de-seeded and sliced into thin strips
1 tbsp finely chopped parsley

Heat the oil in a large saucepan and add the prepared vegetables *except* the strips of tomato. Cook the vegetables over a moderate heat, stirring occasionally to prevent them sticking to the bottom of the pan, for about 10 minutes. Pour in the fish stock, and simmer for 10 minutes. Taste, season with salt and pepper and stir in the saffron.

Before serving, reheat the soup. Add fish, the shellfish and the tomato strips, and simmer the soup very gently for 5 minutes. Just before serving, stir the chopped parsley through the soup. If you like, serve with toasted pieces of French bread floating on the surface, and a bowl of garlic mayonnaise well spiked with Tabasco sauce to spoon into the soup on top of the bread.

Game Soup

This is a warming, delicious soup to drink in the winter. Years ago, I read in a recipe of Katie Stewart's the tip of putting a small amount of liver in game soup. Now I never make it without liver – it rounds off the flavour and the texture perfectly. The soup is made in two stages – first the stock, then the soup.

The stock is best made with uncooked birds, but more usually I find myself using cooked carcasses. Cut any cooked meat off and keep it for the soup. A variety of carcasses is best, say, pheasant, duck and grouse – this is a good way of using up old grouse.

Serves 6

For the stock:

2–3 game bird carcasses

2 small onions, unskinned, with half a dozen cloves stuck in each

2 carrots, peeled and roughly chopped

1 or 2 sticks of celery, chopped

A few strips of orange and lemon rind

Bouquet garni

Some black peppercorns

Salt

For the soup:

2 oz/56 g butter

2 rashers bacon, cut in bits

8 oz/225 g game or lamb's liver, trimmed and cut in bits

2 medium onions, skinned and chopped

1 carrot, peeled and chopped

2 potatoes, peeled and chopped

1 garlic clove, skinned and finely chopped

1 rounded tbsp redcurrant jelly

2½ pints/1.4 litres game stock

2 strips of orange rind

1 strip of lemon rind

Salt and freshly ground black pepper

Any left-over bits of cut-up cooked game

5 fl oz/140 ml port

Put the carcasses into a large saucepan, cover with water and add the rest of the stock ingredients. Bring the stock to the boil, then cover the pan tightly and simmer gently for 3 hours. Cool, and skim off any fat from the top. When quite cold, strain.

To make the soup, melt the butter in a saucepan. Add the chopped bacon and the pieces of trimmed liver. Cook over a moderate heat until the liver is cooked through, then remove the liver from the saucepan and keep on one side till later. Lower the heat under the saucepan and add the chopped vegetables and garlic. Cook gently, stirring from time to time, for 10 minutes. Then stir in the redcurrant jelly, the stock, orange and lemon rind and seasoning. Bring to the boil, cover with a lid, and simmer gently for 45 minutes, until the vegetables are soft. Remove from the heat and cool.

When cold, purée the soup in a blender, adding the cooked liver and game meat to the soup as you purée it. Stir in the port and reheat.

Ham and Bean Soup

This is a sustaining meal in a soup. It needs long, slow cooking and is therefore very convenient in that it has to be made in advance. I prefer to use a smoked ham hock, but it can be very salty so I soak it overnight and throw away the water before simmering it with the other ingredients of the soup.

Serves 6–8

1 ham hock, smoked or unsmoked, whichever you prefer, soaked overnight if salty

1 lb/450 g haricot beans, soaked overnight

2 onions, skinned and neatly chopped

2 cloves of garlic, skinned and chopped finely

3 leeks, washed, trimmed and thinly sliced

2 sticks of celery, washed, trimmed and thinly sliced

4 pints/2.3 litres water

4 medium to large potatoes, peeled and diced

Freshly ground black pepper

Salt, if needed

Put the soaked ham hock and the beans into a large saucepan with the onions, garlic,

leeks and celery. Add the water and simmer very gently, with the pan uncovered, for 2 hours. Then let the soup cool. Skim off any fat from the surface. Remove the ham hock. Add the potatoes to the soup and simmer for a further hour. Cut the meat off the ham hock and throw away the bone and fat.

Put the cut-up ham meat into the soup 10 minutes before serving, and at the same time check the seasoning – add pepper, and salt only if you think it is needed.

Jerusalem Artichoke Soup

The Jerusalem artichoke is a winter vegetable which grows like a weed and has one of the most subtle flavours I know: I find people either love it or loathe it. These lovely vegetables are rather knobbly and so a fiddle to peel, but worth every minute of the time it takes. They make a most delicious simple soup, which also freezes well. It is good accompanied by any of the breads in this book, but especially the Granary Bread on page 368.

Serves 6

2 oz/56 g butter

1 onion, skinned and chopped

1 lb/450 g Jerusalem artichokes, peeled and roughly chopped

2 pints/1.1 litres chicken stock

Salt and freshly ground black pepper

6 tbsp single cream

Finely chopped parsley or chives

Melt the butter in a saucepan, add the onion

and cook over a gentle heat, stirring from time to time, until it is soft and transparent. Add the chopped artichokes, cook for a minute or two, then pour on the stock. Bring to the boil, cover the pan and simmer gently for 30 minutes. Remove from the heat, cool and purée in a blender.

Season and reheat to serve. Just before dishing up the soup, add a spoonful of single cream and some finely chopped parsley or chives to each plateful.

Julienne of Root Vegetables Soup

In the autumn, winter and early spring months I love to make the most of the wide variety of root vegetables available both in the garden and on the shelves of shops and supermarkets. This soup uses as wide a range as you can get, all very finely sliced into matchsticks – which takes no time at all if you have a mandolin. The basis of this soup is a good chicken stock – or, if you are cooking for non-meat eaters, a vegetable stock. The soup can be made two or three days in advance and kept in a covered container in the fridge, or it can be frozen if you are trying to get well ahead with your cooking. Allow it to thaw overnight in the fridge.

This is good served with Cheese, Mustard and Garlic Granary Bread.

Serves 6

3 tbsp sunflower oil

2 onions, skinned and finely sliced

1 carrot and 1 parsnip, peeled and sliced into fine matchsticks

2 leeks, trimmed, washed and sliced into thin strips

4 sticks of celery, washed, trimmed and sliced into thin strips

3 beetroots (raw), peeled and sliced into thin matchsticks

½ lb/225 g Jerusalem artichokes (if you can get them – if not, increase the carrots and parsnips), peeled and thinly sliced

½ head of celeriac, peeled and sliced into fine matchsticks

1–2 garlic cloves, skinned and finely chopped

2 pints/1.1 litres good chicken or vegetable stock

Salt and freshly ground black pepper

Heat the oil in a large saucepan and add the finely sliced onions. Cook for 3–5 minutes, stirring occasionally, till the onions are soft and transparent-looking, then add the rest of the prepared vegetables and the garlic. Cook, stirring from time to time, for about 10 minutes, then pour in the stock. Season with salt and pepper, half-cover the pan with its lid and simmer the soup very gently for half an hour.

Either cool completely before storing the soup in the fridge – or freezing it – or keep it hot till you are ready to ladle it into soup plates or bowls. It really doesn't need anything in the way of a garnish, because the vegetables themselves are so good colourwise.

This soup has the added benefit of being so low in calories that it is a real bonus for those who, like me, are perpetually totting up their calorie intake.

Leek and Bacon Soup

This is really one of those delicious thick soups that are ideal for lunch on a chilly winter's day. You can either liquidize it for a smooth soup or serve it with the leek and bacon chunks still identifiable. It will keep for a couple of days in the refrigerator.

Serves 6–8

2 oz/56 g butter

2 tbsp oil (I use sunflower)

2 onions, skinned and chopped

4 oz/112 g smoked bacon (you can use green if you like), chopped

6 good-sized leeks, washed, trimmed and fairly finely sliced

4 medium potatoes, peeled and chopped

Two 15-oz/420-g tins of tomatoes (liquidized if you are serving a chunky, unliquidized soup)

1½ pints/850 ml chicken or vegetable stock

Salt and freshly ground black pepper

Heat the butter and oil in a saucepan. Add the onions and sauté for a few minutes until they are soft and transparent. Add the bacon and cook for a further few minutes, then stir in the leeks and potatoes. Cook for about 5 minutes, then pour on the tomatoes. Stir in the stock, season with salt and pepper, and bring to boiling point. Simmer very gently with the pan uncovered, for 30–40 minutes, until the pieces of potato are almost falling apart. Allow to cool a little. Liquidize the soup if you want a smooth texture. Reheat to serve.

Leek, Mushroom and Madeira Soup

These flavours go together extremely well. This soup has the added bonus of being very low in calories, yet it is satisfying to eat. As with all soups, the stock is all-important. I prefer to use chicken stock, but a good vegetable stock is a close second.

Serves 6–8

3 tbsp olive or sunflower oil + 1 oz/28 g butter

1 lb/450 g mushrooms, each wiped and chopped quite small

6 leeks, washed, trimmed and sliced thinly

2 pints/1.1 litres good stock, chicken or vegetable

3 oz/84 g long grain white rice, e.g. Basmati

Salt and freshly ground black pepper

A grating of nutmeg

¼ pint/140 ml Madeira

Heat the oil and melt the butter together in a saucepan and cook the mushrooms till they almost squeak – this improves their taste no end. Scoop them out of the pan and add the leeks to the pan. You may need to add another tablespoon of oil, as the mushrooms do rather tend to absorb it. Cook the leeks for a couple of minutes, then replace the mushrooms and stir in the stock, rice, salt, pepper and a grating of nutmeg.

Simmer the soup very gently for about 15–20 minutes. Just before ladling it into bowls, stir in the Madeira.

Leek and Potato Soup

This, if I am pushed to choose a favourite soup above all others, would have to come top of my list. I love it in all its different ways of making – cold and velvety-smooth in the hot summer evenings, with snipped chives stirred through, or hot and smooth on chilly evenings, or, as in this case, half smooth and half chunky, which I think makes it perfect supper food. Anyone who doesn't like either curry powder or celery must be reassured that although both feature in the list of ingredients for this, my version of leek and potato soup, they need not worry – neither is discernible as such, but both go to make a whole, as it were, flavour-wise.

Serves 6

1 oz/28 g butter + 2 tbsp sunflower oil

1 onion, skinned and chopped

1 stick of celery, washed and trimmed and very finely sliced

4 leeks – more if they are small – washed and trimmed, and sliced diagonally (because it looks nicer) into thin strips

4 medium potatoes, peeled and diced neatly

1 tsp medium-strength curry powder

2 pints/1.1 litres good chicken or vegetable stock

Salt and freshly ground black pepper

1–2 tbsp finely chopped parsley (optional)

Melt the butter and heat the oil in a saucepan and add the chopped onion. Cook for 2–3 minutes, till the onion is soft and transparent, then stir in the celery and leeks, and cook for a further few minutes. Add the diced potatoes, stir in the curry powder, cook all together for a minute or two, then pour in the stock.

Simmer very gently for 25 minutes. Cool, liquidize half the soup, return it to the saucepan with the remainder of the soup and stir all together well. Taste, and season with salt and pepper. If you like, just before serving stir through the soup the finely chopped parsley.

This soup can be made in advance by two or three days and reheated to serve, or it can be frozen – thaw overnight.

Leek and Smoked Haddock Chowder

I have only fairly recently realized just how good are leeks with any smoked fish. This soup is a meal in itself. I like to liquidize half the potato and leeks in their fishy milk and water, and then leave the rest of the soup in chunks of potato and sliced leeks, with the cooked fish flaked through. This gives a fairly thick base to the soup, yet provides a contrasting texture with the bits of fish, potato and leek at the same time. The chopped parsley must be added at the last moment, to preserve its colour and flavour.

Serves 6–8

1½ lb/675 g smoked haddock (or smoked cod)

3 pints/1.7 litres milk and water mixed – I leave the ratio up to you

3 tbsp sunflower oil + 1 oz/28 g butter

1 onion, skinned and neatly chopped

3 good sized leeks, washed well and trimmed,
    and sliced about 1 inch/2.5 cm thick

5–6 potatoes, peeled and neatly chopped

Freshly ground black pepper

A grating of nutmeg

2 tbsp finely chopped parsley

Feel the fish on a board, and remove all bones – it is much easier to do this before the fish is cooked, I have discovered. With a very sharp knife, remove the skin from the fish. Put the fish in a saucepan with the milk and water, and over a moderate heat let the liquid come to simmering point. Take the pan off the heat and let the fish cool in the liquid.

Meanwhile, heat the oil and melt the butter together in a large saucepan. Cook the chopped onion for a couple of minutes, then stir in the sliced leeks and chopped potatoes. Cook for about 10 minutes – you will need to stir fairly frequently to prevent it all from sticking. Season with pepper and nutmeg, and pour in the strained fish liquid. Cook this gently, with the liquid barely simmering, till the pieces of potato are soft when you squish them against the side of the saucepan with the back of your wooden spoon.

Cool the soup a bit, then liquidize half the contents of the saucepan and return the smooth soup to the pan. Flake the cooked fish and stir that, too, into the soup. Taste, add more pepper if you think it is needed, and reheat gently before serving. Just before you ladle the soup into the bowls or soup plates, stir the chopped parsley through.

Leek and Tomato Soup

This soup tastes wonderful, combining the flavours of leeks, tomatoes, onions and garlic! It doesn't take a second to make and is low in calories, so it makes a good first course when what is to follow is filling.

Serves 6–8

2 tbsp olive oil

2 medium onions, skinned and chopped small

8 medium leeks, trimmed and thinly sliced

2 garlic cloves, skinned and finely chopped
    (optional for non garlic lovers)

1 pint/570 ml chicken or vegetable stock

Two 15-oz/420-g tins of tomatoes

Salt and freshly ground black pepper

Heat the oil in a saucepan and add the onions. Sauté for about 5 minutes, stirring once or twice so that they cook evenly, then add the leeks and garlic. Cook for another 5 minutes, then pour on the stock. Liquidize and sieve the tinned tomatoes and add to the saucepan. Season with salt and pepper, cover the pan with a lid and simmer gently for 30 minutes.

Mint, Pea and Lettuce Soup

One of my all-time favourite soups. I have used mangetout and sugarsnaps when making this, but you do need to sieve the

Beetroot Soup with Crème Fraîche ▶
page 20

soup if you use either of these pod-and-pea types rather than the frozen or fresh peas referred to in the ingredients.

Serves 6

2 oz/56 g butter

2 onions, skinned and chopped

1 garlic clove, chopped (optional)

2 potatoes, peeled and cut into small pieces

2 handfuls of lettuce leaves – the outer leaves are fine for soup

4 oz/112 g fresh shelled or frozen peas

1½ pints/850 ml chicken stock

A handful of mint leaves, preferably applemint

Salt and freshly ground black pepper

6 tbsp single cream

Finely chopped parsley

Melt the butter in a saucepan, add the onions, garlic and potatoes, and cook over gentle heat for about 10 minutes, stirring from time to time to prevent sticking. Add the lettuce and peas to the saucepan and stir in the stock. Bring to the boil and simmer very gently for 30 minutes, until the pieces of potato are soft. Remove the saucepan from the heat and leave to cool.

Purée the cooled vegetables in a blender, together with the mint leaves. Season with salt and freshly ground black pepper, pour the puréed soup into a bowl and chill. To serve, spoon the soup into soup plates, pour a spoonful of cream on top of each and add a sprinkling of finely chopped parsley.

◀ Fish and Vegetable Chowder
page 26

Parsnip, Lemon and Ginger Soup

Soup is a wonderful light supper food. Easy to prepare, it can be made up to a couple of days in advance and kept in a covered container in the fridge. It combines with bread, cheese and fruit to make a light but satisfying meal. This parsnip soup has all the things I like in a soup – I love the flavour of parsnips, and here it is complemented very well by the lemon and fresh ginger in the recipe. Soup – any soup – is elevated to being something really special if good stock is used to make it. Personally, chicken stock is the one for me, but a good vegetable stock (remember not to include any potato or turnip peeling in it – they make it bitter) comes a close second.

Serves 8

3 oz/84 g butter, or 4 tbsp oil (sunflower, if possible)

2 medium onions, skinned and chopped

4 good-sized parsnips, peeled and chopped

Pared rind of half a lemon – I use a potato peeler to avoid getting any of the pith

A piece of fresh ginger root about 2 inches/ 5 cm long, peeled and chopped

2 pints/1.1 litres good chicken stock

Juice of ½ lemon

Salt and freshly ground black pepper

2 tbsp finely chopped parsley

Melt the butter (or heat the oil) in a large saucepan, and add the chopped onions. Cook for 5 minutes or so, stirring occasionally. Then add the chopped parsnips, the lemon peel and the ginger. Cook for a further 5 minutes, then pour on the stock. With the saucepan half-covered with a lid, simmer gently till the pieces of parsnip are soft. Then cool the soup a little before liquidizing and sieving into a clean bowl or saucepan. Season with lemon juice, salt and pepper to taste.

Reheat to serve. I like to stir a couple of tablespoons of finely chopped parsley through the soup just before serving – it does wonders for its appearance!

Pea, Apple and Mint Soup

This simple recipe combines the best of summer flavours – peas, apples and mint. For any recipe which uses mint, I do prefer to use applemint, the rather hairy, broad-leaved type which I think has a far superior flavour to the more common spearmint. This is a good way of using up garden peas which are still good, but on the large side to serve as a vegetable. The apples just add the touch of tartness and sweetness that this soup needs and the hint of curry powder isn't detectable as such but does add a certain something to the overall flavour. This soup freezes well and can be served hot or chilled.

Serves 6–8

2 oz/56 g butter

3 onions, skinned and chopped

2 eating apples, chopped (skin, core and all – the soup will be liquidized and sieved)

1 rounded tsp curry powder

1 lb/450 g shelled peas

2 pints/1.1 litres good chicken or vegetable stock

Salt and freshly ground black pepper

2 handfuls of mint

Thinly sliced apples for garnish

Melt the butter in a saucepan and add the onions. Sauté for about 5 minutes, stirring occasionally, then add the chopped apple. Cook for a further minute or two, then stir in the curry powder. Add the peas and stock. Season with salt and pepper, and stir in half the mint. Cover the pan and simmer gently for 20 minutes. Draw the pan off the heat and leave to cool. Add the remaining mint to the cooled soup and liquidize. Pour the liquidized soup through a sieve for a really velvety texture.

Either serve chilled or reheat to serve hot. Whether you are serving the soup cold or hot, thinly slice a couple of apples, brush them with lemon juice and garnish each plateful with three or four slices.

Pheasant and Mushroom Soup

In the autumn and winter, when pheasants are plentiful and can be bought so easily these days even by those who don't live in the country, it is good to make the most of them. Pheasants are only mildly gamey in their taste, and their flavour combines very well with mushrooms. This soup has a small amount of Madeira which further enhances the taste. The rice adds substance.

Serves 6–8

1 pheasant, as much fat cut off as possible

4 onions, 2 cut in half (skin on), 2 skinned and
   chopped neatly

2 carrots

2 sticks of celery

4–6 cloves

1 tsp rock salt and several black peppercorns

2 tbsp olive oil

4 oz/112 g long grain rice, such as Basmati

1½ lb/675 g mushrooms, wiped and chopped
   quite small

¼ pint/140 ml Madeira

Salt and freshly ground black pepper

Wash the pheasant and put it into a large saucepan with the onion halves, carrots, celery, cloves, salt and peppercorns. Cover with 3 pints/1.7 litres of cold water and bring slowly to simmering point. Cover the pan with a lid and simmer all together very gently for 2 hours. If you have an Aga or a Rayburn you can do this inside, rather than on top of the cooker. Let it all cool, then take the pheasant out of the stock and cut off the meat, chopping it into small pieces. Strain the stock and reserve.

Make the soup by heating the oil and adding the chopped onions. Cook over a moderate heat for several minutes, then add the rice. Cook for a further couple of minutes, stirring, then add the chopped mushrooms and 2 pints/1.1 litres of the reserved stock. Simmer gently for 45 minutes, stirring occasionally. Add the cut-up pheasant meat and the Madeira 10 minutes before serving, and at the same time check the taste and season accordingly.

Red Onion Soup with Balsamic Vinegar and Goats' Cheese Croûtons

I ate this soup – or one similar – in the Malmaison Hotel in Leith, at an excellent bar lunch. I thought it would be fun and good to experiment with the theme, which is a variation on the Onion Soup with Toasted Cheese in Seasonal Cooking. *I do love the mild flavour of red onions, and their caramelizing as they sauté is complemented by the Balsamic vinegar (but you do have to beware not to use too much). I love Balsamic vinegar, used sparingly, and I tend to include a teaspoonful or two in most casseroles of meat or game. The goats' cheese is far better than Cheddar cheese would be with these flavours.*

Serves 6

1 oz/28 g butter

2 tbsp oil

6 fairly large red-skinned onions, each skinned
   and sliced as finely as you can

1–2 garlic cloves, skinned and finely
   chopped

1½–2 pints/850–1.1 litres beef stock – you can
   use canned consommé – or good vegetable
   stock

2 tsp Balsamic vinegar

12 slices from a stick of French bread

8 oz/225 g soft goats' cheese

Freshly ground black pepper

Salt

A grating of nutmeg

Heat the butter and oil together in a large saucepan, and stir in the red onions. It will look a lot, but as they cook they reduce right down in quantity. Cook them over a moderate heat, stirring from time to time, for 12–15 minutes. Stir in the garlic and cook for a further 2–3 minutes, then stir in the stock and balsamic vinegar. Simmer all together, with the pan half-covered with its lid, for about 30 minutes.

While the soup cooks, prepare the croûtons by spreading goats' cheese on each slice of bread, grinding black pepper on top, then grilling for 45–60 seconds – just till the surface begins to speckle brown. Keep the croûtons warm in a low oven.

Before serving, season the soup with salt, pepper and nutmeg. Ladle it into bowls or soup plates, and put two goats' cheese croûtons on each serving.

Smoked Haddock Soup

This is a traditional Scottish soup, called Cullen Skink. It is exquisitely flavoured, simple to make and greatly enjoyed by all who like fish. I don't call it by its traditional name because this is my version: the diced tomatoes and parsley are my additions, and also the onions. This soup looks most attractive as well as tasting delicious.

Serves 6

1½ lb/675 g smoked haddock

2 pints/1.1 litres milk and water mixed

2 onions, skinned

1 blade of mace

2 oz/56 g butter

3 medium potatoes, peeled and chopped

2 tomatoes, skinned, de-seeded and chopped into neat dice

Freshly ground black pepper

1 rounded tbsp finely chopped parsley

12 dssp single cream

Chopped parsley or chives, to garnish

Feel the fish on a board – and remove all the bones. Then put it in a saucepan and cover with the milk and water. Add a whole onion and the mace. Over a gentle heat bring slowly to the boil, simmer very gently for barely 5 minutes, then remove from the heat and leave to stand for 10 minutes. Strain off the liquid and reserve.

Chop the second onion. In another saucepan, melt the butter, add the chopped potatoes and onion, and cook for about 10 minutes over a gentle heat, stirring from time to time, until the onion begins to soften. Add on the strained fish liquid and simmer gently until the pieces of potato are soft. Remove from the heat, cool, and purée in a blender.

Rinse out a saucepan. Put the puréed soup into it. Flake the cooked fish, removing the skin, and stir the fish into the soup. Stir in the chopped tomatoes and black pepper to taste and reheat gently.

Add the finely chopped parsley just before serving. Into each plateful of soup put 2 dessertspoons of cream and sprinkle with a little more parsley, or chives, to garnish.

Spicy Tomato Soup with Avocado Cream

Serves 8

2 oz/56 g butter or 3 tbsp oil (I use olive)

2 medium onions, skinned and chopped

1 carrot, peeled and chopped

2 leeks, trimmed and chopped

1 stick of celery, chopped

Two 15-oz/420-g tins of tomatoes

1 tsp sugar

Salt and freshly ground black pepper

2 dried chillies

2 pints/1.1 litres good chicken stock

For the avocado cream:

2 avocados, stoned, flesh scooped out

1 whole small garlic clove, or ½ larger clove, skinned and chopped

Lemon juice to taste – about 2 tsp

A pinch of salt and a grinding of black pepper

Melt the butter or heat the oil in a large saucepan, add the chopped onions and cook for about 5 minutes, stirring occasionally. Then add the other chopped vegetables to the pan and continue to cook for a further 5–10 minutes. Add the tinned tomatoes, the seasonings, the chillies and the chicken stock. Half-cover the saucepan with a lid, and let the soup simmer gently for about 45 minutes. Cool, liquidize, and sieve it into a bowl if you are going to keep or freeze it.

Make the avocado cream by simply whizzing all the ingredients together until smooth. Keep covered till required.

Reheat the soup to serve, with 2 tea-spoons of avocado cream in the middle of each plateful.

Spinach, Tomato and Garlic Soup

This is one of the soups I like best, combining as it does three of my favourite flavours – spinach, tomato, and garlic. It is extremely low in calories and makes a wonderful first course for a dinner party or main course soup for lunch. It is very easy and quick to make. I use frozen chopped spinach so I don't bother to liquidize the soup, and the spinach and the pieces of tomato which are stirred through it give it a nice texture. I don't think it needs a garnish – the chopped tomato does double duty as part of the soup and as garnish.

Serves 6–8

3 tbsp olive oil

2 medium onions, skinned and finely chopped

2 garlic cloves, skinned and finely chopped

2 lb/900 g frozen chopped spinach, thawed and drained

2 pints/1.1 litres chicken or vegetable stock

Salt and freshly ground black pepper

4 tomatoes, skinned, de-seeded and chopped

Heat the olive oil in a saucepan and add the onions. Sauté for about 5 minutes, stirring occasionally to make sure that they cook evenly. Add the chopped garlic, and cook for a further minute or two before stirring in the spinach and the stock. Simmer the soup gently for 15 minutes, season to your taste and stir in the chopped tomatoes – check the seasoning again after the tomatoes have been added, and serve. You can make the soup, tomatoes and all, the day before you want to use it, just reheating gently to serve.

Fish, Poultry and Meat

Crab-Filled Tomato and Cream Cheese Ring
·
Marinated Cod with Sweet Pepper and Garlic Sauce
·
Smoked Haddock Croquettes
·
Kipper Fillets Marinated in Lime
·
Oysters in Cream with Lemon and Chives
·
Smoked Salmon, Dill and Cream Cheese Triangles
·
Crab Mousse
·
Smoked Haddock and Parsley Mousse
·
Smoked Trout and Horseradish Mousse
·
Mushroom and Sardine Pâté
·
Prawn, Bacon and Cream Cheese Pâté
·
Smoked Fish Pâté
·
Smoked Mackerel and Walnut Pâté
·
Chicken Liver and Pecan Pâté
·
Chicken Livers with Calvados and Cream
·
Coarse Pork Terrine
·
Tomato Jelly Ring with Watercress and Crispy Bacon

Crab-Filled Tomato and Cream Cheese Ring

This makes a good buffet dish as well as a convenient first course, because it is very decorative. It is also a good main course for lunch – in fact, a most versatile dish! The ring mould is made of tomatoes and cream cheese, flavoured with garlic and flecked with chopped parsley. The parsley provides a good colour contrast. The centre of the ring is filled with a mixture of fresh crab and rice, bound together with a little mayonnaise. The ring mould can be made a day in advance.

Serves 6–8

For the ring mould:

6 tomatoes, liquidized and sieved, to give
    roughly ¾ pint/420 ml purée

1 oz/28 g powdered gelatine

½ pint/285 ml freshly squeezed orange juice

Salt and freshly ground black pepper

1 tbsp Worcestershire sauce

1 large garlic clove, skinned and chopped

2 tbsp finely chopped parsley

8 oz/225 g cream cheese

For the filling:

4 oz/112 g cooked Basmati rice

1 lb/450 g crab meat, white and brown meats
    mixed

2 tbsp mayonnaise

Salt and freshly ground black pepper

Put the puréed tomatoes into a food processor or large bowl. Sprinkle the gelatine on to the orange juice in a saucepan and heat until it has dissolved completely,

taking care not to let the orange juice boil.

Add the seasonings, Worcestershire sauce, garlic, parsley and cream cheese to the puréed tomatoes. Blend or whisk, gradually pouring in the orange gelatine mixture, until you have a smooth mixture. Pour into a 9-inch/22-cm ring mould, and leave in the fridge to set overnight.

To turn out, dip the ring mould into a bowl of hot water for a few seconds. Cover with a plate, invert giving a gentle shake, and the cream cheese and tomato mould should come easily out of the tin.

Mix all the ingredients for the filling together well, and pile them into the centre of the cream cheese and tomato ring mould. Leave in a cool place until you are ready to serve.

Marinated Cod with Sweet Pepper and Garlic Sauce

This is a most convenient first course as the whole thing is prepared in advance. The fish 'cooks' in the acid of the lemon juice.

Serves 6

1½ lb/675 g filleted cod, sliced into neat dice
    about the size of a fingernail

Juice of 4 lemons

For the sauce:

2 red and 2 yellow peppers

6 garlic cloves

¼ pint/140 ml extra virgin olive oil

Pepper, salt and lemon juice to taste – I use
    the juice of half a lemon

Chopped coriander leaves or flat-leafed
parsley, to garnish

Marinate the cod in the lemon juice for at least 4 hours.

Halve and de-seed the peppers and put them, skin sides uppermost, under a hot grill until the skin forms black blisters. Then put them into a polythene bag for 10 minutes, after which the skins should slip off easily. Simmer the cloves of garlic in their peppery skins for 5 minutes, then peel them.

Put the skinned pepper halves and skinned poached garlic into a Magimix and whiz. Still whizzing, gradually add the oil drop by drop – as if you were making mayonnaise – and season with salt, pepper and lemon juice to your taste.

Drain the cod very well and pat it dry. Divide the fish between six serving plates or dishes. Cover each serving with sauce. Scatter chopped coriander over each, if you like, or substitute flat-leafed parsley if you prefer the taste.

Smoked Haddock Croquettes

These may be made and cooked the day before if you are going to serve them cold. If to be served hot, they can be shaped and coated, ready for frying at the last minute.

Makes about 30

2 lb/900 g smoked haddock fillets

1 pint/570 ml milk

Salt and freshly ground black pepper

2 oz/56 g butter

2 oz/56 g plain flour

2 tbsp chopped fresh parsley

2 tbsp capers, chopped

2 tbsp mayonnaise

4 eggs, beaten

8 oz/225 g fresh white breadcrumbs

Oil for deep frying

Put the haddock fillets into a large saucepan with milk and seasoning. Cover and cook gently for about 2 minutes, milk barely simmering, until the haddock flakes easily.

Strain the stock from the haddock into a measuring jug and make up to 12 fl oz/340 ml with extra milk if necessary. Remove the skin and bones from the haddock, then flake the flesh.

Melt the butter in a saucepan, and stir in the flour, then gradually stir in the fish stock. Bring to the boil, stirring all the time until the sauce thickens. Reduce the heat and simmer very gently for about 10 minutes, stirring frequently. Add the flaked fish, parsley, capers and mayonnaise to the fish sauce and beat well together until smooth. Season. Spoon the smoked haddock mixture on to a plate. Allow to cool, cover with clingfilm, and then refrigerate for at least 2 hours, until well chilled.

Shape the chilled haddock mixture into small balls, about 1 inch/2.5 cm in diameter, with wetted hands. Return the fish balls to the refrigerator to firm up again.

Coat the fish balls with beaten egg and breadcrumbs, then deep fry in hot oil, in batches, for 3–4 minutes, until golden brown. Drain well on absorbent paper.

Serve hot or well chilled. These chilled fish

balls may be speared on to cocktail sticks, and arranged with other savouries on sticks.

Kipper Fillets Marinated in Lime

Too many recipes go in fashions of usefulness. Marinated kipper fillets are such a dish, and yet what a waste of a good recipe! It is one of the most convenient and delicious first courses, and not at all difficult or time-consuming to make. I like to use the distinctive flavour of limes in the marinade – we can even buy limes in the Co-op in Broadford, Skye, so I would think they are obtainable in all parts of rural Britain, too!

Serves 6

6 plump kippers

¼ pint/140 ml extra virgin olive oil

3 limes, well washed and dried to remove their preservative, then the rinds finely grated and the juices squeezed

1 tsp grainy mustard – either Moutarde de Meaux, or Isabella's Mustard Relish, from Ellon in Aberdeenshire

1–2 tbsp finely chopped parsley and snipped chives, mixed

Put each kipper on a board. With a very sharp knife slice the kipper flesh from the bones and skin. You will inevitably get some shredded looking bits of kipper but it doesn't matter – it's impossible not to. Slice the bigger bits of kipper flesh into thin strips and put all the kipper flesh into a shallow dish.

Mix together the olive oil, lime rinds and juices, mustard and chopped parsley and chives and pour this over the strips of kipper, mixing it in well – I find a fork easiest to use for this. Cover the dish, and leave in a cool place to marinate for at least 24 hours, forking the marinade through the kipper strips two or three times during the marinating.

Serve on individual plates with a small heap of salad and brown bread and butter.

Oysters in Cream with Lemon and Chives

There are those who think they don't like oysters. But I feel sure that they are people who imagine that oysters can only be eaten raw. They are delicious cooked, providing they have the briefest cooking time which just firms up the flesh and keeps the silky consistency of the oyster. This couldn't be simpler.

Serves 6

1 pint/570 ml double cream

Juice of 1 lemon

A pinch of salt and plenty of freshly ground black pepper

24 oysters, and 24 shells

About 3 tbsp snipped chives

Tip the cream into a sauté pan with the lemon juice, and season with salt and pepper. Let the cream bubble till fairly thick, and then slip in the oysters with their liquor. Let them bubble for no more than

41

30 seconds. Stir in the chives. Spoon an oyster back into each shell and spoon a small amount of the sauce over each oyster. Serve.

Smoked Salmon, Dill and Cream Cheese Triangles

This makes a change from the endless triangles of smoked salmon which turn up at drinks parties. It is also much more convenient to make, and tastes so much better. The smoked salmon is cut into fine dice and mixed into the flavoured cream cheese. This is spread on bread (I like to use granary bread), then each slice is cut into triangles.

Makes about 48 triangles

1 lb/450 g smoked salmon

1 lb/450 g cream cheese

Juice of 1 lemon

1 good handful of dill fronds

Plenty of freshly ground black pepper

1 loaf of granary or other good bread

Slice the smoked salmon in thin strips, then chop these by slicing them the other way. Put the cream cheese into a food processor and whiz till smooth. Then whiz in the lemon juice, adding it slowly, and the dill, and season with black pepper. Turn this cream cheese mixture into a bowl, and mix in thoroughly the shredded smoked salmon.

Spread this on the sliced bread, cut off the crusts, and cut each slice into triangles. You can do this in the morning, provided you cover the serving plates with clingfilm till just before your guests arrive.

Crab Mousse

I love crab, but I feel strongly that both white and brown meat should be used in all crab recipes. The white meat has a pleasing texture, but the brown meat has the flavour.

Serves 6

1 sachet of gelatine (½ oz/14 g)

½ pint/285 ml fish or vegetable stock

Juice of 1 lemon

A good dash of Tabasco

1 lb/450 g half brown and half white crabmeat

A pinch of salt and plenty of freshly ground black pepper

½ pint/285 ml crème fraîche

2 egg whites

Dill, or thinly sliced cucumber, to garnish (optional)

Dissolve the gelatine gently in the stock in a saucepan and leave to cool, stirring in the lemon juice and the Tabasco. When it is quite cold, fold in the crabmeat and season with salt and pepper. Fold the crème fraîche into the crab mixture, and, lastly, in a clean bowl, whisk the egg whites till they are stiff. Use a large metal spoon to fold them quickly and thoroughly through the creamy crab mixture. Pour into a glass or china bowl to set.

Garnish, if you like, with dill or with thinly sliced cucumber. Serve either as a first course, with warm toast or sesame sticks, or as a main course for four people, with salad.

Smoked Haddock and Parsley Mousse

This makes a very good main course for supper in warm summer months. (Incidentally, it makes a very good first course at any time of the year.) As with every recipe which calls for smoked haddock, the end result will be the better for the smoked haddock being really plump and juicy – and undyed, it goes without saying. Also, you can substitute smoked cod for the smoked haddock – I love smoked cod, with its great succulent flakes of fish, and these days we can usually choose which we prefer. The parsley flecks the mousse with green, and looks much more interesting than just the plain pale yellow mousse. Looks do matter, and a visually appealing dish will entice the reluctant eater!

It needs only a salad and warm granary bread as accompaniments.

Serves 6

2 lb/900 g smoked haddock (or cod)

2 pints/1.1 litres milk and water mixed

1 onion, skinned and cut in half

2 sticks of celery, washed and broken in half

1 sachet of gelatine (½ oz/14 g)

6 tbsp mayonnaise

¼ pint/140 ml fromage frais

Plenty of freshly ground black pepper

3 tbsp finely chopped parsley

2 egg whites

Put the fish into a large saucepan with the milk and water and the onion and celery. Put the pan over a moderate heat and heat till the liquid just begins to heave under a skin, then take the pan off the heat, and leave to get completely cold.

Measure ¼ pint/140 ml of the liquid the fish was cooked in into a small saucepan, and sprinkle in the gelatine. Warm – take care not to let it boil – till the gelatine granules dissolve completely, then set aside to cool.

Flake the fish, removing all bones and skin. Mix together the mayonnaise and fromage frais, stir in the cooled gelatine mixture and season with pepper. Fold in the flaked fish and the chopped parsley. Lastly, whisk the egg whites in a bowl till they are stiff, then, with a large metal spoon, fold them quickly and thoroughly through the fish mixture.

Scrape the mousse into a serving bowl, cover, and leave in the fridge till you want to serve it. This can be made a day in advance.

Smoked Trout and Horseradish Mousse

This is a rich first course. I like to make it in ramekins and unmould each on to a serving plate. Serve brown toast or bread to accompany the mousse. It is delicious served with grated apples and horseradish mixed into crème fraîche as an accompanying dressing.

Serves 8

3 smoked trout

½ pint/285 ml single cream

4 tbsp lemon juice

2 tbsp cold water

1 sachet of gelatine powder (½ oz/14 g)

4 tsp grated horseradish (preferably not
horseradish sauce)

Freshly ground black pepper

½ pint/285 ml double cream, whipped

2 large egg whites

2 tbsp chopped parsley

Flake the fish from the smoked trout, removing all bones and skin. Put the flaked fish into a food processor. Whiz, adding the single cream, until you have a smooth purée.

Measure the lemon juice and cold water into a small saucepan and sprinkle the gelatine over the liquid. Let it soak, then heat gently to dissolve the gelatine in the liquid, taking care not to let the liquid boil. Cool for several minutes, then, with the food processor turned on, pour it into the smoked trout and cream mixture. (If you pour it straight from the heat, the mixture tends to curdle.) Add the horseradish and pepper to taste and whiz to blend them in. Add the whipped cream. Turn the mixture into a bowl.

Whisk the egg whites until they are stiff. Using a large metal spoon, fold the whites and parsley quickly and thoroughly through the mousse.

Wipe out eight ramekins with sunflower oil and divide the mixture evenly between them. Cover and leave in the refrigerator for several hours to set. Dip each ramekin in very hot water for a few seconds to unmould.

Mushroom and Sardine Pâté

This is a most unusual paté. Don't be put off by the sardines. My husband loathes sardines, but loves this paté. It doesn't freeze very well – it goes watery – but you can make it three or four days in advance and keep it in the refrigerator.

Serves 6–8

3 oz/84 g butter

8 oz/225 g mushrooms, sliced

Two 4½-oz/125-g tins sardines, drained of their
oil

8 oz/225 g cream cheese

2 tbsp lemon juice

Salt and freshly ground black pepper

Melt the butter in a frying pan and sauté the mushrooms. Mix with the rest of the ingredients in a food processor or blender, and season with a little salt and lots of freshly ground black pepper. Pile into a serving dish and chill.

Serve with wholemeal toast.

Prawn, Bacon and Cream Cheese Pâté

Shellfish and bacon go well together. This pâté is very quick and easy to make, and is heavenly to eat. We get huge, delicious prawns, up to 3 inches/7.5 cm long. Sometimes we get squat lobster tails, which are very good for this recipe.

Serves 6

3 oz/84 g cooked, shelled prawns
3 rashers bacon
8 oz/225 g cream cheese
1 garlic clove, skinned and very finely chopped
Freshly ground black pepper
1 tbsp lemon juice
1 rounded tbsp finely chopped parsley

Chop the prawns. Fry the bacon until crisp, drain it on kitchen paper and break it into small pieces. If you have a food processor, put the cream cheese in and whiz until smooth. Otherwise put the cream cheese into a bowl and pound it until it is as smooth as possible.

Don't add the rest of the ingredients to the food processor, because the whole pâté will become too smooth – one of its attractions is the different textures. So scoop the smooth cream cheese into a bowl, and add the rest of the ingredients, mixing them together well.

Heap into a serving dish and serve with brown bread or toast.

Smoked Fish Pâté

You can use any smoked fish for this pâté – smoked salmon, smoked trout, Arbroath smokies, or kippers (smoked and cured herrings). It is a delicious pâté served with brown toast, or it can be used as a filling for baps or rolls for an up-market picnic, with chopped or sliced tomatoes.

Serves 6–8

4 kippers, or 3 smoked trout, or 12 oz/340 g smoked salmon, or 3 Arbroath smokies
2 oz/56 g butter
6 oz/170 g cream cheese
Freshly ground black pepper
Juice of 1 lemon
1 tbsp chopped flat-leafed parsley

If you are using kippers, poach them in a shallow pan of water for 5 minutes, then drain well. If you are using kippers, Arbroath smokies or smoked trout, flake the fish, removing all the skin and bones. Put the flaked fish – or chopped smoked salmon – into a food processor.

Melt the butter over a low heat, then set the pan aside to cool slightly. Whiz the fish in the food processor, slowly adding the melted butter – if you add the butter when it is too hot, the mixture tends to curdle. Add the cream cheese and pepper to taste and whiz until all is smooth. Still whizzing, slowly pour in the lemon juice and add the parsley.

Scrape the pâté into a serving dish, cover, and keep in the fridge till required.

Smoked Mackerel and Walnut Pâté

The toasted walnuts provide a good texture in this pâté, and their flavour goes very well with the rich smoked mackerel. The pâté is improved by a lot of lemon. Although I'm suggesting it here as a first course, which is where you usually find pâtés, I also like to serve it with granary bread or toast and a salad as a main course for lunch, in larger quantities than if it were a first course.

Serves 6–8

1½ lb/675 g smoked mackerel, skin and as
    many bones as possible removed

1 garlic clove, skinned and chopped

Juice of 2 lemons and grated rind of 1 lemon

1 tbsp Worcestershire sauce

Freshly ground black pepper

10 oz/285 g cream cheese

2 oz/56 g walnuts, toasted for 5–10 minutes,
    cooled and broken into bits

Put the smoked mackerel into a blender or food processor, and add the chopped garlic, lemon juice and rind, Worcestershire sauce and black pepper. Blend until smooth. Add the cream cheese and blend again until all is thoroughly incorporated. Turn the pâté into a bowl and fold in the cooled walnut bits. Don't add them to the pâté at the blending stage or they become ground to the same texture as the pâté.

This pâté keeps well in a covered bowl in the fridge for 3–4 days.

Chicken Liver and Pecan Pâté

Serves 8

4 oz/112 g chopped pecan nuts

½ tsp salt

3 oz/84 g butter

1 small onion, skinned and chopped finely

2 lb/900 g chicken livers, carefully picked over
    and any greenish bits removed

4 tbsp Madeira, or brandy

Lots of freshly ground black pepper

½ pint/285 ml double cream

Roast the pecan nuts by shaking them in a saucepan with the salt, over a moderate heat, for 5 minutes. Set aside.

Melt the butter and add the finely chopped onion. Cook for about 5 minutes, stirring from time to time so that the onion doesn't burn. Then add the chicken livers and cook for a couple of minutes. Then pour in the Madeira. (You can substitute brandy if you prefer, but the Madeira is, I think, much nicer.) Let the chicken livers and Madeira cook together for 2–3 minutes, then take the saucepan off the heat and season with lots of freshly ground black pepper.

Liquidize the mixture, adding the cream as you do so, then stir in the pecans. Pour into a serving dish. Cover with clingfilm when the pâté is quite cold, and store in the fridge for 3–4 days, or freeze.

Serve with Cumberland Jelly (see page 309).

Chicken Livers with Calvados and Cream

This makes a delicious first course, if rather rich, and takes literally minutes to make. I like to serve it with hot garlic bread or brown rolls.

Serves 6–8

2 oz/56 g butter

1 tbsp oil (I use sunflower)

1 small onion, skinned and finely chopped

2 lb/900 g chicken livers, picked over and any
   greenish bits removed

3 fl oz/84 ml Calvados, or other apple brandy

½ pint/285 ml double cream

Salt and freshly ground black pepper

1 tbsp finely chopped parsley

Heat the butter and oil together in a saucepan or frying pan and add the finely chopped onion. Sauté for about 5 minutes, stirring occasionally, until the onion is soft and transparent. Add the chicken livers and cook for 2–3 minutes, continuing to stir – just long enough to seal them. Pour on the Calvados and light with a match immediately. Let it flame for a few seconds then pour on the cream. Season with salt and pepper, and let the cream bubble away for 2–3 minutes.

Stir in the chopped parsley just before serving on warmed plates, accompanied by the garlic bread or rolls.

Coarse Pork Terrine

This terrine can be made several days in advance and stored, tightly wrapped in clingfilm or foil, in the fridge. It also freezes well, but not for long. Serve accompanied by a small amount of mixed leaf salad, with a vinaigrette or Balsamic vinegar-flavoured dressing. Toasted granary bread is an optional accompaniment.

Serves 10–12

For lining the tin:

3 bay leaves

8 rashers streaky bacon

For the terrine:

2 oz/56 g butter

2 medium onions, skinned and chopped finely

3 spring onions, sliced thinly – green stalks as
   well as bulbs

1½ lb/675 g good pork sausagemeat

½ lb/225 g lambs' liver, trimmed and chopped
   finely (slithery but possible)

1 lb/450 g lean pork meat, minced

½ tsp thyme

A good pinch of salt and plenty of freshly
   ground black pepper

2 tbsp chopped parsley

2 large eggs, beaten

Carefully (because foil seems so thin these days, and it is easy to stick your finger through it) line a loaf or terrine tin about 10 inches/25 cm long and 3 inches/7.5 cm wide with foil. Place the bay leaves on the base. Then stretch the bacon rashers with the blunt edge of a knife, and line the tin widthwise with them.

In a large bowl, mix together all the terrine ingredients really well. The *only* way to do this job thoroughly is the messy way, by using your hands!

Put the mixture into the prepared tin. Fold the ends of the bacon rashers over the top. Cover the terrine tightly with foil and put it into a roasting tin, with enough hot water to come halfway up the sides.

Cook in a moderate oven – 350°F/ 180°C/Gas Mark 4 – for 2 hours.

Take the terrine out of the oven and leave it overnight in a cool place, with weights on top. Turn it out on to a serving plate, and peel the foil off the terrine. Surround, if you like, with salad leaves.

Tomato Jelly Ring with Watercress and Crispy Bacon

The jelly for this delicious appetizer has a base of fresh tomato purée (made by liquidizing tomatoes, then sieving them) which is then liquidized again with garlic, cream cheese and dissolved gelatine to set it. Turned out from its ring mould, with a filling of watercress and crispy bacon dressed in a thin cream cheese coating, it will provide an attractive light first course or enhance a buffet table.

Serves 6–8

For the tomato jelly:

6–7 tomatoes, depending on their size

4 fl oz/112 ml water or chicken stock

2 sachets of powdered gelatine (1 oz/28 g)

7 fl oz/200 ml orange juice (preferably freshly squeezed, but you can use canned)

1 garlic clove, skinned and finely chopped (or less, if you prefer a less pronounced flavour)

Salt and freshly ground black pepper

5 oz/140 g cream cheese

For the filling:

3 oz/84 g cream cheese

Milk

5 oz/140 g smoked streaky bacon, thinly sliced

2 handfuls of watercress

Liquidize, then sieve, the tomatoes – you will need about ¾ pint/420 ml of purée. Sprinkle the powdered gelatine over the water or chicken stock in a saucepan, then warm gently over a low heat until the gelatine has dissolved completely.

In a food processor or liquidizer, combine the tomato purée, orange juice, finely chopped garlic and dissolved gelatine. Season with salt and pepper, whiz, and add the cream cheese. Pour the mixture into a 9-inch/23-cm ring mould and leave to set in a cool place. It can be made 2–3 days in advance of serving.

Make the filling as follows. In a food processor, whiz the cream cheese to the thickness of pouring cream by thinning it down with milk until it reaches the right consistency. Grill the bacon till it is evenly crisp, drain it well on kitchen paper, then break it into bits. Tear up the watercress, put it into a bowl, and mix in the broken bits of bacon. Then mix in the thin creamy cheese dressing.

To serve, turn out the ring mould on to a serving dish and pile the filling into the centre.

Vegetables and Salads

Apple, Chicory and Celery Salad with Tarragon Cream
•
Artichoke Hearts in Olive Oil
•
Marinated Grilled Aubergines
•
Avocado with Spinach and Garlic Mayonnaise
•
Avocado and Tomato Dip
•
Hummus
•
Mushrooms in Garlic Butter
•
Marinated Mushrooms
•
Deep-Fried Mushrooms with Tartare Sauce
•
Tomatoes Stuffed with Avocado Pâté
•
Asparagus Mousse
•
Roast Red Pepper Mousse with Black Olive Relish
•
Avocado Terrine
•
Spinach and Garlic Terrine
•
Watercress and Lime Mousse with Creamy Red Pepper Sauce
•
Asparagus Timbales with Hollandaise Sauce
•
Jerusalem Artichoke Timbales with Sauce Bercy
•
Warm Chicken Liver Salad

Apple, Chicory and Celery Salad with Tarragon Cream

This salad makes a delicious first course in the winter months. Use a good eating apple like Cox's Orange Pippin. I leave the skins on, but you may prefer to peel them.

Serves 6

3 eating apples, cored and diced

3 heads of chicory, cut into 1-inch/2.5-cm lengths

6 sticks of celery, very finely sliced

For the Tarragon Cream:

1 tub (10.6 oz/300 g) crème fraîche, full fat, preferably

Several sprigs of tarragon, finely chopped

Salt and freshly ground black pepper

Blend together the ingredients for the Tarragon Cream and season to taste. Mix the apples, chicory and celery together in a bowl and stir in the Tarragon Cream until everything is well blended. Serve on small plates accompanied by Hot Cheesy Scones with Poppy Seeds (see page 374).

Artichoke Hearts in Olive Oil

Serves 8

1½ tbsp lemon juice

8 globe artichokes

1½ tbsp olive oil

½ garlic clove, peeled

Salt and freshly ground black pepper

Add ½ tbsp of the lemon juice to a large bowl of cold water. Remove the stems and outer leaves from the artichokes. Using a sharp stainless steel knife, slice off the remaining leaves to within ½ inch/1 cm of the heart. Remove the chokes with a teaspoon. As the artichoke hearts are prepared, plunge them quickly into the acidulated water to cover them completely. This will prevent them discolouring. Place ¾ pint/420 ml water in a saucepan with the remaining lemon juice, the olive oil, garlic and seasoning. Bring to the boil, then add the artichoke hearts and simmer for 20–25 minutes, until tender.

Remove the artichokes with a slotted spoon. Boil the cooking liquid until reduced by half, then strain a little over the artichoke hearts. Leave to cool, then cut the hearts into quarters.

Marinated Grilled Aubergines

I love aubergines, and I ate the most delicious marinated aubergines one recent November in a small restaurant in a tiny back street in the middle of Rome. We went back to the same restaurant the following February and the same marinated aubergines were again part of the excellent antipasto served as a first course. This is how I reconstructed them.

Serves 6

3 fairly large, firm aubergines

Salt

Olive oil

For the marinade:

¾ pint/420 ml of the best extra virgin olive oil

2 garlic cloves, poached in their skins for 1
minute, then skinned and chopped finely

A handful of parsley, chopped quite fine

½ tsp salt and plenty of freshly ground black
pepper

A sprig of fresh thyme, the tiny leaves
stripped from the stalks

Slice off both ends of the aubergines. Cut lengthways into slices about ¼ inch/5 mm thick and sprinkle with salt. Leave till little beads of dark liquid bubble up then wipe them dry with absorbent paper. Brush each slice on both sides with olive oil then grill or – nicest – barbecue the slices, or fry them, till they are tender. This doesn't take a minute once you have turned them as they cook.

Mix together the marinade ingredients. As the aubergine slices are cooked, put them on to a large serving plate or ashet. Pour the marinade over them and leave for several hours, or overnight.

These are delicious served with Black Olive, Sun-Dried Tomato and Garlic Bread.

Avocados with Spinach and Garlic Mayonnaise

You can make the sauce in the morning for dinner the same evening.

Serves 6

8 oz/225 g fresh baby spinach, well drained

1 tbsp lemon juice

A dash of Tabasco

1 clove of garlic, peeled

6 tbsp mayonnaise, either a good bought
variety or homemade

3 large, ripe avocados

A few chopped peeled prawns, to garnish
(optional)

This recipe is best made in a food processor. Put the spinach into the processor, together with the lemon juice, Tabasco and garlic. Whiz until you have a smooth spinach purée. Add the mayonnaise, and whiz again. Put this mixture into a bowl, cover with clingfilm, and put it in the refrigerator until you are ready to use it.

A couple of hours before serving, cut the avocados in half, carefully easing out the stones with the tip of the knife – if they are ripe the stones will flick out easily. Peel off the skin and put each half, hole side downwards, on to individual plates. Spoon over the sauce, dividing it between the plates. If you like, a few prawns sprinkled on top of each avocado both taste delicious and look nice. Serve with warm brown rolls.

Avocado and Tomato Dip

This is my version of guacamole. I like it much better than any I have either bought in a supermarket or eaten in a restaurant and I have come to the conclusion that there are two things I don't like in guacamole: raw onion, in however infinitesimal amounts, and mayonnaise. Now, I can hear people saying that a true guacamole doesn't have mayonnaise in, but several versions do, and the combination of avocado and mayonnaise is, to me, soapy. This is such a simple and useful dish – you can either serve it as a first course, or as a dip – and I like the crème fraîche which to my taste cuts the denseness of the avocado as well as greatly complementing the flavour, and the chopped tomatoes. I use snipped chives instead of chopped onions.

Serves 6

3 good ripe avocados – it's always better to buy 4, because you can never tell whether one may be fibrous inside

2 tsp lemon juice

2 tubs of crème fraîche (10.6 oz/300 g each)

3 tomatoes, each skinned, cut in half and de-seeded, and the tomatoes chopped into neat dice

About 1 tbsp snipped chives

A good dash of Tabasco sauce

Salt and freshly ground black pepper

Salad leaves, to serve

Cut the avocados in half and scoop their flesh into a food processor. Add the lemon juice and whiz to a smooth purée. Add the crème fraîche and briefly whiz, just enough to combine everything. Scrape this mixture into a bowl, and stir in the diced tomatoes, the snipped chives, Tabasco, salt and pepper. Cover the bowl with clingfilm and leave it in the fridge till you are ready to dish up.

Arrange a small heap of salad leaves on serving plates and put a mound of the avocado and tomato pâté in the middle of each. Do this as near to eating as you can, to let the avocado discolour as little as possible.

Hummus

Serves 6

6 oz/170 g dried chickpeas, soaked overnight

1 garlic clove, skinned + 2 large garlic cloves, poached in their skins for 1 minute

¼ pint/140 ml tahini paste – this is sesame seed paste

¼ pint/140 ml olive oil

1 tbsp lemon juice

Salt and plenty of freshly ground black pepper to your taste

¼ pint/140 ml fromage frais

2 tbsp finely chopped parsley – this 'lifts' the colour of the hummus, as well as adding its fresh flavour

Simmer the chickpeas with the skinned clove of garlic for 1½–2 hours. Drain any excess liquid from them before putting them into a food processor. Snip the ends off the poached cloves of garlic and squeeze – the garlic should pop out of its skin into the processor. Add the tahini. Whiz, adding the olive oil drop by drop at first (as for making mayonnaise), then in a thin trickle. Whiz in the lemon juice, season with salt and pepper, and whiz in the fromage frais and the parsley. Spoon and scrape this into a serving bowl.

Hummus can be made a day or more before it is needed and kept, covered, in the fridge. It can be used as a dip for pitta bread, and makes a delicious filling for potatoes baked in their jackets.

Mushrooms in Garlic Butter

This is a useful dish because you can get it ready an hour or so in advance, and keep it warm until you are ready for dinner.

Serves 6

1 lb/450 g mushrooms

6 oz/170 g butter

2 garlic cloves, skinned and very finely
  chopped

1 dssp lemon juice

Salt and freshly ground black pepper

A pinch of grated nutmeg

2 oz/56 g fresh breadcrumbs, brown or white

2 rounded tbsp finely chopped parsley
  (optional)

Count an even number of mushrooms per head and put them in a buttered ovenproof dish. Or slice the mushrooms and divide them between shallow individual dishes. Cream the butter, add the chopped garlic and beat in the lemon juice, the salt, pepper, nutmeg, breadcrumbs and parsley.

Cover the mushrooms as evenly as possible with the butter mixture and cook in a fairly hot oven, 400°F/200°C/Gas Mark 6, for 7–10 minutes, until the butter is melted and bubbling and the mushrooms are soft.

Serve with wholemeal rolls to mop up the garlic butter.

Marinated Mushrooms

It sounds rather a lot of mushrooms in this recipe, I realize, but they do go down so much as they cook. It is worthwhile cooking the mushrooms in the olive oil till they are crisp – their flavour is very much better. This is a tip passed on to me by Brigadier Ley, one of the best cooks I know, and such a source of inspiration and culinary know-how. You may need more olive oil to sauté the mushrooms than I say – this depends on your sauté pan; a non-stick pan will need less oil than a non non-stick one! This is awfully good.

Serves 6

2 lb/900 g mushrooms, wiped, stalks
  trimmed level with the caps and the
  mushrooms sliced quite thickly

5–6 tbsp olive oil – don't add it to the sauté
  pan all at the beginning, start with 3 tbsp
  and add more as you need it

For the marinade:

4 tbsp extra virgin olive oil

1–2 garlic cloves, skinned and chopped
  finely

½ pint/285 ml chicken (or vegetable) stock

¼ pint/140 ml dry white wine

½ tsp dried thyme or a good sprig of fresh,
  tiny leaves stripped from it

Salt and freshly ground black pepper

3 tomatoes, skinned, cut in half and
  de-seeded, and the tomatoes finely diced

Torn-up basil leaves

Cook the sliced mushrooms in relays, in a sauté pan with the olive oil. Cook them till they are almost crisp, then remove them to a shallow, wide serving dish. As they are sautéing, make the marinade.

Into a wide shallow pan put the olive oil, chopped garlic, stock and white wine, thyme, salt and pepper. Bring to simmering point and simmer gently for 5 minutes. Take it off the heat and leave to cool completely. Then stir in the diced tomatoes and the torn-up basil. Pour this over the sautéed mushrooms and leave overnight in a cool larder or the fridge.

I like to arrange the marinated mushrooms on plates, spooned, with the marinade, over lettuce leaves. Accompany, if you like, with warm bread or with the Sesame Toasts on page 82.

Deep-Fried Mushrooms with Tartare Sauce

How many mushrooms you serve per person depends on how big the mushrooms are – if they are the huge flat ones, which are the nicest, I allow 2–3 per person. If they are the more usual small variety, then 5–6 per person. Simply wipe each mushroom and remove the stalk – there is no need to peel them.

Serves 6–8

Mushrooms (see above)

Oil for deep-frying

Shredded lettuce, to garnish

Tartare Sauce (page 311)

For the batter:

6 oz/170 g plain flour

3 large egg yolks, + 2 egg whites

8 fl oz/225 ml milk

2 tbsp oil (I use sunflower)

Salt and freshly ground black pepper

To make the batter, whiz together in a liquidizer or food processor everything except the egg whites. A couple of hours before cooking, whisk the whites till stiff, with a large metal spoon, fold them quickly and thoroughly through the batter. Cover the bowl with clingfilm.

If you haven't got a deep fryer, heat oil (again, I use sunflower) in a deep saucepan, to a depth of 3 inches/7.5 cm. Dip each mushroom in the batter, and lift it out using two forks. Cook them, no more than three or four at one time, in the hot oil, till they are golden brown and puffed up. Keep them warm, on several thicknesses of kitchen paper, in a low oven till you are ready to dish up. They keep warm quite well for about 20 minutes.

Serve on individual serving plates, accompanied by shredded lettuce if you like, with a good spoonful of Tartare Sauce at the side of the mushrooms.

Tomatoes Stuffed with Avocado Pâté

This simple first course also makes a good main course for lunch or supper, served with accompanying salads. It looks so pretty, too – the red tomatoes contrasting with the pale green avocado filling and the black olives. I like to serve these on a bed of shredded lettuce or spinach.

Serves 6

12 good-sized tomatoes

3 avocados

1 garlic clove, skinned and chopped

8 oz/225 g cream cheese (or a low-fat
   substitute)

Salt and freshly ground black pepper

3 tbsp lemon juice

4 oz/112 g black olives

Cut the tops off the tomatoes, and a tiny slice from the base so that they stand up. Carefully scoop out the seeds. Wipe out the inside of each tomato with a piece of kitchen towel to absorb excess moisture, and leave the hollowed-out tomatoes upside down on a baking tray lined with kitchen paper while you prepare the avocado filling.

Cut each avocado in half and scoop the flesh into a bowl or food processor. Add the chopped garlic, cream cheese, salt and pepper, and mix or process until smooth. Add the lemon juice, tasting to get it to the right sharpness for you. The stuffing will be coarser if you mix it by hand. Stuff the tomatoes with the avocado mixture – the easiest way is to use a piping bag. Garnish each tomato with a black olive and the lid of the tomato, if you like.

If you stuff the tomatoes much more than 2 hours before serving, cover the dish or serving plate with a loose layer of clingfilm to help prevent the avocado filling discolouring too much – the more lemon juice you put in, the less it will discolour anyway.

Asparagus Mousse

This is easy and delicious. If you like, you can make it in ramekins and turn out each mousse on individual serving plates. Serve it with either a small heap of steamed asparagus at the side, or with a tangled small heap of strips of smoked salmon or eel, or with a small amount of dressed salad leaves.

Serves 6

¼ pint/140 ml good chicken stock or vegetable
   stock

1 sachet of powdered gelatine (½ oz/14 g)

1 lb/450 g asparagus, steamed or microwaved
   till just tender when you stick a fork into the
   thickest part of each stem, then with cold
   water run through to refresh its colour

Salt and freshly ground black pepper

A grating of nutmeg

2 pots of crème fraîche (10.6 oz/300 g each)

2 egg whites

Put the stock into a small saucepan and heat it, then sprinkle the gelatine over it. Shake the pan, taking care not to let the liquid boil, till the gelatine dissolves completely and you can see no granules. Let this cool.

Put the cooked asparagus into a processor and whiz till as smooth as you can get it. Whiz in the stock and gelatine mixture, then push this through a sieve, for the smoothest texture. (This depends how sharp the blades of your processor are!) Season the purée with salt and pepper, and a grating of nutmeg. Fold the crème fraîche through the purée.

In a bowl, whisk the egg whites till very

stiff, then, with a large metal spoon, fold them quickly and thoroughly through the purée. Pour the mousse mixture into a serving bowl, cover, and leave to set in a cool place, a fridge or larder.

If you want to set it in ramekins, rub each out with a very small amount of oil – I use sunflower for this – before putting the mousse mixture in. To turn them out, I run a knife around the inside of the ramekins, and the contents should then turn out easily. This can be made a day in advance.

Roast Red Pepper Mousses with Black Olive Relish

Serves 8

3 red peppers

½ pint/285 ml chicken stock

1 sachet of powdered gelatine (½ oz/14 g) or
**   4 leaves gelatine**

1 garlic clove, skinned (optional)

Salt and freshly ground black pepper

2 tubs of crème fraîche (10.6 oz/300 g each)

2 egg whites

For the relish:

1 tin of good black olives

1 garlic clove, skinned and chopped

2 anchovies

4 tbsp olive oil

Freshly ground black pepper

Prepare 8 ramekins by rubbing a minute amount of olive oil thoroughly round the inside of each.

Halve each red pepper and scoop away the seeds. Put the peppers, skin side uppermost, under a hot grill till great black blisters form. Then put the pepper halves into a polythene bag for 10 minutes, after which the skins should peel away easily.

Heat the stock in a small saucepan. When it is hot, sprinkle in the gelatine (or feed in the leaves) and shake the pan till it has dissolved. Leave to cool.

Put the pepper halves into a food processor, with the garlic if used, and whiz till smooth. Season with salt and pepper and whiz in the cold gelatine stock, then the crème fraîche. Tip this into a bowl and set it quickly, if you like, in a larger bowl containing ice cubes and water.

When the stock is beginning to gel, whisk the egg whites until stiff in another bowl, and then use a large metal spoon to fold them thoroughly through the red pepper mixture. Divide the mixture between the ramekins and leave to set.

To turn them out, run the blade of a knife around the inside of each ramekin and shake the mousse on to an individual serving plate.

To make the relish, de-stone the olives, put them into a food processor with the garlic and anchovies, and whiz until everything is pulverized. Then drip in the olive oil while you continue to process, as if you were making mayonnaise. Finally, season with pepper.

Serve the relish in tiny spoonfuls beside each mousse.

Avocado Terrine

*This terrine is very easy to make, and it
provides a wonderfully savoury and
decorative first course for a dinner party.
Or it could be a vegetarian main course,
too, for a summer party, if you replace the
chicken stock with vegetable stock.
Through the middle of the terrine are
avocado halves, which look very attractive
as the terrine is sliced. Serve with a tomato
and basil salad – it contrasts well with the
pale green of the terrine and the flavours
are excellent together – and warm brown
rolls.*

Serves 8

6 medium avocados

Lemon juice

¼ pint/140 ml dry white wine

½ pint/285 ml chicken stock

2 sachets of gelatine (1 oz/28 g)

1 large garlic clove, skinned and chopped

**3 tbsp lemon juice, plus some to brush the
  avocado halves with**

A dash of Tabasco

1 tbsp Worcestershire sauce

Salt and freshly ground black pepper

**½ pint/285 ml double cream, whipped, or you
  can substitute mayonnaise if you happen to
  be on a dairy-free diet**

Line a 9-inch/22-cm loaf or terrine tin with
clingfilm, pressing it carefully into the
corners with your fingertips. Cut each
avocado in half, and carefully remove the
skin from the back of the three most perfect
halves – if they are properly ripe it should
come away easily. Cut the tops off the three
halves and set aside with the unpeeled
halves. Brush the three perfect halves with
lemon juice to prevent the flesh turning
brown. Scoop the flesh out of the other
avocado halves into a liquidizer or food
processor, taking care not to miss the
brightest green and most nutritious flesh,
which lies next to the skin.

Put the white wine and chicken stock
together in a saucepan and sprinkle on the
gelatine. Heat gently until the gelatine is
completely dissolved. Add this to the
avocado flesh in the blender or processor,
and add the chopped garlic, lemon juice,
Tabasco, Worcestershire sauce, salt and
pepper. Blend until you have a very smooth
purée. Then add the whipped cream to the
mixture and blend again until the cream is
thoroughly incorporated.

Pour half the purée into the prepared loaf
or terrine tin. Arrange the avocado halves
nose to tail along the centre of the tin, and
pour the rest of the purée on top. Cover with
clingfilm, and put the tin into the refrigerator for several hours to set.

Just before serving, take the tin out of the
refrigerator, dip it into a bowl of hot water
for a very few seconds and turn it out on to
a serving plate. Peel the clingfilm off the
terrine. Cut it into slices about ½ inch/1 cm
thick. Serve with a tomato salad which has
plenty of torn-up fresh basil leaves mixed in.
If you can't get fresh basil, mix 2 teaspoons
of pesto into the vinaigrette dressing for the
salad.

Spinach and Garlic Terrine

A really useful recipe which tastes good – this can be used as a first course, served with tomato salad, or it can be a main course loved by vegetarians and carnivores alike. It's useful for a buffet lunch or supper party because it's easy to serve and easy to eat with just a fork, and it looks appetizing. It can be made two or three days in advance. All in all, it's a winner. Adjust the amount of garlic to suit your own taste.

Serves 8

1½ lb/675 g frozen chopped spinach, thawed and squeezed of any excess liquid

4 large eggs

2 garlic cloves, skinned and chopped

4 oz/112 g well-flavoured Cheddar cheese, grated

Salt and freshly ground black pepper

Lots of freshly grated nutmeg

A good dash of Tabasco sauce

Line the short sides and base of a terrine or loaf tin with siliconized greaseproof paper. Put the spinach into a liquidizer or food processor and blend. Add the eggs, one at a time, blending continuously. Add the garlic, cheese and seasonings.

Pour the mixture into the prepared terrine and cover with a piece of siliconized grease-proof paper. Stand the terrine in a roasting tin with water coming halfway up the sides of the terrine. Bake in a moderate oven – 350°F/180°C/Gas Mark 4 – for 1½ hours. Take it out of the oven and leave to cool completely.

To serve, run a wetted palette knife down the long sides of the terrine, put a serving plate over the top and invert the whole thing. The terrine should come out with no trouble. Peel off the lining paper. Slice the terrine to serve. Serve with a tomato salad, perhaps with a sweet and mustardy vinaigrette dressing.

Watercress and Lime Mousse with Creamy Red Pepper Sauce

This is simple to make, can be done ahead of time, and is easy and very good to eat. Watercress is a great favourite of mine, with its distinctive, slightly peppery taste, and it is so good for us, being full of vitamin C.

Serves 6

1 pint/570 ml good chicken stock

1½ sachets of gelatine

2 bags (3 oz/84 g each) watercress, stalks and all

Juice of 1 lime and its finely grated rind

Salt, freshly ground black pepper, a dash of Tabasco sauce

2 pots of crème fraîche (10.6 oz/300 g each)

2 egg whites

Measure half the stock into a saucepan and warm gently. When the stock is hot – but not boiling – sprinkle in the gelatine and shake the pan carefully till the gelatine dissolves completely. Put the watercress into a processor with the rest of the stock and whiz till pulverized. Mix together the water-cress liquid with the gelatine liquid, and stir in the grated lime rind and juice and the seasonings.

Leave till it is beginning to gel – you can hurry this by putting the bowl into a wash-ing-up bowl containing water and ice cubes, and stirring the contents of the watercress bowl to prevent a solid jelly forming in the base. It gels quite quickly, especially if it is in a metal bowl. Then take the watercress bowl out of the ice cubes and fold the crème fraîche into the watercress jelly.

In a separate bowl, whisk the egg whites till very stiff, and, using a large metal spoon, fold them quickly and thoroughly through the watercress. Pour into a glass or china serving bowl. Cover with clingfilm and keep in the fridge till you are ready to eat.

Creamy red pepper sauce

4 red peppers, or 3 if they are large

½ pint/285 ml extra virgin olive oil

2 tsp Balsamic vinegar

Salt and freshly ground black pepper

Cut each pepper in half and scoop out the seeds. Put them skin side uppermost on a baking tray under a hot grill. When great charred blisters have formed on the pepper skins, take them out from under the grill and put them in a polythene bag, or wrap them in clingfilm and leave for 10–15 minutes. Then unwrap them and their skins should peel off easily.

Cut the peppers up roughly, put them into a food processor and whiz, adding the oil literally drop by drop – as for making mayonnaise. Lastly, add the Balsamic vinegar and the salt and pepper. Scrape this sauce from the processor into a bowl and store in the fridge, with the bowl covered, till you are ready to serve it with the Watercress and Lime Mousse.

Asparagus Timbales with Hollandaise Sauce

If you grow your own asparagus or have access to a plentiful supply (what bliss!) you may find yourself looking for different ways of cooking it. These timbales are an unusual dish, but easy to make.

Serves 8

1 lb/450 g asparagus

4 large eggs, beaten

½ pint/285 ml single cream

Salt and freshly ground black pepper

Freshly grated nutmeg

Hollandaise Sauce (page 301)

Butter eight large ramekins. Steam the asparagus until it is tender, then blend it to a purée in either a food processor or a liquidizer. Sieve the purée (I know this sounds a fiddle, but it really doesn't take a second and it's worth doing for a smooth and velvety textured purée). Return the purée to the food processor or liquidizer, and blend in first the beaten eggs and then the cream. Season with salt, pepper and nutmeg.

Spoon this mixture into the buttered ramekins, and stand the ramekins in a roasting tin. Pour hot water into the tin so that it comes halfway up the sides of the ramekins. Bake in a moderate oven – 350°F/180°C/Gas Mark 4 – for 25 minutes, or until the asparagus mixture feels quite firm to the touch. Take the tin out of the oven and take the ramekins out of the tin. Let them sit for 10 minutes before turning them out on to serving plates. To turn them out, run the tip of a knife round the edge of the timbale, cover the ramekin with a plate, invert both plate and ramekin and the timbale should come out easily and in one piece.

Serve with Hollandaise Sauce.

Jerusalem Artichoke Timbales with Sauce Bercy

Jerusalem artichokes have one of the most delicious tastes I know. They also have two drawbacks. One is that they are undeniably a fiddle to prepare – they are so knobbly there really is no quick way to peel them (personally I don't begrudge a moment spent in the peeling because they are so good to eat). Their other drawback comes after they are eaten – they are one of the most wind-provoking of all vegetables, even more so than cabbage, onions and beans, and that is really quite something! But they are well worth a little discomfort afterwards. These timbales served with Sauce Bercy are very easy to make and are a really good first course for a dinner party.

Serves 8

2 lb/900 g Jerusalem artichokes
2 pints/1.1 litres chicken stock
4 large egg yolks and 2 egg whites
Salt and freshly ground pepper
Freshly grated nutmeg
⅓ pint/200 ml double cream, whipped
Sauce Bercy (see page 299)

Peel the artichokes (leaving you with about 1½ lb/675 g) and cook them in the chicken stock until tender. Drain the chicken stock (and use it for soup later), and put the artichokes into a food processor or liquidizer. Process or blend the artichokes to a smooth purée, then add the egg yolks, one by one.

Turn the purée into a bowl, season with salt, pepper and nutmeg, and fold in the whipped cream. Whisk the egg whites and fold them into the purée with a metal spoon.

Divide the mixture between eight buttered ramekins. Stand the ramekins in a roasting tin, and pour boiling water into the tin around them. Bake in a moderate oven – 350°F/180°C/Gas Mark 4 – for about 25 minutes, until the mixture is firm to the touch. Take them out of the oven and leave to stand for 5–10 minutes. Turn the timbales out of the ramekins on to serving plates. Pour a spoonful of Sauce Bercy over each timbale and serve.

Warm Chicken Liver Salad

This is so good – the other parts of this salad are tiny cubes of bread, shallow-fried in butter and oil (the oil prevents the butter from burning), and small bits of crisply cooked bacon, preferably smoked bacon. If you make a French dressing with grainy mustard, stirring it in well, it seems to enhance the flavours of this first course salad.

Serves 6

4 oz/112 g butter + 4 tbsp sunflower oil

3 slices of bread, crusts cut off and bread cut into cubes as small as possible

6 slices of smoked streaky bacon, grilled till crisp, then broken into small bits

1½ lb/675 g chicken livers

Assorted salad greenery

2 tbsp finely chopped parsley and snipped chives, mixed

French dressing made with 1 tsp grainy mustard

In the morning you can make the croûtons and grill the bacon – both will reheat before supper. Melt 2 oz/56 g of the butter and heat 2 tablespoons of the oil in a frying pan and fry the bread cubes, turning them continually to prevent them from burning, and cooking them till they are golden brown. As they cook, scoop them on to a plate with two or three thicknesses of kitchen paper, to absorb excess grease.

Pick over the chicken livers, removing any unpleasant bits and chopping any large bits of liver.

Before serving, arrange the salad greens on six plates. Melt the rest of the butter and heat the remaining oil in a frying pan and when they are hot, add the prepared chicken livers. Cook them till they are sealed, but still pink inside. Distribute them evenly between the plates, and scatter the warmed croûtons and bits of bacon over them. Scatter the parsley and chives over each plateful, and serve with the mustardy French dressing handed separately in a jug, with a spoon to stir up the contents.

Eggs and Cheese

Cheese Beignets with Tomato Sauce
·
Egg, Cucumber and Dill Mousse
·
Eggs Niçoise
·
Eggs Stuffed with Tunafish Pâté
·
Pipérade with Garlic Croûtes
·
Quails' Eggs, Artichoke Hearts and Smoked Salmon Salad
·
Quails' Eggs with Stilton and Celery Dip

Cheese Beignets with Tomato Sauce

This is a great favourite when it is on the menu here at Kinloch. The delicious crispy little balls of deep-fried cheesy goo are complemented by the sauce which accompanies them. They are very easy to make, and very convenient – the sauce can be made a day or two in advance and the cheesy choux paste can be made in the morning for cooking the same evening. The deep-frying can be done up to two hours in advance, and the beignets kept warm in a low oven on a dish lined with absorbent kitchen paper. They lose none of their crispiness while they keep warm.

I allow 5–6 beignets per person, trying to make each beignet about the size of a walnut.

Serves 6

2½ oz/70 g butter

¼ pint/140 ml water

3 oz/84 g flour

1 tsp dry mustard powder

2 large eggs

1 garlic clove, skinned and finely chopped

A dash of Worcestershire sauce

A dash of Tabasco sauce

3 oz/84 g Cheddar cheese, grated

Oil for deep-frying (I like to use sunflower oil because it is so light and tasteless)

Tomato Sauce (see page 305; you will need half the quantity given in the recipe)

Cut the butter into the water in a saucepan and melt over a low heat. Don't let the water boil before the butter has melted completely.

Meanwhile sieve the flour and mustard powder together. As soon as the water and butter begin to boil, draw the pan off the heat and add the sieved flour and mustard. Stir and then beat into a paste until it comes away from the sides of the pan. Allow it to cool slightly and then beat in the eggs, one at a time. Add the garlic, seasonings and grated cheese.

Heat the oil in a saucepan to a depth of about 2 inches/5 cm and drop in teaspoonfuls of the mixture. When they are golden brown all over, remove them from the oil with a slotted spoon, and keep them warm on a dish on several thicknesses of absorbent kitchen paper.

Egg, Cucumber and Dill Mousse

This mousse has two different textures, the grated cucumber and the chopped eggs. It is sumptuous, and makes a perfect main course on warm summer evenings as well as an ideal first course.

Serves 6–8

¼ pint/140 ml chicken stock with 1 sachet (½ oz/ 14 g) of gelatine sprinkled in and dissolved over gentle heat

1 cucumber, with peel, grated and sprinkled with salt and left to sit for 30 minutes

8 hardboiled eggs, shelled and chopped

6 tbsp mayonnaise

½ pint/285 ml creamy fromage frais (as opposed to the low-fat kind)

1 tbsp white wine vinegar

1 tsp sugar

1 large handful dill, chopped

2 tbsp snipped chives

Salt and freshly ground black pepper

When the stock and gelatine mixture has cooled completely, stir it into the mayonnaise and add the chopped eggs and the drained grated cucumber. Fold in the fromage frais, the wine vinegar, sugar, chopped dill and chives and put this mixture into a glass or china serving dish, having first tasted to see if there is enough seasoning for your liking. If not, just add a bit more salt and some freshly ground black pepper.

Eggs Niçoise

This is a most popular first course here at Kinloch Lodge. It can also be a summer lunch dish, served with a tomato salad and brown bread rolls. It can be made the day before it is required and kept, covered, in the refrigerator. You can adjust the amount of anchovy essence to suit your taste – we like rather a lot. Do not be tempted to add salt, as both the anchovy essence and the chicken stock are quite salty, and will probably be enough for most palates.

Serves 6

1 level tbsp powdered gelatine

½ pint/285 ml warm chicken stock

8 hardboiled eggs, roughly chopped

8 tbsp mayonnaise

¼ pint/140 ml double cream, whipped

1 dssp anchovy essence

Freshly ground black pepper

A 2-oz/56-g tin anchovy fillets, drained and cut lengthwise into strips

10 black olives, halved and stoned

Dissolve the gelatine in the chicken stock. Stir until there are no granules left and leave to cool. When quite cold and just beginning to set, stir in the chopped hardboiled eggs. Stir together the mayonnaise and the whipped cream. Add the anchovy essence and some black pepper, then fold into the egg mixture. Pour into a dish to set.

When set, garnish the top with strips of anchovies arranged in a lattice design on top, and put half a black olive in each space. If you find anchovies too salty, drain them from the oil in their tin and leave them to soak in a small dish of milk for a few hours. Pat dry before cutting into strips to garnish the finished Eggs Niçoise.

Eggs Stuffed with Tunafish Pâté

These stuffed eggs can be used as a first course, looking impressive but involving minimum effort. Or they can be the main part of a lunch dish, accompanied by salads.

Smoked Haddock and Parsley Mousse ▶
page 43

You can make this in advance, filling the egg halves 2–3 hours before dinner.

Serves 6

| 6 eggs, hardboiled |
| A 7-oz/200-g tin tunafish |
| 6 oz/170 g cream cheese |
| 1 tsp anchovy essence |
| A dash of Tabasco sauce |
| Lots of freshly ground black pepper |
| A few black olives or some finely chopped parsley, for garnish |

Halve the hardboiled eggs lengthwise and cut a tiny sliver off the bottom of each white half, so that they will sit securely. With the tip of a knife, gently ease the yolk out of each half, trying not to split the white.

If you have a food processor, put the yolks into it, and add the tunafish, cream cheese and seasonings. Whiz until the mixture is smooth. If you have no food processor, pound the ingredients together in a bowl, using the end of a rolling pin.

Fit a piping bag with a wide star-shaped nozzle, and fill the piping bag with the mixture. Arrange the whites around a flat plate or shallow dish, and pipe the filling into each hollow. When piping, try to follow the shape of the white, rather than making a tall blob in the hole. If you prefer, fill the egg whites using two teaspoons, scooping the mixture with one, and pushing

◀ Mixed Fish Mayonnaise
page 73

it into the white with the other. Garnish by dusting the eggs with finely chopped parsley, or by putting a piece of black olive on each stuffed egg half.

If you have used a sufficiently large dish, and have a space in the middle, you can fill this with shredded lettuce or tomato wedges.

Pipérade with Garlic Croûtes

As well as a first course at dinner (halving the quantities given below), this also makes a very good lunch or supper dish. The pepper, onion and garlic mixture can be cooked in the morning and reheated before the eggs are scrambled through it. I also like to skin, de-seed and slice tomatoes in thin strips to stir into the cooked scrambled eggs, and I fry the small triangles of bread in olive oil with lots of garlic, then drain them on several thicknesses of kitchen paper. These can be kept warm for up to 1½ hours.

Serves 8

| 16 triangles of bread, white or brown |
| 1 garlic clove, skinned |
| 4 tbsp olive oil, plus extra for frying the croûtes |
| 2 medium onions, skinned and sliced thinly |
| 3 red and 3 yellow peppers, halved, grilled till black-blistered, then skinned and chopped finely |
| 1 garlic clove, skinned and chopped finely |
| 16 large eggs, beaten together |
| 4 tomatoes, skinned, de-seeded and sliced |
| Salt and freshly ground black pepper |

Fry the triangles of bread in extra virgin olive oil, with the whole skinned garlic clove. When the croûtes are golden on both sides, take them out of the oil, drain and keep them warm on several thicknesses of kitchen paper.

Heat the 4 tablespoons of oil in a saucepan and add the onions, peppers and the finely chopped garlic. Cook over a moderate heat till they are all soft. You can get the pipérade to this stage in the morning. Reheat the mixture before adding the beaten eggs, and scramble these with the cooked onion and pepper mixture.

When the eggs are scrambled, stir the sliced tomatoes through them just before serving. Season to taste with salt and pepper and serve either piled on an ashet, with the garlic croûtes all round, or on warmed individual plates.

Quails' Eggs, Artichoke Hearts and Smoked Salmon Salad

Salads with strong individual characters, as it were, as their components, make my favourite first courses. They are convenient in that they can be prepared well in advance, only needing to be assembled before supper-time. In this salad the tastes of the quails' eggs, the artichoke hearts (well drained of their brine) and the smoked salmon all complement each other.

Serves 6

Mixed salad greens

2–3 artichoke hearts per person

18 quails' eggs, boiled for 4 minutes, cooled and shelled

12 oz/340 g thinly sliced smoked salmon

2 tbsp finely chopped parsley and snipped chives, mixed

French Dressing (see page 289)

On six serving plates distribute the salad greenery. On top arrange the artichoke hearts, each cut in half, the shelled and halved quails' eggs and the smoked salmon, cut into thin strips. Scatter the parsley and chives over the surface of each, and hand around the French dressing in a jug with a spoon for serving, so that guests can help themselves as they like – some, or none at all.

Quails' Eggs with Stilton and Celery Dip

Quails' eggs are now widely available, and this makes an ideal first course which can be eaten in the fingers with a drink in hand. Very finely sliced celery is stirred through the smooth Stilton cream dip, providing a good contrasting crunch. I like to stir snipped chives through, too, for the appearance as well as the flavour.

Serves 4–6

Quails' eggs (allow 3–4 per person)

For the dip:

4 oz/112 g Stilton cheese

3 fl oz/84 ml single cream

Half a good stick of celery, sliced as finely as possible

2 tsp snipped chives

Boil the eggs for 4 minutes. Cool and shell them.

Put the Stilton in a food processor and whiz, gradually pouring in the single cream. When it is all a smooth thick mixture, pour it into a serving bowl, and stir through the finely sliced celery and snipped chives. Cover the dip with clingfilm till you are ready to serve it.

Many recipes elsewhere in this book, particularly in the Fish section, can be adapted as first courses simply by serving smaller quantities. Any of the following would work equally well scaled down. The Egg chapter and the Barbecues and Picnics chapter, too, both contain first-course possibilities.

Prawn Curry Mayonnaise • Prawns in Piquant Dressing • Marinated Diced Salmon • Scallop and Leek Salad • Diced Fish Marinated in Fromage Frais with Herbs • Avocado and Salmon Terrine • Smoked Salmon Terrine with Red Pepper Sauce • Smoked Haddock Timbales with Watercress Sauce • Herb Crêpes with Smoked Salmon and Cucumber • Smoked Eel and Cucumber Profiteroles • Oysters on Mushrooms with Hollandaise Sauce • Salmon and Dill Tart • Squid with Garlic and Parsley in Olive Oil • Squid with Tomatoes and Black Olives • Invergarry Crab

Fish and Shellfish

There are recipes for a tremendous variety of fish and shellfish in this chapter, some suitable for a light lunch or supper if accompanied by bread and a salad, others more substantial, or appropriate for special occasions. I have included everyday food such as Fish Cakes and Fish Pie, and also many recipes suitable for entertaining, or for family occasions which require something special. Dishes such as Baked Fillet of Cod with Parsley and Basil Mousseline, or Smoked Salmon Terrine with Red Pepper Sauce, fall into this category.

This chapter includes many recipes which haven't featured in my other books. Perhaps in cooking fish, above all other types of food, I continue to experiment. If I had to choose one food above all others that I couldn't do without, it would have to be fish, in all its many forms, whether smoked or unsmoked, or shellfish. Fish is real convenience food. It is truly fast food, dispelling, I hope, the connotation of hamburgers that the words conjure up. Fish is very easily ruined by overcooking, but that is also the reason why it is such a time-saver as a main course. You can prepare it in advance, cutting it into chunks or just leaving it in fillets, depending on what you are making, and then cook it in two or three minutes just before eating.

I think the preparation of fish for cooking is all-important. What puts people off eating fish above all else is the fear of finding a bone in their mouthful. This fear can be eliminated if you feel the raw fish all over with your fingertips, on a board. You can feel bones where you can't see them, and then you can either pull them out, in the case of fish such as cod, which has large bones, or with haddock, for example, you can use a sharp knife to cut on either side of a row of tiny bones and remove them like that. Feeling the fish while it is still raw is much better than trying to remove bones from it once it is cooked, as I discovered a few years ago. You can then reassure your family or guests that the fish is truly bone-free.

We are told, officially, that we should include fish in our diet at least three times a week, particularly oily fish such as herring, mackerel, sardines, salmon and halibut. This is no hardship! But there are people who genuinely can't bear to touch fish – I have encountered a number of them at cooking demonstrations. It helps, I hope, to remember that fish live in water, whether sea water or fresh. For this reason I never mind cleaning a fish, although I realise that the majority of buyers want their fish ready cleaned (gutted), filleted and even, occasionally, skinned. A pair of rubber gloves worn by the gutter helps the task for the squeamish.

I am impressed by the expanding selection to be found on wet fish counters in some supermarkets. I am so lucky in where I live, because we are almost opposite Mallaig, one of the two main fishing ports on the west coast of Scotland (the other being Inverbervie), and it is from Mallaig that we buy much of the fish we use here at Kinloch, and the rest of our excellent fish comes from our local town, Broadford, from John Gilbertson's fishing boats. We use only wild salmon here, and yet I do like some farmed salmon. There is a difference in the quality, of course, as with anything farmed, but some farmed fish are of an excellent quality. However, I do still prefer wild fish overall.

I believe that the best fish in the world is to be found off the shores of Britain – yet to some people fish means either haddock or cod (both excellent fish, although I prefer my haddock smoked), dipped in batter and deep-fried. I hope that some of these fish-based recipes will whet reluctantly fish-inclined appetites, and will gladden the hearts of all those who – like me – love fish.

Mixed Fish and Shellfish in Dill Sauce

•

Mixed Fish Mayonnaise

•

Prawn Curry Mayonnaise

•

Prawns in Piquant Dressing

•

Marinated Diced Salmon

•

Scallop and Leek Salad

•

Diced Fish Marinated in Fromage Frais
with Herbs

•

Crab Soufflé

•

Crab Florentine with Sesame Toast

•

Plaice on Spinach in Cheese Soufflé

•

Avocado and Salmon Terrine

•

Smoked Salmon Terrine with Red Pepper
Sauce

•

Smoked Haddock Timbales with
Watercress Sauce

•

Herring Roes with Sesame Toast and
Grilled Bacon

•

Herb Crêpes with Smoked Salmon
and Cucumber

•

Baked Fillet of Cod with Parsley and
Basil Mousseline

•

Cod with Parsley and Garlic in Filo Parcels

•

Cod and Smoked Haddock Puffed Pie

•

Smoked Eel and Cucumber Profiteroles

•

Smoked Haddock Gougère

Baked Hake Fillets in Parsley, Garlic and Olive
Oil Paste with Tomatoes

•

Monkfish in Saffron Cream Sauce

•

Monkfish with Tomatoes, Garlic and
Black Olives

•

Oysters on Mushrooms with Hollandaise
Sauce

•

Stir-Fried Oysters with Ginger
and Spring Onions

•

Sautéed Plaice Fillets with Parsley
and Lemon Juice

•

Salmon and Dill Tart

•

Fillet of Salmon in Filo Parcels with Dill Butter

•

Salmon with Julienne Vegetables under a
Puffed Crust

•

Baked Salmon with Sesame Vegetables

•

Scallops with Julienne Vegetables
under a Puffed Crust

•

Scallops in Saffron and White Wine Sauce

•

Fillet of Sea Bass with Almonds

•

Squid with Garlic and Parsley in Olive Oil

•

Squid with Tomatoes and Black Olives

•

Fish Stir-Fried with Leeks and Ginger

•

Fish Cakes

•

Invergarry Crab Cakes

•

Fish Pie

•

Seafood Puff Pastry Turnovers

Mixed Fish and Shellfish in Dill Sauce

This is a delicately flavoured cold fish and shellfish main course – perfect food for summer eating.

Serves 6

1¼ lb/570 g salmon

1 lb/450 g halibut (or turbot or monkfish, also firm-fleshed white fish)

½ lb/225 g (shelled weight) prawns, or Morecambe Bay shrimps if you can get them

6 scallops

Dill Sauce (see page 300)

A few fronds of dill, to garnish (optional)

For the court bouillon:

¾ pint/420 ml water

Fish skins and bones

5 fl oz/140 ml dry white wine

A handful of parsley stalks

½ onion, skinned and halved

1 stick of celery, washed and chopped

⅛ bulb of fennel

A few black peppercorns

½ tsp rock salt

Fillet the salmon (or ask your fishmonger to do this for you) and skin it, and the halibut or other fish. Cut the fish into bite-sized chunks. Trim the dark tube off each scallop, and cut each scallop in half (leave the corals whole).

Put all the ingredients for the court bouillon into a saucepan and bring to simmering point. Simmer gently, with the saucepan covered, for about 40 minutes, then take the pan off the heat. Let the liquid cool completely, then strain.

Reheat the court bouillon to a simmer, and poach small amounts of the fish and shellfish for no more than 30 seconds in the simmering liquid – fish cooks very quickly and is ruined if overcooked. By cooking the fish in small amounts, you avoid under-cooking some pieces and overcooking others. Remove the fish with a slotted spoon from the cooking liquor and leave to cool.

Make up half the quantity of Dill Sauce given on page 300. Pour it into a large bowl and carefully mix the fish into the sauce. Divide between six serving plates (making sure that each person gets a scallop!), or serve on an ashet, garnished with fronds of dill.

Mixed Fish Mayonnaise

You can combine any fish you like, really, in this dish. The more special the occasion it is intended for, the higher the ratio can be of shellfish to white and smoked fish. It makes a delicious main course for summer parties, one of my favourites of the recipes in this book! Also one of the simplest.

Serves 8

2 lb/900 g smoked haddock or cod

1½ lb/675 g cod or hake

Milk and water to cover the fish

1 onion, skinned and cut in half

1 stick of celery, chopped in bits

For the sauce:

¼ pint/140 ml double cream, whipped

¾ pint/420 ml good mayonnaise

1 tsp medium strength curry powder

1 tbsp lemon juice

Freshly ground black pepper

6 oz/170 g cooked prawns, shelled

A few mussels, cooked and shelled (optional)

4 anchovy fillets, patted dry

2 tbsp finely chopped parsley and chives,
  mixed

Feel the fish with your fingertips and remove all bones. Put into a saucepan with milk and water to cover, and the onion and celery.

Heat till the milk and water just begins to simmer. Cook for 2 minutes, then take the pan off the heat and leave till the fish is cool enough to handle. Flake the fish, carefully removing the skin. Reserve the flaked fish.

Mix together the cream, mayonnaise, curry powder and lemon juice. Season with plenty of black pepper. Fold in the cooked flaked fish, the prawns, and the mussels if you are using them. Chop the anchovies and fold them in with the rest of the fish. Arrange on a serving dish or plate, and scatter the chopped parsley and chives over.

Serve with boiled Basmati rice, dressed with a few tablespoons of French dressing as soon as it is drained.

Prawn Curry Mayonnaise

This delicious cold prawn curry makes a wonderful main course dish for a summer party. The sauce can be made two or three days in advance, and then combined with the mayonnaise and prawns on the day of the party. Serve the prawns on a bed of cooked boiled Basmati rice mixed with a handful of raisins and tossed in a little vinaigrette dressing.

Serves 6

1½ lb/675 g prawns or chopped langoustine,
  weighed when shelled and cooked

For the sauce:

2 tbsp sunflower or olive oil

1 onion, skinned and finely chopped

1 apple, cored and chopped

1 rounded tbsp curry powder

2 tbsp mango chutney

1 x 15-oz/420-g tin of tomatoes, or 6 fresh
  tomatoes, liquidized and sieved

For the mayonnaise:

6 tbsp mayonnaise

Juice of half a lemon

Salt and freshly ground black pepper

A dash of Tabasco sauce

Chives and parsley, to garnish

Make the sauce by heating the oil in the saucepan and sautéing the onion for about 5 minutes, stirring occasionally. Add the apple (skin and all) and cook for another 2–3 minutes. Stir in the curry powder, cook for another couple of minutes and then stir in the chutney and the tomatoes. Half cover the saucepan and simmer gently for 30 minutes. Cool, liquidize and sieve the sauce.

Mix together the mayonnaise, lemon juice, seasoning and Tabasco sauce, and stir this into the sieved sauce. Stir in the prawns, and put the bowl to chill in the fridge until you are ready to serve.

On a serving dish arrange cooked Basmati rice mixed with raisins and tossed in vinaigrette dressing, and spoon the prawn curry over the rice. Dust with chopped parsley mixed with chopped chives and serve.

Prawns in Piquant Dressing

Prawns need very little cooking – they can so easily become overcooked and mushy. They are very filling, so you don't need much more than ½ lb (in their shells) per person as a main course. The whole dish can be prepared in the morning and kept covered in a cool place for serving that evening.

Serves 6

6 lb/2.7 kg prawns, in their shells

For the dressing:
½ onion, very finely chopped

6 tbsp olive oil

3 tbsp white wine

Dash of Tabasco sauce

Juice of half a lemon

Salt and freshly ground black pepper

1 tbsp finely chopped parsley

Half fill your largest saucepan with water and bring it to the boil. Put half of the prawns into the boiling water and bring the water almost back to simmering. Using a slotted spoon, scoop the prawns out of the water. Let the water boil up again, then put the remaining prawns in and cook as the first batch. Drain these. Allow the prawns to

cool slightly, then, when cool enough to handle, peel them.

Put the ingredients for the dressing, except the parsley, into a saucepan and bring to simmering point. Simmer for about 5 minutes. Pour the dressing over the peeled prawns. Mix well together, then mix in the parsley. Put in a serving dish and chill until you are ready to serve.

Marinated Diced Salmon

The small cubes of fish are 'cooked' not by any heat source but by marinating for several hours in an acid mixture of lime or lemon juice and white wine vinegar. Purists or foodies say this recipe should be made with shark. Well, I find shark rather hard to come by and so, I should think, do most people who don't live within a stone's throw of Billingsgate! You can, in fact, use any white fish, although the firmer fleshed the better. In this recipe I use salmon. In this case the salmon is served with a tomato and cucumber mayonnaise, which not only tastes delicious but provides a contrasting crunchy texture.

Serves 6–8

3 lb/1.35 kg salmon, filleted, skinned and cut into ½-inch/1-cm cubes or strips

¼ pint/140 ml lime or lemon juice

¼ pint/140 ml white wine vinegar

Grated rind of 1 lemon

½ tsp salt and freshly ground black pepper

2 rounded tbsp finely chopped parsley and coriander, to garnish

Tomato and Cucumber Mayonnaise (see page
  292)

Mix well together the cubed salmon, the lime
or lemon juice, wine vinegar, grated lemon
rind, salt and pepper in a wide shallow dish.
Leave in a cool place for at least 4 hours.
From time to time stir the salmon around, so
that it marinates as evenly as possible.

To serve, drain the salmon of its
marinade, and arrange on a serving dish.
Sprinkle over the mixed parsley and
coriander. Serve the Tomato and Cucumber
Mayonnaise in a bowl or sauce boat.

Scallop and Leek Salad

*This is a simple dish, if a rather special one.
The tastes of the leeks and scallops go so
very well together. The sliced leeks are
cooked with a very small amount of
chopped fresh ginger in butter and sunflower oil, then the sliced scallops are
added to the frying pan. After a brief
cooking the contents of the frying pan are
transferred into a serving dish and a
fromage-frais-based sauce is spooned over,
and the leeks and scallops left to cool.*

*It can be made in the morning for a
supper the same evening, when it needs
only warm bread, white or granary, and
salad to accompany it. You can, if you like,
substitute sliced monkfish for the scallops.*

Serves 6

18 large scallops

2 oz/56 g butter + 1 tbsp sunflower oil

6 medium to large (but not woody) leeks,
  washed, trimmed, and sliced thinly on the
  diagonal

A 1-inch/2.5-cm piece of fresh root ginger,
  pared of its skin and finely chopped

½ pint/285 ml fromage frais

½ tsp salt and plenty of freshly ground black
  pepper

1 tbsp lemon juice

1 tbsp each snipped chives and finely
  chopped parsley

Trim the dark tube off each scallop and slice
into about three (leave the corals whole). In
a large sauté or frying pan, melt the butter
and heat the oil together and cook the sliced
leeks over a gentle heat, with the chopped
ginger, for about 5–7 minutes – till the leeks
feel tender. The ginger will lose its ferocity
as it cooks. Then add the sliced scallops and
cook them, stirring them around, raising the
heat under the pan to moderate. When the
slices of scallop turn opaque, 3–4 minutes at
the most, scoop the contents of the pan into
a serving dish.

Mix together the fromage frais, salt, pepper and lemon juice, and pour this over the
leek and scallops mixture. Scatter the chives
and parsley over the surface. Leave to cool
completely, then serve.

Diced Fish Marinated in Fromage Frais with Herbs

*This is a perfect dish for a hot summer's
evening. It has to be prepared several hours
in advance, so you can get it ready in the
morning. I like to serve it with either warm*

granary bread or Black Olive, Sun-Dried
Tomato and Garlic Bread (see page 368). It
needs only mixed green salad leaves as an
accompaniment apart from the bread.

Use any fish you like, but it is important
to have smoked fish as half the fish quantity.
Feel with your fingers for bones, and cut
them out with a very sharp knife. This is the
only sure way to discover all the bones.

Serves 6

1 lb/450 g each smoked haddock and firm-
fleshed white fish such as cod, hake, or
monkfish

½ pint/285 ml creamy fromage frais

1 tbsp lemon juice

1 tsp sugar

½ pinch of salt – the smoked haddock is quite
salty

Plenty of ground black or white pepper

4 tbsp chopped dill

With a very sharp knife, slice the fish, both
smoked and unsmoked, into small dice,
about ¼ inch/0.5 cm in size. Put the diced
fish on to an ashet or large serving plate.

Mix together the fromage frais, lemon
juice, sugar, salt, pepper and dill weed, and
spread this over the fish, stirring it all up.
Leave for several hours, at least six, and stir
it up once or twice in that time. Serve.

Crab Soufflé

This dish is very straightforward and simple to make. Crab is extremely filling, and
if the amount of crab in this recipe seems a
bit mean to you, it is because a little goes a
long way. It needs only warm bread or
rolls, preferably granary, and a mixed leaf
salad to accompany it.

Serves 6

Freshly grated Parmesan cheese

2 oz/56 g butter

2 tbsp flour

1 tsp mustard powder

¾ pint/420 ml full fat milk (much nicer than
skimmed for this dish)

2 tbsp dry sherry

A pinch of salt and plenty of freshly ground
black pepper

A grating of nutmeg

A dash of Tabasco sauce

5 large eggs, separated

1 lb/450 g crabmeat, and I prefer half white
and half brown

Butter a large soufflé dish, or any ovenproof
dish (such as Pyrex), and dust the dish with
freshly grated Parmesan cheese.

Melt the butter in a large saucepan and
stir in the flour and mustard. Let this cook
for a minute before stirring in the milk,
adding it gradually and stirring all the time
till the sauce simmers. Draw the pan off the
heat and stir in the sherry, salt, pepper,
nutmeg and Tabasco sauce. Beat in the
yolks, one by one. Cover the surface of the
sauce with damp greaseproof paper and
leave to cool – the paper will prevent a skin
forming; if you prefer you can use clingfilm
instead of the greaseproof. When it is cold,
beat in the crabmeat – you can do all this the
previous day if it is more convenient for you.

In a clean bowl whisk the whites till they are very stiff and, with a large metal spoon, fold them quickly and thoroughly through the crab mixture. Pour and scrape this into the prepared soufflé dish and bake in a hot oven, 425°F/220°C/Gas Mark 7, for 30–35 minutes.

Serve immediately, with a green salad.

Crab Florentine with Sesame Toast

I love crab. In this dish the flaked crab-meat, a mixture of white and brown meat, is on a bed of steamed spinach with a faint seasoning of nutmeg – a spice which enhances the taste of both the crab and the spinach – with cheese on top. The cheese sauce is set with the addition of egg, so that the whole thing isn't too runny.

The recipe for Sesame Toast is on page 82. It can be made in advance and reheated to serve. Store it in an airtight container.

Serves 6

3 lb/1.35 kg fresh spinach – this seems an
    awful lot, I realize, but I reckon on 1 lb/450 g
    fresh for two servings; once it is steamed, it
    diminishes by about four-fifths
Grated nutmeg
Salt and freshly ground black pepper
1 lb/450 g crabmeat, white and brown mixed

For the cheese sauce:
2 oz/56 g butter
2 oz/56 g flour
1 pint/570 ml milk
4 oz/112 g grated Cheddar cheese
Salt and freshly ground black pepper
1 whole egg + 2 large egg yolks, beaten
    together

Butter an ovenproof dish. Steam the spinach till it wilts, then, in a bowl, chop it with a very sharp knife, and mix in a grating of nutmeg, a pinch of salt and some black pepper. Chop it as finely as you can, but don't be tempted to purée it – I personally like the texture of the chopped spinach with the flaked crab and without it the whole dish tends to be rather mushy eating. Put it into the buttered dish and distribute the crab over it.

Make the cheese sauce by melting the butter in a saucepan and stirring in the flour. Let it cook for a minute or two, then gradually add the milk, stirring all the time till the sauce boils. Take the pan off the heat and stir in two-thirds of the grated cheese, season with salt and pepper, and beat in the egg and egg yolks mixture. Pour this over the crab and sprinkle the remaining cheese over the surface.

Bake in a moderate oven, 350°F/180°C/Gas Mark 4, till the cheese sauce is just set – about 20–25 minutes.

Serve with Sesame Toast.

Plaice on Spinach in Cheese Soufflé

This is really a version of eggs florentine using fish instead of eggs, and the whole cooked in a cheese soufflé rather than with just a cheese sauce poured over. I love plaice, and I always think it grossly unfair that dreary old lemon sole gets a far higher rating than the humbler plaice. Plaice has far more taste than lemon sole, and I can only think that lemon sole's higher status is because the name 'sole' has connotations in people's minds with the far more worthy and aristocratic Dover member of the family.

The spinach in this recipe can be prepared well in advance. So can the cheese soufflé mixture for that matter – it won't come to any harm provided it is kept closely covered with clingfilm.

Garlic bread or warmed granary bread or rolls go very well with this.

Serves 6

| 3 lb/1.35 kg fresh spinach |
| 2 oz/56 g butter |
| Salt and freshly ground black pepper |
| A grating of nutmeg |
| 1½ lb/675 g filleted, skinned plaice |

For the cheese soufflé:

| 2 oz/56 g butter |
| 2 oz/56 g flour |
| 1 pint/570 ml milk |
| 6 oz/170 g good Cheddar cheese, grated |
| Salt and freshly ground black pepper |
| A grating of nutmeg |
| 4 large eggs, separated |

Steam the spinach till it wilts. Then put it into a food processor and whiz it, adding the butter, salt, pepper and nutmeg. Butter a wide ovenproof dish and spread the puréed spinach over the base of this dish. When the spinach has cooled, put the plaice in a thick layer on top of it.

Make the soufflé by melting the butter and stirring in the flour. Cook for a minute, then, stirring continuously, gradually add the milk. Stir till the sauce boils. Take the pan off the heat and stir in the grated cheese, stirring till it melts, and stir in the salt, pepper and nutmeg. Beat in the egg yolks, one by one. Lastly, whisk the whites till they are very stiff, adding a pinch of salt (which gives increased volume), and then, with a large metal spoon, fold the whites quickly and thoroughly through the cheese mixture. Pour this over the fish.

Either cover the dish with clingfilm ready to cook two or three hours later, or bake it straight away in a hot oven, 420°F/220°C/Gas Mark 7, for 25 minutes. Serve immediately.

Avocado and Salmon Terrine

I like to make this in a Pyrex terrine-shaped dish. Even though I line the dish with clingfilm, I find that if I make it in a metal loaf or terrine tin lined with clingfilm the avocado turns brown in a much more marked fashion that it does with the clingfilm and the Pyrex. As I bought my Pyrex terrines in the hardware shop in Kyle of Lochalsh, I'm quite sure they would be easily obtainable in other places!

This smooth avocado mixture has a

layer of flaked salmon in the middle. It is quite filling, and needs only a green or mixed salad and warm bread to go with it.

Serves 6–8

½ pint/285 ml good chicken stock and ¼ pint/140 ml dry white wine
1½ sachets of gelatine (¾ oz/21 g), or 6 leaves
1 lb/450 g salmon, poached, skinned, bones removed and flaked
½ tsp salt
1 tbsp finely chopped parsley and 1 tbsp snipped chives
4 avocados of the dark knobbly sort (I think these have the best taste) or 3 of the larger smooth-skinned type
1 garlic clove, skinned and finely chopped
A dash of Tabasco sauce
2 tbsp Worcestershire sauce
½ pint/285 ml crème fraîche
Salt and freshly ground black pepper

Line a 2½-pint/1.5-litre Pyrex terrine (11 inches/28 cm long) with clingfilm, carefully pushing it into the corners of the dish as neatly as you can.

In a saucepan warm together the stock and wine. When they are hot but nowhere near boiling, sprinkle in the gelatine and shake the pan gently till it has dissolved completely. Pour a quarter of this liquid into a bowl containing the flaked salmon, and stir in the half teaspoon of salt, the parsley and chives, mixing all together well.

Scoop out the flesh from the avocados into a food processor. Add the chopped garlic, cooled gelatine, stock and wine mixture, Tabasco and Worcestershire sauces and whiz all together till smooth. Add the

crème fraîche, whizzing it in briefly. Taste, and season with salt and pepper.

Scrape half this avocado mixture into the lined Pyrex terrine. With a fork, put the salmon and herbs mixture over the avocado mixture in the terrine, and scrape the remainder of the avocado mixture on top. Bang the terrine – carefully! – a couple of times on a work surface. Cover the dish with clingfilm and store in the fridge till you are ready to turn it out.

To turn out, dip the Pyrex dish in a basin of very hot water for 2–3 minutes, then turn it out on to a serving plate. Peel off the clingfilm at the very last minute before serving it, in thick slices.

Smoked Salmon Terrine with Red Pepper Sauce

Serves up to 10

About 6 oz/170 g smoked salmon slices
Another 1¼ lb/560 g smoked salmon – pieces will do
½ pint/285 ml single cream
5 fl oz/140 ml cold water
2 sachets of powdered gelatine (approx. ½ oz/14 g each)
5 fl oz/140 ml boiling water
Juice of 1 lemon
Freshly ground black pepper
½ pint/285 ml double cream, whipped
1 large egg white
Red Pepper Sauce (page 59)

Trim the smoked salmon slices and use them to line a 10-inch/25-cm-long loaf tin or terrine as neatly as you can. Set aside.

Put the smoked salmon pieces into a food processor and whiz, pouring in the single cream as you do so, until smooth.

Pour the cold water into a bowl, sprinkle over the gelatine, then pour on the boiling water and stir until the gelatine has dissolved. Mix the lemon juice into the dissolved gelatine, and when it is cool, pour this into the processor, whizzing as you do so. Season with pepper to taste.

Turn this smoked salmon mixture into a bowl and fold in the whipped cream. Whisk the egg whites till very stiff, then, with a metal spoon, fold them quickly and thoroughly through the smoked salmon mixture. Pour it all into the tin lined with smoked salmon, cover it with clingfilm, and put it in the fridge for several hours.

To turn out the terrine, run a knife down the sides, invert it on to a board, and slice it. Serve each slice with a good spoonful of Red Pepper Sauce.

Smoked Haddock Timbales with Watercress Sauce

These make a most delicious as well as convenient lunch or supper. You can make up the smoked haddock mixture in the morning ready to bake later, but keep it in a jug and stir it up well with either a fork or a flat wire whisk before pouring it into the oiled ramekins. They take exactly half an hour to bake in a moderate oven, and they are no problem at all to turn out.

They look so pretty surrounded by watercress sauce, and the taste of the sauce, too, is very complementary to that of the smoked fish.

With this main course, I feel a need for a crunchy vegetable, and my favourite with just about everything is sugarsnap peas, each pea sliced diagonally into about three bits, and stir-fried with finely chopped garlic and fresh ginger which has already been given a head start in the frying pan of about 3 minutes before the peas are added – the peas need the briefest cooking time, about 30 seconds.

Serves 6

2 lb/900 g smoked haddock
1½–2 pints/850 ml–1.1 litres milk and water mixed
8 large eggs
¾ pint/420 ml single cream
Plenty of freshly ground black pepper
A grating of nutmeg

For the watercress sauce:

A 3-oz/84-g bag of watercress
½ pint/285 ml milk
2 oz/56 g butter
½ tsp cornflour
1 whole egg + 2 yolks
Salt and freshly ground black pepper
A grating of nutmeg

Feel down the centre of each fillet of fish and carefully cut away the bones. Cut the fish into bits about 1 inch/2.5 cm in size and put them into a saucepan with the milk and water mixture. Bring the liquid around the fish to the point where a skin forms on the surface, then drain the fishy liquid away (keep it for soup) and put the partially cooked pieces of fish into a food processor. Whiz, gradually adding the eggs and cream. Season with pepper and a small amount of freshly grated nutmeg.

Oil twelve large ramekins and pour in the mixture. Carefully put each ramekin into a large, deep baking tray. Pour water into the tray around the ramekins. Bake in a moderate oven, 350°F/180°C/Gas Mark 4, for 30 minutes.

Put the ingredients for the sauce into a liquidizer and whiz till smooth. If you have a microwave oven, put the sauce into a Pyrex bowl on a medium heat for 2 minutes. Whisk well, then repeat the cooking process. Do this a third time, and the sauce should be thickened. If you don't have a microwave oven, put the bowl over a pan of simmering water, with the water coming up the sides of the bowl. Stir it with a whisk from time to time as it cooks – it will take 20–25 minutes, depending on the depth of the water around the bowl.

Turn out the timbales by running a knife around the inside of each ramekin and turning out two on each serving plate. Pour the sauce around the timbales, and serve. They will sit without deteriorating too much for 10 minutes or so – much longer than that and they seem to lose their initial airy texture.

Herring Roes with Sesame Toast and Grilled Bacon

Herring roes are not readily found, but when they are, seize the chance and buy as much as you can eat for several days! They are best eaten with bacon, especially I think smoked bacon – the flavour of both smoked and unsmoked bacon goes so very well with all things fishy, and this is no exception. The Sesame Toast adds a good crisp and crunchy texture to the whole. The toast can be made ahead, and warmed up, if it's more convenient for you.

Serves 6

12 rashers of smoked back bacon, grilled to the degree that you like
2 oz/56 g butter + 1 tbsp sunflower oil
1½ lb/675 g herring roes

For the sesame toast:

6 slices of bread, brown or white, crusts cut off
3 oz/84 g butter, melted
6 tbsp sesame seeds mixed with 1 tsp salt

Melt the butter and heat the oil in a large pan, and gently fry the herring roes until firm.

Brush each slice of bread with melted butter, on each side. Press the salted sesame seeds into each buttered side, and toast under a hot grill, till the slices are golden brown on each side. If you prefer, before toasting you can cut the bread into strips, about three per slice.

Arrange the fried roes, grilled bacon and toast on six plates or a warm serving dish.

Herb Crêpes with Smoked Salmon and Cucumber

Serves 8

For the crêpes:

2 large eggs

4 oz/112 g plain flour

½ pint/285 ml milk and 2 tbsp water

1 oz/56 g butter, melted

Fresh herbs – any or all of parsley, snipped
chives, chervil, dill – about a handful of
herbs in total

Salt and freshly ground black pepper

Butter, for frying crêpes

For the filling:

½ lb/225 g smoked salmon, finely diced

½ pint/285 ml crème fraîche

½ cucumber, skinned, de-seeded, and diced
finely

Freshly ground black pepper

8 sprigs of dill, to garnish

To make crêpes, the batter for which can be mixed a day in advance and kept in the fridge, put the eggs into a food processor and whiz, gradually adding the flour, milk and water, and melted butter. Whiz in the herbs and add the salt and pepper. Leave this batter to stand for at least 30 minutes before making it up into crêpes.

To make the crêpes, melt a small amount of butter in a crêpe pan. Stir the batter well, then pour a good tablespoonful into the pan, and tilt the pan to spread it. Cook for a few seconds, then, with your fingertips uppermost and thumbs under the crêpe, flip it over to cook on its other side for a few seconds. Slip the cooked crêpe on to a plastic tray or a cloth-covered board to cool (they stick to wood) and repeat the process. When cold, stack them with a strip of baking parchment between each. Make them in the morning for dinner the same day.

To assemble, mix together the ingredients for the filling. Put a spoonful – a generous one! – on one half of each crêpe. Fold the other half over, to form a half-moon shape, and put two of these on each plate, straight sides together so that they form a whole. I put a sprig of dill between the two. The herbs give a bright fresh colour to the crêpes, as well as adding flavour.

Baked Fillet of Cod with Parsley and Basil Mousseline

This is simple to make, and can be made in advance and kept covered, in the fridge. Allow 25–30 minutes at room temperature before cooking.

Serves 8

8 pieces of filleted cod, each weighing about
4 oz/112 g, bones removed

½ pint/285 ml dry white wine, or less

For the mousseline:

8 oz/225 g cod, boned and cut into bits

4 good handfuls of parsley, preferably flat-
leafed, and a couple of good sprigs of basil

2 large egg whites

Salt, freshly ground black pepper and a
grating of nutmeg

8 tbsp crème fraîche

Put the pieces of fish into an ovenproof dish with the white wine.

To make the mousseline, put the cut-up bits of cod into a food processor with the parsley, basil, egg whites, salt, pepper and nutmeg, and whiz till smooth – you will need to scrape down the sides of the bowl once or twice. Then whiz in the crème fraîche. Divide this between the four pieces of fish and pat evenly over each piece – dampen your fingers to make this easier. Or you can pipe the mousseline mixture over the surface of each, using a star-shaped wide nozzle. This gives an undeniably more professional finish, but is purely optional.

Bake in a moderate oven, 350°F/180°C/Gas Mark 4, for 20–25 minutes. How long exactly depends upon the thickness of the fish.

This is good served with very creamily beaten mashed potatoes and a crisp green vegetable – such as stir-fried sugar snap peas with garlic and ginger.

Cod with Parsley and Garlic in Filo Parcels

You can use any firm-fleshed white fish for this recipe – e.g. hake, turbot, or halibut. But it's hard to beat fresh cod, and I see it as one of my roles in life to dispel its image in the eyes of some as a dismal, Friday-school-lunch fish of yesteryear.

Serves 8

8 sheets of filo pastry

4 oz/112 g butter, melted

8 filleted and skinned pieces of cod, bones removed

For the parsley and garlic paste:

4 large handfuls of parsley

6 garlic cloves, poached in boiling water, in their skins, for 2 minutes

Salt and freshly ground black pepper

8 tbsp olive oil

Start by making the parsley and garlic paste. Put the parsley into a food processor. Chop the ends off the poached garlic cloves, squeeze each clove, and the flesh should pop out straight into the processor. Season with salt and pepper and whiz, gradually adding the olive oil. Scrape this paste from the processor into a small bowl.

Lay out a sheet of filo, brush it all over with melted butter, cover with a second sheet of filo and brush that with butter. Cut in half widthwise. Lay a piece of cod in the middle of each half. Spread a quarter of the parsley paste on each bit of cod. Fold up like a parcel, put each parcel on to a buttered baking tray, and brush each parcel with melted butter. Repeat the process three more times, using the remaining fish, pastry and butter. At this stage you can leave the tin in the fridge till you are ready to cook the fish.

To cook, bake in a hot oven, 425°F/225°C/Gas Mark 6, for 15 minutes. Serve immediately.

Cod and Smoked Haddock Puffed Pie

You can use any firm-fleshed white fish for this pie, but it is essential to include smoked fish as well. This is really an upmarket fish pie, and the puff pastry top makes a delicious change from the more usual mashed potatoes.

Serves 6–8

2 lb/900 g cod (or other firm-fleshed white fish)

2 lb/900 g smoked haddock

2 onions, skinned and left whole

1 stick of celery

1 bayleaf

A few peppercorns

2 pints/1.1 litres milk

3 oz/84 g butter

3 oz/84 g flour

Freshly grated nutmeg

Freshly ground black pepper

1 lb/450 g puff pastry

1 egg, beaten, for glazing the pastry

Feel the fish with your fingertips and remove all the bones. Place in a large saucepan, together with the onions, celery, bayleaf and peppercorns, and pour on the milk. Add enough water so that the liquid covers the fish, and put the pan on a gentle heat. Bring very slowly to simmering point, simmer for 3–4 minutes, then take off the heat and let the fish cool in the liquid. When it is quite cold, strain off and set aside the liquid. Flake the fish, removing the skin.

Melt the butter and stir in the flour. Cook for a couple of minutes, then gradually add the reserved strained liquid, stirring all the time until the sauce boils. Season with nutmeg and pepper. Stir in the flaked fish, and pour into a large pie dish.

Roll out the puff pastry to cover the pie. Crimp the edges (I always think a set of false teeth would do this job perfectly), slash the surface of the pastry with the beaten egg and bake in a hot oven – 400°F/200°C/Gas Mark 6 – for about 35 minutes, until the pastry is well risen and golden brown. Keep the pie warm until you are ready to serve it.

Smoked Eel and Cucumber Profiteroles

These can be prepared entirely in advance – the profiteroles can even be made and frozen, but I recommend that you put them in a solid box or container in case they get bashed in the freezer. If they have been frozen, they are much nicer if baked in a moderate oven for 7–10 minutes.

These profiteroles need no further stodge in the form of bread to accompany them, just a green salad and a tomato salad.

Serves 6

For the profiteroles:

½ pint/285 ml water

5 oz/140 g butter, cut into bits

7 oz/200 g plain flour; remove 2 tsp flour and add 2 tsp mustard powder

1 large clove of garlic, skinned and finely chopped (optional)

A dash of Tabasco sauce

3 oz/84 g grated Cheddar cheese

3 large eggs or 4 smaller ones

For the filling:

1 cucumber

1 lb/450 g smoked eel, sliced into slivers

2 tubs of crème fraîche (10.6 oz/300 g each)

Plenty of freshly ground black pepper

Rinse a baking tray with water. Put the ½ pint/285 ml water and bits of butter into a saucepan over moderate heat and let the butter melt in the water as it heats. Take care not to let the liquid come to the boil till the butter has melted completely. Meanwhile, sieve the flour and mustard twice into a bowl. Once the butter has melted, let the liquid in the pan come to a rolling boil and add the flour and mustard all at once. Take the pan off the heat and beat like mad till the dough rolls away from the sides of the pan – this only takes a minute. Beat in the chopped garlic and the Tabasco sauce and grated cheese, and then the eggs, one by one, beating really well between each. You should end up with a glossy dough.

Now, by far the easiest method of getting even-sized profiteroles is to pipe them on to the damp baking tray, using a wide star-shaped nozzle. Don't be put off at the thought of washing up the piping bag afterwards, all you need do is slice off the choux mixture and then chuck it in the washing machine with your next very hot wash. It's much easier and less messy than using two teaspoons to get the profiteroles on to the baking tray.

Bake in a hot oven, 425°F/220°C/Gas Mark 7, for 10–15 minutes, then check them and slash each in the middle with a knife tip to release the steam that collects inside them. Bake for a further 10 minutes, or till they are quite firm to the touch. Use a palette knife to lift them from the baking tray on to a cooling rack.

Peel the cucumber with a potato peeler (this takes seconds). Cut it into chunks, and then cut each chunk in half lengthways. Scoop out the seeds, and cut each piece into fine dice – without the seeds the diced cucumber won't seep liquid.

Mix together the slivers of eel, the diced cucumber, crème fraîche and pepper. Cut each profiterole in half and divide the filling among them.

Serve on a large plate, surrounded, if you like, by an assortment of lettuce leaves.

Smoked Haddock Gougère

You can make this dish with any fish (or ham or chicken), but I like it best with smoked haddock. We are great fish eaters in our family, and we are lucky enough to get really good fish from our fish merchant in Mallaig. His haddock is undyed – undyed smoked fish is well worth hunting out in preference to the garish, vivid yellow dyed smoked fish so widely marketed. Large stores are becoming aware of the harm the chemicals used in dyeing can do to us, and many now sell smoked undyed fish.

The gougère bit of this recipe is simply a cheesy choux pastry – I say 'simply' because some people have a hang-up about making choux pastry, although it is extremely easy. This dish is very convenient and won't come to any harm if it is frozen before it is cooked.

Serves 6–8

For the cheese choux pastry:

4 oz/112 g butter, cut into pieces

½ pint/285 ml water

6 oz/170 g strong plain flour

1 heaped tsp dry mustard powder

Salt and freshly ground black pepper

Freshly grated nutmeg

4 large eggs

4 oz/112 g strong Cheddar cheese, grated

For the smoked haddock sauce:

2 lb/900 g smoked haddock

2 pints/1.1 litres milk

1 onion, skinned and cut in half

1 stick of celery

2 oz/56 g butter

2 oz/56 g flour

Freshly grated nutmeg

Freshly ground black pepper

Melt the butter in the water over a moderate heat. Sieve the flour and mustard powder together. When the butter is completely melted, bring the liquid to boiling point. As the first bubbles appear, add the flour and mustard powder all at once.

Draw off the heat and beat hard until the mixture comes away from the sides of the pan. Beat in the seasonings and leave to cool for about 10 minutes. Then beat in the eggs, one by one, and lastly beat in the grated cheese, reserving 2 tablespoons for the top of the gougère.

Butter an ovenproof dish and spoon in the cheesy mixture, heaping it up round the sides, and putting a thin layer over the bottom of the dish.

Feel the fish with your fingertips and remove any bones. Put it into a large saucepan with the milk, onion and celery. Bring slowly to simmering point and simmer gently for 5 minutes. Leave to cool in the milk. When it is cool, strain off 1½ pints/850 ml of the cooking liquor.

To make the sauce, melt the butter in a saucepan and stir in the flour. Cook for a couple of minutes, then gradually add the strained milk from the fish, stirring all the time until the sauce boils. Let it boil for one minute, then draw the pan off the heat, and stir in the grated nutmeg and freshly ground black pepper (no salt is needed because the fish is usually salty enough). Flake the fish from the skin and stir the flaked fish into the sauce. Pour the sauce into the middle of the dish of cheesy pastry, and sprinkle it with the remaining grated cheese.

If you want to freeze it, do so at this point. If not, keep it in the fridge until you are ready to bake it. It takes about 35 minutes in a hot oven – 425°F/220°C/Gas Mark 7 – until the pastry is puffed up and golden brown. Serve immediately.

Baked Hake Fillets in Parsley, Garlic and Olive Oil Paste with Tomatoes

The basis of this recipe was given to me by my friend Jemima who, with her husband Rupert, runs Borealis, the aroma-therapeutic cosmetic shop in Broadford. For many years they lived in Spain, and she was taught to cook fish like this by a

Spanish friend in the hills above Granada. I have heard that aromatherapy massage should be conducted in silence – of this I am incapable, and Jemima and I natter on about food whenever I indulge myself in one of her brilliant massages – never as frequently as I would like!

Serves 6

6 good pieces of filleted and skinned firm-fleshed white fish
6 large cloves of garlic
About ½ lb/225 g parsley
½ pint/285 ml olive oil
Salt and freshly ground black pepper
6 tomatoes, skinned and sliced

Run your fingers over the fish, feel for any bones and, with a sharp knife, cut them out. Feeling for bones is a sure way of removing them – even the keenest eyesight can't expect to see the bones. Put the fish into a large, shallow, ovenproof dish.

Put the unskinned cloves of garlic into a saucepan with water and bring to simmering point. Simmer for 1 minute, then drain. With scissors snip off their ends – when you squeeze them the garlic should pop out of the skin and into your food processor. Add the parsley and whiz till the mixture forms a paste, then, still whizzing, add the olive oil drop by drop initially, increasing gradually to a thin trickle. Season with salt and ground black pepper and spread this paste over the surface of the fish.

Lay the skinned tomato slices over the entire surface and bake in a moderate oven, 350°F/180°C/Gas Mark 4, for 20–25 minutes, till the fish flakes.

Monkfish in Saffron Cream Sauce

I blush when I think back nearly a quarter of a century, when we first began to run Kinloch, our home, as a hotel. I had never even heard of monkfish then – my only consolation is that neither had most other people, because monkfish, for the most part, used to be thrown back by the fishermen, in those far-off days, with the exception of the less than scrupulous who used to buy it, dip it in breadcrumbs and freeze it, and pass it off as scampi tails. That gives you an idea of the texture of monkfish – it is a robust fish, and now fetches a very high price in the fish markets. It is much sought after, and I prize it highly for its versatility.

Here it is in a rich and delicious sauce, flavoured with that aromatic spice saffron, the most exotic of all spices – and the most expensive. It is only worth buying the strands of saffron; the powdered stuff is adulterated and bulked up by other powder than pulverized saffron. Saffron complements the flavour of fish and shellfish.

Serves 6

1 pint/570 ml fish stock
2 oz/56 g butter
2 onions, skinned and very finely chopped
2 good pinches saffron
½ pint/285 ml double cream
1½ lb/675 g trimmed monkfish tails, each cut into bits about 1 inch/2.5 cm long
Salt and freshly ground black pepper

Fish stock can be bought in some supermarkets if you don't make your own, although if you have a microwave you can do this in 25 minutes by putting fish bones and skin, any chopped vegetables, and crushed parsley stalks into a bowl of water, to cook in your microwave on medium-high setting. It is so easy.

In a good wide and heavy-based sauté pan, melt the butter and cook the chopped onions for several minutes – till they are soft and beginning to turn golden. Pour in the stock, and let this simmer, with the saffron stirred in, till it has reduced by about two-thirds, then stir in the cream. Stir in the chopped monkfish at this stage, too, and let the cream bubble – the sauce will thicken as the cream boils, but have no fear of it curdling: it won't if the cream is double rather than single. In the 2–3 minutes that the sauce bubbles the monkfish will cook – stir it all around gently, so that it cooks evenly. Taste, and season with salt and pepper to your liking. The sauce will have the rich golden hue of saffron.

This is nicest served with rice, which I like to stir chopped parsley through just before serving, to make its appearance more interesting. Sugar snap peas are my ideal vegetable accompaniment – particularly if they are sliced and stir-fried with grated ginger.

Monkfish with Tomatoes, Garlic and Black Olives

Monkfish is a most useful fish because it keeps its shape while it cooks, unlike cod, for example, which readily falls into flakes. This dish can be just as delicious eaten cold, on warm summer evenings, in which case drizzle a bit more olive oil over the fish, tomatoes and olives before serving.

Serves 6

2 lb/900 g trimmed monkfish tails
3 tbsp good olive oil
2 medium red onions, skinned and sliced finely
1 large garlic clove, skinned and chopped finely
8 tomatoes, skinned, sliced in wedges and seeds thrown away
8–12 good black olives, stoned and chopped
A pinch each of sugar, salt and freshly ground black pepper
1 tbsp chopped fresh basil

If the monkfish isn't trimmed of its membrane, do this using a really sharp knife. Cut each monkfish tail into chunks about 1 inch/ 2.5 cm in size. Heat the olive oil and sauté the sliced onions over a moderate heat till they are really soft – about 5–7 minutes – stirring from time to time to prevent them from turning too golden brown. Add the garlic, cook for a minute then add the fish. Stir till the fish turns opaque, then add the tomatoes. Cook for a further couple of minutes and stir in the olives, sugar, salt and pepper. Just before serving stir in the chopped basil leaves. If you are making this in the winter months, you can substitute pesto for fresh basil, using a good teaspoon-ful.

This is good served with either new potatoes, boiled Basmati rice, or with spaghetti, tossed when cooked in olive oil with chopped parsley and with more finely chopped garlic, too, if you like – I do!

Oysters on Mushrooms with Hollandaise Sauce

As cultivated shellfish becomes so much more readily available to us, I love to make the most of it. For most people shellfish is a very real treat, and therefore perfect for a main course for more than just the family. For the unfortunate few who are allergic to shellfish, or to one species of shellfish (because I know people who can't eat prawns, or crab, but who can eat other types of shellfish), it is only fair to warn anyone for whom you haven't cooked very frequently if you intend to give them shell-fish; they will instantly tell you if they can or can't eat it. Oysters used to be such a staple diet for the British, and I sincerely hope that they will become so again, as the cultivated oysters increase in quantity year by year. I loathe raw oysters, but love them cooked. In this recipe they are briefly cooked beneath the Hollandaise Sauce under a hot grill.

This is a rich dish, and I think it is best accompanied by warm bread or rolls, and a good salad.

Serves 6

Depending on their size, allow 5–6 oysters per person; they are, like all shellfish, filling

2 oz/56 g butter + 1 tbsp sunflower oil

1 small onion, red if possible, skinned and finely chopped

1 lb/450 g mushrooms, wiped, stalks trimmed level with the caps, and finely chopped

Salt and freshly ground black pepper

Hollandaise Sauce (see page 301)

Shell the oysters. Have six individual oven-proof dishes warmed.

Melt the butter and heat the oil in a frying pan and cook the finely chopped onion for a minute or two, stirring so that it cooks evenly. Then turn up the heat and add the chopped mushrooms and, stirring slowly but continuously, cook the mushrooms well. Season with salt and pepper, and put some of this mushroom mixture in the base of each serving dish, spreading it evenly. Put the oysters, evenly spaced, on the mushroom mixture.

Make the Hollandaise Sauce and pour it over the oysters and mushrooms.

Heat a grill till very hot and pop the dishes on a baking tray under the grill for about 20–30 seconds. Serve as soon as you possibly can.

Stir-Fried Oysters with Ginger and Spring Onions

This takes literally minutes to cook. You can shell the oysters and keep them in a covered bowl in the fridge till you are

ready to cook. *And you can peel and chop the ginger, and trim and slice the spring onions and keep them, too, in a covered bowl in the fridge, so all you need do just before eating is to cook them.*

This is good with boiled Basmati rice, and a crunchy salad of sliced sugar snap peas, crisply cooked bacon and watercress. One of the good things about cooking with spring onions, quite apart from their flavour, is that their green colour intensifies in cooking.

Serves 6

Depending on their size, allow 5–6 oysters
  per person (for a main course; 3 for a first
  course)
About 2 inches/5 cm fresh ginger
18–20 good spring onions – not those weedy
  grass-thin ones
3 tbsp sunflower oil
½ pint/285 ml single cream
Salt and freshly ground black pepper

Shell the oysters. Pare the skin from the ginger and cut it into fine slivers. Trim the spring onions and slice them diagonally about ¼ inch/½ cm thick.

Heat the oil in a wide shallow pan – a sauté or frying pan – and cook the ginger and spring onions, stirring continuously, for about 3 minutes. Then add the oysters and cook for a few seconds before pouring in the cream. Let the cream bubble for about a minute, season with salt and pepper, and tip into a warmed serving dish. Serve as soon as possible.

Sautéed Plaice Fillets with Parsley and Lemon Juice

Unlike most of my recipes, this is not suitable for making in large quantities, but it provides such a quick and delicious individual meal that I felt I had to include it. It is one of the nicest ways I know to eat fish – I buy filleted plaice, but you could use any white fish. If you use cod, or any other thicker-fleshed fish than plaice or lemon sole, you will need to cook it for slightly longer.

Serves 1

2 or 3 filleted plaice, depending on the size of
  the fish and your appetite
1 tbsp flour, sieved on to a plate with a little
  salt
1 oz/28 g butter + 2 tsp sunflower oil
Another 1 oz/28 g butter
2 tsp lemon juice
Freshly ground black pepper
1 tbsp finely chopped parsley

Dip both sides of each fillet in the sieved flour. Melt 1 oz/28 g butter and the oil in a frying pan and cook the fish – it will take less than a minute each side. Dish the fillets on to a warmed serving plate.

Add the rest of the butter to the frying pan, with the lemon juice, pepper and chopped parsley. Let this bubble briefly, then pour it over the fish and serve immediately.

This is good with a vegetable like courgettes cooked with garlic, or steamed broccoli, and creamily mashed potatoes.

Salmon and Dill Tart

I made this once for an elegant picnic competition sponsored by a champagne firm. I was among four contestants selected by the judges to take part in the finals at Henley, in the beautiful garden of some very kind people who had lent their house and garden for the occasion. I travelled down from Skye by plane for the event, with some of my picnic food made (bread, spinach terrine) and I got up early to make the tart. I thought it ideal picnic food for a smart occasion, but my three fellow contestants were Real Chefs, who arrived with stage props undreamt of by me – flower arrangements as for a wedding, hatstands laden with stripey blazers and boaters, spun sugar helmets to put over their pudding concoctions, and two of them really amazed me when I saw that they had brought portable ovens in which to cook their main courses! I was not in the same league at all, with my tablecloth on a rug, fat white pot of garden roses in the middle, and picnic food which could be cooked by anyone but which did not involve baking duck breasts on the spot!

Serves 6–8

For the pastry:

4 oz/112 g chilled butter, cut in pieces

6 oz/170 g plain flour

1 heaped tsp icing sugar

Salt and freshly ground pepper

For the filling:

1 lb/450 g salmon, cut into 1-inch/2.5-cm
    chunks

3 large egg yolks + 1 whole large egg

1 pint/570 ml single cream

A good pinch of salt and plenty of freshly
    ground black pepper

A handful of dill fronds – less if you prefer, but
    dill and salmon are so delicious together
    that, for me, the more the better!

Put the pastry ingredients into a food processor and whiz till the mixture looks like fine crumbs. Pat them round the sides and base of an 8–9 inch/20–23 cm flan dish, and put the flan into the fridge for at least half an hour before baking it in a moderate oven – 350°F/180°C/Gas Mark 4 – for 20–25 minutes, till the pastry is golden and cooked. Take it out of the oven.

Put the chunks of salmon into the cooked pastry shell. Beat together the egg and yolks, and beat the cream into this. Season with salt and pepper and pour over the salmon. Place the dill fronds over the surface, and bake the tart in a moderate oven – 350°F/180°C/Gas Mark 4 – until the filling is just set when you touch it with your finger or when you gently shake the flan dish – 20–25 minutes. Take care not to overcook it, and remember that it will go on cooking a bit once it is taken out of the oven.

Fillet of Salmon in Filo Parcels with Dill Butter

This is a most convenient main course as well as being quite delicious. But it is a filling dish, and I prefer to serve two vegetables, such as steamed sugar snap peas and, perhaps, lemon-glazed carrots;

potatoes are, I think, surplus to require-ments. But that is a decision only you can make.

Serves 4

4 salmon fillets, skinned and bones removed, each weighing 4–6 oz/120–150 g

4 sheets of filo pastry

2 oz/56 g butter, melted

For the dill butter:

4 oz/112 g butter

A good handful of dill fronds, finely chopped

1 tsp lemon juice

Freshly ground black pepper

Make the dill butter by beating the 4 oz/112 g butter until soft and creamy. Add the chopped dill, lemon juice and pepper. It should be spreadable.

Lay a sheet of filo on a work surface and brush it all over with the melted butter. Cover with a second sheet of filo and brush this too with butter. Cut it in half width-ways. Lay a piece of salmon in the middle of each half. Spread a good teaspoonful of dill butter over each bit of salmon. Fold the filo like a parcel and brush all over with melted butter. Put the parcels on to a buttered baking sheet. Repeat the process with the rest of the filo and salmon. At this stage you can cover them with clingfilm and keep the baking tray in the fridge till you are ready to cook the fish.

To cook, bake the parcels in a hot oven, 425°F/220°C/Gas Mark 7, for 15 minutes. Serve as soon as possible.

Baked Salmon with Sesame Vegetables

For this I cook the salmon in the best way I know, as taught me by John Tovey.

Serves 6

1½–2 lb/675–900 g fresh salmon, filleted, boned, skinned and cut into 6 equal-sized pieces

6 oz/170 g butter

1 tbsp sesame oil

2 inches/5 cm fresh root ginger, pared of its skin and very finely chopped

1 clove garlic, skinned and very finely chopped

3 leeks, trimmed and sliced into very fine strips

2 carrots, peeled and sliced as finely as possible

6 oz/170 g sugar snap peas, sliced diagonally (because it looks nicer)

Salt and freshly ground black pepper

Put the pieces of salmon on a baking tray (unbuttered) and put a 1-oz/28-g piece of butter on top of each. Bake in a hot oven, 400°F/200°C/Gas Mark 6, for 5 minutes.

Heat the oil in a non-stick frying or sauté pan and, over high heat, add the ginger, garlic, leeks and carrots to the pan. Stir-fry for about 4–5 minutes, then add the sliced sugar snap peas. Cook, stirring, for a further minute or two, season to your taste, and serve a spoonful of the sesame vegetables beside each piece of salmon, for a delicious but very healthy main course.

Scallops with Julienne Vegetables under a Puffed Crust

In this recipe the scallops steam as the pastry cooks. I think by cooking them like this the maximum taste of the scallops is complemented by the vegetables on which they sit.

Serves 6

3 oz/84 g butter

3 carrots, peeled and cut into the finest julienne

3 sticks of celery, trimmed and cut the same size as the carrots

4 Jerusalem artichokes, peeled and cut into fine strips

Salt and freshly ground black pepper

Flat-leafed parsley, chopped quite coarsely

12 large scallops with dark tube trimmed away, each chopped, the corals left whole

1 lb/450 g puff pastry

1 beaten egg to glaze the pastry

Melt the butter in a sauté pan and cook the prepared vegetables in the butter over a gentle to moderate heat, stirring, for about 5 minutes. Season with salt and pepper. Leave to cool. When cold, stir in the chopped parsley, and divide the mixture evenly between six scallop shells. Arrange the chopped scallops on the vegetables.

Roll out the pastry and cut circles large enough to cover the shells. Dampen the edges and press the pastry firmly on to the edges of the shells. Slash in two or three places with a sharp knife. Brush each with beaten egg.

Bake in a hot oven, 425°F/220°C/Gas Mark 7, for 15 minutes, or till the pastry is golden brown and well puffed. Serve immediately.

Scallops in Saffron and White Wine Sauce

This makes a delicious, fragrant main course. I allow 4 average-sized scallops per person.

Serves 8

32 scallops, with the tube at the end of the coral trimmed away

2 oz/56 g butter

For the sauce:

3 oz/84 g butter

1 onion, skinned and chopped finely

2 oz/56 g flour

½ pint/285 ml dry white wine

1 pint/570 ml fish or vegetable stock

Salt and freshly ground black pepper

About 1 tbsp lemon juice

1 packet of saffron (not the powder, the strands)

Make the sauce first – this can be done in the morning for dinner that evening, or the day before, and kept in the fridge. If you do make it in advance, wring out a piece of greaseproof paper in water and cover the surface of the sauce with it.

Melt the butter for the sauce in a saucepan, and add the finely chopped onion. Cook for 5 minutes or so, giving the onion an occasional stir. Then stir in the flour, and let it cook in the butter for a minute, before stirring in the white wine and stock. Stir till the sauce boils, then take it off the heat, and season to taste with salt, pepper and lemon juice. Stir in the saffron.

Shortly before dinner, melt the 2 oz/50 g butter in a frying pan and gently cook the scallops, for a minute – half a minute each side. Pour them and the butter in which they cooked into the sauce, and reheat the sauce. Try not to let the scallops sit in the hot sauce for too long before eating, as they tend to toughen and shrink.

I like to serve these scallops with Basmati rice.

Fillet of Sea Bass with Almonds

I love the way people are eating so much more fish these days. Along with our growing appreciation of fish has come a desire to experiment with the different types of fish we cook. It is several years since we first cooked sea bass, a firm-fleshed fish which is versatile because of its robustness. In this recipe it is baked on a bed of parsley, then served with a creamy mushroom and almond sauce. It's quick to cook, but makes a delicious and elegant main course for a special lunch or dinner.

Serves 6

2–3 good handfuls of parsley

2½–3 lb/1–1.35 kg filleted sea bass

Butter

For the sauce:

2 oz/56 g butter + 1 tbsp sunflower oil

1 red onion, skinned and finely chopped

½ lb/225 g mushrooms, wiped, stalks cut level with each cap, and chopped

3 oz/84 g flaked almonds, toasted till pale golden

½ pint/285 ml single cream

Salt and freshly ground black pepper

Butter a Pyrex or similarly ovenproof dish well. Put the parsley over the base of the dish, and lay the fillets of sea bass on the parsley. Dot with bits of butter and cover the dish with foil, tightly. You can prepare the fish to this stage in the morning, all ready to pop the dish into the oven – but if you can, take the dish out of the fridge an hour before you cook it, otherwise the fish will take longer to cook, straight from fridge to oven. Bake in a moderate oven, 350°F/180°C/Gas Mark 4, for 15–20 minutes – till the fish is cooked when you gently stick a fork in the thickest bit.

To make the sauce, melt the butter and heat the oil together in a saucepan. Add the finely chopped onion and cook for several minutes, stirring, till the onion is soft, transparent-looking and beginning to turn golden. Add the mushrooms, and cook till they are well done. Add the almonds, the cream, a pinch of salt and lots of black pepper. Simmer the sauce for a minute or two, then pour it into a warmed serving bowl. Alternatively, serve the fish on warmed plates with the sauce spooned over it.

Squid with Garlic and Parsley in Olive Oil

This is a great family favourite for a special occasion, luckily for me, not only because I, too, love squid cooked this way, but also because it is just so simple and quick to cook.

Squid can be bought ready cleaned, but although this takes all effort out of their preparation bar the actual slicing, I think they taste better when bought whole. They come in a variety of sizes, but the cleaning is the same whatever the size! If you are faintly squeamish wear rubber gloves to clean them.

You will be faced with a grey-film-covered squid. Look around the open end for the end of the 'quill', so named because that is exactly what it resembles. It appears to be of plastic, but it isn't! Pull the end of this clear quill, and the whole innard should emerge with it. Rinse it out under cold running water to clean it thoroughly. Pull off the film from the outside, and you will have a clean white tube, closed at one end. Pat it dry with kitchen paper and slice in bits about ½ inch/1 cm wide (use the tentacles, chopped or whole, if you wish).

Serves 6

| 4 tbsp best extra virgin olive oil |
| 2 lb/900 g squid, cleaned and sliced |
| 2 garlic cloves, skinned and finely chopped |
| 3 tbsp finely chopped parsley |
| Plenty of freshly ground black pepper |
| Lemon quarters to serve with the cooked squid |

Heat the oil in a wide frying or sauté pan. Add some of the squid and garlic and cook till the pieces of squid turn opaque – depending on the amount in the saucepan, this can take as little as 30 seconds. Keep one lot warm while you cook the rest. But don't overcook it, because this is what makes squid tough and chewy. It should be tender when cooked briefly.

With the last lot, stir in the chopped parsley and season with pepper. Dish this in with the already cooked squid and mix it all together well. Serve as soon as possible, with lemon quarters on the side, pouring the olive oil from the pan over the contents of the dish.

Squid with Tomatoes and Black Olives

We both love squid, as do most of our friends and, judging by how popular it is when we put it on the menu here, a great many of our guests. It is so easy and quick both to prepare and cook. This dish can be served hot or cold, and is equally good either way. I am generally governed by the weather – serving it cold on very hot evenings and hot on one of those chilly summer evenings.

Serves 6–8

| 2 lb/900 g squid |
| 5 tbsp olive oil |
| 2 garlic cloves, skinned and finely chopped |

Herb Crêpes with Smoked Salmon and ▶ Cucumber, page 83

½ tsp salt

Lots of freshly ground black pepper

Juice of half a lemon

5–6 tomatoes, skinned, halved, de-seeded and cut into wedges

12 black olives, stoned and halved

1 tbsp finely chopped parsley

Clean the squid by pulling out the plastic-like quill and innards – they should come out easily (see the introduction to the previous recipe). Wash the squid and pat them dry with kitchen paper. Cut the tentacles into 1-inch/2.5-cm lengths and the bodies into rings about ¼ inch/6 mm thick.

Heat the oil in a frying pan and add the garlic and squid. Sauté, stirring so that the squid cooks evenly, until it has turned opaque, about 2–3 minutes. Season with salt and pepper and the lemon juice. Stir in the tomato wedges and halved black olives, and cook for a minute or two more.

Turn on to a serving dish to serve hot, or leave to cool and serve cold. Sprinkle with the finely chopped parsley before serving.

Fish Stir-Fried with Leeks and Ginger

Improbable as it may sound, this is an extremely popular dish not only with our own children but with any of their friends

◀ Monkfish with Tomatoes, Garlic and Black Olives, page 89

who like fish. Don't be put off by the leeks and ginger – the heat of the ginger is so decreased in its cooking and its flavour goes so very well with that of the leeks, that they both complement the fish very well, if surprisingly so.

I like to serve this with plain boiled Basmati rice, into which I stir lots of chopped parsley.

Serves 6

2 lb/900 g firm-fleshed white fish, such as hake; cod will do, but it will fall into flakes as it cooks

1 tsp cornflour

3 tbsp dark soy sauce

2 tsp sesame oil

1 pint/570 ml vegetable stock

3 tbsp sunflower oil

4 leeks, trimmed and sliced thinly

About 1 inch/2.5 cm fresh ginger, peeled and grated or finely chopped

1 clove of garlic, skinned and chopped finely

First, put the fish on a board and feel it all over to find bones. Remove them. Then cut the fish into 1-inch/2.5-cm bits.

Mix the cornflour with the soy sauce, sesame oil and stock. Then, in a large heavy-based sauté pan, heat the sunflower oil and stir-fry the leeks, chopped ginger and chopped garlic till the leeks are really soft – about 5 minutes over a moderately high heat. When you are sure the sliced leeks are really soft, add the cut-up fish and stir in the cornflour liquid. Cook over high heat till the sauce bubbles. The fish will then be cooked, too. Serve as soon as possible, to prevent the fish overcooking in the heat of the sauce.

Fish Cakes

These are very different from the bought type of fish cake, which is bright orange because of its coating, and which consists of vastly more potato than fish. I only ever make fish cakes using smoked haddock or cod, because their flavour is so much better. Whether it is their flavour, or their crispy coating once fried, I don't know, but they are tremendously popular with all our family. My only problem is actually having enough.

I like to serve these fish cakes with a tomatoey sauce, and a vegetable such as peas cooked with sautéed onions and garnished with crispy bits of bacon – bacon complements the taste of all fish and shellfish.

Serves 6

2 lb/900 g smoked haddock
Milk to cook the fish
2 lb/900 g potatoes, weighed when peeled, boiled till tender, then mashed well
2–3 tbsp finely chopped parsley – this is important, it really improves the appearance of the fish cakes once they are cut open
Freshly ground black pepper
Flour for dusting
2 eggs, beaten, on a plate
About 6 oz/170 g day-old baked bread, whizzed to fine crumbs
Sunflower oil + butter for frying

Feel the raw fish all over on a board. Remove any bones you feel – this is the only sure way to find bones and to be able to reassure those eating the fish cakes that they are truly bone-free. Cut the fish into bits and put them into a saucepan. Cover with milk, and over moderate heat bring to a gentle simmer. Take the pan off the heat and leave the fish to cool in the milk.

Remove the fish from the cooled milk (strain the milk and use it to make smoked haddock flavoured soup, using sautéed onions and diced potatoes as the bulk of the soup), and mash the cooked fish into the potatoes, adding a small amount of the milk – you have to be careful not to make the potato and fish mixture too damp to form into fish cakes. Beat in the parsley and the pepper. Dip your hand in flour and form the mixture into cake shapes of even size. Dip each into the beaten egg, then into the crumbs, coating each cake on each side. Put them on to a tray lined with baking parchment. Cover the finished trayful with clingfilm and either store in the fridge till you are ready to fry them, or freeze them.

To fry them, heat a small amount of sunflower oil and melt butter – in a non-stick frying pan, if at all possible, because that way you use much less oil. Fry them till they are golden brown on each side. As they cook, remove them from the frying pan to a dish lined with kitchen paper to absorb excess grease.

These fish cakes are very good with tomato sauce, homemade or ketchup. There is no need for added potato, rice or pasta, but a salad or green vegetable, or the peas described above, is a good accompaniment.

Invergarry Crab Cakes

I generally prefer eating crab cold, but crab cakes are the exception. They are very good served with either tartare sauce, or with a homemade tomato sauce. Crab cakes freeze well, for up to 3 months. This quantity makes about 6 large cakes, or more small ones. They are very filling!

Serves 4–6

1 lb/450 g crabmeat
3 slices of brown bread, crusts removed and the bread made into crumbs
2 heaped tbsp mayonnaise
2 rounded tsp English mustard
1 tbsp Worcestershire sauce
4 tbsp oil + 2 oz/56 g butter for frying

For the coating:

1 egg, beaten
6 rounded tbsp brown breadcrumbs

Mix together the crabmeat, breadcrumbs, mayonnaise, mustard and Worcestershire sauce until well combined. Shape the mixture into cakes about ¾ inch/2 cm thick. This is easier to do if you dip your hands in flour. If you are going to freeze them, put them on a paper plate, wrap well and freeze them at this stage. Thaw for an hour or two before coating and frying them.

To coat, dip each crab cake in the beaten egg and then in the breadcrumbs, and leave on a tray in the fridge for 2–3 hours. Then heat the oil and butter in a large frying pan, and fry the crab cakes for 3–5 minutes on each side until golden brown. Drain on absorbent paper and serve with a green salad.

Fish Pie

So many people are put off fish pie for life by ghastly experiences during school-days. It is, sadly, one of those dishes which can be positively vandalized by institution cooks, which is such a pity, because a good fish pie is not only delicious, but versatile. It is the sort of dish which can be dressed up or down. You can take the basic combination of white and smoked fish and add hardboiled eggs and parsley, with a creamy mashed potato top for a family lunch; or you can add a few prawns, sliced mushrooms, and a dash of white wine, with a puffed pastry lid, for a more elegant dish.

This is a more everyday type of fish pie, though with a puff pastry finish. A substitute for potato or pastry is a thick layer of crushed, plain salted potato crisps – this is a great favourite with children. The chopped tomato and parsley in the sauce save the pie from looking too anaemic.

Serves 6–8

1½ lb/675 g white fish, such as haddock or cod
1 lb/450 g smoked haddock
2 pints/1.1 litres milk
1 onion, skinned
1 blade of mace
3 oz/84 g butter
3 oz/84 g flour
2 oz/56 g cheese, grated
3 tomatoes, skinned, de-seeded and chopped
Salt and freshly ground black pepper
2 hardboiled eggs, shelled and chopped

2 rounded tbsp finely chopped parsley

12 oz/340 g puff pastry

Milk for glazing

Feel the raw fish all over on a board and remove any bones. Put the fish, milk, onion and mace together in a large saucepan and, over a low heat, bring gently to the boil. Simmer for 2 minutes, then remove the pan from the heat, and cool for 20 minutes or so. Strain off the cooking liquid. Remove the skin from the fish and flake the flesh. Discard the onion and mace.

Melt the butter in a saucepan and stir in the flour. Let it cook for 2 minutes, then gradually pour on the milk from the fish, stirring all the time until the sauce boils. Take it off the heat and stir in the grated cheese and the flaked, cooked fish. Stir in the chopped tomatoes, a little salt and pepper, and the hardboiled eggs and parsley, and pour the mixture into a 3½-pint/2-litre pie dish.

Roll out the puff pastry and cover the pie. Stick the point of a sharp knife through the pastry in two or three places, to let the steam out while the pastry is cooking. Decorate the surface of the pie with leftover pastry cut into leaf shapes. Brush the pie with milk.

Bake in a hot oven, 425°F/220°C/Gas Mark 7, for 15 minutes, then lower the heat to 375°F/190°C/Gas Mark 5 and cook for a further 30 minutes, until the pastry is puffed up.

Seafood Puff Pastry Turnovers

You can vary the contents of your turnovers to suit the availability of ingredients where you live, but these days it is getting easier and easier to buy shellfish, due to the increase in cultivated items like scallops, mussels and oysters, and it is really almost easier in some parts of Britain to buy these than any fish slightly out of the ordinary, such as hake or monkfish. As the fish cooks in the pastry it steams, really the best way to cook shellfish and fish.

With these turnovers there is no need for potatoes, or any other form of starch, but a vegetable such as my current favourite, sugar snap peas (I never want to see another mangetout, they are so dreary in comparison with the sugar snaps), and a good herb-filled green salad would be ideal accompaniments.

Serves 6

1½ lb/675 g puff pastry

6 scallops, dark tubes removed

1½ lb/675 g trimmed monkfish, cut into
    1-inch/2.5-cm bits

18 shelled mussels

½ lb/225 g large prawns, cooked for
    30 seconds in boiling water then shelled,
    and each cut in half – weighed after shelling

2 oz/56 g butter, melted, then cooled just
    enough before it firms up

2 tbsp chopped parsley

1 tbsp chopped dill

1 egg, beaten

Roll out the pastry and cut out six large circles, each about 6 inches/15 cm in diameter. Cut each scallop in three bits. Mix together in a bowl all the fish and shellfish, the cooled butter, parsley and dill. Spoon this mixture on to one side of each circle. Fold the other over, and stick it down with a little beaten egg. Put each turnover on a baking tray – no need to butter or oil it first – and brush each one with the beaten egg.

Bake in an oven at 400°F/200°C/Gas Mark 6, for 20 minutes. If you like, serve with Sauce Bercy (see page 299).

Poultry and Game

Chicken is still a universal favourite in Britain, and our household is no exception. There are so many ways to cook chicken – the breasts in particular – and I have included a wide selection here, in the hope that everyone will find something to their taste. Whole chickens, for roasting, or jointing for stews, are now some of the cheapest food available, but do try to buy free-range chickens if you can – the flavour is incomparably better so it is worth paying a little bit extra.

I have included the recipe for Roast Turkey with Pork Sausagemeat and Chestnut Stuffing because even though we still tend to associate turkey with Christmas, smaller birds are available throughout the year and can provide a welcome alternative to roast chicken for a special occasion. (Turkey meat *products* have become very popular, because the meat is so lean, but they can often be dry and tasteless – even fresh minced turkey loses the flavour and character of the original bird.)

Game is useful, varied and accessible. No longer is it the prerogative of country dwellers – you can see a selection of types of game in good supermarkets in most city centres, and often at very low prices. As winter progresses, pheasants, for example, become very inexpensive indeed, and pheasant is so lean a meat that it is very healthy eating. I think that people who are not used to eating game are wary of buying and trying it, in case it is very strong in taste. Some is, but not the kind sold in supermarkets. Pheasant can be so mild in flavour as to be almost like chicken.

Game includes venison, of course, a red meat, but a very lean one. There are several recipes where venison gives much more interesting results than beef would if cooked in the same manner – Venison Braised with Beetroot, into which crème fraîche is stirred before serving, and Venison with Soured Cream and Pistachios, are two good examples.

So whether you want a light but tasty supper of Baked Chicken Breasts with Chutney and Mustard, something more substantial such as Chicken, Leek and Parsley Pie, an elegant dish like Spinach and Parmesan Cheese Stuffed Chicken Breasts which has an accompanying sauce of cream and saffron containing onions stewed in chicken stock – a delicious dish for any time of the year – or something slightly more traditional such as Roast Duck with Apple and Cream Gravy or Roast Pheasant with Bread Sauce and Game Chips, in this chapter you should find something for every taste and occasion.

Chicken Breasts with Aubergines, Tomatoes and Garlic

•

Baked Chicken Breasts with Chutney and Mustard

•

Baked Chicken Breasts with Garlic, Onions and New Potatoes in Olive Oil

•

Chicken Breasts Baked with Mushrooms

•

Spinach and Parmesan Cheese Stuffed Chicken Breasts with Saffron Sauce

•

Roast Chicken with Creamy Saffron and Lemon Sauce

•

Pot-Roasted Chicken with Root Vegetables

•

Chicken and Broccoli in Mayonnaise Cream Sauce

•

Cold Chicken in White Wine and Parsley Jelly

•

Chicken Stew with Parsley and Chive Dumplings

•

Chicken or Turkey or Pheasant Fricassée

•

Chicken and Mushroom Filo Pastry Parcels

•

Pancakes Stuffed with Chicken and Mushrooms

•

Chicken, Leek and Parsley Pie

•

Chicken Liver and Rice Balls with Tomato Sauce

•

Sautéed Chicken Livers with Green Peppercorns

•

Roast Turkey with Pork Sausagemeat and Chestnut Stuffing

Roast Duck with Apple and Cream Gravy

•

Wild Duck with Apricot and Lemon Sauce

•

Wild Duck with Cider and Apples

•

Wild Duck Paprika

•

Pheasant Breasts with Creamy Bacon Sauce

•

Pheasant Breasts with Orange and Chestnuts

•

Pheasant Casseroled with Bacon, Shallots and Mushrooms in Red Wine

•

Pheasant with Cream and Brandy

•

Pheasant with Fresh Ginger

•

Roast Pheasant with Bread Sauce and Game Chips

•

Marinated Pigeon Breasts with Port and Redcurrant Jelly Sauce

•

Pigeon and Steak Pie

•

Rabbit and Paprika Casserole

•

Venison Fillet with Port and Redcurrant Jelly

•

Venison Steaks in Red Wine and Vegetable Sauce

•

Venison Braised with Beetroot

•

Venison Ragoût with Chestnuts, Port and Orange

•

Venison with Soured Cream and Pistachios

•

Venison and Leek Pie

•

Game Pudding with Lemon Suet Crust

Chicken Breasts with Aubergines, Tomatoes and Garlic

This dish combines truly Mediterranean tastes with chicken. It can be made in advance and reheated – in fact, I think it is better made ahead. It really is necessary to cut up the aubergines and leave them to sit for half an hour before cooking them – the juices which seep out of them are bitter and indigestible, and the aubergines are so much nicer given this treatment. As they cook they collapse and their pulp gives a substance as well as a delicious flavour to the tomatoes, garlic and chicken in the olive oil.

This is good served with steamed new potatoes or baked jacket potatoes, and a salad.

Serves 6

2 medium aubergines – 3 if they are small
Salt
6 chicken breasts, with skin
2 tbsp flour sieved with ½ tsp salt and black pepper
4 tbsp olive oil plus extra if needed
2–3 cloves of garlic, each skinned and finely chopped
8 tomatoes, skinned, cut in wedges and the seeds removed

Slice the aubergines in half lengthways and cut them into chunks, about 1 inch/2.5 cm in size. Put them in a wide shallow bowl and sprinkle them with a little salt. Leave them for 30 minutes, then drain off the liquid which will have seeped out of them, and pat the chunks of aubergine dry with absorbent kitchen paper. Meanwhile, press each chicken breast in the seasoned flour.

Heat the oil in a wide saucepan – a deep frying pan or a sauté pan ideally – and brown the chicken on each side. Remove the chicken to a warmed casserole dish. Add the chunks of aubergine to the oil in the pan, add more oil if necessary, and cook over a moderate heat, stirring occasionally, till the aubergine is beginning to brown, about 10 minutes. Stir in the chopped garlic and the tomatoes, and pour the mixture over the pieces of chicken.

Cover the dish and bake in a moderate oven, 350°F/180°C/Gas Mark 4, for 30 minutes if you intend to serve it straight away, or for 20 minutes if you intend to cool it and re-cook it at a later date. Re-cook it by taking the dish into room temperature an hour before cooking, and cooking it in a moderate oven till the juices bubble, then let them bubble for 10 minutes.

If you have some basil, just before serving stir a few leaves, torn rather than chopped with a knife (which turns the leaves brown), through the chickeny stew.

Baked Chicken Breasts with Chutney and Mustard

This is one of those extremely easy dishes which taste very good. The sooner the chicken breasts are smeared with the chutney mixture, the better – in the morning for supper that evening, or, even better, the previous day and kept, covered, in the fridge. The mustard used is grainy mustard, and the chutney I use is mango, but I don't see why you couldn't substitute any other type of fruity chutney. It is essential to use chicken breasts which have their skin on – the skinless type dry out during cooking.

This is good served with a green vegetable, such as steamed broccoli or stir-fried cabbage, and mashed potatoes.

Serves 6

6 tbsp chutney (mango, for example)

3 tbsp grainy mustard (Moutarde de Meaux)

6 tbsp olive oil

6 chicken breasts with their skin on

Mix the chutney, mustard and oil together and smear this mixture over the chicken breasts in an ovenproof dish. Do this several hours in advance, and keep the dish, covered, in the fridge. An hour before cooking, take the dish out of the fridge and leave in room temperature.

Bake in a hot oven, 400°F/200°C/Gas Mark 6, for 25 minutes – stab a chicken breast and check that the juices which run from it are clear to see if it is cooked through. This cooking time is right for the average-sized chicken breast. If you think the mixture is getting rather too brown for your liking, put a piece of greaseproof paper (or a butter paper) over the top.

Baked Chicken Breasts with Garlic, Onions and New Potatoes in Olive Oil

This is one of the dishes most chosen by our children throughout the year when I give them the chance! It couldn't be simpler, but you have to beware not to overcook the chicken breasts. There is no need to overcook them, providing you sauté the sliced onions first in the olive oil. The small new potatoes take the same amount of time to cook as do the chicken breasts. Another point is to use the chicken breasts with skin on, not the skinless ones which would dry up horribly. Adjust the quantity of garlic cloves you include to suit your tastes. We love it!

Serves 6

4 tbsp olive oil

3 onions, skinned and finely sliced

1½ lb/675 g tiny new potatoes, scrubbed

6 chicken breasts, with skin

6–12 garlic cloves, each skinned and left
   whole

Salt and freshly ground black pepper

¼ pint/140 ml olive oil

Heat the 4 tbsp olive oil in a heavy, shallow casserole or ovenproof sauté pan. Add the sliced onions and cook till they are just turning colour. Put the new potatoes in with the onions, turning them over so they get coated in oil, and put the chicken breasts on top of the potatoes. Scatter the skinned garlic cloves around the chicken. Season with salt and pepper and pour the olive oil over the lot in a thin trickle.

Cook, uncovered, in a hot oven, 400°F/200°C/Gas Mark 6, for about 30–35 minutes, till when you stick a fork in a potato it feels tender. Stab a chicken joint with the point of a sharp knife – any juices should run clear. This dish keeps warm in a cool oven satisfactorily for about 15–20 minutes.

Chicken Breasts Baked with Mushrooms

Chicken, in whatever form, is universally popular with children. Whenever one of ours is given the choice of what to make for lunch or supper, the decision is invariably chicken in some form or other. This baked chicken dish is simplicity itself to make, and how much garlic you include depends entirely on the general fondness for garlic in your family – with all of us, our liking for garlic amounts almost to addiction.

The ideal accompaniments for this baked chicken dish are either baked jacket potatoes, or steamed (or boiled) new potatoes, with a green salad.

Serves 6

3 tbsp olive oil

6 chicken breasts, with the skin on (it helps prevent shrinkage in cooking)

2 onions, skinned and finely sliced, or chopped if you prefer

1–2 garlic cloves, skinned and finely chopped

½ lb/225 g mushrooms, wiped, stalks trimmed, and sliced

Scant tbsp flour

1 pint/570 ml chicken stock

Salt and freshly ground black pepper

¼ pint/140 ml double cream

Heat the oil in a heavy ovenproof sauté pan and brown the chicken breasts on their skin sides. Remove them, once browned, to a warm dish. Gently sauté the sliced onions till they are really soft – this takes about 5 minutes. Then add the chopped garlic and the sliced mushrooms to the pan – you may need to add more olive oil as the mushrooms tend to take up a lot of oil – and sauté for a couple of minutes before stirring in the flour. After a further minute's cooking time stir in the stock and keep stirring till the sauce simmers. Replace the browned chicken breasts in the gently simmering sauce, skin side uppermost. Cover with a lid and bake for 30 minutes in a moderate oven, 350°F/ 180°C/Gas Mark 4.

Take the sauté pan out of the oven and put it back on a gentle heat. Season with salt and pepper to your taste, and stir in the cream – there is no fear of curdling with double cream, so don't worry. Serve as soon as you like, but this dish will keep warm very satisfactorily in a low temperature oven for 20–30 minutes.

Spinach and Parmesan Cheese Stuffed Chicken Breasts with Saffron Sauce

This is a convenient dish in that the stuffing can be made a day in advance, and the chicken breasts flattened and spread with the spinach and Parmesan mixture and left in its dish in a cool place (fridge or larder) until the evening, when all you need do is pop it in the oven. The sauce, too, can be made in advance and reheated to serve with the chicken. They are a most delicious combination.

Serves 6

4 oz/112 g fresh spinach

2 garlic cloves, skinned and chopped

2 oz/56 g grated fresh Parmesan cheese

A good grating of nutmeg

Juice of 2 lemons

6 chicken breasts, without skin, and all bones removed

2 tbsp olive oil

Saffron Sauce (see page 304)

Put the spinach, garlic, Parmesan cheese and grated nutmeg into a food processor and whiz, adding half the lemon juice.

Lay the chicken breasts on a board and flatten them as much as you can. Spread the spinach mixture thinly over each, roll or fold in half, and stick a wooden toothpick through, or tie with string or cotton.

Put the chicken breasts into an ovenproof dish and pour the rest of the lemon juice over them, plus the olive oil. Bake for 40–45 minutes in a moderate oven – 350°F/ 180°C/Gas Mark 4.

Take the toothpicks out of the cooked chicken or cut off the string or cotton before dishing up. Serve each chicken breast with spoonfuls of Saffron Sauce over and around it. I like to serve this with new potatoes oven-roasted in olive oil till crisp, and with a green vegetable.

Roast Chicken with Creamy Saffron and Lemon Sauce

Straight roast chicken is the favourite of just about everyone, provided, that is, that the chicken is really good, as free-range as it is possible to procure where you live. Straight roast chicken needs bread sauce as its accompaniment, and possibly rolls of bacon too, if we are being strictly correct. But I don't much like rolls of bacon, because I don't like the way that the bacon inside the roll doesn't crisp up – it can't. So for my taste, and very luckily for the tastes of all seven of our immediate family, I like to make this simple sauce to accompany roast chicken – simple it is, but indulgent in its components. The saffron and lemon and cream all complement each other and the chicken.

Serves 4

1 chicken weighing about 3 lb/1.4 kg

1 lemon, cut in half

About 2 oz/56 g softened butter

Salt and freshly ground black pepper

For the sauce:

2 oz/56 g butter

1 onion, skinned and very finely chopped

½ pint/285 ml good chicken stock

2 good pinches of saffron strands

Grated rind and juice of 1 lemon

½ pint/285 ml double cream

Salt and freshly ground black pepper

Put the chicken into a roasting tin with the lemon halves inside it. Rub it with softened butter and season it with salt and pepper. Roast in a hot oven, 425°F/220°C/Gas Mark 7, for 20 minutes, then reduce the heat to 400°F/200°C/Gas Mark 6 for a further 25 minutes or so – till when you stick the point of a knife into the bit between the leg and the body the juices run clear. Leave the chicken in a low temperature oven, once cooked, for 10 minutes, to let the juices settle.

Make the sauce by melting the butter in a sauté pan and cooking the very finely chopped onion over moderate heat till it is really soft. Add the chicken stock and saffron and simmer till the stock has reduced by more than half. Add the lemon rind and juice and reduce for a further couple of minutes' cooking. Pour in the cream – it must be double, the danger with single cream is that it can curdle, or split. Double won't. Let the sauce bubble till it has the texture of thick cream. Season with salt and pepper.

Serve the sauce in a bowl to accompany the sliced roast chicken. The sauce will be a golden colour, from the saffron. Don't be tempted to substitute saffron powder, which is generally adulterated – only the strands will do!

Pot-Roasted Chicken with Root Vegetables

This is a true winter dish, making the most of the lovely root vegetables which are in season during the winter months. This is also one of those convenient one-pot dishes where the vegetables are cooked with the meat. All that is needed to accompany the pot roast is a dish of baked potatoes. Any vegetables left over from the pot roast can be liquidized into a delicious soup made with stock from the chicken carcass. If this is to serve six, it is really better to use two small chickens – use any leftovers for soup.

Serves 4–6

4 tbsp oil (I like to use olive or sunflower)

1 large or 2 small chickens, cleaned, wiped and with giblets removed

4 onions, skinned and thinly sliced

1 lb/450 g carrots, peeled and either sliced in rounds or cut in 2-inch/5-cm chunks and quartered

1 lb/450 g parsnips, peeled and cut to match the carrots

1 lb/450 g leeks, washed, trimmed and cut into 2-inch/5-cm lengths

8 oz/225 g turnips, peeled and cut into smallish chunks

1 lb/450 g celeriac, peeled and cut into smallish chunks

2 garlic cloves, skinned and chopped

Salt and freshly ground black pepper

Heat the oil in a large casserole, and brown the chicken all over. Remove the chicken and keep it warm in a low oven while you brown the vegetables.

First add the onions to the casserole and cook for 4–5 minutes, stirring occasionally. Then add all the remaining vegetables – it looks a lot, but they reduce in quantity as they cook, and they do double duty in flavouring the chicken deliciously and as its accompaniment. Cook the vegetables for 10 minutes or so, stirring from time to time, then add the garlic and season with salt and pepper to taste.

Replace the chicken, making a nest for it in the vegetables. Cover the casserole first with foil and then with a tightly fitting lid. Cook in a moderate oven – 350°F/ 180°C/Gas Mark 4 – for 1½ hours. Test to see whether the chicken is cooked by piercing a thigh with a sharp knife – if the juices run clear, the chicken is cooked. Put the casserole back to cook for a bit longer if the juices are at all tinged with pink.

This dish keeps hot very satisfactorily for an hour or so. The vegetables make a surprising amount of liquid, and I like to serve baked potatoes to soak up the juices.

Chicken and Broccoli in Mayonnaise Cream Sauce

The sauce for this dish has some rather unlikely sounding ingredients in it. Don't be put off, because it is a most useful recipe. It can be made several hours ahead and reheated when needed. It also has the vegetable in with the chicken and the sauce, making extras unnecessary. Although the ingredients sound odd, their combination is quite delicious, giving a lovely velvety textured, tasty sauce.

Serves 6

A 4-lb/1.8-kg chicken
1 onion, skinned and quartered
1 carrot, peeled and cut in chunks
Bouquet garni
Salt
A few black peppercorns
2 lb/900 g frozen broccoli
2 oz/56 g butter
2 oz/56 g plain flour
1 rounded tbsp curry powder
A 7-oz/200-g tin evaporated milk
4 tbsp mayonnaise
2 tbsp lemon juice
2 oz/56 g Cheddar cheese, grated
Salt and freshly ground black pepper
4 rounded tbsp breadcrumbs, or 2 small packets potato crisps, crushed

Put the chicken in a large saucepan and cover with water. Add the onion, carrot, bouquet garni, salt and peppercorns. Bring to the boil, cover with a lid and simmer gently for 1 hour or until the juices run clear when the point of a knife is stuck into the thigh. Leave to cool in the stock.

Put the broccoli into a saucepan of boiling salted water, and boil until the stalks are just tender. Drain, and refresh under running cold water, which will bring back the green colour. Butter a wide, shallow 3-pint/1.7-litre ovenproof dish, and put the drained broccoli spears in it. When the chicken is cool enough to handle, remove it from the stock, take off the skin and strip the meat from the bones. Spread the chicken meat evenly over the broccoli.

Melt the butter in a saucepan and stir in the flour and curry powder. Cook over a gentle heat for 1–2 minutes, then gradually stir in 1 pint/570 ml of the stock in which the chicken cooked. Stir until the sauce boils. Remove from the heat and add the evaporated milk, mayonnaise, lemon juice and the grated cheese, stirring until the cheese has melted. Check the seasoning, and add some salt and pepper if needed. Pour the sauce over the chicken in the dish and sprinkle either breadcrumbs or crushed potato crisps over the surface.

Bake in a moderately hot oven – 375°F/190°C/Gas Mark 5 – for 30 minutes, or until the sauce is just bubbling, and serve with creamily mashed potatoes and a vegetable with contrasting colours – perhaps lemon-glazed carrots.

Cold Chicken in White Wine and Parsley Jelly

This jellied chicken tastes as good as it looks at any party. It's ideal for a buffet because it is easy to eat with just a fork. The jelly is made of dry white wine and chicken stock, and is flecked with bright green parsley.

Serves 6–8

For the chicken:

**2 small chickens, each weighing
  2½–3 lb/1.25–1.35 kg**

3 medium onions, skinned and halved

3 carrots, peeled and halved

2 sticks of celery, leaves and all

2 leeks, washed, trimmed and chopped

2 bay leaves

½ tsp salt

12 black peppercorns

2 egg whites

For the jelly:

1 pint/570 ml dry white wine

**½–1 oz/14–28 g powdered gelatine (see the
  note about gelatine on page 14)**

**1 pint/570 ml clarified stock, from the chicken
  liquid (see method)**

Salt to taste

**4 tbsp finely chopped parsley, preferably
  flat-leafed, for a better flavour**

Put the chickens into a saucepan or casserole, cover with water and add the prepared vegetables, bay leaves, salt and peppercorns. Bring to the boil and simmer gently, half covered, for about 2 hours. Test the chickens by piercing a thigh with a very sharp knife – if the juices run completely clear they are cooked, if they run at all pink the chickens need longer. Then take the pan off the heat, and leave the chickens to cool in their cooking liquid.

When the chickens are cold, remove from their liquid and strip the meat, cutting it into evenly sized 1-inch/2.5-cm pieces. Return the bones – but not the skin – to the stock, and bring back to the boil. Simmer for another hour. Strain the stock, and put it back in the saucepan.

To clarify the stock, first bring it to the boil. Whisk egg whites until stiff and whisk them into the boiling stock. Let the stock simmer under the egg whites, which will collect all the bits in the stock, for 15–20 minutes. Then strain the stock through a large sieve lined with two thicknesses of kitchen paper into a bowl.

To make the jelly, measure the wine into a saucepan and sprinkle in the gelatine. Let the wine sponge up the gelatine, then measure the chicken stock into the saucepan. Heat gently, just enough to dissolve the gelatine granules completely. Taste and add salt as necessary. Take the pan off the heat and allow to cool. When the liquid is beginning to gel, add the chopped chicken and parsley – don't be tempted to add the parsley when the liquid is at all warm or the parsley will lose some of its fresh bright colour.

Pour into a bowl or mould (this jelly doesn't turn out well from an elaborate mould because of the chunks of chicken in it, and the best thing is a plain oval mould). Put it in the fridge to set for 2–3 hours or overnight. When it is quite firm, dip the mould into hot water for a few seconds and turn it out on to a serving plate. Garnish, if you like, with bunches of fresh crisp parsley.

Chicken Stew with Parsley and Chive Dumplings

This is one of those dishes which you think of longingly when on an endless cold and wet walk. It's the sort of dish which conjures up the image in your mind of an appreciative family sniffing in anticipation as the mother lifts the lid from the casserole! My family is never that idyllic – I am usually yelling at them that supper is ready and to hurry up!

The dumplings make any accompanying starch unnecessary, but because of the root

vegetables in the stew I do like to serve a green vegetable alongside.

Serves 6

| 1 chicken, about 3½ lb/1.6 kg |
| 2 onions, skinned and cut in half |
| 2 leeks, washed, trimmed and chopped |
| ½ tsp rock salt |
| A handful of peppercorns |

For the stew:

| 2 oz/56 g butter + 2 tbsp sunflower oil |
| 2 onions, skinned and finely chopped |
| 3 carrots, peeled and chopped |
| 4 medium leeks, washed, trimmed and sliced |
| 4 sticks of celery, washed, trimmed and sliced |
| 4 parsnips, peeled and chopped |
| ½ medium turnip, peeled and chopped |
| 2 tbsp flour |
| 2 pints/1.1 litres chicken stock, from the chicken liquid (see method) |
| Salt and freshly ground black pepper |

For the dumplings:

| 1 tbsp sunflower oil |
| 1 onion, skinned and very finely chopped |
| 12 oz/340 g self-raising flour sieved with ½ tsp salt and ground black pepper |
| 1 tbsp each chopped parsley and snipped chives |
| 3 tbsp grated suet |
| ½ pint/285 ml milk |

Put the chicken into a saucepan with the first lot of onions and leeks, and the rock salt and peppercorns. Cover with water, bring to simmering point, then cover with a lid and simmer gently for 1 hour. Stick a knife into the chicken's thigh – if the juices run clear, the chicken is cooked; if they are even slightly tinged with pink, continue to simmer for a further 5 or 10 minutes.

Take the pan off the heat and let the chicken cool in the liquid. Then lift it out and cut all the meat from the carcass. Set the meat aside. Replace the carcass in the stock and boil gently, pan uncovered, for 45 minutes. Strain.

To make the stew, melt the butter and heat the oil together in a large casserole. Add the chopped onions and cook them till they turn soft and transparent-looking, then stir in the other vegetables and cook, stirring from time to time, for about 10 minutes. Stir in the flour, cook for a minute, then add 2 pints/1.1 litres of the stock, stirring all the time till the mixture comes to boiling point. Season with salt and pepper.

Cover with a lid and cook in a moderate oven, 350°F/180°C/Gas Mark 4, for 35–40 minutes. The vegetables should be soft when you stick a fork into them – try a piece of carrot, they take the longest to cook.

To make the dumplings, heat the sunflower oil and cook the very finely chopped onion in it till soft. Cool, then mix well with the seasoned flour, herbs and suet, and then mix in the milk to bind it all together.

In a saucepan of fast-boiling water or stock, cook spoonfuls of this mixture – they swell during cooking – for 10 minutes each. Lift them out with a slotted spoon, and put them into the vegetable stew. Carefully stir in the chicken, and reheat till the whole stew simmers gently for about 10 minutes. Serve.

Chicken or Turkey or Pheasant Fricassée

A fricassée is viewed by some as a sort of dustbin dish. This view is taken by those for whom a fricassée means a thick white sauce containing chopped leftover chicken or turkey – and leftovers which haven't been carefully trimmed of gristle and other unappetizing bits of skin and fat, a trimming most important to make a good and appealing fricassée.

This is the way I make a fricassée, and a pheasant fricassée is the very first thing I cooked by myself. I think it is essential to have leftover fat from the roasting tin, and the jellied juices which you will find under the fat – both have all the flavour of the bird and, if it was stuffed, of the stuffings too.

Serves 6

3 tbsp (approx.) dripping from the roasting tin

2 medium onions, skinned and finely chopped

2 sticks of celery, washed, trimmed and very finely sliced

3 rashers of back bacon, trimmed of most of its fat and sliced

2 carrots, peeled and chopped into very small dice

2 teaspoons medium curry powder (this isn't enough to be detected by avowed curry haters)

2 oz/56 g flour

1¼ pints/710 ml chicken stock, or 1 pint/570 ml + 2–3 tbsp jellied stock from the roasting tin

2 oz/56 g raisins or sultanas (optional, but I always add them)

Salt and freshly ground black pepper

About 1 lb/450 g chopped, trimmed leftover chicken, turkey or pheasant – more, if possible; if less, use an extra carrot

Put the dripping into a saucepan and add the finely chopped onions, finely sliced celery and bacon and finely diced carrots. Cook all together for about 8–10 minutes, stirring from time to time to prevent the vegetables and bacon from sticking, and to make sure that they cook evenly. Stick a fork into a bit of carrot – it should feel just tender. If it doesn't, cook for a further few minutes. The carrots are the part of this mixture which need most cooking, and as they won't get any length of cooking time after this stage they need to be cooked through now.

Stir in the curry powder, then the flour, and cook for a minute or two before pouring in the stock, gradually, and stirring continuously till the sauce bubbles. Stir in the raisins, and season with salt and pepper. If you intend to eat this immediately, stir in the chopped chicken or turkey or pheasant, whichever you are using, and reheat gently, in the saucepan, letting the sauce bubble very gently for 10 minutes. Don't let it boil fast because that will reduce your leftover chicken to shreds – not the aim. If you want to make up the mixture in advance, let it cool completely before adding the leftover chicken, to avoid reheating it more than once.

Serve with boiled Basmati rice, and a mixture of cooked root vegetables such as julienne strips of parsnip, Jerusalem artichokes and celeriac, or with a green vegetable like courgettes sautéed in olive oil with chopped garlic. Or, if you have tastes like my family (what an admission, this), with frozen peas cooked with mint and half a teaspoon of sugar.

Chicken and Mushroom Filo Pastry Parcels

A pile of these on a dish accompanied by a good salad makes a perfect lunch. You can prepare the parcels right up to the moment before you bake them, leave them covered with clingfilm on their baking tray in a cool place or a fridge, then just bake them before serving them hot. How many you allow per person does depend on appetites. This recipe makes 48 parcels.

Serves 6–8

12 sheets of filo pastry

Melted butter – about 6 oz/170 g

For the filling:

4 tbsp sunflower or olive oil and 4 oz/112 g butter

2 lb/900 g mushrooms, wiped and chopped as finely as you can

4 garlic cloves (optional)

1 lb/450 g reduced or full-fat cream cheese

2 lb/900 g cooked chicken breast, diced as small as you can, which will depend on how sharp your knife is

8 rashers of smoked streaky bacon, grilled till crisp then crumbled

To make the filling, heat the oil and melt the butter together in a frying or sauté pan.

When it is very hot add the chopped mushrooms, and cook them till they are almost crisp. Peel the garlic and chop it very finely and stir that, too, in amongst the mushrooms. Take the cooked mushrooms off the heat and cool them. In a quite large bowl beat the cream cheese till soft, and mix in the diced chicken, cooled mushrooms and garlic mixture, and the crumbled bacon.

Lay a sheet of filo on a table and brush it carefully all over with melted butter. Cover it as exactly as you can with a second sheet of filo and brush that, too, with melted butter. With a sharp knife cut the buttered filo in half, then cut each half in two strips, so you have four broad strips. Put a spoonful of filling in the bottom right corner of each strip. Fold into triangle shapes up to halfway up the strip, then cut across. Brush the triangle with melted butter and put it on a butter-brushed baking tray. Put a spoonful of filling in the bottom right hand corner of the halved strips and fold into triangles again. Brush the parcels with butter and put them on the baking tray. Repeat with the remaining sheets of filo.

Cover the baking tray with clingfilm and store the tray in the fridge till you are ready to bake the parcels. Put it into a hot oven, 425°F/220°C/Gas Mark 7, for 7–10 minutes, or till the filo is golden brown and crisp. Serve hot.

Pancakes Stuffed with Chicken and Mushrooms

Pancakes can be a marvellous way to dress up leftover fish or meat. There is a certain panache attached to a dish composed of pancakes (especially if they are referred to as crêpes!) and a small quantity of leftover chicken, for example, can be padded out with a good tasty sauce.

Serves 8

For the pancakes (makes 16):

4 oz/112 g plain flour
2 eggs
¼ pint/140 ml milk
3 tbsp melted butter, or sunflower oil
¼ tsp salt
Butter for cooking the pancakes

For the filling:

3 oz/84 g butter
1 medium onion, skinned and very finely chopped
8 oz/225 g mushrooms, sliced
3 oz/84 g plain flour
1½ pints/850 ml milk
2 tbsp sherry
Salt and freshly ground black pepper
A pinch of grated nutmeg
4 oz/112 g cooked chicken, diced fairly small (or use leftover ham or salmon)
2 oz/56 g grated cheese

Work the ingredients for the pancakes in a blender until smooth, and leave the mixture to sit for 1–2 hours.

When you are ready to start making them,

drop a piece of butter, about a small tea-spoonful, into a 7-inch/18-cm frying pan. (Do not be tempted to substitute margarine. The pancakes will stick to the pan.) Melt the butter, swirling it around until the pan is well-greased all over. Take a large table-spoonful of the pancake batter and pour it into the pan, tilting the pan to cover the surface with a thin layer of batter. Cook on a moderate heat until the bottom of the pancake is golden brown. Then I find that the easiest way to turn the pancake over to cook on the other side is to carefully use my fingers.

When the pancake is cooked on both sides, slip it on to a cooling rack.

When you have 16 cooked pancakes, make the filling. Melt the butter in a saucepan, add the finely chopped onion and cook over a gentle heat, stirring from time to time, until the onion is soft but not turning colour. Add the sliced mushrooms to the pan and cook for a further 2 minutes, then stir in the flour. Gradually add the milk, stirring all the time, until the sauce comes to the boil.

Take the pan off the heat and stir in the sherry and seasoning. Leave the sauce to cool completely before adding the chicken.

Butter a shallow ovenproof dish. Divide the cold filling between the pancakes, rolling each one up and laying them in rows in the dish. Sprinkle the grated cheese over the top and bake in a moderate oven – 375°F/190°C/Gas Mark 5 – for 40 minutes.

You can get this dish ready to bake in the morning, so all you need to do later is pop it in the oven. Serve with warm brown rolls and a green salad.

Chicken, Leek and Parsley Pie

This is a marvellous pie, extremely popular with adults and children alike.

Serves 8

1 large chicken, about 4½ lb/2 kg
2 onions, skinned
1 carrot, peeled and cut in chunks
1 bouquet garni
Salt, and a few black peppercorns
3 oz/84 g butter
4 good-sized leeks, washed, trimmed and cut into ½-inch/1-cm pieces
1 rounded tsp curry powder
2 oz/56 g plain flour
1 pint/570 ml milk
½ pint/285 ml chicken stock from the chicken liquid (see method)
Salt and freshly ground black pepper
2 rounded tbsp finely chopped parsley
12 oz/340 g puff pastry
Milk for glazing

Put the chicken in a large saucepan and cover with water. Add one onion, cut in quarters, the carrot chunks, bouquet garni, salt and peppercorns. Bring to the boil, cover with a lid and simmer gently for 1 hour or until the juices run clear when the point of a knife is stuck into the thigh. Cool the chicken in the stock in which it cooked. When cool, remove from the stock, strip all the meat from the bones, and put it in a deep 3½-pint/2-litre pie dish. Strain the stock and reserve.

Melt the butter in a saucepan. Add the sliced leeks and the second onion, chopped, and cook gently for about 10 minutes, when they should be soft and transparent. Stir in the curry powder and the flour. Cook for 1–2 minutes longer, then gradually blend in the milk and ½ pint/285 ml of the reserved chicken stock, stirring until the sauce boils. Season with salt and pepper. Stir in the finely chopped parsley. Pour over the chicken meat in the pie dish, and mix well.

Roll out the puff pastry, and use it to cover the pie. Decorate the pie with pastry leaves and brush the surface all over with milk. Bake in a hot oven, 425°F/220°C/Gas Mark 7, for 20 minutes, then lower the heat to 350°F/180°C/Gas Mark 4 for a further 20 minutes, or until the pie is golden brown.

Serve, if you like, with baked jacket potatoes and a green vegetable; purple sprouting broccoli is good.

Chicken Liver and Rice Balls with Tomato Sauce

I like chicken liver and rice balls as a main course, with a green salad to accompany it, for supper for just Godfrey and me. But it can also be a first course for 6–8 if you allow 4–5 balls per person. Use Arborio rice if you can get it – it just makes the chicken liver and rice balls that little better than ordinary long-grained white rice.

Serves 2

1–1½ pints/570–850 ml chicken stock (or
  water plus a chicken stock cube)

½ lb/225 g rice (Arborio if possible)

1 oz/28 g butter

1 medium onion, skinned and very finely
  chopped

½ lb/225 g chicken livers, picked over and any
  bitter green or yellow bits removed

Salt and freshly ground black pepper

A pinch of fresh or dried thyme

1 egg, well beaten

2 tbsp freshly grated Parmesan cheese

2 tsp finely chopped parsley

2–3 tbsp breadcrumbs, made from day-old
  baked bread as opposed to steamed, sliced
  bread

Oil for deep-frying (I like to use sunflower)

Simple Tomato Sauce (see page 305)

Put the chicken stock into a saucepan and bring to the boil. When it is boiling, reduce the heat to simmer and add the rice, stirring for a minute. Simmer gently until the rice is just tender. Drain the rice and leave it to cool.

Melt the butter in a frying pan and add the onions. Sauté for 5–7 minutes, stirring occasionally to prevent the onions burning. Chop the chicken livers and add them when the onions are soft and transparent. Continue cooking, stirring from time to time, for a further 4–5 minutes. Season with the salt, freshly ground black pepper and thyme. Stir first the liver and onion mixture into the rice, and then half the beaten egg. Stir in the grated Parmesan cheese and parsley.

With wet fingers, shape the mixture into evenly sized balls. Roll each ball first in the breadcrumbs, then in the remaining beaten egg, and finally in breadcrumbs again. Arrange the breadcrumbed balls on a baking tray, and chill in the fridge.

When you are ready to eat, take the chicken liver and rice balls out of the fridge, and heat the oil for deep-frying in a saucepan to a depth of about 3 inches/7.5 cm. Deep-fry the balls until they are golden brown. Keep them warm in an ovenproof dish lined with two or three thicknesses of kitchen paper in a low oven and serve as soon as possible, with the tomato sauce.

Sautéed Chicken Livers with Green Peppercorns

The combination of green peppercorns and chicken livers is so good. I serve it on a bed of plain boiled Basmati rice, with either a green vegetable or a salad to accompany it.

Serves 6

1½ lb/850 g chicken livers
2 oz/56 g butter
1 tbsp oil (I use sunflower)
3 onions, skinned and very finely sliced
1 garlic clove, skinned and finely chopped
¼ pint/140 ml medium dry sherry
2 tsp green peppercorns, drained of their brine
Salt

Pick over the chicken livers, throwing out any green bits – these taste bitter when cooked. Chop the livers roughly and set aside.

Heat the butter and oil together in a frying pan. Add the onion and sauté for 5–7 minutes, stirring occasionally so that it cooks evenly. Add the chopped garlic and pour on the sherry. Let it bubble away for about 3 minutes, by which time the liquid will have virtually evaporated. Over a fairly high heat, add the chicken livers to the frying pan. Add the peppercorns and cook, stirring from time to time, until the livers are

just pink in the middle, about 5–7 minutes. Season to taste with salt.

Serve on a bed of boiled Basmati rice, topped with a dusting of parsley, and with a vegetable in a creamy white sauce, such as steamed leeks, or cauliflower.

Roast Turkey with Pork Sausagemeat and Chestnut Stuffing

This amount of stuffing will fill a turkey weighing 12–15 lb/5.4–6.7 kg. Surplus stuffing can be baked in an ovenproof dish, uncovered – it is delicious. Any left over is very good eaten cold, too.

If you prefer, rather than the tinned chestnuts you can use the equivalent amount of vacuum packed chestnuts (the nicest of the lot of preserved chestnuts) or fresh, skinned chestnuts (an awful fiddle to prepare), but don't try to reconstitute dried chestnuts which, however carefully I simmer them in the chicken stock or the like, always end up tasting of cardboard.

For the stuffing:

3 lb/1.35 kg good quality pork sausagemeat (I buy sausages and slit the skins, which then peel off in a matter of seconds)
2 tbsp sunflower oil
2 onions, skinned and chopped very neatly and finely
1 garlic clove, skinned and finely chopped (optional)
Two 15-oz/420-g tins of unsweetened chestnuts
Plenty of freshly ground black pepper (no need for salt, it's in the sausages)

119

Heat the oil and sauté the finely chopped onions, and the garlic if used, for several minutes till they are very soft. Cool them completely.

Skin the sausages into a bowl and add the chestnuts (if they are tinned, drain off the brine) and the pepper. When the onions are cool, mix them into the stuffing – the only way to do this thoroughly is with your hands.

If you want to freeze the stuffing, pack it into a polythene bag and, most important, label it clearly. It is frightening how anonymous food becomes once frozen! Thaw it for 36–48 hours and be sure it is quite thawed before you stuff the turkey with it.

To roast the turkey

Most books tell you that a turkey needs 20 minutes' cooking time per lb/450 g. If you are cooking a bird weighing about 10 lb/ 4.5 kg that is quite right, but if you cooked a 20-lb/9-kg bird for the equivalent time it would be uncarvable – the meat would drop off the bones. When cooking a large bird it is inevitable that the breast will be slightly overdone if the thighs are to cook thoroughly, but this is how I cook a turkey.

I make a cross out of two thick pieces of foil (you have to double it up these days because it tears so easily) and place it in a roasting tin. I rub butter all over the turkey, sprinkle it with salt, and grind black pepper over it. Then I put the turkey, *breast side down*, into the tin and wrap it well – this is a tip I learned from John Tovey several years ago, and I have followed it ever since. The juices run down during the cooking, preventing the bird from drying out. It does nothing

for the shape of the bird when cooked, but who is going to look at it? It is going to be carved and eaten!

I roast the turkey in a hot oven – 400°F/200°C/Gas Mark 6 for about 3½ hours. After 3 hours I stick a sharp knife into the thigh – if the juices are still pink it will need more cooking.

When the bird is cooked I take it out of the oven and let it sit on top of the cooker, wrapped in its foil, for about half an hour. It doesn't get cold, and resting it makes it much easier to carve.

Roast Duck with Apple and Cream Gravy

Duck is a great favourite on the menu here at Kinloch and for a special-occasion lunch party. So many people love duck that I can't think why you don't find it eaten more often in homes. It is thought of far more as a restaurant food. It's so easy, I mean, all you need is a really sharp pair of game shears to cut the duck in quarters. But how I loathe undercooked duck. Duck flesh should be cooked through without being shredded, and the skin should be crisp – utterly delicious. What is to me quite repellent is duck, whole or just duck breasts, undercooked with that layer of fat just under the surface of the skin. Can anyone seriously enjoy their duck like this? I can't think so. It's just a case of people not daring to admit it!

Serves 8

Allow 2 ducks for 8 people (if you are
   only 6, cold roast duck is delicious eaten
   up the next day)

1 quantity Apple and Cream Gravy (see below)

Put the ducks in a roasting tin in a hot oven,
425°F/220°C/Gas Mark 7, and roast them
for 1 hour and about 10 minutes.

When done, cut each duck in half with a
very good pair of scissors or, better still,
game shears. Trim off the legs at the tops
and cut down either side of the backbone for
a neater appearance. Serve with the warm
Apple and Cream Gravy.

Apple and cream gravy

*The creamy content of this gravy is actually
crème fraîche, which is less rich – slightly!
– than cream, and which has the right
acidic kick to sharpen up the sauce to
complement the rich roast duck meat.*

2 oz/56 g butter

1 onion, skinned and very finely chopped

3 good eating apples – Cox's would be ideal –
   skinned, cored and chopped as finely as
   possible

1 tsp flour

½ pint/285 ml dry cider – as dry as you can get

½ pint/285 ml crème fraîche

Salt and freshly ground black pepper

Melt the butter in a sauté pan and gently
sauté the chopped onion till it is really soft,
about 5 minutes. Then add the chopped
apples to the sauté pan, stir in the flour and

pour in the cider. Simmer till the cider has
reduced by about half. Stir in the crème
fraîche, and season with salt and pepper. Let
the sauce bubble for a few minutes. Keep the
sauce warm till you are able to serve it with
the duck.

Wild Duck with Apricot and Lemon Sauce

*Both roast wild duck and domestic duck are
good with this sauce. (If you use domestic
duck you don't need to rub them with butter
before roasting, as they have their own fatty
layer beneath the skin.) I like to serve a
green vegetable, such as celery with walnuts
and orange segments, with the duck, and
perhaps sautéed potatoes.*

Serves 6

3 mallard duck, approximately 1½–2 lb/
   675–900 g each

2 oranges

2 oz/56 g butter

Apricot and Lemon Sauce (page 298)

Put half an orange inside each duck, and rub
the ducks all over with butter. Roast in a hot
oven, 400°F/200°C/Gas Mark 6, for about
45 minutes. Keep them warm, then carve the
breasts, and serve them with the Apricot and
Lemon Sauce, which can be made in
advance if necessary.

Wild Duck with Cider and Apples

You can, if you wish, leave the cream out of this recipe, to make it a fairly low-calorie dish. But I think it is much nicer with the cream! Serve with a purée of celeriac and crunchy stir-fried cabbage, both of which complement the wild duck and apples particularly well.

Serves 6

2 wild duck (mallard), approximately 2 lb/900 g each

2 small onions, skinned, and 1 apple, halved, to stuff the ducks

3 oz/84 g butter

1 tbsp sunflower oil

2 medium onions, skinned and thinly sliced

1½ lb/675 g apples – a mixture of eating, such as Cox's, and cooking apples – peeled, cored and sliced

Salt and freshly ground black pepper

1 pint/570 ml dry cider

¼ pint/140 ml double cream

Stuff each duck with a whole skinned onion and half an apple. Heat the butter and oil together in a heavy casserole, and brown the ducks well, all over. Take them out of the casserole and keep them warm. Add the onions to the casserole and sauté for about 5 minutes, stirring occasionally to prevent them sticking. Add the apples. Season with salt and pepper, and stir in the cider. Return the mallards to the casserole, pushing them down into the oniony apple mixture.

Cover the casserole with a tightly fitting lid and simmer very gently for 1 hour, or until the juices run clear when you stick the point of a sharp knife into the duck flesh. The cooking apples will have become mush, but the eating apples should have retained their shape.

Just before serving, stir in the cream and check the seasoning. Carve the ducks, and spoon the sauce around the slices of duck.

Wild Duck Paprika

This recipe was given to me by my sister, Olivia Milburn. It is extremely good and I am complimented on it when I make it, but the credit must go to Liv, not to me!

Serves 4–6

2 wild duck (mallard), approximately 1½–2 lb/ 675–900 g each

3 onions, skinned

1 carrot, peeled and quartered

1 bouquet garni

1 orange, quartered

3 oz/84 g butter

1 garlic clove, peeled and finely chopped

1 rounded tbsp plain flour

1 rounded tbsp paprika

1 rounded tbsp redcurrant jelly

¼ pint/140 ml red wine

4 tbsp sour cream

Salt and freshly ground black pepper

Put the ducks in a deep roasting tin. Pour water into the tin to come halfway up the inside. Put 1 onion, the carrot, bouquet garni and orange into the tin around the ducks.

Cover the roasting tin with a double thickness of foil, and cook in a moderate oven, 350°F/180°C/Gas Mark 4, for 1½ hours. Remove from the oven, and cool. When cold, remove the ducks from the stock, carve them and put them on to an ovenproof serving dish.

Slice the remaining onions. Melt the butter in a saucepan and add the sliced onions and the garlic. Cook gently for 15 minutes, stirring occasionally, until the onions are soft. Stir in the flour, cook for 1–2 minutes, then add the paprika, redcurrant jelly, red wine and 1 pint/570 ml of the stock the duck cooked in. Stir until the sauce boils. Stir in the sour cream, salt and black pepper and pour over the duck in the serving dish.

Cover the serving dish with either a lid or foil, and reheat in a moderate oven, 350°F/180°C/Gas Mark 4, for 45 minutes. The sauce should be bubbling.

I like to serve this with well beaten mashed potatoes, which gives them a creamy texture, and with a vegetable such as sautéed courgettes, with or without garlic, depending on your taste.

Pheasant Breasts with Creamy Bacon Sauce

You can substitute chicken breasts for the pheasant in this recipe. On the other hand, pheasants are ever-increasingly easy to buy, even if you don't have access to them on a ready basis. This simple recipe transforms a pheasant breast into a special occasion supper. There is no doubt that the flavours of the smoked bacon, the pheasant and the cream all enhance each other quite wonderfully! And don't be aghast at the cream in the ingredients – remember that 1 pint/570 ml is divided between six people and is single cream at that, so it isn't nearly as harmful as it might seem!

Serves 6

6 good-sized pheasant breasts
2 tbsp plain flour, sieved
2 oz/56 g butter + 2 tbsp sunflower oil
6 rashers of smoked back bacon, trimmed of fat and cut into small dice
1 pint/570 ml single cream
Plenty of freshly ground black pepper – the bacon is usually sufficiently salty for most people's tastes

Dip the pheasant breasts in the flour, coating each side. Melt the butter and heat the oil together in a wide frying or sauté pan. Cook the pheasant breasts, browning on each side, till they are cooked through – this will take about 15 minutes. Stick a knife in the middle of one, to test that it is cooked – the juices should be clear. If they are tinged with pink, give them a bit longer.

Then remove the cooked pheasant breasts to a warmed serving dish and add the diced bacon to the pan. Cook, stirring, for 2–3 minutes, then pour in the cream, season with pepper, and let the cream bubble for a couple of minutes. Pour it and the bacon over and around the pheasant breasts in the serving dish.

Keep it warm till you are ready to serve – this is good with well-mashed potatoes, and a green vegetable.

Pheasant Breasts with Orange and Chestnuts

This is a real treat if you are eating alone. From about December onwards it is possible to buy pheasant breasts in butchers' shops and most supermarkets. They do shrink as they cook, so if they look small, buy two. This recipe combines the pheasant with the complementary flavours of orange and chestnuts. To save opening a tin of whole chestnuts and freezing what you don't use, buy fresh chestnuts and boil them for 10 minutes. They should then be ready to have their skins nicked and cut off. They taste much nicer than tinned ones! Alternatively, use vacuum-packed chestnuts. Avoid dried ones like the plague: they have the taste and texture of cardboard.

Serve this casserole with mashed potatoes and with finely sliced cabbage stir-fried with grainy mustard.

Serves 1

1 or 2 pheasant breasts
1 tbsp flour mixed with salt and ground black pepper
2 tbsp sunflower oil
1 onion, skinned and chopped
¼ pint/140 ml red wine, or stock if you prefer
About 6 chestnuts, shelled and chopped
1 orange, peel cut off with a serrated knife, and flesh chopped
Salt and freshly ground black pepper

Coat the pheasant breasts in the seasoned flour. Heat the oil in a casserole dish, and brown the pheasant breasts on each side.

Remove them to a warm dish. Add the chopped onion to the casserole and cook for a few minutes, till the onion is soft. Stir in the red wine or stock, the chopped chestnuts and the chopped orange. Replace the pheasant breasts in the casserole.

Cover with a lid and bake in a moderate oven, 350°F/180°C/Gas Mark 4, for 20 minutes. Take out of the oven, season with salt and pepper, and eat as soon as you can.

Pheasant Casseroled with Bacon, Shallots and Mushrooms in Red Wine

This is really like coq au vin only with pheasant instead of chicken. I think it is an awfully good way to use pheasant, which tends to dryness in cooking if you're not careful. Pheasants are widely available in city supermarkets and butchers these days, and their flavour is very mildly gamey. This is a most delicious casserole, full of richly complementary flavours.

Serves 6–8

2 fairly small pheasants
4 tbsp olive oil
1 lb/450 g shallots, skinned
6 slices of the best back bacon you can buy, trimmed of fat
1 lb/450 g mushrooms, each wiped, stalks cut level with the caps, and the mushrooms quartered
1 level tsp flour
1 bottle of red wine, ideally a Beaujolais

Salt and freshly ground black pepper

2 bay leaves

Pull out any fat from inside each pheasant. Heat the oil in a heavy casserole and brown the pheasants all over in the hot oil. As they are browned, put them on to a warm dish. Then add the skinned shallots to the casserole, and cook them gently, shaking the casserole so that they brown all over. Meanwhile slice the bacon into thin strips and add those to the shallots. Cook for several minutes, then, with a large slotted spoon, remove the shallots and bacon to the dish with the pheasants.

Turn up the heat under the casserole and sauté the quartered mushrooms till they are almost crisp – this much improves their flavour. Turn the heat back down to moderate, stir in the flour and cook for a moment, then pour in the wine, stirring till the sauce bubbles. Season with salt and pepper. Replace the shallots and bacon in the casserole, and the pheasants, pushing them down amongst the vegetables and bacon. Tuck in the bay leaves.

Cover the casserole with its lid and cook in a moderate oven, 350°F/180°C/Gas Mark 4, for 1 hour. Stick the point of a sharp knife into the thigh of one of the pheasants – if the juices run clear, take the casserole out of the oven. Remove the birds and carve them, replacing the pheasant meat in amongst the bacon, shallots and mushrooms in their winey sauce. Keep the carcasses to make stock.

Gently reheat to serve. Either very creamily mashed potatoes, or crisp sautéed potatoes with paprika, are good with this. Or you could – Godfrey would! – have plain boiled Basmati rice. Any green vegetable, such as broccoli or spring greens, goes very well with the pheasant casserole. And it freezes beautifully.

You can make it in advance by a day or two (provided you keep it in a cool place, like the fridge), reheating it till it bubbles very gently – fast boiling spoils the texture of the ingredients and will render the cooked pheasant shredded – for 10 minutes before serving.

Pheasant with Cream and Brandy

Please don't be put off by the cream in this recipe. It is a lovely, rich way of cooking pheasant.

Serves 6–8

2 pheasants

2 oz/56 g butter

3 medium onions, peeled and very thinly sliced

1 rounded tbsp curry powder

2 rounded tbsp plain flour

½ pint/285 ml double cream

6 tbsp brandy

Salt and freshly ground black pepper

In a large, heavy casserole, which has a tightly fitting lid, melt the butter and brown the pheasants well all over. Remove them from the pan and add the thinly sliced onions. Cook gently until the onions are soft, then replace the pheasants in the pan.

Cover with a piece of foil and the lid, and put in a moderate oven, 350°F/180°C/Gas Mark 4, for 1 hour. Test to see if the pheasants are cooked by sticking the point of a sharp knife into the thigh – if the juices run clear and are not tinged with pink, the pheasant is cooked. If necessary, cook a little longer.

Carve the pheasants and keep them warm on a serving dish. Stir the curry powder and flour into the onions in the pan, and cook gently for 2–3 minutes. Stir in the cream and brandy, season and simmer, stirring until the sauce thickens. Pour over the carved pheasant and serve, with boiled rice or with new potatoes, and with a crunchy green vegetable, such as my favourite sugar snap peas.

Pheasant with Fresh Ginger

I used to have to go to great lengths to get fresh root ginger when I first made this recipe. Changed days now – fresh ginger is to be found in the Co-op in Broadford.

Serves 6–8

2 pheasants

3 oz/84 g butter

4 onions, peeled and thinly sliced

1 garlic clove, peeled and finely chopped

1 piece of fresh ginger, about 2 inches/5 cm long, cut in fine slivers

1 cooking apple and 3 sweet apples, all peeled, cored and chopped

1 rounded tbsp plain flour

¾ pint/420 ml dry cider

½ pint/255 ml game stock, or water and 1 chicken stock cube

Salt and freshly ground black pepper

Melt the butter in a large casserole which has a tightly fitting lid. Brown the pheasants really well all over, remove from the pan and keep warm. Lower the heat a little under the pan, and add the thinly sliced onions. Cook, stirring occasionally, until the onions are soft. Add the garlic, slivers of ginger, the chopped apples and the flour, and cook for 1–2 minutes. Then gradually stir in the cider and stock, stirring until the sauce boils. Season to taste.

Replace the pheasants in the casserole and cover with the lid. Cook in a moderate oven, 350°F/180°C/Gas Mark 4, for 1 hour. Test to see if the pheasants are done (see previous recipe). Take them out of the casserole, and carve. Put the carved pheasants into a serving dish, pour over the onion, ginger and apple sauce and serve.

Roast Pheasant with Bread Sauce and Game Chips

This seems rather an obvious item to include in this book – obvious, because to many people straight roast pheasant seems to be so easy. But it isn't often that you come across really good roast pheasant traditionally produced with creamy bread sauce and proper game chips. Game gravy should be thin in texture and intense in flavour – it's a matter of taste, but I generally add port to mine.

Serves 6

**2 pheasants approximately 2–2½ lb/
    900 g–1.1 kg each**

Butter

Salt and freshly ground black pepper

**Several rashers of streaky bacon (smoked if
    possible)**

Bread Sauce (see page 300)

Smear butter over the breasts of the pheasants, season with a little salt and freshly ground black pepper, and cover the pheasants with the streaky bacon. You can do all this in the morning so that the pheasants are ready to pop into the oven before dinner that evening. Roast them in a hot oven – 400°F/200°C/Gas Mark 6 – for 20 minutes, then lower the temperature to 350°F/180°C/Gas Mark 4 and continue to roast the birds for about an hour. Test to see whether they are cooked by piercing a leg at the point where it joins the body – if the juices run clear, and are not tinged with pink, they are ready. I find that dropping the oven temperature prevents the pheasant flesh drying out too much. Keep the pheasants warm until you are ready to carve.

Game chips

Game chips, either wafer-thin slices or matchsticks, can be made in the morning and reheated to serve with the pheasants for dinner.

To make good game chips you really need a mandoline, because you can't slice the potatoes thinly enough by hand – I know, I've tried! The slices have to be thin to stay crisp – if they are too thick, they will go flabby soon after frying. We make matchsticks here for our guests. Our mandoline has a matchstick blade, and the matchsticks don't take a minute to cook.

Serves 6

Fat for deep frying

**1½ lb/675 g potatoes, peeled and cut in
    matchsticks**

Salt

A chip pan with a wire basket is the best utensil for cooking chips. You can use an ordinary saucepan with a metal slotted spoon for fishing out the cooked chips or matchsticks, but you have to be quick about it so as not to burn any in the saucepan.

Pour fat into the pan to a depth of about 4 inches/10 cm and heat until it sizzles when you drop a piece of potato in. Cook your chips or matchsticks, in batches if necessary, until they are golden brown. Drain them, and put them in a roasting tin lined with several thicknesses of kitchen paper to absorb excess grease. Sprinkle them with a little salt, and either leave and reheat to serve or keep warm to serve.

Marinated Pigeon Breasts with Port and Redcurrant Jelly Sauce

We tend to overlook pigeon as a useful and delicious meat. If you're a novice pigeon eater, you'll find some advice on how to prepare them in the introduction to the following recipe.

Serves 2

2 pigeons, breasts separated from the
   carcasses

1 tbsp sunflower oil

1 oz/28 g butter

For the marinade:

2 tbsp olive oil

1 onion, skinned and sliced

1 stick of celery, chopped

A small bunch of parsley, chopped

2 garlic cloves, skinned and chopped

¼ pint/140 ml red wine

For the stock:

The 2 pigeon carcasses

2 onions, skinned and cut in half

1 stick of celery

A few black peppercorns

1 tsp salt

For the sauce:

About ½ tbsp flour

2 juniper berries, crushed (I use a rolling pin)

¼ pint/140 ml strained pigeon stock

¼ pint/140 ml port

2 slightly rounded tsp redcurrant jelly

Salt and freshly ground black pepper

First prepare the marinade. Heat the oil and add the sliced onion, chopped celery, parsley and garlic. Cook for a few minutes, then pour in the red wine. Simmer for 3–4 minutes, then take the marinade off the heat and let it cool. Put the pigeon breasts into a dish and pour the cold marinade over them. Leave for several hours or overnight in a cool place.

Make stock with the two pigeon carcasses. Put them into a saucepan and cover them with cold water. Add the onions, celery, black peppercorns and salt. Simmer for 1 hour, then strain the stock.

Heat the oil and melt the butter together in a saucepan. When it is hot, brown the pigeon breasts on each side, cooking them for 2–3 minutes. How long you cook them depends on how well done you like them. Some people like them very rare – personally I like to eat them just tinged with pink, no redder. Take the breasts out of the pan and put them on a dish to keep warm.

For the sauce, add the flour to the fat in the pan together with the crushed juniper berries. Cook for a minute or two then, stirring all the time, add the stock and port, stirring till the sauce boils. Add the red-currant jelly, and stir till it melts. Season to your taste with salt and pepper.

Pour this sauce over the pigeon breasts in the dish, cover, and keep warm in a low oven till you are ready to eat. To serve, slice the breasts lengthways, in half, or, if you prefer, in three pieces so that they fan out on each plate. Spoon the sauce or gravy over them.

I think they are good served with mashed potato, well beaten, and a mixed leaf salad with a good Balsamic vinegar-flavoured dressing to accompany them.

Chicken, Leek and Parsley Pie ▶
page 117

Pigeon and Steak Pie

Pigeons are wonderful birds to cook and eat. Not only are they delicious, but they need no plucking – if you slit the skin through the feathers, the skin, feathers and all, just peels off, and you can then cut the breasts away from the rest of the bird. Because we somehow never get enough pigeons to make a dish on their own, I usually end up making a pie by adding some rump steak, which goes well with the pigeon meat. (What we call rump in Skye is not a grilling steak; it is a lean braising steak usually sold as topside or silverside in other parts of Britain.)

Serves 8

4 tbsp sunflower oil

4 pigeons, with the breasts separated

2 lb/900 g lean braising steak, cut in pieces about 2 inches/5 cm across

2 rashers of bacon, cut in pieces

2 onions, peeled and thinly sliced

8 oz/225 g mushrooms, sliced

1 rounded tbsp plain flour

½ pint/285 ml stock (you can make this from the pigeon carcasses as described in the previous recipe)

½ pint/285 ml red wine

1 tbsp redcurrant jelly

Salt and freshly ground black pepper

12 oz/340 g puff pastry

Milk for glazing

◄ Venison Fillet with Port and Redcurrant Jelly, page 130

Heat the oil in a saucepan and brown the pigeon breasts and the pieces of steak well on all sides. Remove from the pan. Add the pieces of bacon and fry until brown, then remove them to the dish containing the pigeon and beef. Lower the heat under the saucepan and add the sliced onions to the pan. Cook gently, stirring occasionally, for 10 minutes, until the onions are soft and transparent. Then put the sliced mushrooms in with the onions, cook for 1–2 minutes and stir in the flour. Gradually add the stock and red wine, stirring until the sauce boils. When it has boiled stir in the redcurrant jelly and the seasoning. Put the meat, pigeon breasts and the sauce in a 3½-pint/2-litre pie dish, and leave to cool.

Roll out the pastry and cover the pie. Decorate and brush the pie with milk. Bake in a hot oven, 400°F/200°C/Gas Mark 6, for 20 minutes. Then lower the heat to 350°F/180°C/Gas Mark 4 and cook for a further 30 minutes until the pastry is golden brown.

Any pastry-lidded food has its own in-built starch, so I think that potatoes are unnecessary with this. Instead, I prefer to serve braised celery and a puréed root vegetable: parsnips, carrots or celeriac.

Rabbit and Paprika Casserole

You can buy rabbit in most supermarkets and butchers', and whereas you can use chicken instead of rabbit in this recipe, it does seem a waste not to use rabbit when we can now get it, wherever we live, so easily.

I think that on the whole, rabbit benefits from casserole type of cooking rather than the sauté type.

In this casserole the pieces of rabbit are browned, then cooked in the sauce. When cooked the casserole is cooled, and the rabbit is cut off the bones and reheated in the sauce with sour cream or fromage frais added.

I like to serve this with pasta, like green tagliatelle, and spinach.

Serves 6

6 joints of rabbit
2 tbsp flour mixed with 1 tsp salt and plenty of black pepper
4 tbsp sunflower oil
2 onions, skinned and finely chopped
1–2 garlic cloves, skinned and finely chopped
1 tbsp paprika
1½ pints/850 ml chicken stock
¼ pint/140 ml fromage frais (or sour cream)

Coat the joints of rabbit with the seasoned flour. Heat the oil in a large casserole and brown the pieces of rabbit on each side, removing them as they brown to a warmed dish. Lower the heat a bit and add the chopped onions to the casserole. Cook them, stirring occasionally to prevent them from sticking, till they are just beginning to turn golden at the edges, about 5–7 minutes. Then add the chopped garlic, any remaining flour and the paprika, and stir for a minute before adding the stock, stirring continuously till this sauce boils. Replace the browned pieces of rabbit in the sauce.

Cover with a lid, and bake in a moderate oven, 350°F/180°C/Gas Mark 4, for 1–1¼

hours. Take the dish out of the oven, cool, strip the meat from the bones and reheat it in the sauce. Just before serving, stir in the fromage frais, or sour cream, reheating the sauce gently and trying not to let it boil again. Taste, and add more salt and pepper if you think it is needed. (Reheat it in a moderate oven till the sauce bubbles gently – let it simmer very gently for 10 minutes before adding the fromage frais or sour cream.)

Venison Fillet with Port and Redcurrant Jelly

This is simple food, but excellent ingredients. How long you cook the meat depends on how rare you like to eat the venison. I like it just red in the very centre, but I loathe meat so underdone that it is almost bleeding on the plates.

This is nicest, I think, served with par-boiled potatoes in their skins, chopped and sautéed till crisp, with paprika, and with a purée of root vegetables, such as Jerusalem artichokes or celeriac or parsnips. The best!

Serves 6

2 oz/56 g butter + 2 tbsp sunflower oil
About 2 lb/900 g venison fillet, trimmed and left whole
½ pint/285 ml port
½ pint/285 ml good stock
2 tsp redcurrant jelly – homemade if possible because it is less sweet than commercial
Salt and freshly ground black pepper

In a wide sauté pan, heat the oil and melt the butter. Brown the fillet, turning it over and over so that it cooks evenly. Cook it like this for 10 minutes, then pour in the port and stock and stir in the jelly. Stir till the jelly melts – if it is homemade it will melt much more quickly than bought – and let the liquid bubble away around the meat till it reduces by about a third.

Lift the meat on to a board, and season the sauce in the pan with salt and pepper. Carve the meat into a warmed serving dish and pour the juices, and the small amount of sauce, over the sliced meat.

Venison Steaks in Red Wine and Vegetable Sauce

For this recipe you need to cut thick slices from a fillet of venison. They are cooked in a red wine sauce with tiny onions and julienne strips of carrot and parsnip. The whole dish can be made in advance and reheated to serve.

I think it is nicest served with creamily mashed potatoes with plenty of parsley and chives beaten into them, and with either a green salad or a green vegetable, such as steamed spring greens or stir-fried cabbage, to accompany it.

Serves 6

1 lb/450 g tiny onions

2½ lb/1.25 kg venison fillet, trimmed and cut into thick slices

2 tbsp flour mixed well with ½ tsp salt and plenty of ground black pepper

3–4 tbsp sunflower oil

3 carrots and 3 parsnips, each peeled and sliced into neat matchsticks

1–2 garlic cloves, each skinned and finely chopped

½ pint/285 ml red wine

¾ pint/420 ml water or stock

Skin the onions by pouring boiling water over them in a bowl. Leave them for a minute, drain off the water and snip off their ends – the onions should pop out of their skins when squeezed.

Coat the pieces of meat in the seasoned flour on each side. Heat the oil in a heavy casserole and quickly brown each slice of meat on each side, removing them, as they brown, to a warmed dish. Lower the heat a bit and add the onions, carrots, parsnips and garlic. Cook, stirring occasionally to prevent them sticking, for about 15 minutes – they will be almost cooked through. Stir in the wine and water (or stock), stirring till the sauce bubbles. Replace the meat in the sauce, pushing it down amongst the vegetables.

Cover with a lid, and cook the casserole in a moderate oven, 350°F/180°C/Gas Mark 4, for 25–30 minutes. Alternatively, if you prepare the casserole up to the stage where you replace the meat, you can cool it completely and store it in the fridge, ready to cook that evening. Remember to take it from the fridge into room temperature an hour before cooking it, or if you can't, give it an extra 20 minutes' cooking time.

Venison Braised with Beetroot

Beetroot is an under-used vegetable which, in my opinion, deserves a far higher profile. It complements the taste of all game, and venison is no exception. And it has a tenderizing effect on the meat – it contains the same enzyme as papaya, which is used specifically as a meat tenderiser.

Serves 6–8

2 tbsp flour

Salt and freshly ground black pepper

2½ lb/1.125 kg venison, trimmed of fat and cut in pieces about 1 inch/2.5 cm in size

4 tbsp sunflower oil

2 oz/56 g butter

3 medium onions, skinned and finely sliced

1–2 garlic cloves, skinned and finely chopped

3 uncooked beetroots, peeled and sliced into julienne strips about the thickness of a little finger

1½ pints/850 ml beef or venison stock

¼ pint/140 ml port

¼ pint/140 ml (small pot) crème fraîche

Put the flour, salt and pepper into a polythene bag and shake the cut-up venison in this till all the bits are well covered.

Heat the oil and melt the butter together in a heavy casserole and brown the venison on all sides. Remove to a warm dish as the pieces brown. Add the onions, and cook till they are soft and just turning golden at their edges. Add the garlic and the beetroots, and cook for several minutes, stirring from time to time. Stir in any flour left in the bag. Stir

in the stock and port, and stir till the liquid simmers. Replace the meat and cover with a lid.

Cook in a moderate oven, 350°F/180°C/Gas Mark 4, for 1½ hours. Take out of the oven and serve, with a spoonful of crème fraîche on each serving.

The casserole keeps warm very well without spoiling in the least. It also reheats beautifully, and, like all casseroles, is better in flavour when reheated. Take it from the fridge an hour before giving it a further 35–40 minutes reheating in a moderate oven. It should be very gently simmering.

I like to accompany this with either jacket potatoes or with very well mashed potatoes, and a green vegetable, such as Cabbage Fried with Grainy Mustard (see page 221).

Venison Ragoût with Chestnuts, Port and Orange

This is a perfect dish for chilly weather. It both tastes good and is convenient in that, like all casseroles, it benefits from being made a day or two in advance. On the other hand, you can make it several weeks ahead and freeze it (it freezes beautifully). If you can't get venison, you could substitute beef, but venison is now very widely available, and can be found in the butchery departments of many good supermarkets.

Serves 5–6

2 lb/900 g venison, trimmed and cut in chunks about 1½ inches/3.5 cm in size

1 heaped tbsp plain flour

¼ tsp salt and lots of freshly ground black pepper

Oil in which to brown the meat (I use sunflower oil, about 1 tbsp to start with)

¼ pint/140 ml port

2 tsp redcurrant jelly

2 medium onions, skinned and sliced finely, or ½ lb/225 g small whole onions, skinned

1 pint/600 ml vegetable stock

A few drops of Balsamic vinegar

Grated rind and juice of 1 small orange

Half a 15-oz/420-g tin of whole chestnuts in brine, unsweetened, or the same weight of vacuum-packed chestnuts (but *not* dried chestnuts)

Start by coating the chunks of venison in the flour, seasoned with salt and pepper. Heat the oil in a large saucepan or casserole, and brown the meat, in small amounts at a time so as not to lower the temperature in the pan – which would let the juices run from the meat and therefore stew them to a greyish hue rather than browning them nicely and sealing in the flavour. Add more oil to the pan as you think necessary. As the meat browns, keep it warm on a dish in a low oven.

While the meat is browning, measure the port and redcurrant jelly into a saucepan, and melt the jelly in the port over a moderate heat. Set to one side.

When all the meat is browned, add some more oil, lower the heat a bit under the pan or casserole, and add the finely sliced onions. Cook them for about 10 minutes, stirring occasionally so that they cook evenly. Then dust in 2 tsp of the seasoned flour, cook for a further minute, before

gradually adding the strained vegetable stock and the Balsamic vinegar, stirring continuously until the sauce boils. Stir in the grated orange rind and juice, the port and redcurrant jelly, and the chestnuts. Replace the meat in the casserole or stew pan, and cover with a lid.

Cook in a moderate oven, 350°F/180°C/Gas Mark 4, for 2 hours. Cool completely, and either keep in a cold larder or fridge, or freeze it.

Before serving, give the casserole a further 1½ hours, simmering in a moderate oven. If you are putting it in the oven from the fridge, put it in 2 hours before you intend to serve it, to let it come to simmering point. If it is in a dish covered with foil, it will need a longer cooking time, because foil is such a rotten conductor of heat that it takes ages for the contents of what it is covering to come to simmering point.

This is nicest accompanied by creamy mashed potatoes and braised celery or leeks.

Venison with Soured Cream and Pistachios

This is a rich and delicious dish that makes a wonderful main course. Be careful about adding any salt to the dish – the pistachios are salty enough for most tastes. I like to serve this with creamy mashed potatoes, and glazed carrots and parsnips.

Serves 6–8

2 oz/56 g butter

2 tbsp oil (I use sunflower)

2½ lb/1.125 kg venison, trimmed and cut into
   chips about ½ inch/1 cm thick

2 medium onions, skinned and very thinly
   sliced

1 tbsp flour

Freshly ground black pepper

1 pint/570 ml vegetable stock

¼ pint/140 ml dry white wine

Juice of 1 lemon

½ pint/285 ml double cream

4 oz/112 g shelled pistachio nuts

Heat the butter and oil together in a casserole. Brown the thin chips of venison, a few at a time. Keep the browned meat warm as it is done.

Add the onions to the casserole. Cook them, stirring occasionally to prevent them sticking, for about 5 minutes. Stir in the flour and pepper. Cook for a further minute or two, then gradually add the stock and white wine, stirring until the sauce boils. Add the browned meat to the sauce, cover the casserole with a tightly fitting lid and cook in a moderate oven, 350°F/180°C/Gas Mark 4, for 45 minutes.

Just before serving, stir the lemon juice into the cream and add to the casserole together with the pistachios. Reheat, being careful not to let the sauce boil once the cream has been added, and serve.

Venison and Leek Pie

This is a great favourite of our family. It is really a shepherd's pie made from minced leftover venison. You can make it with fresh venison mince, too. The venison filling has steamed leeks in a white sauce on top. Served with baked potatoes and a salad or a steamed green vegetable, it makes a delicious dish for lunch or supper in the long winter months.

Serves 6–8

For the meat filling:

3 oz/84 g venison or beef dripping, or
   6 tbsp oil (sunflower, if possible)

3 medium onions, skinned and finely chopped

3 carrots, peeled and finely diced

3 parsnips, peeled and finely diced

2 lb/900 g lean venison, minced

1 rounded tbsp flour

1½ pints/850 ml stock or dry cider

3 tsp redcurrant jelly

4–6 tbsp Worcestershire sauce (depending on
   your taste)

Salt and freshly ground black pepper

For the topping:

8 medium leeks, washed, trimmed and cut into
   ½-inch/1-cm slices

2 oz/56 g butter

1 medium onion, skinned and fairly finely
   chopped

2 oz/56 g flour

1 pint/570 ml milk

Salt and freshly ground black pepper

Freshly grated nutmeg

3 oz/84 g grated Cheddar cheese

First make the filling. Heat the fat in a heavy casserole. Add the onions, carrots and parsnips. Sauté for 7–10 minutes, stirring from time to time so that the vegetables cook evenly and don't stick. Add the minced venison. Cook for a minute or two, then stir in the flour. Cook for a further few minutes and then stir in the stock or cider, red-currant jelly, Worcestershire sauce, and salt and pepper. Let the meaty mixture simmer for a few minutes, then take it off the heat and leave to cool completely.

To make the topping, first steam the sliced leeks for a few minutes until they are soft. Melt the butter in a saucepan and stir in the onion. Sauté for 5 minutes, stirring from time to time, then stir in the flour. Cook for a couple of minutes, then gradually add the milk, stirring until the sauce boils. Season with salt, pepper and nutmeg. Stir the steamed leeks into the sauce, and allow to cool completely before spooning it over the cooled venison mixture. Sprinkle with the grated cheese.

Cook in a moderate oven, 350°F/180°C/ Gas Mark 4, for 30–35 minutes, or until the cheese has melted and the whole pie is bubbling and golden.

Game Pudding with Lemon Suet Crust

The lemon in the crust of this pudding greatly complements the game. It is a most richly satisfying main course – no potatoes needed with this!

Serves 6

For the suet crust:

12 oz/340 g self-raising flour

6 oz/170 g shredded suet

Grated rind of 1 well washed and dried lemon

Salt and freshly ground black pepper

For the filling:

1½ lb/675 g game meat – hare, old grouse, venison, or a mixture, cut off the carcass and cut into neat pieces as nearly equal in size as possible

2 tbsp flour

Salt and freshly ground black pepper

1 onion, skinned and chopped finely and neatly

1 pint/570 ml water and red wine or port – I leave the ratio up to you

1 tbsp redcurrant jelly

Mix together the pastry ingredients and stir in enough cold water to mix to a dough – about ¼ pint/140 ml. Roll out two-thirds of the dough and line a large pudding bowl with it – a boilable plastic bowl with a snap-on lid is the ideal – capacity 3 pints/1.7 litres. The pastry won't fill it.

Mix together well the pieces of game, flour, seasoning and chopped onion. Pack this into the pastry-lined bowl. Measure half the water and wine (or port) into a small saucepan and stir in the redcurrant jelly. Heat till the jelly dissolves, then mix it with the rest of the liquid and pour this into the game mixture.

Roll out the remaining pastry into a circle to fit on top of the game. Cut a circle of baking parchment to fit on top, making a small pleat in the middle of its diameter. Snap on the lid and put the bowl in a large pan with water coming halfway up the sides of the bowl. Cover the pan with a lid, and bring the water in the pan to a gently simmering point. Cook like this, with the water barely simmering, for 3½–4 hours. Check the level of the water from time to time.

To reheat, steam for a further 2 hours. If you intend to serve the pudding after one steaming, steam for 5 hours.

Have a jug of hot water or stock to hand – game consommé is the best for this – to top up the liquid level inside the pudding as you spoon out its content.

This is good served with Cabbage Fried with Grainy Mustard (page 221), or with purple sprouting broccoli. Serve, too, with rowan or redcurrant jelly.

Meat

You will see that this chapter is subdivided into sections for Beef, Lamb and Pork. Meat is rather a contentious subject at this moment in 1997, and it has been since March 1996 when the truly dreadful BSE crisis began. I have always felt that I would rather buy top-end-of-the-market beef, for example, and eat it less often. And provided you know the origin of your beef (if you are ever in doubt, just ask your butcher), you are safe.

I have also been very wary of pork, and of the content of lower-end-of-the-market sausages. With sausages it truly is a case of you get what you pay for. Cheaper sausages contain finely minced parts of the pig which I certainly wouldn't want to eat whole – parts such as lips, eyelids and ears, to remain at the head end of the animal. I leave other parts to your imagination, but they, too, are minced and go into sausages. Ugh.

A good-quality sausage, on the other hand, is delicious. They contain pork meat, minced, and sometimes combined with other flavourings. In fact, I think that some sausage-makers are getting rather too ambitious with their flavourings. As our son Hugo said plaintively the other day, after we had had some orange and basil sausages for supper: 'I do wish sausages tasted of sausage.' I know what he meant.

I think we have the best lamb, here in the north of Scotland, to be found anywhere. Our lamb is getting on in months – the average weight for a leg of lamb of the sort we buy is about 7 pounds (just over 3 kilos). I deplore baby meat of whatever type. I think that flavour and texture develop with maturity (quite the opposite in vegetables). I also deplore boned meat because, quite apart from shrinkage, I reckon that the bones impart a depth of flavour to the meat. I know that carving is easier with, for example, a boned and rolled sirloin of beef, but some of the taste is sacrificed for easier carving.

There is better pork much more widely available these days, thanks to many pigs being reared in a more natural way. Travelling from Nairn towards Aberdeen is a hazard for those who, like me, love pigs. You drive past field after field full of pigs, and it is hard not to let your eyes swivel from side to side. Naturally raised pigs produce pork of a type as different as chalk is from cheese from the pork from intensively reared animals. And, thankfully, it is now so much easier to find and buy bacon which is as bacon used to be – by which I mean that it isn't shot through with phosphates, and it doesn't leave a curd-like liquid in the pan when the bacon is grilled.

Although my family and I, like so many other families in Britain, eat fewer meat-based meals each week, I could never give up eating meat. It wouldn't be fillet steak that would be so irresistible, though. Should I ever declare that I am giving up meat, Godfrey would only need to grill bacon for me to be convinced by the smell that I just couldn't live without a bacon sandwich fairly regularly in my life.

Offal is a food that produces extremes of like and dislike. Those who love liver, kidneys, sweetbreads and brains do so with a passion. Those who don't, shudder at the very mention of the words. Offal in its various forms, though, can be extremely nutritious and economical, and I *love* it, particularly kidneys and liver. I often think that there are people who think they don't like offal but who haven't actually tried it. Perhaps they will be tempted by one of my favourite recipes, to be found in this section.

Beef

Peppered Fillet Steak with Stilton Cheese and
Chive Butter

·

Stir-Fried Rump Steak with Sweet Peppers
and Ginger

·

Beef Casserole with Beer and Onions

·

Braised Beef in Beaujolais

·

Casserole of Beef with Mushrooms and
Black Olives

·

Casserole of Beef with Pickled Walnuts and
Prunes

·

Beef Stew with Mustard Dumplings

·

Braised Brisket with Root Vegetables

·

Silverside of Beef with Root Vegetables,
Dumplings and Horseradish Dressing

·

Baked Minced Beef Ragù with Aubergines

·

Meatballs in Tomato Sauce

·

Oxtail Stew

·

Calves' Liver with Mousseline Potatoes,
Sautéed Baby Onions and Spinach with
Fried Pinenuts

·

Livi's Liver

·

Steak, Kidney and Mushroom Puff Pastry Pie

·

Steak and Kidney Pudding with
Lemon Suet Crust

Peppered Fillet Steak with Stilton Cheese and Chive Butter

I must give credit to the New Club in Edinburgh for this special dish. We eat an inordinate amount of ground black pepper, and the coarser the grind, the better. So you can imagine how much we love anything au poivre. I crush black peppercorns with the end of a rolling pin, or in my pestle and mortar, and press them on to either side of the steaks, and then fry the meat in a non-stick frying pan with a very small amount of olive oil.

The Stilton cheese and chive butter can be made two or three days in advance and kept, rolled in greaseproof paper, ready to slice in rounds about ¼ inch/0.5 cm thick straight from the fridge, and a piece put on top of each cooked steak.

Serves 6

6 pieces of fillet steak (this is for a *very* special occasion!)

About 2 tbsp black peppercorns, crushed to the degree of fineness that you like

2 tbsp olive oil

For the butter:

3 oz/84 g butter

2 oz/56 g Stilton cheese

2 tsp snipped chives

First beat together the butter, Stilton cheese and chives till they are very well mixed. Roll into a fat sausage shape between sheets of greaseproof paper and put in the fridge.

Pepper the steaks and cook them in the olive oil to the degree of doneness that each family member likes – these vary vastly in our family, from being so rare as to only need passing through the kitchen on a plate, this for Godfrey and Meriel (our third daughter), to medium cooked for the remaining four of us.

Just before serving, slice the butter evenly and put a piece on top of each steak.

Stir-Fried Rump Steak with Sweet Peppers and Ginger

This recipe takes only minutes to cook, and rather longer to prepare, but the preparation can be done several hours in advance. It really is a dish which can be categorized as convenience food, with none of the unhealthy connotations usually ascribed to the term! The combination of flavours is delicious. I like to serve Basmati rice with this stir-fry.

Serves 8

2½ lb/1.125 kg rump steak

3 red and 3 yellow sweet peppers, cored and de-seeded

12 spring onions

A 2–3 inch/5–7.5 cm piece fresh root ginger

Sunflower oil

5 tbsp good soy sauce

Freshly ground black pepper

Be sure to use a very sharp knife for the preparation as it takes all the effort out of the fine slicing which follows. Slice the steak into thin matchsticks. Slice the peppers into thin strips. Trim the spring onions but leave as much green stalks as possible and slice them into thin slivers. Peel the ginger and slice it into slivers.

In a wok, if you have one and gas flames to cook on, or in a large frying pan, heat enough sunflower oil to very thinly cover the bottom of the pan, until the oil is smoking hot. Cook the beef, turning it (stir-frying it) until it is sealed all over, removing it to a warm dish as it is browned. Cook the peppers, onions and ginger, for 2 minutes over a really high heat, then return the beef to the pan. Measure in the soy sauce, and cook for a further 1–2 minutes. Season with a good grinding of pepper (no salt as the soy sauce is salty enough), and serve.

Beef Casserole with Beer and Onions

This is a good dish for an informal party in the winter. The secret of success with this recipe lies in browning the meat really well all over. If possible, make this the day before it is needed, leave overnight, and reheat in a moderate oven for 45 minutes. It is good served with baked potatoes, and with Cabbage Fried with Grainy Mustard, as much or as little mustard as you like.

Serves 6

2 tbsp oil
1 oz/28 g butter
2½ lb/1.125 kg lean braising beef, cut into 1½-inch/4-cm cubes
4 onions, peeled and thinly sliced

1 garlic clove, peeled and finely chopped
1 rounded tsp sugar
1 heaped tbsp plain flour
¾ pint/420 ml beer
½ pint/285 ml water
A bouquet garni
Salt and freshly ground black pepper

Heat the oil and butter together in a casserole. Add the meat, a little at a time, and cook until well browned all over. Remove the meat to a separate dish and keep warm.

Lower the heat, add the onions and garlic to the pan, and cook, stirring from time to time, until the onions are soft and transparent. Sprinkle over the sugar, and cook for a further minute, then stir in the flour. Cook for another couple of minutes, then gradually pour on the beer and the water, stirring all the time until the sauce boils.

Add the bouquet garni and seasoning to the pan, replace the meat in it, cover with a lid and cook in a slow to moderate oven, 325°F/170°C/Gas Mark 3, for 1½ hours. Remove the bouquet garni before serving.

Braised Beef in Beaujolais

The joy of this is that it can be made the day before and reheated to serve. As with virtually all casseroles, the flavour is very much better if it is made in advance. It is well worth taking the time to make the stew correctly, cutting no corners. The cooking of the onions at the beginning of any casserole, stew, or soup is, I think, all-important to the flavour of the end result. I loathe the taint of the taste of undercooked onions.

This is delicious served with either creamily mashed potatoes, or baked sliced potatoes, or sautéed potatoes.

Serves 6

1 lb/450 g tiny onions
3 lb/1.35 kg braising steak, trimmed and cut into 1½-in/4-cm chunks
2 tbsp flour with ½ tsp salt and plenty of ground black pepper mixed into it
2 oz/56 g butter + 2 tbsp sunflower oil
6 rashers of back bacon, cut into small dice
½ lb/225 g mushrooms, wiped and sliced
2 garlic cloves, skinned and finely chopped
1 bottle of Beaujolais
Bouquet garni made by tying together a few parsley stalks, a sprig of thyme and a bayleaf

Skin the onions by pouring boiling water over them in a bowl, leaving for 1 minute, then draining. Snip the ends off the onions and they should pop neatly out of their skins with no trouble.

Coat the cut-up meat in the seasoned flour. Heat the oil and melt the butter together in a heavy casserole and brown the steak, a small amount at a time, removing it to a warm dish as it browns. If you try to brown the whole lot at one go it won't brown, it will lower the temperature in the casserole and the meat will stew in its juices. Once the meat is all browned, lower the temperature a bit and add the skinned onions and the diced bacon. Cook, stirring

occasionally, till the onions are just beginning to turn colour, about 5–7 minutes. Add the sliced mushrooms and the chopped garlic, and cook for a few minutes before pouring in the wine. Stir till the sauce bubbles, then add the bouquet garni, replace the meat and cover the casserole with a lid.

Cook it in a moderate oven, 350°F/180°C/Gas Mark 4, for 1 hour. Cool, and store it in the fridge. To reheat, take it out of the fridge and into room temperature for an hour before putting it back into a moderate oven for a further hour's cooking.

Serve with Basmati rice, or with baked sliced potatoes. I also like a salad with it, dressed with vinaigrette.

Casserole of Beef with Mushrooms and Black Olives

As with every recipe which calls for black olives, this one needs the very best black olives, those preserved with herbs and not the black olives preserved in brine, which impart a very strong and not altogether pleasant flavour to this or any other dish for that matter. This casserole has rather Mediterranean flavours, and is delicious. I like to serve it with creamy mashed potatoes or with Basmati rice, and with a green vegetable or with a salad. As with virtually all casseroles, it benefits from being made in advance and reheated – somehow the flavours seem to mingle better than eating it after its initial cooking.

Serves 6

2 lb/900 g stewing beef, or rump, trimmed and
cut into 1-inch/2.5-cm bits

2 tbsp flour sieved with ½ tsp salt and lots of
ground black pepper

4 tbsp olive oil

2 onions, skinned and finely sliced

½ lb/225 g mushrooms, wiped and chopped

1–2 garlic cloves, skinned and finely
chopped

About 12 black olives, stones removed and
olives chopped

1 tbsp tomato purée

½ pint/285 ml red wine

¾ pint/420 ml water

Toss the cut-up meat in the seasoned flour. Heat the olive oil in a heavy casserole and brown the meat, a little at a time. Remove the browned meat to a warm dish.

Lower the heat a bit and add the onions, cooking them till they are transparent – about 5 minutes. Scoop them into the dish with the meat and raise the heat under the casserole. Fry the chopped mushrooms almost till they are crisp – this greatly improves their flavour. Lower the heat again, and add the chopped garlic, the olives, the tomato purée, and, stirring all the time, the wine and water. Replace the onions and meat.

Put a lid on the casserole, and cook it in a moderate oven, 350°F/180°C/Gas Mark 4, for 1¼ hours. Take it out of the oven, cool completely, and store it in the fridge. Before reheating, take the casserole out of the fridge and into room temperature for an hour, then reheat in a moderate oven for 30 minutes. The sauce should be gently simmering around the meat.

Casserole of Beef with Pickled Walnuts and Prunes

The sharpness of the pickled walnuts complements the flavour of beef extremely well, and the prunes are a surprisingly delicious complementary flavour to both.

Serves 6

2–2½ lb/900 g–1.25 kg beef, trimmed and cut
into cubes about 1 inch/2.5 cm in size

2 tbsp plain flour sieved with ½ tsp salt and
plenty of ground black pepper

3–4 tbsp sunflower oil

2 onions, skinned and finely sliced

1 garlic clove, skinned and finely chopped

1½ pints/850 ml stock and ¼ pint/140 ml red
wine

Contents of 1 x 15-oz/420-g jar of pickled
walnuts, drained of their preserving liquid,
and the walnuts chopped

4 oz/112 g soaked and de-stoned prunes,
chopped

Toss the cut-up meat in the seasoned flour. Heat the oil in a heavy casserole and brown the floured pieces of meat, a small amount at a time, and removing the meat as it browns to a warm dish.

When all the meat has browned, lower the heat a bit under the casserole and add the sliced onions, cooking them till they are soft and transparent-looking. Add the chopped garlic, replace the browned meat in the casserole, and stir in the stock and wine, and the chopped pickled walnuts and prunes. Stir till the liquid comes to simmering point, then cover the casserole with its lid and cook it in a moderate oven, 350°F/180°C/Gas

Mark 4, for 45 minutes. Take it out of the oven and let it cool completely before storing the casserole in the fridge.

Before serving, take it out of the fridge and into room temperature for an hour, then re-cook it in a moderate oven, as above, for a further 45 minutes – stick a fork into a piece of meat to check that it is tender.

By cooking it twice, as with all casserole and stewed dishes, the flavour is so much better than if it has had only one cooking.

Beef Stew with Mustard Dumplings

You don't need anything other than what is in this casserole. There is no need for jacket potatoes, or bread, because the combination of the meat, the variety of root vegetables and the mustard-flavoured dumplings with their hint of lemon, all go together so well, and in themselves provide the starch and protein and taste essential for a good and sustaining cold-weather meal.

Serves 6

4 tbsp sunflower or olive oil

2½ lb/1.125 kg stewing beef, trimmed of fat and gristle and cut into 1-inch/2.5-cm chunks

2 tbsp flour

Salt and freshly ground black pepper

2 onions, skinned and chopped

1–2 garlic cloves, skinned and chopped finely

2 carrots, peeled and chopped in chunky dice about ½ inch/1 cm in size

2 parsnips, peeled and cut as the carrots

Half a small turnip, peeled and cut as the carrots

2 leeks, washed, trimmed and sliced quite thinly

2 sticks of celery, washed, trimmed and sliced

2 beetroots, raw, peeled and chopped as the other root vegetables

2 pints/1.1 litres stock, vegetable or beef (or use a good tinned consommé)

For the dumplings:

8 oz/225 g self-raising flour

4 oz/112 g shredded suet

Grated rind of 1 lemon

3 tsp dry mustard powder

½ tsp salt and a good grinding of black pepper

Heat the oil in a large and heavy casserole. Meanwhile shake the pieces of beef with the flour, salt and pepper in a large polythene bag till all the bits of beef are well coated. Brown the beef in the hot oil, a little at a time, till it is all browned on all sides. Remove to a warm dish, using a slotted spoon to drip off as much oil as possible back into the casserole.

Cook the chopped onions in the oil till they are just beginning to turn golden. Stir in the garlic, cook for a minute, then add all the prepared vegetables. Pour in the stock, and stir till the stock simmers around the vegetables. Replace the browned meat amongst the vegetables, cover the casserole with its lid, and cook in a moderate oven, 350°F/180°C/Gas Mark 4, for 2 hours. Then take it out of the oven and cool it completely before storing it in the fridge.

Reheat in a moderate oven till the contents simmer – about 30 minutes, providing you put the casserole in at room temperature, but add 20 minutes more if you put it in straight from the fridge. Let it cook from simmering point for a further 20 minutes.

Mix all the dry ingredients for the dumplings together well, then add just enough cold water to bind to a stiff dough. Flour your hands (to stop the dough sticking to them) and shape the dough into even-sized blobs. Push them down amongst the hot contents in the casserole, replace the lid, and put the casserole back in the moderate oven for a further 45 minutes.

Braised Brisket with Root Vegetables

Brisket is a fatty cut of meat, cut from the breast of the animal. It needs to be braised or pot-roasted, cooled, and when cold the fat skimmed from the surface. But it has a very good flavour, and makes a really good supper main course, especially when braised with a variety of root vegetables, as in this recipe.

It needs only baked potatoes as an accompaniment, and any left over can either be taken out of the vegetables and sliced, and served cold, or reheated in the vegetables. If you serve it cold, you can whiz the remains of the vegetables into soup.

This may sound a lot for six, but the meat shrinks dramatically during cooking.

Serves 6

2 tbsp sunflower oil

4 lb/1.8 kg brisket, boned and rolled, which is how it is usually bought

3 onions, skinned and chopped

3 leeks, washed, trimmed and sliced

3 carrots, peeled and chopped

3 parsnips, peeled and chopped

Half a medium to small turnip, skin cut off and chopped

4 sticks of celery, washed, trimmed and sliced

2 tbsp tomato purée

2 tbsp flour

1 can lager

1 pint/570 ml water

Salt and freshly ground black pepper

You will see, when you have prepared the vegetables, that it looks rather a large amount. Don't worry – they, like the meat, go down by about half during cooking time. But you do need a fairly large casserole to cook this in.

Heat the oil in the casserole and brown the meat all over. Take it out of the casserole and put it on a warm dish. Add the onions to the casserole and cook them, stirring occasionally, till they are transparent, then add the rest of the vegetables. Cook them, stirring from time to time, for about 10 minutes, then stir in the tomato purée and the flour. Cook for a minute then stir in the lager and the water, stirring till bubbles appear. Replace the meat, pushing it down amongst the vegetables, season with salt and pepper and put the lid on the casserole.

Cook in a slow to moderate oven, 300°F/150°C/Gas Mark 2, for 2 hours, then take the casserole out of the oven, let it cool completely and store it in the fridge. Before serving, take it out of the fridge and into room temperature for an hour before putting it back into an oven, at a moderate temperature this time, 350°F/180°C/Gas Mark 4, for a further 1½ hours' cooking. Before replacing it in the oven, skim any fat from the surface.

To serve, lift the meat on to a board, cut away the string, and slice the meat, spooning the vegetables and the juices around.

Silverside of Beef with Root Vegetables, Dumplings and Horseradish Dressing

Silverside is a lean meat, unlike the much fattier brisket, which could be used for this dish instead of the silverside. But I prefer the silverside because of its leanness. The vegetable content of this dish is quite enough – there is no need to have any other vegetable accompaniment. The dressing is best made with creamy Moniack horse-radish, far and away the best horseradish sauce to be bought.

Serves 6

3 lb/1.35 kg rolled silverside

Cold water to cover the meat – about 4 pints/2.3 litres

6 onions, skinned

6 carrots, trimmed, peeled and left whole

About half a turnip, peeled and sliced in neat strips

6 potatoes, peeled and left whole – try and use potatoes of as near the same size as you can

3 large parsnips, trimmed, peeled and each cut in half lengthwise

6 leeks, washed and trimmed to the same length

Salt and freshly gound black pepper

For the dumplings:

8 oz/225 g self-raising flour

Salt and freshly ground black pepper

4 oz/112 g shredded suet

Finely grated rind of 1 lemon

For the dressing:

½ pint/285 ml of the best horseradish sauce you can find

1 tub of crème fraîche (7 fl oz/200 ml)

Put the meat into a large casserole and cover with cold water. Over a moderate heat bring the water slowly to the boil – this should not be hurried. Skim off, with a metal spoon, any scum which forms on the water. The water should take 25–30 minutes to reach a gentle bubble. Put the onions, carrots and turnip into the casserole with the meat and simmer all very gently for an hour, skimming the surface clean as it is needed. Then add the potatoes, parsnips and leeks, season with salt and pepper and cook gently for a further 30 minutes.

To make the dumplings, sieve the flour, salt and pepper together and mix with the suet and grated lemon rind. Mix in just enough cold water to form a dough, and, with floured hands, form the dumplings into small balls about the size of a ping-pong ball. Drop them into the simmering liquid, amongst the vegetables, and simmer for a further 20–25 minutes cooking.

Lift the meat from the casserole and on to a warmed serving plate. It should be very tender. Carve, and serve with the vegetables and dumplings.

Mix the ingredients for the dressing together well, and serve in a separate bowl.

Baked Minced Beef Ragù with Aubergines

If you think, as I used to, that frying aubergines requires a vat of oil, then read on . . . I discovered a year or two ago that by dipping the slices of aubergine first in sieved flour then in beaten egg (yes, I really do mean in that order!) they absorb a scant amount of oil as they fry. I really prefer to 'mince' my own beef in my food processor. This dish can be made in advance and reheated to serve, and it freezes.

Serves 6

2 aubergines, sliced lengthways into slices about ¼ inch/0.5 cm thick
3–4 tbsp olive oil
1½–2 lb/675–900 g beef, stewing steak or rump, trimmed of fat and gristle and 'minced' in a processor but not pulverized
2 onions, skinned and finely chopped
2 carrots, peeled and diced small
3 back bacon rashers, trimmed of fat and diced quite small
1–2 garlic cloves, skinned and finely chopped
2 tbsp tomato purée
A 15-oz/420-g tin chopped tomatoes
¾ pint/420 ml red wine
Salt and freshly ground black pepper
2–3 tbsp olive oil – for cooking the aubergine slices
Flour to coat the aubergine slices, sieved
1 egg, beaten
4 oz/112 g Cheddar cheese, grated

First, put the aubergine slices on a large plate or tray and sprinkle them with salt – not too thickly. Leave for 20–30 minutes, then pat dry with absorbent kitchen paper – drops of brownish liquid will have appeared on the slices.

Next, make the meaty sauce by heating the first amount of oil in a saucepan and browning the minced beef, removing it as it browns to a warmed dish, with a slotted spoon to drain as much oil as is possible back into the saucepan. Lower the heat and put the chopped onions and diced carrots into the oil. Cook, stirring, for about 5 minutes, adding the bacon and garlic halfway through. Stick the point of a knife into a bit of carrot – it should feel tender. If it doesn't (people's ideas of 'fine' dice differ!), continue to cook for a further few minutes. Then stir in the tomato purée and the chopped tomatoes, replace the browned minced beef, and add the wine, salt and pepper. Bring this mixture to a very gentle simmer, and cook for 30 minutes, with the pan half-covered with a lid.

Meanwhile, heat the second amount of oil, dip the aubergine slices first into the sieved flour, then into the beaten egg on a plate, and fry the slices in relays in the oil in a frying or sauté pan. Take them out as they turn pale golden on each side, and put on a warmed dish with a couple of thicknesses of kitchen paper to absorb any excess oil.

Cover the base of a shallow ovenproof dish with a layer of aubergine, then with a layer of the meat mixture. Repeat the layering. Sprinkle with the grated cheese, and bake in a moderate oven, 350°F/180°C/Gas Mark 4, for 25–30 minutes. The cheese should be melted and the meaty sauce bubbling gently.

This is good served with baked potatoes and a green salad.

Meatballs in Tomato Sauce

When you make your own meatballs you can turn a mundane dish into something really special. I like to use half beef – and as for hamburgers, I buy rump steak and pulverize it in the food processor rather than buy ready-minced beef – and half good-quality pork sausagemeat. The sausagemeat keeps the meatballs juicy and the flavours of both meats and the other ingredients make a delicious combination. The meatballs freeze very well in their tomatoey sauce. The only drawback is that you always need more meatballs than you imagine you will. They really are a hit, particularly with children.

Serves 6

1½ lb/675 g rump steak, trimmed of excess fat and all gristle

2 tbsp olive oil

2 onions, skinned and as finely chopped as you can manage

1½ lb/675 g best quality pork sausages, each slit with a sharp knife and the skins peeled off – this takes seconds

2 tbsp finely chopped parsley and snipped chives, mixed

A dash of Tabasco sauce

A couple of pinches of salt and freshly ground black pepper

Flour for dusting

Olive oil for frying the meatballs – you need little oil if you have a non-stick pan

Simple Tomato Sauce (see page 305)

Put the trimmed beef into a processor and pulverize, but not too finely. Heat the olive oil in a saucepan and gently fry the finely chopped onions till they are really soft – this takes about 5 minutes. Let them cool completely. With your hand, mix together the skinned sausagemeat and the pulverized beef, and mix in the cooled onions, parsley and chives, Tabasco sauce, salt and pepper.

Have a bowl of flour to dip your hands into as you form the mixture into small balls, about the size of a ping-pong ball. Roll each in flour and lay them on a baking-parchment-lined tray. When you have made up the mixture into meatballs, heat olive oil in a frying or sauté pan, using as little oil as you can, and fry the meatballs, turning them carefully (I use two forks for the turning) so that they brown all over. As they brown, remove them to a large warm plate lined with a couple of thicknesses of kitchen paper, to absorb excess grease.

When all are made, cover them with Tomato Sauce.

Oxtail Stew

To my mind, this is the best casserole of any meat. An oxtail has to be cooked long and slowly, and as with all casseroles this benefits greatly from being cooked and reheated. This allows you to skim off any excess fat when it has cooled after its first cooking, and it also lets the flavours of the meat and vegetables mingle together. An oxtail stew is a rich and deeply satisfying dish, and absolutely perfect for a special occasion main course on a chilly winter's day. Beware, though, of ever buying a frozen oxtail. They are horrible – why oxtails don't freeze successfully raw I don't know, they are the only cut of meat I can think of which doesn't. But when cooked, oxtail freezes as well as any other casserole or stew.

Serves 6

2 oxtails (any left over can either be reheated and eaten up, or made into soup)
4 tbsp olive or sunflower oil
3 medium onions, each skinned and finely chopped
3 carrots, peeled and chopped neatly
Half a turnip, peeled and diced neatly
1 clove of garlic, skinned and chopped finely
2 fairly level tbsp flour
2 tbsp tomato purée
1 can of lager + 1–1½ pints/570–850 ml water
Salt and freshly ground black pepper

With a very sharp knife (which will make the task quicker), trim as much fat and gristle off each oxtail as you can and then cut them into pieces. Heat the oil in a heavy casserole and brown each piece of oxtail all over, removing the pieces to a warm dish as they are browned.

Lower the heat a bit under the casserole and sauté the chopped onions for several minutes, stirring occasionally, until they are really soft and beginning to turn golden at the edges. Then stir in the chopped carrots and turnip, and the garlic. Cook for a couple of minutes, then stir in the flour and cook for a further couple of minutes.

Stir in the tomato purée, lager and 1 pint/ 570 ml of the water, stirring till the liquid begins to bubble gently. Then season with salt and pepper and replace the pieces of browned oxtail in the casserole, pushing them down amongst the vegetables in the sauce.

Cover the casserole with its lid and cook in a fairly low temperature oven, 250°F/ 120°C/Gas Mark ½, for 3 hours. Take it out of the oven and let it cool completely – store it in a cool place like a larder or fridge. Skim any fat from the surface.

Reheat by taking the casserole out of the fridge and into room temperature for an hour before putting it into the oven, this time a moderate oven, 350°F/180°C/Gas Mark 4, for 2 hours. Check the liquid and stir in a bit more water as it cooks if you think it is needed. If you put the casserole straight from the fridge into the oven, add 30 minutes on to the reheating and cooking time.

I like to serve this with very creamily mashed and beaten potatoes, and the vegetable which I like best with oxtail is either cabbage or spring greens.

Calves' Liver with Mousseline Potatoes, Sautéed Baby Onions and Spinach with Fried Pinenuts

This was my tip-top favourite supper when I was a child. Luckily, so it was for my two sisters as well, and this is the supper we had without fail on our first night home from school, when we lived in Rome, and on the last night of the holidays. It is vital that calves' liver be cooked briefly – as with squid, it is ruined by overcooking.

Serves 6

2½–3 lb/1.125–1.35 kg calves' liver, trimmed of any bits of tube and cut into as neat slices as is possible

2 oz/56 g butter + 2 tbsp sunflower oil

For the potatoes:

12 medium potatoes, peeled and halved

2 oz/56 g butter

½ pint/285 ml warmed milk

Salt and freshly ground black pepper

2–3 tbsp chopped parsley and snipped chives, mixed

For the onions:

1–1½ lb/450–675 g small onions – the little pickling ones

Butter and sunflower oil for frying

For the spinach:

3 lb/1.35 kg fresh spinach

Salt and freshly ground black pepper

Grated nutmeg

3 oz/84 g pinenuts

1 oz/28 g butter

Cook the liver by heating the butter and oil in a wide shallow pan – a frying pan would be ideal. When the fat is very hot, cook each piece of liver on one side till it just 'seizes', till it is firm. Turn it over, and give it about 30 seconds on the other side. Remove the pieces of liver to a warmed serving plate as you continue to cook the remainder.

Boil the potatoes in salted water till just soft, then mash them with the butter, beat in the warm milk with a wooden spoon, and season with salt and black pepper. Just before transferring them to a warm dish for serving, beat in the parsley and chives.

Skin the onions – an easy way to do this and avoid an agonizing weep as you do so is to put them into a bowl and pour boiling water over them. Leave them for a couple of minutes, then slice off the ends of each onion, and the skins should pop off with no effort at all – rather like skinning tomatoes. Cook them in a frying or sauté pan in a mixture of butter and sunflower oil, shaking the pan, and cooking them till they are golden brown, and tender when you stick a fork into the biggest one.

Steam the spinach till it wilts, then chop it with a sharp knife, and season it with salt, pepper and a grating of nutmeg. Fry the pinenuts in the butter till golden brown and scatter them over the spinach.

The onions will keep warm without spoiling, the potatoes need only the herbs beaten into them just before serving, and the spinach and calves' liver both take seconds to cook – the pinenuts can be fried in advance – so this is not a meal which is going to take you ages in preparation, but the memory lingers on. As is so often the case, the simplest food is the best.

Livi's Liver

It sounds corny, I know, and too good (or bad) to be true, but my sister Livi is one of the best cooks I know. She has a winning way with liver, and this is her recipe. You can use either calves' or lambs' liver – calves' liver is that bit more delicious, but lambs' liver is nearly as good. We can't buy calves' liver locally anyway, and there must be many people in Britain in the same boat. I like to serve this dish with creamy mashed potatoes and spinach.

Serves 6

2 lb/1.125 kg calves' or lambs' liver
2 oz/56 g butter
1 tbsp oil (I use sunflower)
1 rounded tbsp flour
¾ pint/420 ml chicken or vegetable stock
3 fl oz/84 ml medium dry sherry
3 tsp redcurrant jelly
Salt and freshly ground black pepper
3 fl oz/85 ml sour cream
2 tbsp finely chopped parsley, to garnish

Slice the liver very thinly, trimming away any bits of tube. Heat the oil and butter together in a frying pan. When it is frothy hot but before it turns brown, toss in the liver and cook for just long enough on each side to turn the liver golden brown – about

half a minute each side. Do the liver in relays, so that the heat in the frying pan stays high. (If you try to cook all the liver at once, the heat in the frying pan is reduced and the liver stews rather than seals.) Keep the cooked liver warm in an ovenproof serving dish in a low oven.

Stir the flour into the remaining fat in the frying pan and cook for a minute or two. Then stir in the stock, sherry and redcurrant jelly. Stir until the sauce boils and the jelly melts. Season with salt and pepper, return the liver to the sauce and cook for 2–3 minutes. Just before serving, stir in the sour cream and sprinkle with the parsley.

Steak, Kidney and Mushroom Puff Pastry Pie

Steak and kidney is a combination made in heaven, but it is enhanced by the flavour of the mushrooms. It might be worth mentioning for any first-time steak and kidney cooks that you can only use ox kidney in the long and slow cooking that is needed by a pie or pudding. It is perfectly safe to use ox kidney providing you ask your butcher as to its origins. Faith in your butcher is vital! If you use lambs' kidneys the flavour borders on the revolting once they have cooked for the length of time necessary.

Serves 6

2 lb/900 g beef steak – stewing or rump
1 lb/450 g ox kidney
2 rounded tbsp flour

Salt and plenty of freshly ground black pepper

3 tbsp sunflower oil, use more if necessary – it depends whether your pan is non-stick

1 onion, skinned and very finely chopped

1 lb/450 g mushrooms, wiped and cut in quarters, stalks trimmed but not removed

1 can lager + 1 pint/570 ml vegetable or beef stock

1 lb/450 g puff pastry

Milk or 1 beaten egg to brush the pastry

Trim the steak and kidney of fat or gristle and cut the meat into 1-inch/2.5-cm bits. You will have to cut the kidney as you can, but try to make the bits as uniform in size as possible. Toss the cut-up meat and kidney in the flour seasoned with salt and pepper.

Heat the oil and brown the meat and kidney in small amounts, making sure that each is well browned before removing it to a warm plate and browning the rest. Next, cook the chopped onion, till it is transparent. Then scoop it into the browned meat. You may need to add more oil, but turn up the heat and brown the mushrooms very well – the more they cook, till they are almost crisp, the better will be their flavour.

Return the browned meat, kidney and onion to the saucepan or casserole and stir in the lager and stock, stirring till the sauce around the meat comes to boiling point. Cover the pan or casserole with a lid, and cook in a moderate oven, 350°F/180°C/Gas Mark 4, for 45 minutes.

Take it out of the oven and pour the meat into a pie dish. Leave to cool before rolling out the pastry and covering the pie as neatly as you can. Decorate the pastry with roses or how you like, and press a fork around the edges of the pie. Brush with either milk or beaten egg. Slash the top of the pastry in several places – this is important, to let out any steam accumulating as the pastry cooks.

Bake in a hot oven, 425°F/220°C/Gas Mark 7, for 15 minutes, then reduce the heat to moderate and cook for a further 20–25 minutes, till the pastry is well puffed up and golden brown. (Cook the pie from room temperature.) You can cover it and prepare it for cooking several hours in advance, but you will need to give it longer cooking time if you cook it straight from the fridge.

Steak and Kidney Pudding with Lemon Suet Crust

The lemon in the suet crust makes the flavour of this pudding much more interesting. A savoury pudding is such an excellent dish, and so simple to make, that I can't think why more people don't make them more often! They are always greeted with such appreciation.

Serves 6

For the suet crust:

12 oz/340 g self-raising flour

6 oz/170 g shredded suet

Grated rind of 1 well washed and dried lemon

Salt and freshly ground black pepper

For the filling:

2–2½ lb/900g–1.125 kg lean stewing steak

½ lb/225 g ox kidney

1 onion, skinned and chopped finely and
   neatly

2 tbsp flour

Salt and freshly ground black pepper

1 pint/570 ml water and red wine or port –
   I leave the ratio up to you

1 tbsp redcurrant jelly

Mix together the pastry ingredients and stir in enough cold water to mix to a dough – about ¼ pint/140 ml. Roll out two-thirds of the dough and line a large pudding bowl with it – a boilable plastic bowl with a snap-on lid is ideal – capacity 3 pints/1.7 litres. The pastry won't fill it.

Mix the pieces of meat, flour and seasoning and chopped onion together well. Pack this mixture into the pastry-lined bowl. Measure half the water and wine into a saucepan and stir in the redcurrant jelly. Heat till the jelly dissolves, then mix this with the rest of the liquid and pour it all into the meat mixture.

Roll out the remaining dough to the size of the lid of the bowl you are using and put on top of the meat, pinching around the sides of the pastry to seal.

Cut a circle of baking parchment to fit the top of the bowl, making a small pleat in the middle of its diameter. Snap on the lid and put the bowl in a large pan with water coming halfway up the sides of the bowl. Cover the pan with a lid, and bring the water in the pan to a gently simmering point. Cook like this, with the water barely simmering, for 3½–4 hours. Check the level of the water from time to time. To reheat, steam for a further 2 hours. If you intend to serve the pudding after one steaming, steam for 5 hours.

Have a jug of hot water or stock to hand to top up the liquid level inside the pudding as soon as you spoon out its content.

Lamb

Lamb Chops Baked with Potatoes, Leeks
and Cream

•

Lamb Cutlets Braised in Red Wine and
Redcurrant Jelly

•

Blanquette d'Agneau

•

Casseroled Lamb with Tomatoes and Pesto

•

Irish Stew with Black Pudding

•

Ragoût of Lamb with Red Wine

•

Winter Navarin of Lamb

•

Leg of Lamb with Lemon and Caper Sauce

•

Roast Rack of Lamb with a Herb Crust

•

Roast Lamb with Anchovies

Roast Leg of Lamb with Herb Jellies

•

Cold Roast Leg of Lamb Flavoured with Garlic
and Rosemary

•

Lamb Cooked with Spices and Apricots

•

Lamb Korma

•

Traditional Shepherd's Pie

•

Shepherd's Pie with Cheese and Oatmeal
Crumble Topping

•

Devilled Kidneys

•

Sautéed Kidneys with Port and Grainy
Mustard Sauce

•

Spinach Roulade with Lambs' Kidneys and
Bacon Filling

Lamb Chops Baked with Potatoes, Leeks and Cream

Leeks and potatoes cooked together complement each other extremely well (think of vichysoisse) and the sweetness of the leeks enhances the flavour of the lamb in this all-in-one dish. The very small amount of medium curry powder won't be noticed by any partaker who thinks they don't like curry, I promise you, but it does just round off the overall flavour well.

Serves 6

6 large, double lamb chops
6–8 medium to large leeks
8 medium potatoes
2 oz/56 g butter + 2 tbsp sunflower oil
1 tsp medium strength curry powder
½ pint/285 ml single cream
Salt and freshly ground black pepper

Trim excess fat from the lamb chops. Wash and trim the leeks, and slice them diagonally into slices about 1 inch/2.5 cm thick. Peel the potatoes and slice them thinly. In a wide shallow pan – a sauté pan or a deep frying pan – melt the butter and heat the oil together. Brown the chops on each side, removing them to a large ovenproof dish as they are browned. Sauté the sliced leeks with the curry powder, stirring occasionally, for about 3–5 minutes. Take the pan off the heat.

Lift up the chops and arrange a layer of sliced potatoes to a depth of about ½ inch/ 1 cm under the chops. Put the sautéed leeks over the chops, and cover with the remaining sliced potatoes. Pour in the cream and season with salt and pepper.

Bake uncovered in a moderate oven, 350°F/180°C/Gas Mark 4, for 25 minutes, then cover the dish and continue to cook for a further 20 minutes.

Lamb Cutlets Braised in Red Wine and Redcurrant Jelly

These are simple to make, good to eat, and convenient in that they can be prepared and baked well in advance of your guests arriving, and covered and kept warm in a low-temperature oven. I like to serve them with very well and creamily mashed potatoes and with leeks in a nutmeg-flavoured creamy sauce. Sautéed parsnips are another delicious and complementary accompaniment.

Serves 6

About 3 tbsp oil – I use sunflower for this
2 onions, skinned and sliced very thinly
12 lamb cutlets – more, if your guests have large appetites
1 bottle of red wine – I use a Beaujolais for this
2 tsp redcurrant jelly – homemade if at all possible, it has a so much better taste
Salt and freshly ground black pepper

In a wide sauté pan heat the oil and sauté the sliced onions till they are just turning golden at their edges. Scoop them into a wide ovenproof dish. Brown the cutlets on both sides and put them, as they brown, on to the onions. Pour the wine into the sauté pan and stir in the redcurrant jelly. Let this bubble for a couple of minutes, and the jelly melt in the wine. Season with salt and pepper and pour this over the chops.

Cover the surface of the chops with greaseproof paper or with butter papers, and bake in a moderate oven, 350°F/180°C/Gas Mark 4, for 40 minutes. The wine will reduce as the cutlets cook.

Then keep the dish warm in a very low-temperature oven till you are ready to eat.

Blanquette d'Agneau

A blanquette is traditionally made with veal, but we can't get veal in Skye so I make it with lamb.

Serves 6

2 lb/900 g boneless leg of lamb, trimmed and cut into 1 inch/2.5 cm cubes

1 onion, peeled and stuck with a few cloves

2 carrots, peeled and sliced

A bouquet garni

Salt and freshly ground black pepper

2 oz/56 g butter

2 level tbsp flour

8 oz/225 g mushrooms, sliced

2 egg yolks

¼ pint/140 ml double cream

Juice of 1 lemon

Put the lamb cubes in a saucepan and cover with cold water. Put the onion stuck with cloves, the sliced carrots, the bouquet garni and a little salt and black pepper in the saucepan and bring to the boil. Then simmer gently for 45 minutes, with the pan uncovered.

Draw the pan off the heat and strain 1 pint/570 ml of the stock into a jug. Leave the meat in the remaining stock to keep warm.

In another saucepan, melt the butter. Stir in the flour and cook over a gentle heat for 1–2 minutes. Then gradually stir in the strained 1 pint/570 ml stock. Bring to the boil and simmer, stirring, for 5 minutes. Put the sliced mushrooms in the sauce and cook gently for a further 5 minutes, stirring. Season with salt and black pepper.

Mix together the egg yolks, cream and lemon juice. Add a little of the hot sauce to this mixture, then stir the egg yolks, cream and lemon juice into the sauce. Reheat gently but don't let the sauce boil again or it will curdle.

Drain the meat from the rest of the stock, put it in a warmed, ovenproof dish and pour the sauce over. Serve with rice and a green vegetable.

Casseroled Lamb with Tomatoes and Pesto

Pesto is a paste made from basil, pinenuts, olive oil and cheese. When basil is growing in the garden you can make your own pesto, but during the winter months I buy it ready-made in jars. It enhances tomato dishes tremendously. I like to serve this casserole with tagliatelle (or any noodles) tossed in cream and freshly grated Parmesan cheese, and a green salad.

Serves 6–8

2 tbsp flour

Salt and freshly ground black pepper

3 lb/1.35 kg good stewing lamb (ask for a piece from the top of the leg), cut roughly into 1-in/2.5-cm chunks and trimmed of excess fat

3 tbsp olive oil

2 medium onions, skinned and finely sliced

2 garlic cloves, skinned and finely chopped

2 x 15-oz/420-g tins of tomatoes

½ pint/285 ml dry white wine

A pinch of sugar

2 tbsp pesto

Season the flour with salt and pepper. Coat the pieces of lamb with the seasoned flour.

Heat the olive oil in a heavy casserole, and brown the pieces of lamb all over, a few at a time. Keep the browned lamb warm in a low oven.

Add the onions to the oil and meat juices in the casserole and sauté for about 5 minutes, until they are soft and transparent. Then add the garlic and the tomatoes, breaking the tomatoes up against the sides of the casserole with your wooden spoon. Stir in the white wine, sugar and pesto, season and bring to the boil.

Return the browned lamb to the casserole, cover with a lid, and cook for 1 hour in a moderate oven, 350°F/180°C/Gas Mark 4. Like so many casseroles, this one tastes even better if made a day in advance, allowing the flavours to mingle and fuse, and then reheated to serve.

Irish Stew with Black Pudding

You really can't overcook this dish, but almost more than with any other casserole, it is essential that it be made, cooled and reheated. The flavour is so very much better.

Serves 6–8

2 lb/900 g neck of lamb, with as much fat trimmed off as possible

½ lb/225 g black pudding, cut into dice about ½ inch/1 cm in size

3 onions, skinned and sliced

6 carrots, peeled and sliced

6 fair-sized potatoes, peeled and sliced

Salt and plenty of black pepper

Layer up the meat, black pudding and prepared vegetables in a heavy casserole, ending with a layer of potatoes. Season with salt and pepper. Pour in cold water to come level with the top layer.

Cover with a lid and cook in a moderate oven, 350°F/180°C/Gas Mark 4, for 2 hours, then reduce the temperature to 300°F/150°C/Gas Mark 2 and cook for a further hour. Take it out of the oven and cool completely. When it is cold, skim any fat off the surface. Cook for a further 1½ hours in a moderate oven, with the casserole uncovered for the last 45 minutes of cooking time.

Ragoût of Lamb with Red Wine

This recipe was given to me by my mother. It is quite delicious, easy to make, and will freeze, though not for much more than a month. The most arduous part of making this lamb ragoût is peeling the small onions, but this task is made much easier by pouring boiling water over them for a few minutes first – their skins then slip off, thereby reducing the crying time considerably. I find, incidentally, that wearing contact lenses helps to prevent the onion fumes from making my eyes stream.

Serves 6

2 oz/56 g butter
2 lb/900 g boneless leg of lamb, trimmed and cut into 1-inch/2.5-cm cubes
8 oz/225 g unsmoked bacon, as lean as possible, cut into 1-inch/2.5-cm cubes
18 tiny onions, peeled
1 rounded tbsp flour
½ pint/285 ml water
¾ pint/420 ml red wine
A bouquet garni
12 oz/340 g mushrooms, sliced
Salt and freshly ground black pepper

Melt the butter in a heavy casserole, add the lamb and the bacon a few pieces at a time and cook until they are well browned all over. Remove from the pan to a separate dish and keep warm.

Lower the heat slightly and add the onions. Cook gently, shaking the pan occasionally, until the onions are golden. Sprinkle in the flour, stir well and cook for a further 2–3 minutes. Then gradually add the water and the wine, stirring all the time until the sauce boils.

Replace the meat in the casserole, and add the bouquet garni, mushrooms, salt and pepper. Cover tightly, and cook in a moderate oven, 350°F/180°C/Gas Mark 4, for 1½ hours. Remove the bouquet garni before serving.

Winter Navarin of Lamb

This is a good dish to serve round Christmas time. A total contrast to turkey, it is a meal in one, that is, all the vegetables are cooked and served together with the meat, so you only need a green salad as an accompaniment. It will also freeze for a short time, 2–3 weeks, but if you are going to freeze it don't add the potato until you reheat it. This version of the classic navarin recipe, which correctly made should have young and tiny spring vegetables in it, is delicious and adapts to winter vegetables with no detriment to the end result.

Serves 8

3 rounded tbsp flour
Salt and freshly ground black pepper
3 lb/1.35 kg boneless leg of lamb, trimmed and cut into 1-inch/2.5-cm cubes
6 tbsp sunflower oil
1 rounded tbsp granulated sugar
A 15-oz/420-g tin of beef consommé, made up to 1½ pints/850 ml with water
About 3 oz/84 g tomato purée
2 garlic cloves, peeled and finely chopped
2 sprigs of thyme, or a pinch of dried thyme

1 bay leaf

6 medium onions, peeled and cut into eighths

8 carrots, peeled and cut into fine strips about
   2 inches/5 cm long

Half a small turnip, peeled and cut into
   1-inch/2.5-cm cubes

4–6 medium potatoes, peeled and cut into
   1-inch/2.5-cm chunks

Season the flour with salt and pepper and toss the prepared meat in the seasoned flour, until it is all thoroughly coated. Heat the oil in a large heavy casserole. Brown the meat, a few pieces at a time, in the hot fat, turning the pieces so that they brown really well all over. As you brown the pieces of lamb, bit by bit, sprinkle a little of the sugar over the meat in the pan. This improves not only the colour but also the taste of the dish. As the meat is browned, remove it to another dish, and keep it warm.

When you have browned the lot, pour the consommé and water into the pan, and stir in the tomato purée, garlic, thyme and bay leaf. Stir, scraping the meat bits off the bottom of the pan, until the liquid boils. Replace the meat in the pan, cover with a tightly fitting lid, and cook in a moderate oven, 350°F/180°C/Gas Mark 4, for 1 hour. Cool the casserole, and skim off any fat which forms on top.

Meanwhile prepare the vegetables. Add them, including the potatoes, to the cooked casserole, pushing them well down into the liquid. Add a little more water (or stock) if necessary. Cook in a moderate oven, 350°F/180°C/Gas Mark 4, for 1 hour, or until the vegetables are tender.

Leg of Lamb with Lemon and Caper Sauce

One of the classic British dishes is boiled leg of mutton with caper sauce. Well, it is almost impossible to buy mutton these days, and I don't much care for the flavour of lamb or mutton on the leg when it is boiled, but this dish is my version of the classic. The lamb we buy is several months old – a leg weighs about 7 lb/3 kg – and as I don't care for baby anything (except vegetables) I think our lamb has a superb flavour. It is hard to find lamb anywhere in the world better in flavour than that raised in the Highlands and Islands.

It is worthwhile seeking out the very best capers you can find – they are a world apart from the run-of-the-mill capers tasting of nothing but the harsh brine in which they are preserved.

Serves 6–8

1 leg of lamb weighing 6–7 lb/2.7–3.15 kg

Butter

½ pint/285 ml red wine and 2 pints/1.1 litres
   water

3 onions, skinned and cut in half

3 carrots, trimmed and chopped

3 sticks of celery, trimmed and chopped

3 leeks, washed, trimmed and chopped

A sprig of rosemary

Game Pudding with Lemon Suet Crust ▶
page 135

For the sauce:

2 oz/56 g butter
2 oz/56 g flour
1 pint/570 ml strained stock from around the cooked meat
3 oz/84 g butter, cut into bits
Grated rind and juice of 1 lemon
½ pint/285 ml double cream
Freshly ground black pepper – taste to see if salt is needed and add it as you like
4 tsp of the best capers you can buy – a good delicatessen should stock salted capers

Trim any excess fat from the lamb and rub it with a small amount of butter. Put it into a deep roasting tin with the wine and water, the vegetables and the rosemary. Put the tin into a hot oven, 400°F/200°C/Gas Mark 6, and cook for 2 hours, basting the meat at regular intervals with the liquid. Halfway through the cooking time put a piece of greaseproof paper or a couple of butter papers over the top of the meat. If you prefer less well done meat, reduce the cooking time – this will give you very slightly pink meat. Lift the meat, once cooked, on to a warmed serving plate. Strain 1 pint/570 ml of the stock from around the meat.

Make the sauce by melting the butter in a saucepan and stirring in the flour. Let it cook for a minute then, stirring continuously – I find a small balloon whisk ideal for this and all sauce-making – add the stock. Stir till the sauce boils. Take the pan off the heat and whisk in the bits of butter, a piece at a time. Whisk in the lemon rind and juice and, lastly, the cream. Season with pepper, add the capers and mix them well into the sauce, then check to see if you think it is sufficiently salty.

Keep the sauce warm as you carve the meat, and serve it separately. The lamb is nicest, I think, with potatoes roast in olive oil with rosemary (cut the potatoes into 1-inch/2.5-cm chunks, or roast new potatoes whole), and steamed sugar snap peas.

Roast Rack of Lamb with a Herb Crust

I have seen – and bought – racks of lamb in butchers' departments of supermarkets and they are so convenient, especially when you are only a few for lunch. They cook so much more quickly than a large leg of lamb. How long you roast it depends on how pink you like to eat your lamb. Do trim as much fat as possible off each rack, because it doesn't get a chance to crisp up under the herb crust. I like to serve this with a sauced vegetable, like leeks in a nutmeg-flavoured creamy white sauce, and with crispy sautéed potatoes with paprika.

Allow 2–3 chops per person, depending on their ages and therefore, to a great extent, their appetites.

Serves 6

◀ Roast Leg of Lamb with Herb Jellies
page 163

2 oz/56 g butter + 2 tbsp olive oil

1 onion, chopped as finely and neatly as
  possible

1 garlic clove, skinned and very finely
  chopped

6 oz/170 g day-old breadcrumbs made from
  baked bread, as opposed to steamed sliced
  bread; cut off the crusts before whizzing the
  bread to crumbs

Salt and freshly ground black pepper

2 tbsp finely chopped parsley, snipped chives
  and chopped tarragon

2 racks of lamb each with 6--7 chops in it

Melt the butter and heat the oil together in a
frying pan and sauté the onion in this till it
is really soft – about 5 minutes. Stir in the
garlic, cook for a minute, then take it off the
heat and stir in the breadcrumbs, salt and
pepper, and lastly the chopped herbs. Mix
all together very well.

Trim all the fat you can from the racks.
Lay them flat so the fat side is uppermost.
Spoon over the herb crust, pressing it down
well, and roast in a hot oven, 400°F/ 200°C/
Gas Mark 6, for 25 minutes – 30 minutes if
you prefer slightly better-cooked lamb.

Roast Lamb with Anchovies

*This may sound rather odd to you, I
realize, but it is a most delicious way to
roast lamb. It is equally good hot and cold
– my sister Camilla and I both love roasting a leg (or two, depending on numbers)
to serve cold for a special occasion. I cook
it the same day that it is to be eaten, and
there is such a variety of vegetables and
salads which embellish a cold roast leg of
lamb.*

*Leeks, for example, can be steamed till
tender, then dressed whilst still very hot
with a good olive oil and plenty of chopped
fresh herbs – the leeks absorb the flavours
of the oil and herbs as they cool. Broccoli
and cauliflower are delicious cooked and
served the same way. But the garlic and
anchovies give the lamb an even better
flavour.*

*Cooking it with red wine in the roasting
tin helps to keep the meat moist.*

Serves 8

1 leg of lamb, weighing about 5 lb/2.25 kg

2 cloves of garlic

1 tin of anchovy fillets

About 2 oz/56 g soft butter

Freshly ground black pepper

½ pint/285 ml red wine

With a very sharp knife, trim as much of the
fat off the lamb as you can. Stick the knife
into the leg of lamb in as many places as you
can. Peel the garlic cloves and cut them into
thin slivers. Cut the anchovy fillets in half.
(If you like you can soak them in milk for
half an hour before using them.) Pat them
dry if you have soaked them in milk, using
absorbent kitchen paper. Stuff the slivers of
garlic and the pieces of anchovy fillet into
the slits in the lamb. Rub the surface of the
lamb with the softened butter, and season
well with black pepper. Put the leg in a
roasting tin and pour the wine around.

Roast in a hot oven, 425°F/220°C/

Gas Mark 7, for 40 minutes, then lower the heat to 375°F/200°C/Gas Mark 5 and continue to roast for a further 45 minutes. If the meat weighs about 5 lb/2.25 kg, this will give you pinkish meat. If you prefer your lamb more pink than this gives you, reduce the cooking time by 15 minutes. If you like it cooked through, add 15–20 minutes to the cooking time. Let the meat cool before serving.

W Carlin

Same-day roast lamb can be served with hot or cold vegetables – for example, spinach cooked just till it wilts, then dressed with the best olive oil, a brief squeeze of lemon juice and plenty of black pepper, and left to cool before eating. Or any Mediterranean way of cooking vegetables, like cauliflower steamed till just tender, then dressed with olive oil and really good capers. A good ratatouille, or baked aubergines, all these and many more are perfect accompaniments to room-temperature roast lamb.

When it comes to roasting the lamb like flying in the face of fashion because do not like lamb roasted rare. It is a shame for those who do, because it is safer, too, to cook meat through. Having said that, I don't like lamb roasted till it is positively grey in colour.

To roast lamb

I trim off excess fat and rub the leg all over with softened butter, then I stick a sharp knife into it in frequent places and stick slivers of garlic in the cuts. I season the leg with salt and plenty of black pepper, and I scatter rosemary over it. I pour about 1 pint/ 570 ml of red wine over the lamb in its roasting tin and roast it for 20 minutes per pound weight in a very hot oven initially – for the first 45 minutes of cooking at 425°F/ 220°C/Gas Mark 7, then I reduce the heat a bit, to 400°F/200°C/Gas Mark 6, for the rest of the cooking time. Allow about 20 minutes after the cooking time is up for the lamb to sit in a very low-temperature oven before carving, if you are serving it hot – this allows

3

the juices to settle and makes carving much easier. Of course this isn't necessary if you are serving the lamb at room temperature.

Rosemary and apple jelly

Makes 3–4 lb/1.4–1.8 kg

2 lb/900 g apples – windfalls, or eating apples with a good flavour

Several sprigs of rosemary

2 lb/900 g preserving or granulated sugar, more or less depending on the quantity of juice

Wash the apples then chop them in chunks, with peel, core, the lot, and put them and the rosemary into a solid and large saucepan with 3 pints/1.7 litres of water. Let them simmer very gently, with the lid on the pan, till the apples are really soft, mushy when pressed against the sides of the pan with your wooden spoon. This can take up to an hour.

Drain the juice of the contents of the pan through a muslin or jelly bag into a bowl – this is best done overnight. Don't be tempted to squeeze the contents of a muslin or jelly bag because that will give you a cloudy jelly. Measure the strained liquid back into a clean pan and add 1 lb/450 g sugar per pint/570 ml. Over a gentle heat, dissolve the sugar in the apple and rosemary liquid, taking great care not to let the liquid reach boiling point till there is no more grittiness under your wooden spoon. Then boil it fast. After 10 minutes' fast boil, draw the pan off the heat, drip some liquid on to a cold saucer and leave the saucer for several minutes. Push the trickle of jelly with your fingertips. If the jelly wrinkles, you have a set. If it is still runny, replace the pan on the heat, bring the contents to the boil and boil fast once more. Repeat the testing after a further 5 minutes' boiling, remembering to pull the pan off the heat.

When you have reached setting point, pot the hot jelly into hot jamjars. Seal. When cold, label and store on a shelf in a cool cupboard or larder.

Mint jelly

This is my favourite jelly for eating with lamb.

Makes 3–4 lb/1.4–1.8 kg

2 lb/900 g apples, half of them cookers and the rest eating apples

Several good handfuls of mint, preferably applemint which has the best flavour

½ pint/285 ml white wine vinegar

2 lb/900 g preserving or granulated sugar, more or less depending on the quantity of liquid

Wash the apples then chop them in chunks, with peel, core, the lot, and put them into a heavy saucepan with half the mint, 3 pints/1.7 litres of water and the white wine vinegar. Cover the pan with its lid and simmer the contents very gently till the apples are really soft, mushy when pressed against the sides of the pan with your wooden spoon. Strain the liquid through a muslin or jelly bag into a bowl – this is best done overnight. Don't be tempted to squeeze the contents of the muslin because that will give you a cloudy jelly.

Meanwhile, strip the remaining mint leaves from the stalks and chop them roughly. Measure the strained liquid back into a clean pan, and add 1 lb/450 g sugar for each pint/570 ml of liquid. Over a moderate heat dissolve the sugar in the liquid, taking great care not to let the liquid boil before the sugar is completely dissolved. Then boil it fast. After 10 minutes draw the pan off the heat and trickle some liquid on to a cold saucer. Leave for several minutes, then push the surface with your fingertip – if it wrinkles, you have a set. If not, re-boil for a further 5 minutes before testing again. Just before the final test, stir the chopped mint through the liquid.

When you have reached a set, pot into clean jars and seal, as above.

Cold Roast Leg of Lamb Flavoured with Garlic and Rosemary

Serves 8

1 leg of lamb weighing about 5 lb/2.25 kg

2–3 garlic cloves, peeled and cut into slivers

Butter

Salt and freshly ground black pepper

Dried rosemary

Trim off as much fat from the lamb as you can. Push the point of a sharp knife into the lamb in several places, and push slivers of peeled garlic cloves into these slits in the meat. Rub butter all over the leg of lamb, grind some salt and pepper over it, and sprinkle over some rosemary. Roast in a hot oven, 425°F/220°C/Gas Mark 7, for 15 minutes to the lb/450 g weight of the lamb.

Take it out of the oven and let it cool completely. Then carve the lamb and arrange it neatly on an ashet or serving plate.

Lamb Cooked with Spices and Apricots

This is a lovely recipe for those who, as I do, like the combination of fruit and meat. I think that the apricots greatly enhance the spices in this dish. I usually serve it with boiled Basmati rice.

Serves 6

2 rounded tsp coriander seeds

2 rounded tsp cumin seeds

2 rounded tsp ground cinnamon

2 oz/56 g lamb dripping, or butter and oil mixed

2 lb/900 g boneless leg of lamb, trimmed and
    cut into 1-inch/2.5-cm pieces

4 large onions, peeled and very thinly sliced

1 garlic clove, peeled and finely chopped

1 rounded tbsp plain flour

8 oz/225 g dried apricots, soaked in
    1 pint/570 ml water for at least 6 hours

Salt and freshly ground black pepper

Put the coriander, cumin and cinnamon together in a pestle and mortar if you have one, to pound them. If you don't have a pestle and mortar, a small deep bowl is just as good, and I use the end of a rolling pin to pound them. You won't be able to break down the cumin entirely, but it doesn't matter, it will break down during cooking.

Melt the dripping in a heavy casserole (using dripping really does make a great deal of difference to the end taste of this casserole), and brown the pieces of lamb well all over, a few pieces at a time. As they brown, remove the pieces of meat and keep warm. When all the meat is browned, lower the heat under the casserole and add the sliced onions and chopped garlic to the fat. Cook gently for 10 minutes or so, stirring all the time, until the onions are soft and transparent. Then stir in the flour and the pounded spices. Cook, stirring from time to time, for about 5 minutes. Then stir in the apricots, and the water in which they soaked, stirring all the time until the sauce boils. Return the meat to the casserole and season with salt and black pepper. Cover with a lid, and cook in a moderate oven, 350°F/180°C/Gas Mark 4, for 1½ hours.

Lamb Korma

This spicy dish isn't at all fiery – it contains no chilli. The blend of spices in this recipe are so complementary to the flavour of the lamb.

Serves 4–5

4 oz/112 g butter

2 lb/1.125 kg good stewing lamb, trimmed of
   fat and gristle and cut in bits about
    1 inch/2.5 cm in size

3 onions, skinned and finely sliced

2 garlic cloves

A 1-inch/2.5-cm piece of ginger

½ pint/285 ml boiling water

Salt and freshly ground black pepper

2 oz/56 g ground almonds

1 tsp cornflour

¼ pint/140 ml plain yoghurt

Juice of 1 lemon

Spices:

1 tbsp turmeric seeds

1 tsp coriander seeds

½ tsp cardamom seeds

2 cloves

1 tsp cumin seeds

½ tsp ground cinnamon

1 tsp paprika

Melt the butter in a sauté pan or stewpan. Brown the lamb on all sides. Remove the meat to a warm dish as it is browned. Then sauté the sliced onions till they are soft and just beginning to turn golden at the edges.

Pound together all the spices using a pestle and mortar, or in a bowl with the end of a rolling pin. Then pound the peeled garlic and skinned ginger together and pour the boiling water over them. Stir the pounded spices into the browned lamb and fry them in the pan with the onions for 1 minute. Then pour in the garlic and ginger and the water, season with salt and pepper, cover and cook gently for 25–30 minutes. You can do this all several hours in advance if it is more convenient for you.

Mix together the ground almonds, cornflour, yoghurt and lemon juice. Reheat the spices, onions and lamb. When the spices and lamb mixture just reaches simmering point, stir a little of the liquid into the yoghurt mixture, then stir the yoghurt mixture into the contents of the stewpan, stirring till it reaches simmering point once more. Keep warm till you are ready to serve it.

I like this with boiled Basmati rice mixed with fried sliced almonds and with raisins.

Traditional Shepherd's Pie

A properly made shepherd's pie is one of the best dishes I know. But I read recipes for shepherd's pie using raw meat, which is not what I have always understood to be proper. Real shepherd's pie should always be made with leftover roast lamb, although I sometimes use roast venison or roast beef. As I understand it, a similar pie made with raw minced beef is known as a cottage pie, and, for my taste, is much less appealing. Good shepherd's pie should be really well flavoured with the ingredients you see in this recipe – tomato purée, well-sautéed onions, Worcestershire sauce, and I like to add a teaspoon of redcurrant jelly.

Serves 6

About 2 lb/900 g potatoes

½ pint/285 ml warm milk

2 oz/56 g butter

Salt and freshly ground black pepper

2 tbsp of lamb dripping, or 4 tbsp olive oil

1 onion, skinned and chopped finely

1½ lb/675 g leftover roast lamb (or beef, or venison), weighed after having been trimmed of all fat and gristle; put the cut-up meat into a processor and whiz, but not too finely

1 tbsp flour

1 tbsp tomato purée

1 tsp redcurrant jelly

3 tbsp Worcestershire sauce (or 3 tsp balsamic vinegar)

1 pint/570 ml lamb, beef, or vegetable stock

Butter for finishing

Peel the potatoes and boil them in salted water till you can easily stick a fork into the biggest bit. Drain them, shaking the pan over heat to steam any excess water off the drained potatoes. Mash them well, then, with a wooden spoon, beat them, adding the warm milk and butter. Season to taste with salt and pepper. Set aside.

Make the base of the pie by melting the dripping or heating the oil in a heavy-based saucepan or casserole. Cook the chopped onion over gentle heat till it is turning golden brown at the edges. Then raise the heat and stir in the processed lamb (or beef, or venison), adding the flour, tomato purée and redcurrant jelly. Cook for 2–3 minutes, taking care not to let the mixture stick to the bottom of the pan. Then stir in the Worcestershire sauce and the stock, and keep stirring till the contents of the pan reach simmering point. Taste, and add salt and pepper. Let this mixture simmer very gently for 10 minutes, then put it into a pie dish and let it cool.

When the base is cold, put the well-beaten potato over the top, using a fork to make long furrowed lines all over the surface. Put little dots of butter over the top of the potato, or alternatively you can brush melted butter over the entire surface of the potato. Reheat in a moderate oven, 350°F/180°C/Gas Mark 4, for 40–45 minutes, or till the meat mixture is bubbling at the edges and the top of the potato is golden brown.

I like a vegetable in creamy white sauce, such as cauliflower or leeks, to go with this shepherd's pie.

Shepherd's Pie with Cheese and Oatmeal Crumble Topping

Shepherd's pie features often on our family menu. We generally eat up the leftovers from the hotel kitchen larder, which usually includes joints of beef, lamb or venison waiting to be made into shepherd's pie or something similar. Sometimes I put leeks in a creamy sauce on top of shepherd's pie instead of mashed potatoes or, another alternative as in this recipe, a sort of savoury crumble of oatmeal and grated cheese.

Shepherd's pie is a rather vague name for any pie dish using leftover meat, but a real shepherd's pie is never made with raw meat – nor with shepherds. One Sunday just before Christmas some years ago, when shepherds were uppermost in our minds in connection with cribs and wise men, our youngest, Hugo, then aged three, hissed at me during the sermon, 'What's for lunch?' 'Shepherd's pie,' said I. 'Real shepherds?' he asked, with glee!

Serves 6–8

For the filling:

2–3 oz/56–85 g dripping or 5 tbsp oil (sunflower, if possible)

2 medium onions, skinned and chopped

4 carrots, peeled and finely diced

2 parsnips, peeled and finely diced

1½–2 lb/675–900 g cooked lamb, beef or venison, off the bone, trimmed of fat and gristle, and finely minced

1 rounded tbsp flour

1 pint/570 ml water or leftover gravy

1 tbsp tomato purée

Salt and freshly ground black pepper

For the topping:

3 oz/84 g plain flour

3 oz/84 g medium oatmeal or porridge oats

4 oz/112 g grated Cheddar cheese

1 rounded tsp mustard powder

Heat the dripping or oil in a casserole and add the onions, carrots and parsnips. Sauté the vegetables for about 10 minutes, stirring from time to time so that they cook evenly. Add the minced meat and cook for another minute or two. Stir in the flour and cook for a further couple of minutes. Pour on the water or gravy and stir it in, together with the tomato purée and salt and pepper. Bring to the boil, stirring all the time. Cover with a lid and simmer gently for 20 minutes or so.

Mix all the ingredients for the crumble together well, rubbing them with your fingertips. Sprinkle the crumble over the meat filling in the casserole, and cook in a moderate oven, 350°F/180°C/Gas Mark 4, for 30–35 minutes, until the crumble is golden brown.

I like to serve this pie with baked potatoes and with cabbage stir-fried with grainy mustard or grated nutmeg.

Devilled Kidneys

I am quite intrigued, when I 'do' kidneys at a cooking demonstration, and ask those present who do not like kidneys to put up their hands, by what a small percentage of the guests don't like them. Four out of the seven in our family absolutely love kidneys, one doesn't mind them, and two actively dislike them. Kidneys are such convenient food (like fish) because they cook so quickly. In fact, overcooked lambs' kidneys become tough and rubbery in texture, and their flavour deteriorates, too, with over-cooking. Devilled kidneys are a perfect brunch dish, because they go so well with any dish containing eggs, or with bacon, sausages and black pudding.

You can core the kidneys – easiest done with a sharp pair of scissors – the night before. Kidneys bought in a butcher's shop are the best. Those prepacked in super-markets tend to seep a lot of blood as they sit, once cored.

Serves 6

2 oz/56 g butter and 1 tbsp sunflower oil

12 lambs' kidneys, each skinned, cut in half and the core snipped out

2 tsp English mustard powder

2 tsp Dijon mustard

2 tsp medium curry powder

1 tbsp Green Label mango chutney, trying not to include actual bits of mango

½ pint/285 ml double cream

Salt and freshly ground black pepper

Melt the butter and heat the oil together in a sauté pan. Over a fairly high heat cook the prepared kidneys till they just curl up, turning them over to let them cook on either side. Move them to a warm dish. Stir in the mustard powder, made-up Dijon mustard, curry powder, chutney, cream, salt and pepper. Let them all bubble briefly, then replace the kidneys in the sauce to reheat. Cook for a minute, then serve in a warm dish.

Sautéed Kidneys with Port and Grainy Mustard Sauce

The great thing to remember when cooking kidneys – and liver, too, for that matter – is not to overcook them. Overcooking makes them tough. This doesn't apply to ox kidney, which is used in steak and kidney pies and puddings, but it certainly does to lamb and calf kidneys. In this recipe the kidneys are sautéed in butter, and served with a delicious sauce of finely chopped onion simmered in port, with grainy mustard and cream stirred in at the end. It is a very easy dish and so good! I like to serve it with creamily mashed potatoes or Basmati rice and a green vegetable, such as Brussels sprouts.

Serves 6

2 medium onions, skinned and very finely chopped

½ pint/285 ml port

2 tbsp grainy mustard

½ pint/285 ml double cream

Salt and freshly ground black pepper

2 oz/56 g butter

18 lamb or calf kidneys, skinned, halved and
    cored (I find a pair of sharp scissors the
    best tool for this job)

Finely chopped parsley, to garnish (optional)

Put the onions and port in a saucepan, and simmer, with the pan uncovered, for 25–30 minutes, until the port is reduced by about two-thirds and the onions are soft. Stir in the mustard, cream and seasoning, and simmer all together.

Meanwhile melt the butter in a frying pan and sauté the kidney halves until the juices just stop running pink.

Serve the kidneys with the sauce poured over them and, if you like, sprinkled with the finely chopped parsley.

Spinach Roulade with Lambs' Kidneys and Bacon Filling

This is a delicious and useful dish with a good combination of complementary tastes and flavours – the spinach goes so well with the kidneys and mushrooms, and the nutmeg in the spinach enhances the lot. It is a useful recipe because it is one of those dishes where the whole course is in one.

If you like, you can serve baked potatoes or warm granary bread as an accompaniment, if you are feeding vast appetites.

Serves 6

For the roulade:

2 lb/900 g frozen leaf spinach, well drained
    when thawed

1 oz/28 g butter

1 garlic clove, skinned and chopped

A 3-oz/84-g carton of cream cheese, or a
    low-fat alternative

4 large eggs, separated

Salt and freshly ground black pepper

A grating of nutmeg

For the filling:

2 oz/56 g butter

6 lambs' kidneys, cored and chopped

½ lb/225 g mushrooms, wiped and chopped

2 oz/56 g flour

1 pint/570 ml milk

6 rashers of smoked or unsmoked back
    bacon, grilled till crisp, then chopped in
    quite small bits

Salt and freshly ground black pepper

Line a shallow baking tray or roasting tin with baking parchment, the tin measuring about 12 x 14 inches/30 x 35 cm.

Put the spinach into a food processor with the butter, garlic and cream cheese, and whiz till smooth, gradually adding the egg yolks, one by one. Season with the salt, pepper and nutmeg. In a bowl, whisk the egg whites with a pinch of salt – to give increased volume – till they are very stiff, then, with a large metal spoon, quickly and thoroughly fold them through the spinach mixture. Pour and scrape this into the paper-lined baking tin, and smooth evenly.

Bake in a moderate oven, 350°F/180°C/ Gas Mark 4, till firm to the touch, 15–20 minutes. Take the tin out of the oven, cover it with a damp teatowel and leave it for 2–3 minutes. Then, holding the shorter ends of the paper under the spinach in either hand, tip it face down on to a fresh piece of baking parchment on a work surface. Carefully peel off the paper from the back of the roulade, tearing in straight strips parallel to the long sides of the roulade. This avoids tearing the roulade up with the paper.

You can make the filling while the spinach is cooking. Melt the butter and cook the chopped kidneys in it till just firm. Scoop them out of the butter and on to a warmed dish. Add the chopped mushrooms to the butter and cook for a minute, then stir in the flour. Cook for a minute, then gradually add the milk, stirring continuously. Stir till the sauce boils, then take the pan off the heat. Stir in the cooked kidneys and the bits of bacon, and season with salt and pepper.

Spread this filling over the roulade, and carefully roll it up, rolling away from you. Slip it on to a warmed serving plate or ashet. Serve as soon as possible – it will keep warm without spoiling for up to 10 minutes or so, but the sooner it is eaten, the nicer it will be.

Pork

Collops of Pork Fillet with Cream, Brandy and
Apple Sauce

•

Pork Fillets with Ginger and Cream

•

Pork Fillets in Mushroom and Soured Cream
Sauce

•

Pork Chops with Tomato and Grainy Mustard
Sauce

•

Roast Loin of Pork with Prune and Red
Wine Sauce

•

Hot Ham Mousse

•

Baked Glazed Ham with Tomato and
Madeira Sauce

•

Pigs in Blankets

•

Sausagemeat and Apple Pie

•

Sausage and Lentil Hot-Pot

•

Toad in the Hole with Onion Gravy

Collops of Pork Fillet with Cream, Brandy and Apple Sauce

This rather rich dish is perfect for a dinner party. Pork fillet is such a tender meat and the flavour of the cream and brandy, with the edge just taken off their richness by the apples, complements it very well. I like to serve this dish with new potatoes and fresh peas with applemint.

Serves 6

| 2 eating apples |
| Juice of 1 lemon |
| 1 tbsp oil (I use sunflower) |
| 2 oz/56 g butter |
| 4 pork fillets, each trimmed and cut into 4, making 16 rounds, or collops, each about 1½ inches/4 cm thick; flatten them with a rolling pin |
| 3 fl oz/84 ml brandy |
| ½ pint/285 ml double cream |
| Salt and freshly ground black pepper |
| Finely chopped parsley, to garnish |

Peel, core and slice the apples, and cover them with lemon juice to prevent them going brown.

Heat the oil and butter together in a large shallow pan, such as a frying pan. Brown and cook the collops of pork fillet in the pan, allowing about 4–5 minutes on each side, turning them fairly frequently to prevent them browning too much. Stick a knife into one to see if it is cooked. When they are cooked, pour over the brandy and ignite it with a match. After a few seconds, pour on the cream. Drain the apple slices and add them to the pork and cream, with the seasoning. Cook all together for about 3 minutes.

Arrange the pieces of pork on a warmed serving dish, with the apple slices down the centre, and the creamy sauce poured over the top. Sprinkle with finely chopped parsley and serve.

The apple slices still have a crunch to them, giving a good contrast in texture as well as adding their flavour to the dish.

Pork Fillets with Ginger and Cream

This simple but delicious dish makes a perfect main course. It is rather rich, so precede it with something fairly plain. I like to serve it with creamily mashed potatoes, and a green vegetable such as spinach.

Serves 6

| 3 large pork fillets |
| 2 tbsp flour, seasoned with salt and freshly ground black pepper |
| 2 oz/56 g butter |
| 1 tbsp oil (I use sunflower) |
| ¼ pint/140 ml green ginger wine |
| 2 tbsp lemon juice |
| 2 fl oz/56 ml water |
| ¼ pint/140 ml sour cream |
| 3 pieces of preserved ginger, drained of their syrup and chopped |

Slice each fillet lengthwise but not right through. Flatten them out and beat them

173

into escalopes. Cut each escalope in half across the centre, making six escalopes. Coat the escalopes with seasoned flour.

Heat the butter and oil in a frying pan. Sauté the escalopes until they are browned on each side and cooked through, about 4–5 minutes. Remove them from the pan and keep them warm on a serving dish in a low oven.

Pour into the frying pan the ginger wine, lemon juice and water, and stir well. Let it boil away until the liquid has reduced by half, then stir in the sour cream and the chopped ginger. Boil again until the sauce has thickened, then pour it over the cooked escalopes and serve. This will keep warm satisfactorily for about half an hour before serving.

Pork Fillets in Mushroom and Soured Cream Sauce

This simple but ritzy main course dish can have chanterelles substituted for the mushrooms if they are available. It is very quick and easy to make, but doesn't reheat very well. Don't be put off making it, though – you can prepare the pork fillets in the morning ready to cook before your guests arrive, and slice the mushrooms all ready to pop into the frying pan. The finished dish can be kept warm for about half an hour in a low oven.

Serves 8

4 pork fillets (each weighing 8–12 oz/
   225–340 g)

2 oz/56 g butter

2 tbsp oil (I use sunflower)

1 medium onion, skinned and finely chopped

1 lb/450 g mushrooms, wiped and sliced
   (keep their stalks for stock)

½ pint/285 ml single cream

¼ pint/140 ml double cream

Salt and freshly ground black pepper

Juice of half a lemon

1 tbsp finely chopped parsley, to garnish

Start by preparing the fillets. Cut each fillet into four thick pieces. Sandwich each piece between two layers of clingfilm and pound gently with a rolling pin to flatten the round piece of pork fillet into an escalope.

Heat the butter and oil together in a large frying pan. Brown the escalopes a few at a time so that the heat in the frying pan isn't reduced too much and the meat can really seal and cook. Cook the escalopes, turning them so that they cook evenly on both sides, for about 5 minutes each side. Test to see if they are done by sticking the point of a sharp knife into the middle of the meat – the juices should run clear. Put the escalopes into a warmed serving dish and keep them warm while you make the sauce.

Add the onion to the fat in the frying pan and cook for about 5 minutes, stirring occasionally so that the onion cooks evenly. Then add the mushrooms, and cook for a minute or two before pouring in the single cream. Let the sauce simmer for 3–4 minutes, then add the double cream and the salt and pepper. Let the sauce boil for a few moments, then add the lemon juice and pour over the pork escalopes in the serving dish. Garnish with chopped parsley before serving.

Pork Chops with Tomato and Grainy Mustard Sauce

The sauce for this recipe can be made in the morning ready to serve with the grilled chops for dinner the same evening. I like to serve a green vegetable with the chops – either stir-fried Brussels sprouts or cabbage. A purée of potato mixed with celeriac makes a delicious accompaniment, too.

Serves 6

2 oz/56 g butter

½ medium onion, skinned and finely chopped

1 rounded tbsp flour

2 rounded tsp tomato purée

2 rounded tsp grainy mustard

¾–1 pint/420–570 ml milk

Salt and freshly ground black pepper

6 pork chops

Melt the butter in a saucepan and add the onion. Sauté for 5–7 minutes, stirring occasionally, until the onion is soft and transparent. Stir in the flour and cook for a minute or two, then add the tomato purée and grainy mustard. Gradually add the milk, stirring all the time until the sauce boils. Season with salt and pepper. If you are not going to serve the sauce immediately, press a dampened piece of greaseproof paper over the surface of the sauce to prevent a skin forming. Reheat to serve.

Snip the fat of the pork chops in several places to prevent them curling up and grill them till they are cooked through. Hand the sauce separately in a jug or sauce boat, or arrange the chops in a shallow serving dish and pour the sauce over them to serve.

Roast Loin of Pork with Prune and Red Wine Sauce

I love pork and judging by its popularity when it is on the menu here, I am not alone. I like it served cold as well as hot, and any leftover pork becomes a meal in itself served with salad, baked potatoes and chutney. For this main course dish I roast pork loin, and accompany it with a red wine and chopped prune sauce. The sauce doesn't take a minute to make, and its sharpness and sweetness go so very well with the rich pork meat.

This is good with potatoes chopped and roasted with onions and paprika in olive oil. Steamed leeks, or braised celery, are also delicious accompaniments.

Serves 6–8

A piece of loin of pork weighing about
   4 lb/1.8 kg

For the sauce:

Fat and juices from roasting the pork

1 medium onion, skinned and finely chopped

1 rounded tbsp flour

½ pint/285 ml red wine

½ pint/285 ml vegetable stock

Salt and freshly ground black pepper

1 tbsp lemon juice

About 8 cooked prunes, stoned and quartered

If the pork has crackling on top (sometimes they are sold without the crackling), rub it with salt.

Roast in a hot oven, 425°F/ 220°C/ Gas Mark 7, for 40 minutes or so, then lower the temperature to 350°F/180°C/Gas Mark 4 and roast for a further hour.

To make the sauce, drain some of the fat and juices from the pork into a saucepan, while the pork is cooking (there is no need to wait until the last minute to make the sauce). Add the onion to the saucepan. Cook over a moderate heat for 5–7 minutes, stirring occasionally, then stir in the flour. Cook for a further couple of minutes, then gradually add the red wine and vegetable stock, stirring continuously until the sauce boils. Season with salt and pepper, and stir in the lemon juice. Finally add the prunes. Keep it warm until you are ready to serve and then pour it into a bowl or sauce boat.

When you are ready to carve the pork, first cut off the crackling to make carving easier. With a very sharp knife, cut the meat off the bone and then carve it into slices. I take the meat off the bone and carve it into thickish slices in the kitchen, arranging them on a warm serving dish. It speeds up the serving of the main course so that the food is hotter when your guests start to eat.

Hot Ham Mousse

This is so easy to make. You can either serve it with Horseradish Sauce (see page 309), or if you prefer something rather less rich, you can substitute Simple Tomato Sauce (see page 305).

Serves 6

1 lb/450 g cooked ham, trimmed of fat

¾ pint/420 ml single cream

A dash of Tabasco sauce

Plenty of freshly ground black pepper

A grating of nutmeg

6 large eggs

2 tbsp dry sherry

Butter a large soufflé dish, or two equal-sized smaller dishes. Put the ham into a food processor and whiz till fine, then, still whizzing, add the cream, Tabasco, pepper and nutmeg. Continue to whiz and add 2 whole eggs, then the yolks of the remaining 4 eggs, and the sherry. In a bowl, whisk the whites with a pinch of salt (to give a greater volume) till they are very stiff. With a large metal spoon fold the whites quickly and thoroughly into the ham mixture and pour this into the buttered dish, or dishes.

Bake in a roasting tin with water in it to a depth of 1 inch/2.5 cm, in a moderate oven, 350°F/180°C/Gas Mark 4, for 55–60 minutes for the large dish or 45–50 minutes if using two smaller ones.

I like to serve leeks and tomatoes in vinaigrette to go with this.

Baked Glazed Ham with Tomato and Madeira Sauce

For those who have family and friends to stay, especially over the Christmas holiday, I can think of no better main course to welcome their arrival. The ham is so delicious served hot, with a wonderful Tomato and Madeira Sauce. And it is endlessly useful afterwards, served thinly sliced with scrambled eggs for breakfast, or with baked potatoes and salads for lunch.

I buy smoked ham, off the bone, which makes carving much easier.

Serves 8

Half a smoked ham, off the bone, weighing about 7–8 lb/3.15–3.6 kg

2 onions, halved

2 carrots

2 leeks

2 sticks of celery

For the glaze:

6 oz/170 g Demerara sugar

2 tbsp Dijon or grainy mustard

Cloves for studding the ham

Soak the ham for 24 hours in water. Then put it in a large saucepan or ham pan and cover it with fresh cold water. Add the onions, carrots, leeks and celery, bring it to the boil, and simmer gently for 2 hours. Let it cool a bit in the liquid (which you can strain off and make into delicious lentil soup). Then skin the ham and score the fat to make a diamond pattern.

Make the glaze by mixing the sugar with the mustard till you have a smooth paste. Spread it evenly over the ham fat and stick a clove in the centre of each diamond.

Roast the glazed ham in a hot oven, 400°F/200°C/Gas Mark 6, for 20 minutes, then lower the temperature to 350°F/ 180°C/Gas Mark 4 for a further 25 minutes.

Carve, and serve with the Tomato and Madeira Sauce on page 306.

Pigs in Blankets

I first ate these in Georgia, USA, when Godfrey and I were staying in the small village of Culloden, for the Culloden Highland Games. We were lucky enough to stay in an old hotel which had been in the same family for over a hundred years. Culloden is just a few miles from Juliette, the small village where Fried Green Tomatoes at the Whistlestop Café *was filmed, and the whole area is enchanting. The earth is a vivid red, there are so many people of Scots ancestry, indeed the county in which Culloden is situated is called Monroe County, and the Games were the best we have ever been lucky enough to attend. The whole atmosphere was one of warmth and friendly informality. And because the Holmes Hotel was small, with a veranda running around the front and one side of the house, we stayed there amongst other very good Macdonald friends – it was really like staying in a very nice house, and we became good friends with our host and hostess, Jimmy and Clarene Wilson.*

For breakfast each day we ate delicious and interesting food, all different to us. Pigs in Blankets was among our favourites! They are so simple, but so good. They consist of small sausages, usually frankfurters (and when I make them at home I always use frankfurters), wrapped in a scone mixture. I was told that the small pigs could have pastry blankets instead of scone-type blankets, but I think the scone mixture is best. They are served with tart jelly – this could be blackcurrant jelly, or even rowan jelly, providing it is made with sweet apples and spiced with a stick of cinnamon.

Be sure to make enough pigs, because they really are very popular, but do watch out not to make the blankets too thick! The first time I made them I made this mistake, and the pigs were fine but their blankets were rather stodgy. They must be thinly rolled out.

Makes 20

12 oz/340 g self-raising flour
½ tsp salt
1 tsp baking powder
1 egg
1 tbsp sunflower oil
Just less than ½ pint/285 ml milk
10 frankfurters, cut in half

Sieve the dry ingredients together into a bowl. Beat together the egg, oil and milk in a mixing bowl. Stir it into the flour mixture, adding a bit more sieved flour if the dough is too sticky. Roll out thinly on a floured surface, into a rectangular shape. Cut into triangles to hold a half frankfurter each, wrapped so the frank is facing opposite corners and the blanket folds point to the middle around the sausage.

Put them on to baking trays and bake in a hot oven, 425°F/220°C/Gas Mark 7, for about 10 minutes. The scone blanket will be puffed up and pale golden. Serve them warm, with a sharp fruit jelly to eat with them.

Sausagemeat and Apple Pie

This is one of those invaluable dishes which freeze well, make an entire meal in one dish, and taste delicious. The idea was my sister Livi's many years ago. I think it matters very much whenever sausages or sausagemeat is used in a recipe to get the very best you can find – I like Marks & Spencer's butcher style or free-range sausages, or their Lincoln sausages. I much prefer to skin my own. The sausages just need to be slit down with a sharp knife and the skins peel off easily.

The chopped apples in this pie go very well with the sausagemeat, and the sautéed chopped onions and the thyme just make all the flavours set each other off perfectly. I like to beat chopped parsley and snipped chives or very finely chopped garlic into the well-beaten mashed potatoes for the top of the pie.

Serves 6

3 tbsp sunflower oil
2 medium onions, skinned and finely chopped
1–2 garlic cloves, skinned and very finely chopped
3 tart eating apples – Granny Smith's are ideal for this (or Cox's), peeled, cored and chopped
2 lb/900 g top-quality pork sausages, each slit and skinned
2 tbsp tomato purée
1 tbsp flour
A good pinch of thyme
½ pint/285 ml dry apple juice (with no sweetener)
½ pint/285 ml chicken or vegetable stock

Salt and freshly ground black pepper

About 1½ lb/675 g well-beaten mashed
potatoes containing chopped parsley and
snipped chives – beating with a wooden
spoon gives a very creamy texture to
mashed potatoes

Butter for the topping

Heat the oil in a heavy saucepan or casserole dish and cook the chopped onions till they are soft and beginning to turn golden. Add the garlic and the chopped apples and cook for a few minutes, then scoop this mixture out into a bowl. Brown the sausagemeat in the pan, stirring all the time to break it up. When you have mashed it up as best you can, and it is browned, replace the onion-and-apple mixture in the pan. Stir in the tomato purée and the flour, and the thyme. Gradually stir in the apple juice and the stock, and stir till the mixture bubbles. Season with salt and pepper, and simmer very gently for 15 minutes, stirring from time to time to prevent the mixture from sticking. Pour into a pie dish and cool.

Cover with the beaten mashed potatoes, forking the surface into a neat pattern. Dot with tiny bits of butter and cook the pie in a moderate oven, 350°F/180°C/Gas Mark 4, for 30 minutes, till the potato is turning crisply golden on its forked pattern, and the filling is bubbling. If you put the pie directly from the fridge into the oven, you will need to add about 20 minutes on to the cooking time.

This is good served with cabbage.

Sausage and Lentil Hot-Pot

This is a kind of soupy stew – one of those convenient all-in-one dishes. It is very warming, just the thing for cold winter days. It is very quick to put together, and can be made a day in advance and reheated to serve. You can substitute beef sausages for the pork ones listed in the ingredients – it is a matter of personal taste.

Serves 6–8

1 lb/450 g pork sausages, cut into
1-inch/2.5-cm chunks

2–3 tbsp oil (I use sunflower)

3 onions, skinned and chopped

4 carrots, scraped and chopped into smallish
chunks

4 parsnips, peeled and chopped into smallish
chunks

4 medium potatoes, peeled and chopped

1 large garlic clove

8 oz/225 g red lentils

2 pints/1.1 litres chicken or vegetable stock

Salt and freshly ground black pepper

Grill the chunks of sausage until they are brown all over (I personally can't bear an unbrowned sausage, however well cooked it is).

Heat the oil in a saucepan or large casserole and add the onions. Sauté for 4–5 minutes, then stir in the carrots, parsnips, potatoes and garlic. Cook for several minutes, then stir in the lentils and the pieces of sausage, the stock and the seasoning.

Cover the saucepan or casserole with a tightly fitting lid, and simmer gently over a low heat for about 45 minutes or until the pieces of vegetable are tender. Serve, or cool and reheat to serve the next day.

Toad in the Hole with Onion Gravy

We all love anything to do with Yorkshire pudding, but I wish I could make a Yorkshire pud which is edible. Meriel, our third daughter, is the Toad in the Hole maker in our family. My contribution to supper or lunch, when Toad in the Hole is the main part, is the Onion Gravy, which, as far as our family is concerned, is an integral part of the meal. For health, a green vegetable is essential. Stir-fried cabbage with grainy mustard is the perfect accompaniment for this dish.

Serves 6

1½ lb/675 g good pork sausages, each cut in
   half, or chipolatas

6 oz/170 g plain flour sieved with a pinch of
   salt and freshly ground black pepper

3 large eggs

½ pint/285 ml milk with 2 tbsp cold water

Grill the sausages or chipolatas till browned – I can't bear the anaemic appearance of ungrilled sausages in Toad or any other dish containing sausages. Put them into a Pyrex or similarly ovenproof dish along with about 2 tbsp of the fat which has come from them as they grill.

Put all the other ingredients into a food processor or liquidizer and whiz. Leave the batter to sit for 30 minutes before pouring it into the sausages. Cook in a very hot oven, 425°F/220°C/Gas Mark 7, for about 30–35 minutes, or till the batter is well puffed up and golden brown. If you cook it in a metal container it will cook quicker – you will need about 5 minutes less cooking time.

Onion gravy

Ideally, some beef dripping, about 2 tbsp;
   as a dripping substitute use 2 tbsp
   sunflower oil + 1 oz/28 g butter

2 onions, skinned and very finely sliced

2 cloves of garlic, skinned and chopped finely
   – optional, but we love garlic and tend to
   put it in everything

1 rounded tbsp flour

1 pint/570 ml chicken, beef, or vegetable stock

Gravy browning, if you think a deeper colour
   is more attractive

Salt and freshly ground black pepper to taste

Melt the dripping or heat the oil and melt the butter together in a saucepan and sauté the sliced onions very well, stirring from time to time, till they are really soft and turning dark golden brown. This takes about 7–10 minutes to do properly – but try not to hurry the procedure because it makes all the difference to the taste of the gravy. Then stir in the garlic and the flour. Let it cook for a moment before stirring in the stock, stirring till the gravy boils. Draw the saucepan off the heat, add the gravy browning if you like, and season with salt and pepper to your taste.

Eggs

Eggs are inexpensive, extremely versatile and they can be the simplest and quickest of all foods, or they can be elegant, as in a soufflé. They are the food at which my father excels. Whenever my mother was away, he fended for himself with eggs, his favourite food, varying only in quantity according to his hunger. I think six was the maximum, and he liked his eggs cooked one way only, coddled, which is to put them into a pan of simmering water, then to take the pan off the heat and leave the eggs in the hot water for a couple of minutes. The result is nectar to him, but not to my taste!

There can be few dishes quicker to prepare than a soufflé, and it doesn't have to be a last-minute concoction, either. If you have a couple of hours' notice of surprise guests, you can prepare the soufflé right up to the folding in of the egg whites, and leave the mixture in its buttered dish, covered, until you are ready to pop it into a hot oven to cook. There are seven soufflé recipes in this chapter, as well as a Sausagemeat Soufflé which isn't a proper soufflé as we know them but is a most convenient dish prepared hours in advance of being cooked. It is more solid than a 'proper' soufflé.

Omelettes are often overlooked as an invaluable lunch or supper dish. There are recipes in this chapter for omelettes that are a far cry from the often leathery and dull offerings which can be the standard fare for unexpected guests who don't eat meat, for whom the word omelette must take on dread dimensions. Scrambled eggs, too, are certainly not just for breakfast eating. One of the scrambled egg recipes in this chapter contains flaked smoked haddock (so much nicer than smoked salmon, but you could substitute the hot smoked salmon, now more widely available, for the smoked haddock), and it makes an excellent lunch or supper, and a perfect brunch. Like the omelettes, it needs only bread and a mixed green leaf salad to accompany it.

Celeriac and Egg Mousse

•

Bacon, Tomato and Cheese Soufflé

•

Goats' Cheese and Hazelnut Soufflé

•

Leeks with Ham in Goats' Cheese Soufflé

•

Mushroom Brunch Soufflé

•

Mushroom, Cheese and Garlic Soufflé

•

Sausagemeat Soufflé

•

Smoked Haddock Soufflé with Tomato Sauce

•

Stilton Cheese and Celery Soufflé

Eggs with Cheese and Onion Sauce

•

Eggs Benedict

•

Scrambled Eggs with Smoked Haddock and
Grilled Tomatoes

•

Scrambled Eggs with Tomatoes, Red Peppers
and Croûtes

•

Chive, Tomato and Cottage Cheese Omelettes

•

Goats' Cheese and Rocket Omelettes

•

Parsley Omelette with Chopped Ham

Celeriac and Egg Mousse

This mousse can conveniently be made a day or two in advance and kept in the refrigerator. The grated celeriac is delicious combined with eggs and mayonnaise, and provides a good contrasting texture. You can decorate the top of the mousse with black olives and anchovies, or do as my sister Camilla does, and serve it with black olive pâté – fairly easily obtainable from delicatessens – spread on slices of toasted French bread. The mousse makes a very good supper dish to follow a hot soup.

Serves 8

1 lb/450 g celeriac, peeled

Juice of 1 lemon

1 sachet of powdered gelatine (½ oz/14 g)

½ pint/285 ml chicken stock

8 hardboiled eggs, chopped

½ pint/285 ml double cream

1 tbsp anchovy essence

A good dash of Tabasco sauce

Freshly ground black pepper

6 tbsp mayonnaise

Black olives or parsley to garnish

Grate or very finely shred the celeriac, and toss it in the lemon juice to prevent the celeriac from discolouring. Sprinkle the gelatine over the chicken stock in a pan and heat gently (watch it doesn't boil) until the gelatine granules have dissolved completely. Leave to cool. When the stock is quite cold, stir in the chopped eggs and the celeriac, and leave until the mixture begins to set. Then whip the cream and fold it together with the anchovy essence, Tabasco sauce, pepper and mayonnaise. Fold this mixture and the egg and celeriac mixture together thoroughly.

Pour into a serving dish and leave to set. If you don't want to bother with the black olives, sprinkle some finely chopped parsley over the mousse and serve.

Bacon, Tomato and Cheese Soufflé

I always think that bits, or to put it more elegantly texture, in a soufflé makes it far more interesting to eat. This soufflé has chopped tomatoes which are skinned and de-seeded (to prevent them being too watery) and diced lean smoked bacon to add interest in texture as well as taste. If you can get good Lancashire cheese the soufflé will be the better for it, but if not, use Cheddar cheese.

Soufflés are more filling than one imagines them to be, and this needs just a salad and warm bread or rolls to go with it.

Serves 6

2 tbsp fresh Parmesan cheese, grated

3 oz/84 g butter

6 rashers of smoked back bacon, trimmed of most of its fat and diced quite finely

1 large garlic clove, skinned and very finely chopped (if you don't love garlic as I do, you can leave this out)

3 oz/84 g self-raising flour

1¼ pints/710 ml milk

8 oz/225 g Lancashire cheese, crumbled

Salt and freshly ground black pepper

A grating of nutmeg

8 large eggs, separated

6 tomatoes, each skinned, cut in half and de-seeded, then cut in neat strips or chopped

Butter two same-sized soufflé dishes or similar ovenproof dishes (of about 2-pint capacity), and dust them out with grated Parmesan cheese.

Melt the butter in a saucepan and add the diced bacon and the finely chopped garlic. Cook, stirring, for several minutes till the bacon is cooked through. Stir in the flour, then gradually add the milk, stirring continuously till the sauce boils.

Take the pan off the heat and stir in the crumbled cheese, the salt, pepper and nutmeg. Beat in the yolks, one by one. Whisk the whites till they are very stiff and, with a large metal spoon, fold them and the chopped tomatoes quickly and thoroughly through the sauce.

Divide the soufflé mixture between the two prepared dishes and either cover them with clingfilm and bake later, or bake them straight away, in a hot oven, 425°F/220°C/Gas Mark 7, for 30–35 minutes. Serve immediately.

Goats' Cheese and Hazelnut Soufflé

This soufflé – like all soufflés – can be prepared, with the egg whites whisked and folded into the mixture and the dish

covered with clingfilm, three or four hours before you want to cook it. The soufflé mixture comes to no harm, and rises as beautifully as if you had whisked the egg whites at the last minute, as I always used to do until this invaluable tip was given to me by my great friend Char Hunt.

1 tbsp ground hazelnuts

1 oz/28 g butter

1 oz/28 g self-raising flour

¼ pint/140 ml milk

Salt and freshly ground black pepper

3 or 4 gratings of nutmeg

2 large eggs, separated

3 oz/84 g goats' cheese, crumbled

Sauce to serve (optional):

4 tbsp double cream

1 tbsp snipped chives

Butter a round ovenproof dish or a soufflé dish of about 1 pint/570 ml capacity. Dust it with the ground hazelnuts.

Melt the butter in a small saucepan and stir in the flour, let it cook for a couple of minutes, then stir in the milk. Stir till the sauce boils, then season with salt, pepper and nutmeg. Take the pan off the heat and beat in the egg yolks, one at a time. Stir in the crumbled cheese, stirring till it melts. Whisk the egg whites till they are very stiff and, with a large metal spoon, fold them quickly and thoroughly through the cheese mixture.

Pour into the prepared dish, cover the dish with clingfilm, and leave. When you think you're almost ready to eat, remove the clingfilm, pop the dish into a hot oven, 420°F/220°C/Gas Mark 7, and bake for 25 minutes. Eat the soufflé immediately. If you like, and I do, you can serve this simple sauce with it. Just warm the double cream in a saucepan with the snipped chives, and serve it around each helping of soufflé.

Leeks with Ham in Goats' Cheese Soufflé

This is a substantial dish, and needs no further accompaniment other than, perhaps, a green or a mixed salad, and warm bread or rolls. For anyone who hasn't had cooked goats' cheese before, the taste is delicious, and it is particularly complemented by leeks.

Serves 6

12 medium leeks, trimmed, well washed, and
    steamed till just tender
12 very thin slices of ham

For the soufflé:
2 oz/56 g butter
2 oz/56 g self-raising flour
¾ pint/420 ml milk
Salt and lots of freshly ground black pepper
A grating of nutmeg
8 oz/225 g goats' cheese, crumbled
4 large eggs, separated

Butter a large oval or oblong ovenproof dish. Wrap each just-cooked leek in a slice of the wafer-thin ham and arrange these in the buttered dish. Make the soufflé by melting the butter in a saucepan and stirring in the flour. Let it cook for a minute before pouring in the milk gradually, stirring

continuously till the sauce boils.

Take the pan off the heat and season with salt, pepper and the nutmeg, and stir in the goats' cheese. Beat in the yolks, one by one, and lastly whisk the whites till they are very stiff. With a large metal spoon, fold the whisked whites quickly and thoroughly through the cheese sauce. Pour this over the ham-wrapped leeks.

Bake in a hot oven, 425°F/220°C/Gas Mark 7, for 30 minutes – the soufflé should be very slightly runny in the middle.

If you want to prepare the soufflé ahead, when you have folded in the whites and poured the sauce over the leeks, cover the dish with clingfilm and leave it in a cool place till you are ready to bake it. Remove the clingfilm and cook it as described. Once cooked, it must be eaten immediately. There can be no sadder sight than that of a slowly but inexorably sinking soufflé!

Mushroom Brunch Soufflé

This is my version of the Sausagemeat Soufflé on page 188, so perfect for those who don't eat meat!

Serves 6–8

6 slices of brown bread, crusts removed, and
    the bread cut into 1-inch/2.5-cm squares
3 tbsp olive oil
1½ lb/675 g mushrooms, wiped and chopped
2 onions, skinned and finely chopped
A grating of nutmeg
Salt and freshly ground black pepper
8 large eggs, beaten with 1 pint/570 ml milk
6 oz/170 g grated cheese

Lightly oil an ovenproof dish with at least a 4-pint/2.25-litre capacity. Put the squares of bread in the bottom.

Heat the oil in a heavy-based sauté pan and cook the chopped mushrooms over a high heat till they are almost crisp – this greatly improves their flavour. Lower the heat, scoop the mushrooms out of the pan and put them in with the bread. Cook the finely chopped onions in the pan (you may need to add another spoonful of oil) till they are really soft and just beginning to turn golden at the edges. Scoop them in amongst the mushrooms.

Mix the nutmeg, salt and pepper in with the eggs and milk and pour this over the bread and mushrooms. Scatter the grated cheese over the surface – it will sink in, but it doesn't matter. Cover with clingfilm and leave in the fridge – overnight if you are planning a brunch.

Three-quarters of an hour before you wish to eat, remove the clingfilm and bake in a moderate oven, 350°F/ 180°C/Gas Mark 4, for 45–50 minutes. It should be well puffed up and firm. Serve immediately.

Mushroom, Cheese and Garlic Soufflé

Many people regard the making of soufflés with awe. They are, quite wrongly, under the impression that soufflés require a lot of skill in their production, and that you have to be some sort of culinary genius to concoct one. I felt just the same about them until I plucked up courage one day and, following a recipe word for word, made a stunning cheese soufflé. Flushed with my success I started experimenting and now when I can't think what to make for supper I opt for a soufflé.

The only thing to remember about soufflés is that they have to be eaten straight from the oven – they just won't wait for anyone, as they quickly lose their glorious, puffy height. So we usually only eat them in the winter months when I can be sure that Godfrey will be having supper at the pre-arranged time. In the months when the hotel is operating unforeseen hitches tend to crop up just as he is having his supper, and sunken soufflé is a sorry sight indeed.

A soufflé is a marvellous last-minute dish for when unexpected visitors arrive. You can nearly always be sure of having an onion, some garlic, a bit of cheese and, of course, eggs in the house. And this is all you need to make a soufflé. Or add some finely chopped mushrooms, as in this recipe.

Serves 4–5

Grated Parmesan cheese (optional)
3 oz/84 g butter
1 onion, peeled and finely chopped
1 garlic clove, peeled and finely chopped
4 oz/112 g mushrooms, finely chopped
3 oz/84 g self-raising flour
¾ pint/420 ml milk
6 large eggs
Salt and freshly ground black pepper
A pinch of ground nutmeg
4 oz/112 g mature Lancashire or Cheddar cheese, grated

Butter a soufflé dish, about 7 inches/18 cm in diameter, and dust with freshly grated Parmesan cheese if you have some.

Melt the butter in a saucepan, add the chopped onion and garlic and cook gently for 7–10 minutes until the onion is soft and transparent. Add the finely chopped mushrooms, and cook for about 1 minute, then stir in the flour. Gradually add the milk, stirring all the time until the sauce boils. Take the saucepan off the heat and leave to cool.

Separate the eggs, putting the whites in a clean bowl and beating the yolks one by one into the cooled sauce. Season with salt, pepper and nutmeg and beat in the grated cheese. Whisk the whites and fold them through the sauce. You can do this two, three or even four hours in advance.

Pour into the prepared soufflé dish and bake in a hot oven, 425°F/220°C/Gas Mark 7, for 40 minutes. If the diners are not quite ready another 5–10 minutes in the oven won't hurt.

Serve immediately – the soufflé will be soft in the centre. Serve with a green or tomato salad, and with warm brown bread or rolls.

Sausagemeat Soufflé

This isn't a soufflé in the real sense, but it is a breakfast dish we enjoyed whilst in Georgia, and one I have made several times since then. It comes in many versions – some have chopped peppers in them – but this is how I make this very good dish. It does make a difference if you use best quality sausages. If you want to eat it for brunch you can prepare the whole dish, cover it with clingfilm and leave it in the fridge overnight, only needing the clingfilm removed before you pop it in the oven. It takes a good 45 minutes to cook.

Serves 6–8

2 tbsp sunflower oil
1½ lb/675 g best quality pork sausages, each slit with a sharp knife and the skins removed
3 tsp made-up mustard, either English or French
A good dash of Tabasco sauce
3 tsp tomato purée
Good brown bread (you can use white if you prefer), crusts removed and the bread cut into 1-inch/2.5-cm squares – you will need 6 slices
8 large eggs, beaten with 1 pint/570 ml milk
Salt and freshly ground black pepper
4 oz/112 g grated cheese

Heat the oil in a heavy sauté pan and cook the skinned sausagemeat, breaking up the sausage shape with your wooden spoon. Cook till the meat looks as if it is beginning to brown. Stir in the mustard, Tabasco and tomato purée.

Lightly oil a 4–5 pint/2.5–3 litre ovenproof dish and put the squares of bread in the bottom. Scatter the cooked sausagemeat over the bread (avoiding any of the grease from the sauté pan). Season the egg and milk mixture, pour this over the sausagemeat and bread, and scatter the grated cheese into the mixture.

Bake in a moderate oven, 350°F/180°C/ Gas Mark 4, for 45–50 minutes. It should be firm and puffed up. Serve immediately. You won't notice the bread – it will have become as one with the other ingredients.

Smoked Haddock Soufflé with Tomato Sauce

Thank heavens that we can all get good smoked haddock these days without having to search too hard for it. It isn't very many years since smoked haddock meant brilliant yellow, rubbery little fillets, whereas what I want – and can now get with comparative ease – is large, juicy, undyed, pale-coloured smoked fish. And I love smoked cod, too, as much as smoked haddock.

This soufflé is a favourite with our family who luckily all love fish. The soufflé is made using the milk in which the fish cooked briefly before being flaked. Serving a sauce with a soufflé can be looked upon as both a garnish and an integral part of the whole.

Serves 6

2 lb/900 g smoked haddock (or cod)
1 onion, skinned and cut in half
2 pints/1.1 litres milk
3 oz/84 g butter
3 oz/84 g self-raising flour
1¼ pints/710 ml of the fish milk
Plenty of freshly ground black pepper (the fish will be sufficiently salty for most palates)

8 large eggs, separated
Simple Tomato Sauce (see page 305)

Put the fish into a saucepan with the halved onion and the milk. Over a moderate heat cook till a skin forms on the milk, then take the pan off the heat, and leave the fish to cool in the milk. Strain 1¼ pints/710 ml of the milk into a jug. Flake the fish, throwing away all bones and skin, into a bowl.

Butter two soufflé dishes, or same-sized ovenproof dishes. Melt the butter in a saucepan and stir in the flour. Let it cook for a minute, then stir in the reserved fish milk, stirring till the sauce boils.

Take the pan off the heat, season with pepper and beat in the egg yolks one by one. Whisk the whites till they are very stiff and, with a large metal spoon, fold them and the flaked cooked fish through the sauce.

Divide this soufflé mixture between the two buttered dishes and bake in a hot oven, 425°F/220°C/Gas Mark 7, for 30 minutes. Serve immediately they are cooked – they should be slightly runny in the middle.

Stilton Cheese and Celery Soufflé

This soufflé has the complementary flavours of Stilton and celery. You can, if you like, substitute any good quality blue cheese – Dunsyre Blue, for instance. Serve with warm bread or rolls, and with a mixed leaf salad.

Serves 8

4 oz/112 g butter	
1 small onion, skinned and chopped finely	
4 sticks of celery, washed and sliced very finely	
4 oz/112 g self-raising flour	
1½ pints/850 ml milk	
Freshly ground black pepper – about 15 grinds	
About ¼ tsp freshly grated nutmeg	
6 oz/170 g Stilton cheese, crumbled	
8 large eggs, separated	

Butter two soufflé dishes, each about 6 inches/15 cm in diameter.

Melt the butter in a saucepan and add the finely chopped onion and the finely sliced celery. Cook over a moderate heat for about 5 minutes, stirring occasionally. Then stir in the flour, and cook for a further couple of minutes. Stir in the milk, adding it gradually and stirring continuously till the sauce boils. Take the pan off the heat, season with the pepper and nutmeg – the Stilton will add enough saltiness – and stir in the crumbled Stilton. Beat in the egg yolks, one at a time. Cool the sauce.

Whisk the egg whites till they are very stiff and, with a large metal spoon, fold the whites quickly and thoroughly through the Stilton sauce. Divide between the two prepared soufflé dishes and cover each with clingfilm. You can then leave them for 3–5 hours before baking.

Remove the clingfilm and bake in a hot oven, 425°F/220°C/Gas Mark 7, for 45–50 minutes. Serve immediately.

Eggs with Cheese and Onion Sauce

This is one of those lovely supper or lunch dishes that can be prepared ahead and heated through in the oven at the last minute. As with all egg dishes, it is very filling. Lancashire cheese is one of the best cheeses for cooking with. The quantities given here are for a main course. If you are making this for a first course, eight eggs would be enough.

Serves 6

12 hardboiled eggs	
3 oz/84 g butter	
2 large onions, peeled and very thinly sliced	
3 oz/84 g plain flour	
1½ pints/850 ml milk	
8 oz/225 g Lancashire cheese, grated	
A little salt and lots of freshly ground black pepper	

Butter a shallow ovenproof dish.

Melt the butter in a saucepan, add the sliced onions and cook, gently, for about 10 minutes, until the onions are soft and transparent. Don't let them turn colour.

Stir in the flour, and cook for 1–2 minutes, then gradually add the milk, stirring all the time until the sauce boils. Take the saucepan off the heat and stir in most of the grated cheese, reserving some for sprinkling on top of the finished dish. Season.

Shell the hardboiled eggs, slice them and arrange them in an even layer over the bottom of the buttered dish. Pour the cheese and onion sauce over them, and sprinkle with the remaining grated cheese. Put the dish in a moderate oven, 350°F/180°C/Gas Mark 4, for 15 minutes, or until the cheese on the top is melted and the sauce is just bubbling gently.

Serve with salad and brown bread, or with rice instead of the bread, if you prefer.

Eggs Benedict

I first ate this most delectable of all brunch food on a far too brief visit to New Orleans what seems – and is – an age ago, in 1967. As with everything you cook, the very best ingredients make the difference between an ordinary result and a super-lative one. I like to use unsmoked roast (or boiled) ham, trimmed of all fat. There is no denying that Eggs Benedict is a last-minute concoction, and there just can't be short cuts. This makes it a special brunch for 2–4 people but it isn't practical to make it for many more, unless, that is, you have help in the making.

Serves 2

4 large egg yolks

6 tbsp white wine vinegar, reduced by two-thirds in a small saucepan with a slice of onion, a bayleaf, a few peppercorns and a couple of crushed parsley stalks (to release their flavour)

8 oz/225 g butter, cut in bits

2 muffins, split and toasted at the last moment – toasted too soon, the muffins turn

unpleasantly leathery in texture – and buttered

4 slices of the best ham

4 large eggs, poached

Whisk the egg yolks with a small balloon whisk, adding the strained, hot reduced vinegar. Put the bowl over a pan of just simmering water and beat in the butter, bit by bit, till all is incorporated and you have a thick and glossy hollandaise sauce.

Put two buttered toasted muffin halves on a warm serving plate for each person. Cover each with a slice of ham. Put a poached egg on top of each slice of ham, and divide the hollandaise sauce between the four eggs, spooning it over them. Eat immediately if you can – it will keep warm for 5 minutes or so without deteriorating too much, but it is really nicest eaten at once.

Scrambled Eggs with Smoked Haddock and Grilled Tomatoes

For this delicious dish, the cooked smoked fish is flaked and stirred into the eggs as they scramble – that way the fish warms up as the eggs cook. The fish can be cooked and flaked in the morning for supper that evening, and the eggs can be beaten with the pepper, Tabasco sauce and milk, all ready to scramble 5 minutes before you eat. The pinch of powdered ginger sprinkled on each tomato before grilling adds an interest which enhances the smoked haddock and scrambled eggs.

This is even better when served with toasted Cheese, Mustard and Garlic Granary Bread (see page 369).

Serves 6

| 12 tomatoes |
| 4 oz/112 g butter |
| Powdered ginger |
| A little sugar |
| Salt and freshly ground black pepper |
| 1 lb/450 g smoked haddock, bones removed |
| 1 pint/570 ml milk and water mixed |
| 12 large eggs |
| ¼ pint/140 ml milk |
| A shake of Tabasco sauce |

Wash the tomatoes, cut them in half and put the halves, cut side up, on a metal tray, with a tiny piece of the butter on each, a pinch each of powdered ginger, sugar and salt, and a grinding of black pepper. This can be done as much as a day in advance, and the tray covered and left in a cool place.

Put the fish in a large pan and pour over the milk and water. Heat gently till a skin forms on the liquid, then take it off the heat. The fish will go on cooking as the liquid cools. When cool, flake the fish into a bowl, removing the skin.

Beat the eggs with the fresh milk, salt (not more than a pinch or two, the fish is quite salty), pepper and Tabasco sauce.

When you are almost ready to eat, begin to grill the tomatoes – they should be cooked until their skins are falling away. Melt the remaining butter in a large saucepan – preferably non-stick. Add the beaten egg mixture and cook it over a gentle heat,

occasionally scraping the bottom of the pan as you stir with a wooden spoon. The secret of scrambling eggs, I'm convinced, is to cook them slowly. As the mixture begins to scramble, stir in the flaked smoked haddock.

Take the saucepan off the heat as soon as the eggs are creamily solid – they will continue to cook for a minute or two after the pan is taken off the heat, and overcooked scrambled eggs take on an unpleasant rubbery texture.

Serve, dividing the eggs between six warmed plates, with grilled tomatoes, and toast and butter.

Scrambled Eggs with Tomatoes, Red Peppers and Croûtes

These both look good and taste good. You can do so much of the preparation the night before – the eggs can be beaten all ready to scramble, the tomatoes can be skinned, de-seeded and chopped, and the peppers can be grilled, skinned and chopped, all ready to fold into the scrambled eggs. The croûtes (fried bread) can be made the day before, too, and reheated.

Serves 6–8

| Butter and olive oil for frying |
| Bread, crusts removed, cut into whatever size |

Collops of Pork Fillet with Cream, Brandy ▶ and Apple Sauce, page 173

you choose – I like to make the croûtes
about 2 inches/5 cm square

3 oz/84 g butter

1 garlic clove, skinned and chopped finely

12 large eggs, beaten well with ¼ pint/140 ml
creamy milk

Salt, pepper and a dash of Tabasco sauce

4 tomatoes, each skinned, de-seeded, and the
flesh chopped neatly

3 red peppers, skinned (see page 56) and
chopped

In a non-stick sauté or frying pan, heat a little butter and oil together. Fry the crustless croûtes till they are golden brown on either side. When they are cooked put them on to several thicknesses of kitchen paper to absorb excess grease. Alternatively, you can brush a baking tray with melted butter, brush the crustless bread with melted butter on both sides, and bake your croûtes – you actually use less butter this way.

Melt the 3 oz/84 g butter in a heavy-based saucepan. Add the garlic and cook for a minute, then add the egg mixture. Cook over a moderate (not high) heat, stirring till the eggs are just softly firm. Take care not to let them get too solid. Then take the pan off the heat, season with salt, pepper and Tabasco (if you haven't already mixed it into the egg mixture), and stir in the chopped tomatoes and peppers. The heat of the eggs should heat through the tomatoes and peppers.

Dish up into a hot shallow dish, with the hot croûtes around the edge of the eggs.

◀ Baked Glazed Ham with Tomato and
Madeira Sauce, page 176

Chive, Tomato and Cottage Cheese Omelettes

It really isn't very practical to plan omelettes for much more than four people, because it means either eating in relays, or, if you eat all at the same time, the last omelette made is perfectly delicious whilst the first and second, which have been keeping warm, are inevitably rather less than perfect! But omelettes for a few people are delicious, and all the preparation can be done several hours ahead. In this case, the tomatoes can be skinned, de-seeded and chopped the previous day, and the chives snipped into the eggs, beaten all ready to be poured into the foaming butter in your omelette pan.

This type of omelette is particularly good with Black Olive, Sun-Dried Tomato and Garlic Bread (page 368) as an accompaniment.

Serves 4

8 large eggs beaten together in a large jug
with 4 tbsp cold water, ½ tsp salt, plenty of
freshly ground black pepper and 4 tbsp
snipped chives

Butter for the omelette pan

8 oz/225 g cottage cheese

6 tomatoes, skinned, de-seeded and chopped
into small dice

If you beat the eggs in advance, you do need to fork through the mixture before making each omelette, to keep the snipped chives evenly distributed throughout.

To make each omelette, put a piece of butter in your omelette pan and swirl it around till it is hot and foaming, then, tipping and tilting the pan, pour in about a quarter of the egg mixture. The tipping and tilting distributes the mixture evenly over the base of the pan. Let it cook, lifting up the edges of the omelette to let the mixture run underneath, and just before it is cooked, while it is still slightly runny on top, spoon on a quarter of the cottage cheese, spreading it over the surface, and scatter a quarter of the diced tomatoes over that. Slip the cooked omelette on to a warm plate and repeat the process.

Goats' Cheese and Rocket Omelettes

To try to turn out omelettes for much more than four obliterates you, the cook, from the sociable side of the meal altogether. I was once at a large party where omelettes were the main part of brunch (it was in New York City) but there were five chefs cooking them, and each had an array of bowls containing different fillings from which the guests chose, for their individual orders! I have never forgotten it.

This recipe makes omelettes for four – keep the first one for your own, as it will have to sit and keep warm the longest.

Serves 4

| 8 large eggs |
| 4 tbsp water |
| A good dash of Tabasco sauce |
| Salt and freshly ground black pepper |
| Butter for the omelette pan |

| 8 oz/225 g soft goats' cheese, broken into quite small bits |
| 3 oz/84 g rocket (or baby spinach), torn into small bits (or chopped) |

If you have a large omelette pan you can make two large omelettes (4 eggs each, and cut each one in half, although individual omelettes do look better). Beat together well the eggs, water, Tabasco sauce, salt and pepper. Heat the crêpe or omelette pan (mine is one and the same pan) with a dab of butter in it. When the butter is foaming pour in about a quarter of the mixture – this is easiest if you mix it up in one of those very large measuring jugs which have a 4-pint/ 2½-litre capacity and which can so well double up as mixing bowls. Lakeland Plastics sell them, but so do a wide variety of other outlets, too, these days.

Cook the mixture briefly in the omelette pan, lifting up the edges to let the runny mixture slip underneath the firm top. When it is mostly firm, scatter a quarter of the broken-up goats' cheese on top, and a quarter of the torn-up rocket (or spinach). Cook for about half a minute longer, then fold over and slip on to a warmed plate. Repeat, till you have made three more omelettes.

These are good served with the Grilled Tomatoes on page 191–2.

Parsley Omelette with Chopped Ham

Omelettes are very satisfying. They can be served folded over their filling or served flat with their filling covering their surface. This omelette has lots of parsley in the egg mixture, which looks pretty and tastes good.

Serves 1

2 eggs, beaten

1 tbsp cold water

Salt, freshly ground black pepper and a dash of Tabasco sauce

1 rounded dssp finely chopped parsley

½ oz/14 g butter

2 oz/56 g chopped ham

Beat together the eggs, water, the seasoning, Tabasco and parsley. In an omelette pan (which should never be washed, just wiped out thoroughly with kitchen paper whilst still warm) melt the butter. When it is foaming, pour in the egg and parsley mixture. Cook over a medium heat, lifting the edges of the omelette from time to time to allow the runny mixture to go underneath. When the omelette is slightly uncooked on top, sprinkle the chopped ham over the surface. Cook a minute or two longer, then fold over and slip on to a warmed plate.

Omelettes are best eaten straight away, but this isn't very sociable. They will keep warm perfectly well in the time it takes to make omelettes for four people. Serve with warm brown garlic rolls and a green salad, and there you have one of the simplest and best meals.

Vegetable Main Courses

When I first came to live in Skye, which feels like yesterday but is in fact 25 years ago, you couldn't buy a tomato in a tin, let alone a fresh one, at the Co-op in Broadford which is my local food mecca. In the intervening years I reckon there has been (and is on-going) a greater revolution in the availability of fresh vegetables than in any other form of foodstuff.

Because we live here, in the most beautiful of all the Hebridean islands, I assume that whatever I can buy locally must be an in-dication of its accessibility elsewhere in even the most rural areas of Great Britain. There are too many food writers who forget just how many of us don't live within a stone's throw of Soho and the wonderful and varied foodstuffs to be found there and in other parts of central London. These days I can buy garlic, aubergines, red, yellow and green peppers (I loathe the green ones), and fresh Brussels sprouts in the winter months – this may not sound remarkable, but not long ago the only sprout you could buy locally was a frozen one.

All over the country, supermarkets are selling vegetables from around the world.

This isn't always a good thing. I feel that when we buy asparagus in November, for example, grown in Kenya, we forget how delicious British asparagus is. Waiting for vegetables to arrive in the season natural to our country used to be one of the treats of life. And there have become accessible some revolting vegetables, epitomized for me by the ubiquitous baby sweetcorn, which I can't bear, and which is to be found only too frequently. Always remembering that taste is a very individual thing, I can't think of a single point in favour of baby sweetcorn except, perhaps, its appearance.

Vegetable main course dishes need to be substantial, and very often they can be very filling eating indeed. A number of these suggested main courses, on the other hand, are elegant. The Asparagus Puff Pastry Parcels with Sauce Bercy, for example, falls into this category. So, too, do the Goats' Cheese Stuffed Crêpes with Leek Purée. Many of them can be perfect first courses, too, if served in smaller quantities.

All in all, I hope that I am right in think-ing that there is something in this chapter to suit every occasion, and the tastes of all.

Asparagus and Mushroom Gratin

•

Asparagus Puff Pastry Parcels with
Sauce Bercy

•

Asparagus Tart with Cheese Pastry

•

Avocado Cheesecake

•

Goats' Cheese Roulade with Cheese and
Walnut Filling

•

Goats' Cheese Stuffed Crêpes with Leek Purée

•

Leek and Cheese Filo Pastry Parcels

•

Marrow Stuffed with Curried Rice
and Vegetables

•

Mushroom and Broccoli Florentine

•

Mushroom and Garlic Roulade

Creamy Mushroom Pie with Almond and
Garlic Crust

•

Onion and Cheese Tart

•

Red Onion and Red Pepper Tart with
Cheese Pastry

•

Spiced Spinach Strudel

•

Spinach and Garlic Tart

•

Spinach and Sweetcorn Fritters

•

Tomato, Basil and Avocado Mousse

•

Tomato, Goats' Cheese and Leek Tart

•

Tomato Tart with Cheese Pastry

Asparagus and Mushroom Gratin

This is rather a rich main course, so I would plan for a fairly light, simple first course and pudding to precede and follow it. I like to serve it with plain boiled brown or Basmati rice.

Serves 8

1 lb/450 g mushrooms, wiped and sliced
2 oz/56 g butter
1 tbsp sunflower oil
8 oz/225 g asparagus, trimmed, and cut in 1-inch/2.5-cm pieces
1 pint/570 ml double cream
12 oz/340 g grated Cheddar cheese
A good pinch of thyme
Juice of half a lemon
Salt and freshly ground black pepper
2 oz/56 g fine breadcrumbs (white or brown)
2 tbsp chopped parsley

Start by cooking the sliced mushrooms. Melt the butter and heat the oil together in a wide saucepan or frying pan, heating till it is very hot. Cook the sliced mushrooms in small amounts till almost browned, then take them out of the pan with a slotted spoon and keep to one side. Steam the asparagus until just tender and set aside also.

Put the cream, 8 oz/225 g of the grated cheese and the thyme into a saucepan and heat over a gentle-to-moderate heat. When the cheese has melted in the cream, take the pan off the heat, and stir in the lemon juice, salt and pepper.

Stir the steamed asparagus and cooked mushrooms into the rich sauce. Pour it into a wide, fairly shallow flame-proof dish, mix the rest of the grated cheese with the crumbs and parsley and sprinkle over evenly. Put under a hot grill till the crumbs brown.

Asparagus Puff Pastry Parcels with Sauce Bercy

This is delicious for carnivores as well as for vegetarians. Although we can buy asparagus all year round, I much prefer to wait till it comes into our natural season to Britain. I think it tastes better.

I don't think these asparagus parcels need potatoes or rice with them, just something like a tomato and basil salad, and perhaps roast aubergines, garlic and peppers.

Serves 6

2 lb/900 g asparagus
2 oz/56 g butter
Salt and freshly ground black pepper
A grating of nutmeg
1½ lb/675 g ready rolled out puff pastry
1 egg, beaten
Sauce Bercy (see page 299)

First, trim any really tough ends off the asparagus stalks. Cut the head off each stalk and set aside. Steam the stalks till barely tender, then put them in a food processor and whiz them with the butter till they are a smooth purée. Season with salt and pepper and a grating of nutmeg. While your steamer is on, steam the heads of the asparagus for 1 minute, no more. Set on one side.

Cut six circles in the pastry. Spread half of each with the asparagus purée, and divide the asparagus heads evenly between them, laying them on top of the purée. Fold the other half of each circle over, and seal with beaten egg, pressing the edges down. Put the semi-circles on a baking tray – no need to butter or oil it. Brush the asparagus parcels with beaten egg.

Bake in an oven at 400°F/200°C/Gas Mark 6 for about 20 minutes, or till the parcels are puffed and golden.

Serve with a spoonful of Sauce Bercy beside each asparagus parcel.

Asparagus Tart with Cheese Pastry

This makes a good vegetarian main course and is also ideal for a picnic. The cheesy pastry complements the delicate taste of the asparagus filling, without overpowering it.

Serves 6

For the pastry:

3 oz/84 g butter, hard from the refrigerator, cut into pieces

3 oz/84 g mature Cheddar cheese, grated

1 rounded tsp dry mustard powder

5 oz/140 g plain flour

Salt and freshly ground black pepper

A dash of Tabasco sauce

For the filling:

1 lb/450 g fresh asparagus, unchewable ends trimmed off, steamed until just tender

2 large eggs + 3 large egg yolks

¾ pint/420 ml single cream (you can use milk if you prefer, but it doesn't really do justice to the dish)

Salt and freshly ground black pepper

Freshly grated nutmeg

If you have a food processor, process all the pastry ingredients together until the mixture resembles breadcrumbs. If not, sieve the flour, mustard and salt into a bowl. Mix in the cheese, pepper and Tabasco sauce. Rub in the pieces of butter with your fingertips until the mixture resembles fine bread-crumbs. Pat the mixture round the sides and base of a 9-inch/23-cm flan dish, and put the dish into the refrigerator for at least half an hour before baking in a moderate oven, 350°F/180°C/Gas Mark 4, for 20–25 minutes, until the pastry is golden brown.

Arrange the steamed asparagus in the flan, with the tips pointing towards the centre.

In a bowl, beat together the eggs, egg yolks, cream or milk, salt, pepper and nut-meg. Pour this over the asparagus, and bake in a moderate oven, 350°F/180°C/Gas Mark 4, for 15–20 minutes, until the filling is just set. Serve warm or cold.

Avocado Cheesecake

This cheesecake has a base of crushed wholemeal bran biscuits, and a smooth filling of puréed avocado mixed with cream cheese and flavoured with garlic. It looks extremely decorative, especially with a garnish of sliced tomatoes around the edge.

Serves 6–8

For the base:

12 oz/340 g wholemeal bran biscuits

3 oz/84 g butter, melted

1 garlic clove, skinned and very finely
   chopped

For the filling:

3 avocados

1 sachet of gelatine (approx. ½ oz/14 g)

¼ pint/150 ml chicken stock

8 oz/225 g cream cheese (or quark if you
   prefer a low-fat cheese)

2 tbsp lemon juice

1 garlic clove, skinned and chopped

A dash of Tabasco sauce

Salt and freshly ground pepper

4–5 tomatoes, skinned and sliced, to garnish

Finely chopped parsley and chives to garnish

First prepare the base. Break the bran biscuits into the food processor and process until fine – the noise is horrendous, but it only takes a minute – or crush them by hand with a rolling pin. Mix together well the crushed biscuits, melted butter and garlic. Press around the sides and base of an 8–9 inch/20–23 cm flan dish. Bake blind in a moderate oven, 350°F/180°C/Gas Mark 4, for 15 minutes. Leave to cool.

Cut each avocado in half, flick out the stone, and scoop out the flesh into a bowl or food processor, taking care to scrape the flesh from the inside of the skin, where the colour is a slightly darker shade of green. Sprinkle the gelatine on the chicken stock, and heat gently until the gelatine has dissolved completely – don't let the stock boil.

Pour the chicken stock and gelatine on to the avocado flesh, and add the cream cheese, lemon juice, garlic, Tabasco sauce, salt and pepper, and mix or process until you have a smooth pale green purée. The purée will be coarser if you mix by hand. Pour on to the cooled biscuit crust and leave for 3–4 hours to set.

Just before you are ready to serve the cheesecake, arrange the sliced tomatoes around the edge. Sprinkle the finely chopped parsley and chives either in the middle of the cheesecake or over the sliced tomatoes, whichever you prefer.

Goats' Cheese Roulade with Leek and Walnut Filling

A cold roulade is both delicious and easy to eat. Goats' cheese, leeks and walnuts are tastes which are made to be combined – they complement each other so well.

Serves 6–8

1 pint/570 ml milk

1 onion, cut in half

1 bay leaf

A stick of celery

A few peppercorns

About ½ tsp rock salt

For the roulade:

2 oz/56 g butter

2 oz/56 g plain flour

The strained flavoured milk

2 oz/56 g grated Cheddar cheese

6 oz/170 g soft goats' cheese, rind removed

Extra pepper, if liked

Grated nutmeg

4 large eggs, separated

Chopped parsley

For the filling:

2 tbsp sunflower oil

**6 medium leeks, washed, trimmed and sliced
thinly**

A 7-fl. oz/200-g tub crème fraîche

**3 oz/84 g walnuts, crushed and dry-toasted in
a saucepan over heat for several minutes,
(shake the pan)**

A pinch of salt, freshly ground black pepper

Put the milk, onion, bay leaf, celery, pepper-corns and rock salt into a saucepan over heat till a skin forms on the surface. Take the pan off the heat and leave to cool completely. The milk will be infused with all the flavours when it has cooled. Strain it when it is quite cold.

Line a baking tray measuring about 10–12 x 12–14 inches (25–30 x 30–35 cm) with baking parchment, putting a dab of butter at each corner to hold the paper firmly in place. Melt the butter in a saucepan and stir in the flour. Let this cook for a minute before gradually adding the strained milk, stirring all the time – I find it best to use a wire whisk – until the sauce boils. Let it simmer gently for a moment, then take the pan off the heat and stir in the grated Cheddar cheese and the goats' cheese. Season with pepper if you think it needs more, and with nutmeg. Beat in the egg yolks, one by one.

Lastly, in a clean bowl whisk the egg whites till they are very stiff, and, with a large metal spoon, fold them quickly and

thoroughly through the sauce. Pour and scrape this into the paper-lined tin and bake in a moderate oven, 350°F/180°C/Gas Mark 4, for 20–25 minutes, till the roulade feels firm to the touch and the surface is puffed up and golden. Take it out of the oven and cover with a slightly dampened teatowel. Leave to cool.

For the filling, measure the oil into a non-stick (if possible) frying or sauté pan and cook the sliced leeks over a moderate heat, stirring, till they are very soft when you stick a fork into a bit. Do try to slice them thinly, because not only do they look and eat better, but they take a very short time to cook – about 4–5 minutes. Let the leeks cool.

Lay a sheet of baking parchment on a work surface or table. Scatter the chopped parsley over it. Take the short ends of paper in either hand and flip the roulade face down, as it were, on to the parsley. Peel the paper off the back of the roulade. Spread the crème fraîche over the surface, then scatter on the cooled nuts. Distribute the leeks over everything. I find a fork the easiest thing to use to do this. Season with a merest pinch of salt and with plenty of freshly ground black pepper.

Roll the roulade up away from you and slip it on to a serving plate. Leave it rolled up in its paper if you do this much more than an hour in advance, and then you can keep it a good rolled shape. Slip it off the paper before serving.

Goats' Cheese Stuffed Crêpes with Leek Purée

These parsley-flavoured crêpes have a filling of goats' cheese and a purée of leeks is served with them. I think the flavour of goats' cheese and leeks is a wonderful combination. You can leave the chopped tomatoes out of the goats' cheese filling if it is winter – tomatoes simply aren't worth their exorbitant cost when there is no flavour to them at that time of the year.

Serves 5–6

For the crêpes:

2 large eggs

4 oz/112 g plain flour

½ oz/14 g butter, melted

7 fl oz/200 ml milk and 3 fl oz/84 ml water, mixed

1 tbsp chopped parsley

Salt and freshly ground black pepper

A little extra butter, or oil, for greasing

For the filling:

12 oz/340 g goats' cheese, weighed before trimming

1 large egg white

Freshly ground black pepper

2 tomatoes, skinned, de-seeded and chopped quite small

For the leek purée:

4 medium leeks, washed, trimmed and sliced

Salt and freshly ground black pepper

Freshly grated nutmeg

1 oz/28 g butter

Put the eggs into a food processor or liquidizer and whiz, gradually adding the flour, melted butter, the milk and water, parsley, salt and pepper. Whiz till all is very well blended. Leave this batter, in a jug, for at least half an hour – you can make up the batter the previous day and keep it in the fridge overnight, but give it a good stir before you make up the crêpes.

Melt a small nut of butter in a pancake pan. When it is very hot, pour in a small amount of batter, swirling the pan with one hand while you pour with the other – as you pour, a thin film of batter covers the bottom of the pan. The aim is to make the pancakes or crêpes as thin as possible. Cook for a minute or two, then, using your fingers and a palette knife, turn over the crêpe and cook it for a minute on the other side.

Slip it on to a plate, and make a second crêpe. Put a disc or rectangle of baking parchment on top of each crêpe as you make them, which prevents them from sticking together. If you make pancakes often, it is well worth while investing in a second pancake pan, which halves the making time of a batch of crêpes such as this.

Cover the finished crêpes with clingfilm, and keep them in the fridge – they keep for several days – before stuffing them. You should allow 2–3 per person.

To make the filling, first de-rind the goats' cheese, then put it into a food processor and whiz, gradually adding the egg white. Season with black pepper. Take the cheese mixture out of the processor, put it into a bowl, then fold in the chopped tomatoes. Put a spoonful – a heaped teaspoon, or two if they are small – in the middle of each crêpe. You can stuff them in the morning ready for dinner that night. Fold over one side, then the next, clockwise till you have folded all the sides over to form a fat rectangular parcel.

Butter an ovenproof dish and lay the stuffed crêpes in it. Brush the crêpes with melted butter or sunflower oil. Heat the crêpes in a moderate oven, 350°F/180°C/Gas Mark 4, for 25 minutes – they will puff up slightly. Serve them hot, accompanied by the following leek purée.

Steam the sliced leeks, and when tender, liquidize or process them with the seasonings and butter. If the blades in your liquidizer or food processor are blunt, you may need to sieve the purée to get rid of the fibres. Put the hot purée into a buttered serving dish, and keep it warm in a low oven until you are ready to dish up the first course.

Leek and Cheese Filo Pastry Parcels

These are delicious and different served with soup, as a first course, especially a soup such as the Leek, Mushroom and Madeira Soup on page 30.

Makes 24 parcels, serving 8

| 4 sheets of filo pastry |
| Melted butter, or sunflower or olive oil |

For the filling:

| 1 oz/28 g butter |
| 2 tbsp sunflower or olive oil |
| 6 medium leeks, washed, trimmed, and cut in 1-inch/2.5-cm slices |
| 1 garlic clove, skinned and finely chopped |
| Salt and freshly ground black pepper |
| Freshly grated nutmeg |
| 3 oz/84 g cream cheese, such as Philadelphia |

Start by making the filling. Heat the butter and oil in a saucepan, and add the sliced leeks and chopped garlic. Cook till the leeks are soft, about 10 minutes over a moderate heat. Season with salt and pepper, and freshly grated nutmeg. Take the pan off the heat and liquidize the cooked leeks to a smooth purée, adding the cream cheese. How smooth a purée you get depends on the sharpness of the blades of your food processor or blender. If you feel the purée is a bit stringy (leeks do vary), sieve it, but if you keep whizzing you should get it smooth enough.

Brush a sheet of filo pastry all over with melted butter or sunflower or olive oil. Put a second sheet of filo exactly over the first, and brush this too with butter or oil. With a sharp knife, cut the filo in half, then cut each half into three even-sized strips. Cut each strip in half widthways. Put a teaspoonful of leek and cheese purée on each piece of filo, and fold into a parcel, brushing each with oil or butter. Repeat the process with the remaining pastry.

Put the parcels on an oiled baking tray, cover the baking tray with clingfilm, and put the tray into the fridge until you are ready to bake the filo parcels. Bake them in a hot oven, 425°F/220°C/Gas Mark 7, for 7–10 minutes, till they are golden and crisp.

Marrow Stuffed with Curried Rice and Vegetables

Marrow can be deadly – often the only thing in its favour is that it contains virtually no calories because it is composed largely of water. But marrow can also be very good, so make the most of them while they are in season in the autumn months. I like them best stuffed because they rely on accompanying vegetables or meat for flavour. The moistness of the marrow makes for a good juicy filling and this one, with curried rice and onions, peppers, garlic and mushrooms, is delicious. Serve with an accompanying cheese or tomato sauce if you like.

Serves 6

4 tbsp oil (I use sunflower)
2 onions, skinned and chopped
1 red and 1 yellow pepper, halved, de-seeded and chopped
2 garlic cloves, skinned and chopped
1 tbsp curry powder
8 oz/225 g mushrooms, wiped and chopped
2 tsp tomato purée
Salt and freshly ground black pepper
8 oz/225 g cooked brown rice
1 large marrow, peeled and halved lengthways, with the seeds scooped out of each half

Heat the oil in a frying pan and add the onions and peppers. Sauté for about 5 minutes, stirring occasionally so that they cook evenly, then stir in the garlic and the curry powder, and cook for a further few minutes. Add the mushrooms and tomato purée. Season with salt and freshly ground black pepper and cook for 2–3 minutes. Mix this together thoroughly with the cooked brown rice.

Oil a large piece of foil, and put one half of the marrow on it. Pack the stuffing into the scooped-out hollow, mounding it up to fill the hollow in the other half which you put on top like a lid. Wrap the foil tightly around the marrow and put the foil parcel in a roasting tin. Bake in a fairly hot oven, 400°F/200°C/Gas Mark 6, for 1¼–1½ hours. Pierce the marrow with a knife to see whether it is soft and cooked.

This dish keeps warm successfully for about an hour before serving. Cut the marrow into thick slices to serve, spooning the stuffing into the middle of each slice.

Mushroom and Broccoli Florentine

Not at all consciously, all of us in our family tend to eat fewer meals with meat as its main theme than we used to. This wholly vegetarian dish is an example. All you need to go with it is a basket of warm granary bread or rolls. If you can get good Lancashire cheese to make the sauce, do, but if not use a good strong Cheddar cheese.

Serves 6

3 bags young spinach, weight 7 oz/200 g each bag
3 tbsp extra virgin olive oil

1 tbsp lemon juice

Salt, freshly ground black pepper, freshly
grated nutmeg

2 lb/900 g broccoli, cut into small florets using
as much stem as possible

2 oz/56 g butter and 3 tbsp olive or sunflower
oil

1 lb/450 g mushrooms, wiped and chopped

2 cloves of garlic, skinned and finely chopped

2 oz/56 g flour

1¼ pint/710 ml milk

5 oz/140 g grated cheese, Lancashire if
possible

Put the bags of spinach into a microwave oven, if you have one, on a high setting for 2 minutes. Then tip the contents into a bowl and chop with a sharp knife, mixing in the olive oil and lemon juice, and some salt, pepper and nutmeg. If you don't have a microwave, put the spinach into a steamer with water, simmering until just before the spinach wilts – 3–4 minutes. Steam the broccoli florets till you can push a fork into the thickest bit of stem. Put the well chopped spinach into an ovenproof dish – a wide and fairly shallow one – and put the steamed broccoli over the spinach.

In a sauté pan melt the butter and heat the oil together and cook the chopped mushrooms till they almost squeak – by cooking them very well their flavour is greatly improved. Add the finely chopped garlic and cook for barely a minute before scattering in the flour. Stir it in well and cook for a further minute before adding the milk, gradually, and stirring continuously till the sauce reaches a simmering point. Simmer for a few moments then take the sauté pan off

the heat, and stir in all but about a tablespoon of the grated cheese, and some more salt, pepper and nutmeg. Pour this sauce over the broccoli and spinach, and sprinkle the remainder of the grated cheese over the surface.

Before serving, put the dish under a hot grill, till the cheese on top melts and turns golden. This should be sufficient time for the contents to heat through. Keep it warm in a low-temperature oven till you are ready to serve.

Mushroom and Garlic Roulade

This roulade is a great favourite here, both with us and our guests. Don't be tempted to skip the flavouring of the milk – it does make all the difference, and makes the roulade taste extra good. The filling is just cream cheese and chopped hardboiled eggs flavoured with crushed garlic and parsley. Alternatively you can use less cream cheese and replace it with a layer of sliced red, yellow and green peppers, first sautéed until soft in olive oil. Both fillings are delicious.

Serves 6–8

For the flavoured milk:

1 pint/570 ml milk

1 onion, skinned and halved

1 celery stick, cut in 3 pieces

1 bay leaf

A few parsley stalks

½ tsp salt

8–12 black peppercorns

For the roulade:

1 lb/450 g mushrooms	
3 oz/84 g butter	
3 oz/84 g plain flour	
The strained flavoured milk	
4 large eggs, separated	
Salt and freshly ground black pepper	
Freshly grated nutmeg	

For the filling:

8 oz/225 g cream cheese (or a low-fat substitute, such as quark)	
1 garlic clove, skinned and chopped	
A few tbsp milk	
2 rounded tbsp finely chopped parsley	
4 hardboiled eggs, chopped	

Put all the ingredients for the flavoured milk into a saucepan and bring to scalding point over a gentle heat. Take the saucepan off the heat and leave to stand for 40–45 minutes. Strain the milk and reserve it for the roulade.

Wipe the mushrooms, put them into a liquidizer or food processor and blend until they are evenly pulverized. Pour the thick mushroom purée into a large sieve lined with two or three thicknesses of kitchen paper to absorb any excess moisture from the mushrooms.

Meanwhile, melt the butter in a saucepan and stir in the flour. Cook for a couple of minutes. Stirring all the time, gradually add the flavoured milk. Stir until the sauce boils. Take the pan off the heat and beat in the egg yolks, one by one. Season with salt, pepper and nutmeg. Line a baking tin or Swiss roll tin, about 12 x 14 inches/30 x 35 cm with baking parchment.

Fold the raw mushroom purée into the sauce. Whisk the egg whites until stiff, and using a large metal spoon, fold them quickly and thoroughly into the mushroom sauce. Pour the mixture on to the lined tin and bake in a moderate oven, 350°F/180°C/Gas Mark 4, for 20–25 minutes or until the roulade feels firm to touch. Take it out of the oven, cover with another piece of baking parchment and a damp teatowel, and leave to cool.

For the filling, put the cream cheese and garlic into a liquidizer or food processor and blend. Thin the mixture with a little milk – just enough to give the mixture a spreadable consistency. Add the chopped parsley and blend again. Turn the mixture into a bowl and mix in the hardboiled eggs.

To assemble the roulade, first remove the teatowel and top sheet of paper. Lay a fresh piece of paper on a table or work surface. Invert the roulade on to this. Carefully peel off the paper, tearing it in strips parallel to the roulade – if you try to pull the whole sheet off at once, it tends to tear the roulade. Spread the roulade with the cream cheese and egg mixture, and roll it up lengthways, like a Swiss roll. Slip it on to a serving dish and serve in 2-inch/5-cm slices.

Creamy Mushroom Pie with Almond and Garlic Crust

This is a rather unusual pie, with bread-crumbs and almonds forming the crust instead of the usual pastry. I like to use nibbed or flaked almonds, as I like the contrasting crunch in texture. We do this here as a first course for our hotel guests, but it can be quite filling, and makes a good lunch dish.

Serves 6

For the base:

6 oz/170 g wholemeal breadcrumbs

2–3 oz/56–84 g nibbed or flaked almonds

A pinch of dried thyme

2 garlic cloves, peeled and very finely chopped

3 oz/84 g butter, melted

For the filling:

2 oz/56 g butter

8 oz/225 g mushrooms, sliced

1 heaped tbsp plain flour

Just less than 1 pint/570 ml milk

Salt and freshly ground black pepper

A pinch of grated nutmeg

2 egg yolks

1 rounded tbsp finely chopped parsley (optional)

Mix the breadcrumbs, almonds, thyme, garlic and melted butter together well, and lightly press round a 9-inch/23-cm flan dish. Bake in a hot oven, 400°F/200°C/Gas Mark 6, for 10–15 minutes, turning the dish round from time to time to brown it evenly. Remove from the oven when the surface feels just crisp.

For the filling, melt the butter in a saucepan, and add the sliced mushrooms. Cook for just 1 minute, then sprinkle on the flour. Stir well and gradually pour on the milk, stirring all the time until the sauce boils. Season with salt, freshly ground black pepper

and nutmeg (freshly grated if possible). Draw off the heat.

In a small bowl beat the egg yolks, pour a little of the mushroom sauce on to them, mix well, then add a little more sauce, mix well, then pour the contents of the bowl into the sauce in the saucepan and stir well. Pour into the flan dish, sprinkle with parsley if you like, and bake in a moderate oven, 350°F/180°C/Gas Mark 4 for 10 minutes.

Onion and Cheese Tart

This tart makes a perfect first course or a light main course for lunch or supper and is lovely to take on a picnic. Onions and cheese are meant for each other – simple but delicious!

Serves 6–8

For the pastry:

6 oz/170 g flour

½ oz/14 g icing sugar

Salt and freshly ground black pepper

4 oz/112 g butter, hard from the refrigerator and cut into pieces

For the filling:

3 tbsp oil (I use sunflower)

4 medium to large onions, skinned and very thinly sliced

2 large eggs + 2 large egg yolks

¾ pint/420 ml milk, or milk and cream mixed

Salt and freshly ground black pepper

Freshly grated nutmeg

4 oz/112 g mature Cheddar cheese, grated

Finely chopped parsley to garnish (optional)

If you have a food processor, process all the pastry ingredients until the mixture is like fine breadcrumbs. If not, sieve the flour, sugar, salt and pepper into a bowl. Rub in the pieces of butter with your fingertips until the mixture resembles fine breadcrumbs. Pat the mixture round the sides and base of a 9-inch/23-cm flan dish. Put the dish into the fridge for at least half an hour before baking blind in a moderate oven, 350°F/180°C/Gas Mark 4, for 20–25 minutes, until the pastry is golden brown. Take out of the oven.

Alternatively make a conventional short-crust pastry flan shell and bake blind until golden brown.

Heat the oil and add the onions. Sauté gently for 25 minutes, stirring occasionally to prevent the onions sticking and to make sure they cook evenly. When they are cooked, spread them over the base of the pastry shell. Beat together the eggs, egg yolks, milk (or milk and cream), salt, pepper, nutmeg and cheese. Pour this mixture over the onions in the flan case, and bake in a moderate oven, 350°F/180°C/Gas Mark 4, for 15–20 minutes, until the filling is just set. Allow to cool a little, and dust with finely chopped parsley if you like before serving.

Red Onion and Red Pepper Tart with Cheese Pastry

I don't think we use red onions enough in our cooking. They are much more widely available to us these days, and their taste is much milder and really nicer for certain dishes by far than the usual onions. In this tart they are gently fried till soft with the skinned red peppers (they go together very well) and then set with a creamy custard. The cheese and mustard in the pastry just round off the flavours, I think. All else you need to complete this supper dish is a good green salad.

Serves 6

For the pastry:

5 oz/140 g plain flour

5 oz/140 g butter, hard from the fridge, cut in bits

2 tsp mustard powder

3 oz/84 g Cheddar cheese, grated

For the filling:

2 red peppers

3 tbsp sunflower oil

6 red onions, skinned and very finely sliced

2 whole eggs beaten with 2 large egg yolks

¾ pint/420 ml single cream

Salt and freshly ground black pepper

Put the flour, butter and mustard powder into a food processor and whiz till the mixture resembles fine crumbs (or see instructions opposite). Then add the Cheddar cheese and whiz very briefly to incorporate it. Pat this firmly around the sides and base of a flan dish measuring approximately 9 inches/23 cm in diameter.

Put the dish into the fridge for an hour before baking, then move it straight from the fridge into a moderate oven, 350°F/180°C/Gas Mark 4, for about 25 minutes, or till the pastry is pale golden. Take it out of the oven.

To make the filling, start by cutting the peppers in half and scooping away their seeds. Put them on a baking tray, skin side uppermost, under a hot grill, and grill till the skin swells into great charred bubbles. Take the peppers out, put them into a polythene bag, and leave for 10 minutes, then skin them. Their skins will peel off easily. Slice the peppers into thin strips.

Heat the oil in a wide-based saucepan and cook the sliced onions over a moderate heat, stirring from time to time so that they don't stick, for about 10 minutes. Then add the sliced peppers and cook for a further 2–3 minutes. Spoon this mixture over the base of the cooked pastry. Mix together the beaten eggs and yolks with the cream, season with salt and pepper, and carefully pour this in with the onions and peppers mixture.

Carefully, so as not to spill the contents, put the flan dish into a moderate oven, 350°F/180°C/Gas Mark 4, till the filling is just set when you gently shake the dish – about 20 minutes.

Serve cold or warm.

Spiced Spinach Strudel

This spinach strudel is made with filo pastry, which is widely available ready-made from delicatessens. If you have to buy more than you need, just wrap up any unused leaves of filo pastry and freeze them.

The spinach filling for the strudel is quite spicy, and I like to serve it with a tomato sauce. The sauce is purely optional, *however, an embellishment rather than an integral part of the dish!*

Serves 8

2 oz/56 g butter
1 onion, skinned and very finely chopped
1 large garlic clove, skinned and finely chopped
2 lb/900 g chopped frozen spinach, thawed and pressed to extract surplus water
1 tsp ground cumin
Salt and freshly ground black pepper
12 sheets of filo pastry
4 oz/112 g melted butter or 6–8 tbsp olive oil

Melt the butter in a saucepan and add the onion. Sauté for 5 minutes, stirring occasionally, then add the garlic and cook for a further couple of minutes. Stir in the well-drained spinach, the cumin, salt and pepper. Cook for about 5 minutes, then take the saucepan off the heat, and cool the spinach mixture. You can make this the day before you want to serve the strudel if it is more convenient, and keep it in a covered container in the refrigerator.

Lay the sheets of filo pastry out, brush each with melted butter or with olive oil and put them in twos, so you have six sheets of double thickness. Divide the spinach mixture among the six sheets, spreading it over the pastry. Roll up each sheet, like a Swiss roll, and lay the rolls on a buttered baking sheet. Brush the rolls with melted butter or olive oil, and bake in a hot oven, 400°F/200°C/Gas Mark 6, for about 15–20 minutes, until the pastry is golden brown.

To serve, cut each strudel into four,

allowing three pieces per person. Serve with Simple Tomato Sauce (page 305) if you like.

Spinach and Garlic Tart

A delicious and convenient lunch or supper dish. The amount of garlic you use depends on your liking of garlic – my liking could more accurately be described as an addiction! The filling for this tart can be made easily in a food processor, with the egg whites then whisked and folded in by hand. I like to serve it with baked potatoes or warm brown rolls and either a tomato salad or a vegetable with a tomato sauce – spinach and tomato are lovely together.

Serves 6–8

One quantity shortcrust pastry (see page 209)

2 lb/900 g frozen spinach, thawed and well
   drained

8 oz/225 g cottage cheese

1 large garlic clove, skinned and finely
   chopped

Salt and freshly ground black pepper

Freshly grated nutmeg

4 large eggs, 2 whole and 2 separated

Roll out the pastry and line an 8–9 inch/20–22 cm flan dish. Prick the bottom of the pastry all over with a fork. Put the flan dish into the refrigerator for at least 30 minutes and then bake blind in a moderate oven, 350°F/180°C/Gas Mark 4, until the pastry is golden brown (about 10 minutes).

Put the spinach into a food processor and process until smooth. Add the cottage cheese

and garlic and blend again. Add the salt, pepper and nutmeg, and, with the processor still going, add the 2 whole eggs and the 2 yolks. If you haven't got a food processor, you can use this method with a liquidizer, pushing the mixture down from time to time with a spatula. Otherwise, use chopped spinach and simply beat the ingredients together in a bowl. Whisk the 2 remaining egg whites until stiff and fold them into the spinach mixture with a large metal spoon.

Pour the spinach mixture into the baked flan case, and bake in a moderate oven, 350°F/180°C/Gas Mark 4, for about 25 minutes, or until the filling feels firm to the touch. The tart will keep warm very well for about 20 minutes, but much more than that and it will begin to dry out.

Spinach and Sweetcorn Fritters

These fritters can either be a supper by themselves, with perhaps a tomato sauce, or they can be served with sausages or bacon. They are quite filling, and you can include the garlic or not, as you like. I do!

Serves 6

4 oz/112 g plain flour

2 large eggs

Salt and freshly ground black pepper

2 lb/900 g fresh spinach, steamed till it just
   wilts, then chopped quite finely, or
   ½ lb/225 g frozen leaf spinach, thawed,
   drained well and chopped

1 garlic clove, skinned and finely chopped

Two 15-oz/420-g tins of sweetcorn kernels,
  drained of their brine

Beat together the flour and eggs, and season them with the salt and pepper. Beat in the well-chopped spinach, the finely chopped garlic and the sweetcorn.

Lightly oil a non-stick frying pan or, if you have an Aga or a Raeburn, lightly oil the cooler hotplate and drop on spoonfuls of the mixture, well spaced out. After a minute or so, turn them over – I use a palate knife to do this. When they are golden brown (well flecked with the green spinach), pile them on to a warmed serving plate or dish and eat as soon as possible.

Tomato, Basil and Avocado Mousse

This is a good dish for light lunch on a summer's day. It can be made the evening before, and it looks good served with a mixed green salad and warm bread or rolls – for my taste, granary bread.

Serves 6

½ pint/285 ml chicken or vegetable stock

1½ sachets (¾ oz/21 g) of gelatine, or 6 leaves
  of gelatine

8 tomatoes, skinned, de-seeded and whizzed
  to a purée – this should yield ¾ pint/420 ml

2 tbsp snipped chives

About 2 tbsp chopped basil leaves

6 tbsp mayonnaise – a good bought one
  if not homemade

Salt and lots of freshly ground black pepper

2 egg whites

3 avocados, skinned, and the flesh chopped
  into neat dice and tossed in 3 tbsp lemon
  juice

Heat the stock and sprinkle the powdered gelatine into it – or feed in the leaves of gelatine. Shake the pan gently till the gelatine dissolves completely. Set the pan on one side till the contents cool. Then stir the cooled stock and gelatine into the tomato purée, along with the snipped chives and chopped basil. When the mixture begins to gel fold in the mayonnaise. Taste, and season with salt and pepper.

Whisk the egg whites till stiff and, with a large metal spoon, fold them quickly and thoroughly through the tomato mousse. Spoon half the mousse into a serving dish or bowl. Cover with the diced avocado, then cover with the rest of the tomato mousse. Cover the bowl with clingfilm and leave to set.

If you like, garnish before serving with diced, skinned and de-seeded tomatoes tossed in a tablespoon of good olive oil, with more chopped basil. Scatter this around the edge of the mousse in its bowl.

Tomato, Goats' Cheese and Leek Tart

The flavours of the tomatoes, goats' cheese and leeks go together so very well that this tart is a great favourite of mine. I use creamy goats' cheese, crumbled. I never used to like goats' cheese until I ate it hot for the first time, and now it is one of my most sought-after food items – but I still prefer it hot to cold.

Serves 6–8

For the pastry:

4 oz/112 g butter, hard from the fridge, cut into bits
6 oz/170 g plain flour
1 tsp icing sugar
½ tsp salt and a good grinding of pepper

For the filling:

2 tbsp olive oil
4 leeks, washed, trimmed and sliced thinly
4 oz/112 g soft goats' cheese, crumbled
2 large eggs + 2 large egg yolks
½ pint/285 ml single cream
A pinch of salt (the cheese will be quite salty) and plenty of pepper
5 tomatoes, skinned, each cut in half, de-seeded and sliced into thin strips

Put all the ingredients for the pastry into a food processor and whiz – or sieve the dry ingredients into a bowl and rub in the butter – till the mixture resembles fine crumbs. Pat this firmly around the sides and base of a 9-inch/23-cm flan dish. Put the dish into the fridge for at least an hour, then bake in a moderate oven, 350°F/180°C/Gas Mark 4, for 20–25 minutes. If the pastry looks as though it is slipping down the sides as it cooks, press it back up using the back of a metal spoon.

Heat the oil in a sauté or frying pan and cook the leeks over a moderate heat till they

are soft. This will only take about 5 minutes at the most – leeks cook more quickly than onions. Scoop them into the cooked pastry base. Distribute the crumbled goats' cheese over the leeks. Beat together the eggs, yolks and cream and season with the pinch of salt and pepper. Pour this in amongst the leeks and goats' cheese. Arrange the strips of tomato on the runny top.

Carefully put the flan dish into a moderate oven (as for the pastry) and cook till the custard filling is just set when you gently shake the dish, about 20 minutes. Serve warm or cold – I think it is nicer warm.

Tomato Tart with Cheese Pastry

This is best made in the summer when tomatoes taste their best. The cheese pastry has its flavour accentuated by the mustard powder – but you don't actually taste the mustard. It's a slightly rich but utterly delicious savoury tart, only needing a green salad to go with it.

Serves 6

For the pastry:

4 oz/112 g butter hard from the fridge, cut into bits
3 oz/84 g grated Cheddar cheese
6 oz/170 g plain flour
Salt and pepper
2 tsp mustard powder

For the filling:

6 tomatoes, skinned, halved and the seeds removed, and the flesh roughly chopped

1–2 cloves of garlic, skinned and finely chopped (optional)

2 large eggs + 2 large egg yolks

½ pint/285 ml single cream

Salt and freshly ground black pepper

Basil leaves, torn up

Put all the ingredients for the pastry into a food processor and whiz – or sieve the dry ingredients into a bowl and rub in the butter – till fine. Mix in the grated cheese. Pat this firmly around the sides and base of the 9-inch/23-cm flan dish and put the dish into the fridge for at least an hour. Then bake in a moderate oven, 350°F/180°C/Gas Mark 4,

till the pastry is pale golden. If you notice the pastry slipping down the sides of the dish as it cooks, press it back up the sides with the back of a metal spoon and continue to cook for a few more minutes. The cooking will take about 20–25 minutes.

Put the chopped tomatoes on the cooked pastry base, and scatter on the garlic if used. Beat together the eggs and yolks, gradually mixing in the cream. Season with salt and pepper and pour this over the tomatoes. Scatter the basil leaves over everything.

Bake in a moderate oven till the filling is just firm, about 20 minutes. Serve warm.

Vegetable Side Dishes

The following chapter contains recipes for vegetables to accompany a main dish. A glance at the huge range included here will show how much more varied the use of vegetables has become in recent years. This makes what we eat far more interesting – and in most cases, better for us, too.

Vegetables in very many of the recipes in this chapter can be a main meal when combined with, perhaps, baked jacket potatoes or with boiled rice (Basmati for my taste). They don't, of course, have to be served as side dishes, they can themselves be centre stage, as it were, in a meal. For example, the Root Vegetable Ragoût or the Spicy Red Cabbage dishes are both substantial and, served in larger amounts with other vegetables to accompany them, could well form a most sustaining lunch or supper.

Though I have made suggestions about which main dishes are complemented by the recipes in this chapter, as with all eating it is very much a matter of individual taste. I have tried to be as general as possible, and not prescriptive, and have recommended more what vegetable I like to eat with meat, game or fish. There are certain vegetables I don't like with fish – red cabbage, for example, and, for the most part, turnip (although personally I do like puréed turnip with salmon – remember, taste is a very individual thing). But I have eaten cod cooked with red cabbage, and that was in a restaurant in the centre of Paris! So it only goes to emphasize just how personal taste is.

Many vegetables do not make solo appearances in this chapter but are of course included in recipes elsewhere in the book, not least the Vegetable Main Course chapter. As you will have gathered, as with most types of foods I do like to cook and serve vegetables in their natural season. Not only do they taste better, but they are far better for us. And I am so thankful that it seems to be ever easier to find organically grown vegetables to buy. We are very fortunate here in Skye to have a number of growers from whom we buy, as well as our excellent new fruit and vegetable supplier, Munro of Tain. In our 24 years of running our home as a hotel, probably the single food item hardest to source has been good vegetables, but thankfully, this problem seems to be easing.

Beetroot Baked in Cream and Lemon

•

Steamed Brussels Sprouts with Bacon Bits

•

Brussels Sprout Purée with Toasted Cashew Nuts

•

Braised Cabbage with Nutmeg

•

Cabbage Fried with Grainy Mustard

•

Braised Red Cabbage

•

Spicy Red Cabbage with Apples, Onions and Raisins

•

Spicy Red Cabbage with Green Grapes

•

Steamed Cauliflower with Fried Parsley and Breadcrumbs

•

Glazed Celeriac, Parsnips and Carrots

•

Purée of Celeriac

•

Braised Celery

Courgettes and Mushrooms in Cream and Soy Sauce

•

Sautéed Spaghetti Courgettes

•

Jerusalem Artichoke, Turnip and Potato Purée

•

Leek and Carrot Ragoût

•

Leeks Braised with Tomatoes

•

Steamed Leeks in White Sauce

•

Sautéed Onions in White Sauce

•

Parsnip Chips

•

Purée of Parsnips with Toasted Cashew Nuts

•

New Potatoes with Dill

•

Purée of Turnips with Cashew Nuts

•

Sautéed Turnips and Onions

•

Root Vegetable Ragoût

Beetroot Baked in Cream and Lemon

If you should happen to be counting calories, you can substitute natural yoghurt for the cream in this recipe. It will give a rather drier result, but is still good. Beetroot goes with all things gamey, and I think its spectacular colour dresses up the contents of a dinner plate like nothing else can.

Serves 6

2 lb/900 g cooked beetroots
Grated rind of 1 lemon
¼ pint/140 ml single cream
Salt and freshly ground black pepper
2 rounded tbsp breadcrumbs

Butter a shallow ovenproof dish. Slice the cooked beetroots evenly about ⅛ inch/3 mm thick. Arrange the slices in the buttered dish, overlapping each other. Sprinkle the grated lemon rind over the beetroot. Pour over the cream and season with salt and black pepper.

Bake in a moderate oven, 350°F/ 180°C/Gas Mark 4, for 20 minutes, then remove from the oven, sprinkle over the breadcrumbs, and put under a hot grill to toast the crumbs. This dish keeps warm very well for about 30 minutes.

Steamed Brussels Sprouts with Bacon Bits

Allow at least 6 medium sprouts per person. Pick them over, discarding any damaged outer leaves, and nick the base of each one.

Steaming Brussels sprouts over water gives a much better flavour than boiling them in water. Steam them until they are just tender when stuck with a fork – no one really likes them underdone.

I serve crisp Canadian streaky bacon with the sprouts, grilled and broken into pieces – you can do this in advance. Mix the bacon bits through the sprouts in their serving dish.

Brussels Sprout Purée with Toasted Cashew Nuts

This purée is enjoyed here by those who don't actually like Brussels sprouts whole. The cashew-nut garnish adds a good contrasting crunch.

Serves 6–8

For the sauce:

1 oz/28 g butter
1 oz/28 g flour
½ pint/285 ml milk

For the purée:

2 lb/900 g Brussels sprouts
Salt and freshly ground black pepper
Freshly grated nutmeg
2 oz/56 g toasted cashew nuts, chopped, to garnish

Melt the butter and stir in the flour to make a roux. Add the milk a little at a time, stirring continuously, bring to the boil, and simmer until the sauce has thickened.

Put the sprouts into a saucepan and pour boiling water over them to a depth of about 1 inch/2.5 cm. Cover the pan with a lid and cook over a high heat for 10–15 minutes, until the sprouts are tender.

Put the sprouts with the hot sauce into a food processor, and season with salt, pepper and nutmeg. Blend until smooth.

Put the purée into a warmed serving dish and sprinkle over the toasted cashew nuts. Keep it warm until you are ready to serve.

This is good with all meat- and game-based dishes, whether roast or stewed (or casseroled).

Braised Cabbage with Nutmeg

Cabbage, however you cook it, goes so very well with any type of meat or chicken or duck. Braised, the cabbage is easier to cook and to keep warm without spoiling.

You will, perhaps, notice that nutmeg is used to season many of these vegetable dishes. I think that nutmeg is the most versatile of all spices, complementing as it does such a wide range of foods, from vegetables to cheese, fish to meat, and soft fruits and cream- and milk-based puddings. Whichever meat I intend this cabbage to accompany, I tend to cook it in chicken stock. You can use vegetable stock if you prefer.

Serves 6

2 oz/56 g butter + 1 tbsp either sunflower or olive oil

1 medium white cabbage, or 2 medium savoys, trimmed of outer leaves and tough stalks, and shredded as finely as possible

1 pint/570 ml chicken or vegetable stock

Salt and freshly ground black pepper

Freshly grated nutmeg

Melt the butter and heat the oil, and stir-fry the cabbage in this till it is all turned in the butter/oil. Pour in the stock, bring it to simmering point, season with salt, pepper and nutmeg, and simmer very gently, stirring occasionally, till the largest bit is tender when stuck with a fork. As it simmers, the stock will reduce. I find the best type of pan to use to cook this is a wide sauté pan – that way the cabbage cooks evenly and the stock reduces.

To keep the cabbage warm cover it, in a warmed serving dish, and keep it in a low temperature oven.

Cabbage Fried with Grainy Mustard

Cabbage is one of those things which conjures up in people's minds awful visions of greatly overcooked mush in a pool of water, with that all-pervading smell which seemed to fill the sort of institution which turned out cabbage like this. Poor cabbage, because it is a delicious winter vegetable, and can be cooked in a number of ways. I think it is very complementary to stewy dishes. This is one of my favourite ways of cooking and eating cabbage.

Serves 6

About half a large cabbage

3 oz/84 g butter

2 rounded tbsp grainy mustard, such as
   Meaux

Salt and freshly ground black pepper

Shred the cabbage finely. Melt the butter in a wide, shallow pan, and stir the mustard into it, then add the cabbage and seasoning. Cook over a gentle heat, stirring occasionally, for up to 30 minutes. How long you cook it depends on how crunchy you like to eat cabbage.

Braised Red Cabbage

Red cabbage cooked in this way is both good to eat and most convenient, because it will keep warm without deteriorating in the slightest.

Serves 6–8

3 tbsp sunflower or olive oil

2 onions, skinned and chopped finely

1 medium red cabbage, chopped neatly

4 good eating apples, e.g. Cox's, peeled,
   cored and chopped

About 5–6 juniper berries, crushed

Salt and pepper

1 tsp soft brown sugar

2 tbsp white wine vinegar, or 2 tsp Balsamic
   vinegar

Heat the oil and cook the chopped onions till they are soft and just beginning to turn golden at the edges. Add the cabbage and apples and the juniper berries.

Cook, stirring occasionally, for about 5 minutes. Then stir in the seasonings, sugar and vinegar.

Cover with a lid, and cook on a gentle heat for 25–30 minutes, taking the lid off from time to time to give it all a good stir, to prevent sticking. This reheats successfully, if you have any left over.

Spicy Red Cabbage with Apples, Onions and Raisins

This is such a convenient vegetable dish to prepare, because it can all be made in the morning and reheated for dinner that night. The flavours of red cabbage, apples and onions all go very well with venison, and with all game.

Serves 6–8

3 tbsp oil

1 oz/28 g butter

2 onions, finely sliced

1 medium red cabbage, trimmed of its outer
   leaves and finely shredded

3 apples, preferably Cox's, cored and chopped

2 oz/56 g raisins

2 tbsp wine vinegar

1 tsp ground all spice

Salt and freshly ground black pepper

Heat the oil in a large saucepan or heavy casserole and melt the butter in it. Add the onions and cook for 2–3 minutes, then add the cabbage, apples, raisins, vinegar, allspice and seasoning. Cook over a gentle heat for about 30 minutes, stirring from time to time so that it cooks evenly.

Spicy Red Cabbage with Green Grapes

The cabbage can be cooked in the morning of the day it is to be eaten. Before serving, add the grapes and reheat in the butter. It is good with the Marinated Pigeon Breasts on page 127.

6 lb/2.7 kg red cabbage, cored and finely shredded
7 fl oz/200 ml red wine vinegar
6 tbsp sugar
Salt and freshly ground black pepper
1 lb/450 g seedless green grapes, or larger grapes halved and de-seeded
4 oz/112 g butter

Put the cabbage into a very large saucepan, or two saucepans. Add ¾ pint/420 ml of water, the vinegar, sugar and seasoning. Cover the saucepan(s) tightly and cook gently for at least 1 hour until the cabbage is tender.

Add the grapes and continue cooking for a further 5 minutes.

Drain the cabbage well in a large colander. Melt the butter in the saucepan(s), then return the drained cabbage to the pan(s) and toss well in the hot butter. Spoon into a hot serving dish and serve hot.

Steamed Cauliflower with Fried Parsley and Breadcrumbs

The garnish is an integral part of this dish, both for taste and texture.

Serves 8

2 medium cauliflowers
4 oz/112 g brown breadcrumbs
A large bunch of parsley
4 oz/112 g butter
8 tbsp oil (I use sunflower)
Salt and freshly ground black pepper

Each medium cauliflower should be enough for four people. Steam them till the stalks are tender – you will find their flavour quite intense in comparison with cauliflower cooked in water.

For the breadcrumb and parsley mixture, whiz together in a food processor or liquidizer the brown breadcrumbs and the parsley.

In a frying pan (preferably a non-stick one) melt the butter and heat the sunflower oil till they are hot. Fry the breadcrumb and parsley mixture, seasoning it with salt and freshly ground black pepper, and turning it over as it cooks so that the crumbs brown and crisp evenly. When it is browned, keep it warm in a dish lined with several thicknesses of kitchen paper, and sprinkle it liberally over the cauliflower on each plate as you dish up.

Glazed Celeriac, Parsnips and Carrots

The flavours of these root vegetables, especially when combined as they are in this dish, seem to enhance and complement venison more than any other vegetables I can think of.

Serves 8

3 oz/84 g butter

3 tbsp sunflower oil

2 medium celeriac, peeled, and cut in fat julienne strips, about ½ inch/1 cm wide

4 medium carrots, peeled and cut in flat, even-sized, julienne strips

4 parsnips, peeled and cut in fat julienne strips

1 tsp sugar

1 pint/570 ml chicken stock

Salt and freshly ground black pepper

In a heavy casserole, melt the butter and heat the oil. Add the prepared vegetables, and sprinkle on the sugar. Cook over a moderate heat for 5 minutes or so, stirring from time to time, so that the vegetables all get coated in the butter and oil. Pour in the stock, season with salt and pepper and let the stock come to simmering point, then cover the casserole with a lid and put it into a low oven, 250°F/125°C/Gas Mark ½, and leave for 1–1½ hours.

Stick the point of a knife into a piece of carrot (the vegetable of the three which takes longest to cook) and test to see if it is tender. If it feels too firm for your liking, put the casserole into a moderate oven, 350°F/180°C/Gas Mark 4, for about 20 minutes.

Purée of Celeriac

Celeriac is one of the seasonal vegetable treats. I love it raw, as in the Celeriac and Egg Mousse on page 184, I love it combined with other root vegetables, and I love this smooth purée.

Serves 8

2 medium celeriac

2 large potatoes

1 tsp salt

4 oz/112 g butter, cut in pieces

2 egg yolks

Salt and freshly ground black pepper

Peel the celeriac and cut them into chunks. Peel the potatoes and cut them into chunks too. Put the cut-up celeriac and potatoes into a saucepan and cover with water. Add the salt and boil the vegetables together till they are tender when you stick a knife into them. Drain, and steam them off over heat to get rid of any excess moisture. Then mash well, and beat the purée with a wooden spoon, adding the pieces of butter and the egg yolk, with salt and pepper to taste.

Butter an ovenproof dish, and put the purée into it. Cool, cover and freeze, or if you are not intending to freeze it, keep it in a warm oven till you are ready to serve it. If you freeze it, allow it to thaw overnight, and reheat in a moderate oven for 20–30 minutes, with small bits of extra butter dotted over the surface.

Eggs Benedict ▶
page 191

Braised Celery

You do have to be careful with celery – it falls into the category of foods which people love or loathe. It goes so well, though, with all manner of meats, and chicken and duck, that if you are sure of the tastes of your guests it is a delicious and convenient vegetable. As its appearance is rather nondescript, it is as well to have something with a splash of colour as another vegetable – like puréed turnip or swedes, or carrots sliced into julienne strips and stir-fried with lemon, and with chopped parsley stirred through just before serving.

Serves 6

2 good heads of celery
2 oz/56 g butter
1 pint/570 ml stock, or ½ pint/285 ml stock + ½ pint/285 ml dry white wine – this combination is particularly good if the celery is to go with chicken
Salt, pepper and nutmeg

Trim the stalk end off the celery, and cut away any outer stalks. Chop off most of the leaves – keep them for stock – but leave some. Strip off any stringy bits. Slice into diagonal bits about 1 inch/2.5 cm long.

Melt the butter in a wide heavy sauté pan and cook the celery in the butter for a couple of minutes, stirring so that each bit of celery is coated. Pour in the stock and season with salt, pepper and nutmeg.

◀ Goats' Cheese Stuffed Crêpes with Leek Purée, page 204

Simmer very gently till the stock reduces and the celery is soft when stuck with a fork. In a warmed dish, closely covered, this keeps warm very successfully without spoiling.

Courgettes and Mushrooms in Cream and Soy Sauce

We grow courgettes, and after the first season, they tend to grow in such abundance that I rack my brains for ideas for cooking them. This is a recipe of my mother's. It is easy, good, and can be used either as a first course, or as an accompaniment; it is especially good with plain grilled chicken or fish.

Serves 6

About 10 medium courgettes
8 oz/225 g mushrooms
3 oz/84 g butter
5 fl oz/140 ml single cream
2 tbsp dark soy sauce
Salt and freshly ground black pepper

Cut the courgettes into 1-inch/2.5-cm pieces and slice the mushrooms.

Melt the butter in a wide, shallow pan, ideally a large frying pan. Put the courgettes into the melted butter, and cook for about 15–20 minutes, over a gentle heat, shaking the pan from time to time, to turn the pieces of courgette as they cook.

Stir in the sliced mushrooms and the cream and soy sauce. Season with salt and pepper, and raise the heat under the pan. Cook, with the cream boiling, for 5 minutes, then turn into a heated serving dish.

Sautéed Spaghetti Courgettes

This really does resemble vegetable spaghetti. A mandoline takes all the effort out of the slicing and takes seconds to render the courgettes into spaghetti-thin strips.

Serves 8

1½ lb/675 g small courgettes, washed, dried
  and trimmed

Olive oil for sautéing

Salt and freshly ground black pepper

Very finely chopped garlic (optional)

These courgettes can be sliced into very thin spaghetti strips with a mandoline or vegetable peeler on the morning of a dinner party, and they take literally only a minute to cook in a few spoonfuls of hot olive oil, seasoned with salt and freshly ground black pepper. If you wish, and you know that all your guests are garlic lovers, add some very finely chopped garlic to the oil, too.

Jerusalem Artichoke, Turnip and Potato Purée

The sweetness of these combined root vegetables goes extremely well with lamb ragoût, or any lamb dish. The purée can be frozen.

Serves 8

1 small turnip, peeled and cut in chunks

8 potatoes, peeled and cut in half

1½ lb/675 g Jerusalem artichokes, peeled,
  and cut up if they are large

Salt, freshly ground black pepper and grated
  nutmeg

3 oz/84 g butter, cut in pieces

2 large egg yolks

Put all the peeled and cut-up vegetables together in a saucepan, cover them with cold water and bring the water to the boil. Add ½ tsp salt, and simmer till the vegetables are tender when a knife is stuck into them. Drain them really well, steam them off over heat, then mash well.

When you have mashed them as well as you can, beat the purée with an electric hand-held beater, beating in the pieces of butter and egg yolks. Season to taste with salt, pepper and nutmeg. Butter an oven-proof dish and pile the vegetable purée into it. Cool completely, cover, and freeze.

Thaw overnight, and reheat in a moderate oven, 350°F/180°C/Gas Mark 4, uncovered, for 20–30 minutes to serve.

Leek and Carrot Ragoût

This can be prepared well in advance without spoiling. It is good with all fish, meat or game.

Serves 8

2 oz/56 g butter or 3 tbsp oil (I use sunflower)

6 medium carrots, peeled and sliced
  diagonally into 2-inch/5-cm lengths

6 leeks, washed, trimmed and cut diagonally
  into 2-inch/5-cm lengths

½ tsp sugar

Salt and freshly ground black pepper

Melt the butter or heat the oil in a cast-iron casserole or similar pan, add the prepared carrots and let them cook for several minutes, stirring occasionally. Put the lid on the casserole and cook over gentle heat for 10 minutes. Then add the sliced leeks to the casserole, mix well into the carrots, season with sugar, salt and pepper, cover, and continue to cook either over gentle heat, in which case stir from time to time, or in a moderate oven, 350°F/180°C/Gas Mark 4, for 30–40 minutes. The ragoût will keep warm for an hour in a low oven.

Leeks Braised with Tomatoes

The leeks and tomatoes can be prepared in advance, so all you need to do when you wish to eat is gently cook them together. It complements plain grilled chicken, or lamb chops, and it is also good with grilled or baked fish.

Serves 6–8

12 medium leeks, washed and trimmed

2 tbsp oil

1 lb/450 g fresh ripe tomatoes, skinned, de-seeded and diced, or a 14-oz/390-g can, drained and chopped

Salt and freshly ground black pepper

Cut the leeks into pieces about 2 inches/5 cm long. Heat the oil in a heavy casserole which has a lid. Add the prepared leeks and cook over a moderate heat for 5 minutes, turning the leeks from time to time. Add the tomatoes and seasoning. Cover with the lid and cook gently for 10–15 minutes. Serve warm.

Steamed Leeks in White Sauce

I think that any vegetable in a creamy well-made white sauce makes a good accompaniment to roast meat, but leeks in white sauce are especially good with Roast Leg of Lamb and with Roast Rack of Lamb with a Herb Crust. They are also delicious with Steak, Kidney and Mushroom Pie, and with Game Pudding, too. It is so much better to steam the leeks rather than to simmer them in water, because, like onions, leeks hold so much water that when they are cooked in it, it is pretty well impossible to drain them. The water seeps out from between the layered leaves of leek and makes the sauce watery. By steaming them you avoid direct water contact with the leeks.

Serves 4–6

6 good medium leeks, each trimmed and washed well and sliced on the diagonal – it looks nicer – about 2 inches/5 cm thick

2 oz/56 g butter

2 oz/56 g flour

1 pint/570 ml milk

Salt and freshly ground black pepper

A grating of nutmeg

Steam the leeks till you can stick a fork in them and they feel tender.

Melt the butter and stir in the flour. Let it cook for a minute before stirring in the milk, adding a small amount at a time. You may find a wire whisk better than a wooden spoon for this. Stir till the sauce reaches simmering point. Let it simmer gently for a minute, then draw the pan off the heat and season with salt, pepper and nutmeg.

Put the cooked leeks into a warmed oven-proof dish and pour the sauce over them. Gently, so as not to break them up, stir the sauce into the leeks. Cover closely to prevent a skin forming if you want to keep the leeks in white sauce warm, which they do very successfully without spoiling. You can actually prepare them the day before and reheat them gently, stirring them occasionally, and my sister has even frozen leeks in white sauce.

Sautéed Onions in White Sauce

Onion sauce is a classic accompaniment for roast lamb, but I much prefer to enlarge the sauce into vegetable status. I don't like to boil the onions – like leeks, onions hold so much water within their layers that they are difficult to drain, resulting in a diluted white sauce. I also find that steaming onions, unless they are very small onions, is a very lengthy process. The result is that for onions in white sauce I sauté them gently in a thick-based pan with the lid on. I pay frequent attention to them, shaking the pan from time to time and checking that the onions within aren't browning too much. Stick a fork into the largest onion, or, if you have cut them in quarters, the largest piece of onion. When it is tender, they are cooked.

Like the leeks, onions in white sauce

reheat well and this dish, too, can be frozen. The sauce, on thawing, looks horribly separated but don't worry, as it reheats it all comes together satisfactorily.

Serves 6

2 oz/56 g butter + 1 tbsp sunflower oil, or dripping from the roast lamb tin

2 lb/900 g onions, skinned and cut in quarters, or left whole, depending which you prefer

For the sauce:

2 oz/56 g butter

2 oz/56 g flour

1 pint/570 ml milk

Salt and freshly ground black pepper

Freshly grated nutmeg

In a large heavy sauté pan, preferably non-stick, melt the butter and heat the oil or dripping together. Over gentle to moderate heat cook the onions, shaking the pan till they are soft – this is speedier if you cover the pan with a lid, but do watch the contents, so as not to burn them.

Melt the butter in a saucepan and stir in the flour. Let this cook for a minute and then gradually add the milk, stirring all the time till the sauce boils. You may find this easier to do with a wire whisk, called a 'batter' whisk – an invaluable piece of kitchen equipment. Let the sauce simmer briefly, then take the pan off the heat and season to your taste with salt, pepper and nutmeg.

Stir the cooked onions into the sauce and pour into a warm serving dish. Cover closely and keep the dish warm till you are ready to serve.

Parsnip Chips

Allow 2 average-sized parsnips per person, peel them and cut them into finger-thick pieces. Heat oil (I use sunflower) in a saucepan to a depth of about 3 inches/7.5 cm and deep-fry the parsnip chips in small amounts, till they are golden brown. Keep them warm on several thicknesses of kitchen paper on an ovenproof dish in a low oven.

Purée of Parsnips with Toasted Cashew Nuts

This is one of Godfrey's favourite vegetable dishes. It goes very well with any meat or fish dish. The toasted, slightly salted cashew nuts add a good contrasting crunch.

Serves 8

8 medium parsnips – a few more if they are
  small

3 oz/84 g butter, cut in pieces

Salt and freshly ground black pepper

Freshly grated nutmeg

2 oz/56 g cashew nuts

1 tsp salt

Peel the parsnips, trim them, and slice quite thickly. Cook them in boiling salted water till they are tender – test by sticking a knife into a fat piece to see if it is cooked. Drain very well, and steam over heat to remove excess moisture. Put the cooked parsnips into a food processor and whiz, adding the butter. Season with salt and freshly ground black pepper, and a couple of gratings of nutmeg.

Butter a vegetable dish and put the purée into it. Cover, and keep warm in a cool oven till you are ready to serve. Dry-fry the cashew nuts in a saucepan with the teaspoon of salt, shaking the pan till the nuts are fairly evenly golden brown. Sprinkle a few over each helping of purée, or sprinkle all the toasted nuts over the dish of parsnip purée if you intend to hand round the vegetables. But don't sprinkle the nuts over the parsnip mixture till just before you serve it, otherwise they soften in the purée.

New Potatoes with Dill

Dill is one of my favourite herbs, and it goes very well with new potatoes – and with salmon. I think that all herbs (with the exception of sage) go together very well, and mixing chopped dill with new potatoes makes a welcome change from mint.

Allow 3–4 average-sized new potatoes per person, more if they are small. Scrub them – in Scotland new potatoes are always cooked unpeeled, which is so much better than scraping off their tasty skins. Put them into a large saucepan with a teaspoonful of salt. Cover with boiling water from a kettle, and simmer till they are tender when stuck with a knife.

Drain well, steam dry, and turn into a warmed serving dish. Dot with bits of butter and sprinkle a tablespoon of chopped dill over them. Mix it into the potatoes, along with the melting butter. Cover the dish and keep it warm till you are ready to serve.

In a covered dish, these potatoes will keep warm in a low oven for over an hour without spoiling. In fact, this gives the flavour of the dill a really good chance to get into the potatoes.

Purée of Turnips with Cashew Nuts

I add a couple of potatoes to the turnip as it cooks, as otherwise the resulting purée can be rather wet. Alternatively, you can steam the turnip and leave out the potato. You could also substitute crisply grilled bacon, shredded, for the cashew nuts.

Serves 8

1 medium turnip, peeled and cut into
   2-inch/5-cm chunks
2 medium potatoes, peeled and cut in half
2 egg yolks
2 oz/56 g butter
Salt and freshly ground black pepper
About 5 gratings of nutmeg
1 oz/28 g butter
Salt
3 oz/84 g cashew nuts

Put the cut-up turnip and the potato halves into a saucepan and cover with cold, lightly salted water. Bring to the boil, simmer till the vegetables are tender, then drain well and steam over heat for several seconds to get rid of any excess moisture. Mash well, or put the turnip and potato into a food processor. Whiz or mash in the egg yolks,

the butter cut in bits, and the seasonings.

Butter an ovenproof dish, and put the purée into it. Cool, cover, and either freeze or store in the fridge.

Melt the butter, add a couple of pinches of salt, and fry the cashew nuts in it till they are golden brown. Drain on kitchen paper, and store in a jar or bowl, covered with clingfilm.

To serve, reheat the turnip purée in a moderate oven, 350°F/180°C/Gas Mark 4, for 30 minutes (or tip it into a saucepan and stir it over gentle heat). Scatter the cashew nuts over the surface before bringing the purée to the table.

Sautéed Turnips and Onions

The sweetness of the turnips and onions go together very well, and they complement duck ideally.

Serves 8

3 medium onions
2 oz/56 g butter
2 tbsp sunflower oil
1½–2 turnips, depending on their size
Salt and freshly ground black pepper

Skin and chop the onions. Melt the butter and heat the oil together in a casserole, add the onions and cook over a moderate heat for 5 minutes. Meanwhile, cut the skin off the turnips, and slice them into ½-inch/1-cm dice. Add the diced turnip to the onions in the casserole, season with salt and pepper, and cook over a moderate heat, stirring from time to time to prevent them from sticking and to make sure that they cook evenly. Stick a knife into a bit of turnip to test whether it is soft and cooked.

This vegetable dish can be cooked, then the casserole covered with a lid, and kept warm for up to an hour before serving. It really comes to no harm being kept warm for such a comparatively long time.

Root Vegetable Ragoût

This is most convenient for all winter eating – a vegetable dish that has to be prepared well in advance because of the length of the cooking time.

Serves 6

2 tbsp oil (I use sunflower)

1 large onion, skinned and sliced finely

2 leeks, trimmed, washed, and sliced in about 1-inch/2.5-cm chunks

3 carrots, trimmed, peeled, and cut in 1-inch/2.5-cm chunks

½ small turnip, skinned and cut in 2 inches/5 cm long and ½ inch/1 cm thick strips

2 parsnips, peeled and cut in thick strips

Salt and freshly ground black pepper

Heat the oil in a heavy casserole-type of flameproof dish. Add the onions, and cook them for about 5 minutes, then add the rest of the vegetables. Season with salt and pepper, and cook on top of the stove for about 15 minutes, stirring from time to time to prevent any sticking and burning.

Then cover the casserole with a lid and cook in a low-to-moderate oven, 325°F/160°C/Gas Mark 3, for about 1½ hours.

Salads

A salad used to mean a pitiful offering consisting of limp lettuce leaves, chunks of cucumber, skin and seeds included, and eggs so over-hardboiled that there was a grey aura around the yolk. Mercifully, these are changed days, and salads come in such wide-ranging variations that they are both exciting to eat, nutritious and convenient. They can form a first course, as in the recipes for Asparagus Salad with Saffron and Lemon or Lime Aïoli, or the Avocado Salad with Tomato Cream. They can be a main course, like the succulent Smoked Chicken and Mango Salad with Curried Mayonnaise, or the Ham and Parsley Jellied Salad. They can be perfect food for those who don't include meat in their diet, for example, the Three Bean, Chive and Tomato Salad with Egg Mayonnaise, or the Roast Vegetable Salad. They can also be an excellent substitute for a hot vegetable, throughout the year; a perfect example of this is the Fennel Salad with Lemon Dressing, which is so good with all fish or chicken dishes. During the winter months we can add a baked jacket potato to a salad such as the Beetroot and Orange Salad, or the Tomato, Watercress and Avocado Salad with its Crispy Bacon Dressing, to make a most delicious main course which is, at the same time, an effortless and delicious way to eat raw vegetables and fruit combinations – which we are supposed to eat all year round but which can fail to entice in cold weather.

There are several dressings and mayonnaises in the sauces chapter to team up with many of the salads in this chapter, and, too, in the chapter on breads and cakes you will find a range of tempting breads and herb or cheese scones which make the perfect accompaniment to many of the salads in this section.

I hope that there will be recipes in this chapter to make even the most reluctant salad-eater (and I am married to just such a one) able to enthuse.

Asparagus Salad with Saffron and Lemon or Lime Aïoli

•

Avocado Salad Dressed with Tomato Cream

•

Avocado and Bacon Salad, with Pinhead Oatmeal and Garlic Bread

•

Grated Beetroot and Carrot Salad

•

Beetroot and Orange Salad

•

Chicken, Ham and Cheese Salad

•

Smoked Chicken and Mango Salad with Curried Mayonnaise

•

Courgette, Celery and Apple Salad

•

Couscous Salad with Red Onions and Peppers, and Lemon and Thyme Dressing

Cucumber and Fennel Salad

•

Fennel Salad with Lemon Dressing

•

Ham and Parsley Jellied Salad

•

Spinach, Bacon, Avocado and Feta Cheese Salad

•

Tomato, Avocado, Orange and Sunflower-Seed Salad

•

Three Bean, Chive and Tomato Salad with Egg Mayonnaise

•

Tomato, Watercress and Avocado Salad with Crispy Bacon Dressing

•

Roast Vegetable Salad

Asparagus Salad with Saffron and Lemon or Lime Aïoli

I think there is something luxurious about a pile of asparagus, and nothing could be simpler to prepare than this salad. The asparagus can be steamed, and the saffron and lemon or lime aïoli can be made in advance. Then all you need to do is arrange the asparagus on a large serving plate and surround it with assorted lettuce leaves. But I do think that sieved hardboiled eggs mixed with snipped chives make a very good garnish – the tastes all go together so well, and it looks good, too.

For a main course allow a generous amount of asparagus per person, about ½ lb/225 g. Steam the asparagus till the thickest stalk is just tender when you push a fork into it. Immediately take the asparagus off the heat and run cold water briefly through it, to refresh the colour. Let it drain, and pat it gently with kitchen paper to absorb excess moisture.

For the garnish, hardboil 3 eggs (for 6 people), shell them, and chop them roughly. Put them into a sieve and push them through – the back of a ladle is best for this. Mix them, using a fork, with 2 tbsp snipped chives, and scatter this over the steamed asparagus in its serving dish with lettuce around.

Saffron and lemon or lime aïoli

Enough for 6 servings

1 whole egg + 1 egg yolk

1 tsp French mustard

½ tsp salt and a good grinding of black pepper

½ tsp sugar

2 garlic cloves, poached for 1 minute, then skinned

¼ pint/140 ml each of olive and sunflower oils, mixed

1 tbsp lemon or lime juice, and the grated rind of 1 lemon or lime

2 generous pinches of saffron threads, soaked in 1 tbsp wine vinegar

Put the egg, yolk, mustard, salt and pepper, sugar and poached garlic into a food processor and whiz, adding the oils drop by drop till you have a thick mayonnaise, then adding them in a steady trickle. In a small pan gently warm the vinegar and the lemon juice and rind with the saffron – the colour will seep from the strands of saffron. Cool this, and whiz it into the mayonnaise. Serve in a bowl to accompany the asparagus salad.

Avocado Salad Dressed with Tomato Cream

This salad has the dressing as a vital part of the dish. You really do need to use a red-skinned, mild onion for this – if you can't, you can substitute finely sliced spring onions. The dressing can be made up ahead if you keep it in a covered bowl in the fridge.

Serves 6

Assorted salad leaves

6 ripe avocados

Lemon juice

For the dressing:

8 tomatoes

¼ pint/140 ml creamy fromage frais

¼ pint/140 ml good mayonnaise

2 tsp very finely chopped red onion

2 tbsp finely chopped parsley

Salt and lots of freshly ground black pepper

Arrange torn-up salad leaves on six individual plates. Peel the avocados, halve them and remove the stones. Slice each one thinly and arrange in a fan shape on top of the leaves on each plate. Brush the slices with lemon juice.

Put the tomatoes into a bowl and stab each one with the point of a knife. Pour over boiling water to cover them, and leave till you see the skins beginning to curl back from the stabbed places – several seconds. Drain the water off the tomatoes and skin them. Cut each in half, scoop away their seeds, and chop the flesh into fine dice. Fold these into the fromage frais together with the mayonnaise, finely chopped red onion, parsley, and salt and pepper to your taste.

Spoon the dressing over the avocados on their plates and serve straight away. This looks and tastes good.

Avocado and Bacon Salad, with Pinhead Oatmeal and Garlic Bread

You can, of course, serve this with any bread or rolls which you happen to have in the freezer, but it is extra delicious with Pinhead Oatmeal and Garlic Bread.

The salad is simplicity itself, and surprisingly filling. Although you can use back bacon, I much prefer to use streaky bacon for this, grilled till crisp.

Serves 6

6 avocado pears

Lettuce leaves

Lemon juice

12 rashers smoked streaky bacon

Really good extra virgin olive oil

Pinhead Oatmeal and Garlic Bread
  (see page 371)

Pare off the skins of the avocado pears, halve them and flick out the stones. Slice the flesh into slivers and arrange these fan-shaped on top of lettuce leaves on six individual plates. Brush them well with lemon juice to help prevent discolouring. Grill the bacon till crisp, then crumble it and divide it between the six plates. Pour olive oil over each.

Serve with the bread of your choice, preferably warm.

Grated Beetroot and Carrot Salad

It is rare to come across grated raw beetroot, but it is so delicious and combines very well with grated carrots in a salad which makes for very good winter suppers. The only thing against grating beetroot is that, whilst peeling and grating, the beetroot inevitably dyes your fingers a handsome shade of burgundy, but as this washes off quite easily it seems a small deterrent. Dressed with a spoonful of French dressing, and served with baked jacket potatoes and Hummus (see page 52), this is a really good supper at any time of the year, but especially for winter months.

Serves 6

3 raw beetroots, each about the size of a
   cricket ball, peeled

5–6 medium carrots, peeled

2 oz/56 g raisins – optional

2 oz/56 g chopped walnuts – optional

French Dressing, with 1 tsp medium curry
   powder shaken in (see page 289)

Grate the peeled beetroot and carrots into a bowl, and stir in the raisins and chopped walnuts (if you are using them). Toss with the curry-flavoured French dressing – you can dress this salad well in advance, unlike a green salad. In fact I think it is nicest dressed well ahead, so that the grated vegetables marinate in the dressing.

Beetroot and Orange Salad

If the thought of grated raw beetroot doesn't appeal to you (although it is in fact delicious), boil the beetroot first. Then, when they are cooked, peel their skins off and cut them into matchsticks. This is good either with baked jacket potatoes and a mixed leaf salad, or with any cold meat or game, especially venison.

Serves 6–8

2 red onions, thinly sliced

2 lb/900 g raw young beetroots, peeled and
   coarsely grated

4 oranges, peeled and segmented

½ pint/285 ml sour cream

2 tsp horseradish sauce

Salt and freshly ground black pepper

3 tbsp snipped chives

Mix together the onions, grated beetroot and orange segments. Mix the soured cream, horseradish sauce and seasoning and stir into the salad just before serving. Sprinkle the top with snipped fresh chives.

Chicken, Ham and Cheese Salad

This is an ideal all-in-one main course. It is to be found on restaurant and hotel menus throughout America, where it is offered with a variety of dressings. The only thing it generally lacks is a contrasting texture, so for a crunch I like to add dry-roasted peanuts, or better still, dry-roasted cashew nuts.

Serves 6

6 oz/170 g cold cooked chicken
6 oz/170 g cooked ham, smoked if possible
6 oz/170 g hard cheese, Edam or Cheddar
1 large crisp lettuce
3 oz/84 g dry roasted peanuts or cashew nuts
4–6 tbsp salad dressing of your choice, either French Dressing (see page 289) or a garlic- and herb-flavoured mayonnaise

Cut the chicken, ham and cheese into fine strips, as evenly as possible. Tear the washed lettuce into bits, using your fingers, and arrange round the sides of a serving bowl.

Put the strips of chicken, ham and cheese in the middle of the bowl. Sprinkle the nuts over the whole bowl. Pour over the dressing, and gently toss the chicken, ham and cheese, trying not to break up the neatly cut strips.

Serve with warm brown rolls.

Smoked Chicken and Mango Salad with Curried Mayonnaise

In this recipe the smoked chicken is chopped into bite-sized pieces along with the mango flesh. The delicious mango taste is accentuated by the addition of lime juice, and then combined with the chicken and the curried mayonnaise. It makes an easy, delicious and slightly unusual chicken salad – a perfect main course for a summer party. I like to serve it with a rice salad – perhaps mixed with fresh peas and toasted flaked almonds.

Serves 6–8

2 smoked chickens, each weighing about 3–3½ lb/1.35–1.6 kg
4 mangoes, skinned
Juice of 1 lime
Curried Mayonnaise (see page 290)
Shredded lettuce and chopped parsley and chives, to garnish

Strip the chicken meat off the carcasses, chopping it into bite-sized pieces. Cut the mango flesh off the stones, chop it and mix it with the lime juice. Combine the chopped chicken and mango flesh. Fold the curried mayonnaise into the mixture and arrange the chicken salad on a serving plate, with the shredded lettuce around the sides and the chopped parsley and chives scattered over.

Courgette, Celery and Apple Salad

The dressing for this crunchy, refreshing salad can be made a day ahead, and kept in the refrigerator. If you like, the courgettes and celery can be steamed briefly and cooled, rather than being used raw in the salad. This is particularly good with cold, rich meats, such as cold roast duck, pork or ham.

Serves 6–8

2½ lb/1.125 kg small courgettes, thinly sliced
10 celery stalks, thinly sliced
4 large crisp green dessert apples, cored and chopped

For the dressing:

½ pint/285 ml Greek strained yoghurt

7 fl oz/200 ml lemon juice

3 tbsp finely grated lemon rind

2 tsp Dijon mustard

3 tbsp chopped thyme

Salt and freshly ground black pepper

Toss the ingredients for the salad together.

Make the dressing by blending the yoghurt, lemon juice and rind and mustard together. Stir in the thyme and seasoning. Pour the dressing over the salad and toss again lightly.

Couscous Salad with Red Onions and Peppers, and Lemon and Thyme Dressing

When cooking couscous I prefer not to buy the quick-cook stuff. As with rice, I find the flavour of the couscous which needs longer cooking so much better. I like to surround this salad with barely steamed sugar snap peas and thin beans – it looks pretty and tastes good all together.

Serves 6

4 tbsp olive oil – I use extra virgin olive oil

3 red-skinned onions, skinned and chopped
   quite small and neatly

12 oz/340 g couscous

2 garlic cloves, skinned and finely chopped
   (optional)

2 pints/1.1 litres water, nearly boiling

3 red peppers, skinned as described on pages
   210–11 and chopped quite neatly

For the dressing:

Finely grated rind of 1 lemon (well washed and
   dried before grating)

A sprig of thyme, its tiny leaves stripped off
   the stalks

A pinch of salt and a good grinding of black
   pepper

Juice of half a lemon

6 tbsp best extra virgin olive oil

Heat the olive oil in a wide heavy-based sauté pan and add the chopped onions. Cook for about 4–5 minutes, stirring from time to time, then stir in the couscous and garlic. Cook, again stirring occasionally, for a further 5 minutes, then pour in the near-boiling water. Stir as the couscous cooks over a moderate heat. The water will be absorbed. When the couscous is quite firm – as opposed to sloppy – stir in the chopped skinned red peppers and the ingredients of the dressing.

Let the couscous cool, forking the mixture through from time to time. It will absorb the flavours of the dressing as it cools. To serve, heap up the couscous on a large serving plate and surround it with barely steamed sugar snap peas, or with assorted lettuce leaves if you prefer.

Cucumber and Fennel Salad

This salad can be prepared entirely several hours before serving, and kept in a cool place. It is ideal for hot, summery days, as it is both cool to look at, and cool and crunchy to eat.

Serves 6–8

4 large cucumbers
Salt
2 heads of fennel, cut into fine shreds
2 bunches of spring onions, finely chopped
1½ pints/850 ml natural yoghurt
Salt and pepper

Thinly peel the cucumbers, cut them in half lengthways and scoop out the seeds. Cut the cucumber halves crossways into slices about ¼ inch/5 mm thick. Put the slices into a large mixing bowl and sprinkle lightly with salt. Cover and leave to stand for at least 1 hour (the salt extracts the excess water, and crisps the cucumber). Rinse the cucumber and drain well in a colander or pat dry with absorbent kitchen paper.

Put the cucumber, fennel and chopped spring onions into a large salad bowl. Add the yoghurt and seasoning. Stir together until well mixed. Cover the salad and refrigerate until ready to serve. It is good with cold fish dishes, such as fish in dill mayonnaise or fish in creamy mayonnaise. But it is also good by itself, with jacket potatoes.

Fennel Salad with Lemon Dressing

This is a deliciously crunchy salad. The lemony dressing complements perfectly the aniseed flavour of the fennel. I like to decorate this salad with fronds from the top of the fennel.

Prepare the salad several hours in

advance. It is particularly good with fish, whether hot or cold, as a side salad.

Serves 6–8

6 large fennel bulbs

For the dressing:

1 tsp sugar
½ tsp salt
Freshly ground black pepper
Finely grated rind and juice of 1 lemon
3 tbsp sunflower or olive oil

Put all the dressing ingredients in a screw-topped jar and shake well. Pour the dressing into a mixing bowl.

Trim any brown outside bits and feathery fronds off the fennel. Cut each bulb into sticks, about ¼ inch/5 mm thick and 2 inches/5 cm long. Toss the sticks of fennel in the dressing, then arrange on a serving plate. Decorate the salad with feathery fronds of the fennel for an attractive garnish.

Ham and Parsley Jellied Salad

I always think that parsley is a greatly underrated herb, too often used only as garnish. I love all parsley, but flat-leafed parsley has by far the best flavour. This salad is good served with a tomato and basil salad and a green salad, and, if you like – I always do like – warm bread. It has to be made a day in advance to let the jelly set.

Serves 4–6

1½ lb/675 g ham, trimmed of gristle and
excess

    fat before weighing, then cut into cubes
about ½ inch/1 cm thick – the better the
ham, either roast or boiled, the better this
salad will be

3 good tbsp chopped parsley, preferably the
flat-leafed type

1 pint/570 ml good vegetable or ham stock,
either freshly made or made using a cube
containing no additives – these are made by
either Kallo or Friggs

2 sachets of gelatine (1 oz/28 g)

½ pint/285 ml dry white wine – if you prefer to
leave out the wine just use an extra ½ pint/
285 ml of stock

Plenty of freshly ground black pepper

Salt if you think it necessary, but taste first –
need or not will depend on how salty your
ham is

Mix together the cubed ham and the
chopped parsley. In a small saucepan heat ½
pint/285 ml of the stock and sprinkle in the
gelatine, shaking the pan gently till it dissolves completely. Then stir this into the rest
of the stock and wine. Season with pepper,
and salt if needed.

Put the ham and parsley into a 2½-
pint/1.5-litre ring mould, or a loaf or terrine
tin, and carefully pour in the stock and gelatine. As it sets, fork it through once or twice
to keep the ham and parsley evenly distributed through the setting jelly. When set,
unmould and surround with lettuce.

Spinach, Bacon, Avocado and Feta Cheese Salad

*I know that the combination of spinach
and avocado is an odd one, but if you add
chopped crisply cooked bacon, and tiny
cubes of feta cheese as well, you have a
main course salad which is sustaining to eat
as well as being delicious – and very good
for you.*

*All that you need besides this salad is
warm bread, either Granary Bread or the
Black Olive, Sun-Dried Tomato and Garlic
Bread on page 368. Use the best spinach
you can find – if you don't grow your own,
that is. Be sparing with the salt in the
French dressing for this, or do as I do and
just pour good olive oil over the salad,
because both the bacon and the feta cheese
are quite salty.*

Serves 6

4 ripe avocado pears

8 oz/225 g feta cheese, cut into small cubes

10 rashers of smoked streaky bacon, grilled
till crisp, then broken into bits

A 2-lb/900-g bag of small spinach leaves, torn
into bits (as soon as they are tossed in oil
they wilt down)

Either French Dressing (see page 289), or
about 4 tbsp good olive oil

Cut each avocado in half and flick out their
stones with the tip of a knife. Slice down
their skins and peel them off – this will be
easy provided the avocados are ripe – and
chop them into cubes. Mix together the
avocado, feta, bacon and spinach leaves
with either the French dressing or just the

olive oil, and serve. Don't dress the salad till just before you eat it, and if you chop the avocados ahead by much more than half an hour, toss them in a tablespoon or two of lemon juice.

Tomato, Avocado, Orange and Sunflower-Seed Salad

This salad both looks pretty, being very colourful, and tastes good. The toasted sunflower-seeds add a slightly contrasting texture, and the port vinaigrette is just a bit different from the more usual dressing. It is very good with cold poultry or game, especially venison, grouse or pheasant.

Serves 6–8

For the salad:

1 head of lettuce, or a combination, such as lambs' lettuce or lollo rosso sliced finely into shreds

6 tomatoes, skinned, de-seeded and halved, and each half cut in 4 wedges

2 oranges, peeled with a serrated knife, and each cut in segments

2 avocados, flesh chopped and tossed in lemon juice

1 tbsp sunflower-seeds, toasted till golden brown in a dry saucepan over moderate heat

For the port vinaigrette:
4 fl oz/112 ml sunflower oil

Half a medium onion, skinned and chopped finely

½ tbsp honey

A pinch of salt

Freshly ground black pepper

½ tbsp lemon juice

3 tbsp port

2 tsp red wine vinegar

Make the port vinaigrette first. Put the oil in a saucepan and add the finely chopped onions. Gently simmer for about 5 minutes.

In a bowl, mix together the honey, salt and pepper, lemon juice, port and vinegar, and then mix in the hot oil and onions. Cool, then store in a jar in the fridge till required.

Mix all the salad ingredients together in a large bowl and toss gently with the vinaigrette before serving.

Three Bean, Chive and Tomato Salad with Egg Mayonnaise

This is a yummy salad. Luckily all our family love it. I first ate something similar in the Laigh Coffee House in Edinburgh one lunch-time, and thought I could concoct something along the same lines, but without the onion and with some tomato. The chives add enough flavour of the onion family for me, without the rather horrid repetitiveness that raw onion seems to give, and not only to me!

Serves 6

6 tomatoes, skinned

1 lb/450 g fresh broad beans, weighed when

shelled, steamed till just tender – the
smaller they are, the nicer they will be

1 15-oz/400-g tin of kidney beans, drained of
their liquid, rinsed under cold water and
patted dry with kitchen paper

¾ lb/340 g 'fine' beans, or French beans, cut
in 1-inch/2.5-cm lengths and steamed till
tender – a brief steaming, refresh under
cold water and pat dry

2 tbsp snipped chives

3–4 tbsp French Dressing (see page 289)

For the egg mayonnaise:

8 hardboiled eggs, shelled and chopped

6 tbsp good mayonnaise, either bought or
homemade – see page 290

Chopped parsley and snipped chives
(optional)

Cut each skinned tomato in half and scoop away the seeds. Chop the tomatoes. Mix together the three types of beans, the chives, tomatoes and French dressing – do this several hours in advance if it is more convenient for you.

Mix together the chopped eggs and mayonnaise, and the herbs if you like.

Arrange the bean salad around a mound of the egg mayonnaise – it looks more attractive than having two separate bowls. Serve with warm bread and, if you like, with salad leaves.

Tomato, Watercress and Avocado Salad with Crispy Bacon Dressing

This salad, padded out with shredded lettuce, is the ace favourite choice for lunch during the summer holidays with all the members of our family. Whenever I am racking my brains and ask what shall we have for lunch, the unanimous answer is tomato, watercress and avocado salad, with the bacon dressing. I really think they would eat it every day for a week if I let them! I like to serve it with warm brown rolls, or the granary bread which we make each day for our guests here at Kinloch.

Serves 6–8

For the salad:

6 good-sized tomatoes, skinned (for guests,
if not for family!) and cut into wedges

4 handfuls of watercress, the thicker stalks
removed and the watercress torn

3 avocados, peeled and cut into ½-inch/1-cm
chunks

For the dressing:

2 tsp mustard powder

½ tsp salt

½ tsp caster sugar

4 tbsp olive oil

1 tbsp wine vinegar (or more – to taste)

6 rashers of bacon, cooked until crisp, cooled
on absorbent kitchen towels, then broken
into bits

In a bowl, mix together the tomato wedges, torn watercress and chunks of avocado. Mix together the first four ingredients for the dressing, then add wine vinegar until the dressing is sharp enough for your taste. Add the crumbled bacon. Pour the dressing over the salad and toss carefully. To serve, divide between six to eight serving plates.

Roast Vegetable Salad

This is a warm salad which is very good with either Black Olive, Sun-Dried Tomato and Garlic Bread on page 368 or Lemon, Thyme and Garlic Bread on page 370. The vegetables need careful watching as they roast – there is a fine line between roasting and burning. A touch of charring here and there is perfectly acceptable, but any over-all surface blackening doesn't make for good eating! Don't be fooled by recipes which tell you to wrap vegetables for 'roasting' in foil – roasting means that the heat should be direct. When the vegetables are foil-wrapped they steam within their parcel. This is simple, but delicious.

Serves 6

6 small red-skinned onions, or 3 larger ones
6 courgettes, as similar in size as possible
6 red peppers
3 yellow peppers
3 aubergines
6 garlic cloves, skinned
8 tbsp very good olive oil
3 tsp Balsamic vinegar
Salt and freshly ground black pepper
Assorted salad leaves

Line a roasting tin with foil – try not to mass the vegetables in the roasting tin, they need space for their roasting. Skin the onions and, if using the large ones, quarter them. Cut the ends off the courgettes and slice each in quarters lengthways. Cut each pepper in half and put under a red-hot grill till the skins char in black blisters, then put the pepper halves into a large polythene bag for 10 minutes; their skins should then peel off easily. Slice each pepper into fat strips. Cut both ends off the aubergines, and cut each in half lengthways. Cut each half in four strips. Chop the skinned garlic roughly.

Mix all the vegetables with olive oil, so each is well coated. Put them on the foil in a hot oven, 425°F/220°C/Gas Mark 7, for 10 minutes. Turn them over and carefully baste with olive oil and replace them in the oven for a further 10 minutes. Stick a fork in a piece of aubergine to test for tenderness – it should feel soft. If it is, take the roasting tin out of the oven. If it isn't, give the vegetables a further 5 minutes' cooking time.

When you take the vegetables out of the oven, carefully stir in amongst them the Balsamic vinegar, salt and pepper. Distribute the roast vegetables on to six large warmed plates, on which you have arranged a bed of assorted lettuce leaves, and spoon over each plateful any olive oil and vegetable juices from the foil.

Pasta and Rice

As with most families throughout Britain, we eat pasta or rice-based main courses several times a week. These dishes can be everyday ones for family eating, such as the straightforward Mushroom Risotto, or they can be 'dressed up' for informal entertaining. The simple risotto can be transformed into such a dish by adding a mixture of wild mushrooms, dried when the natural product is out of season or otherwise unobtainable (we are lucky to have woods beside our house so full of a variety of wild mushrooms, chanterelles in particular, that you positively trip over them), fresh asparagus and saffron.

I don't think I could live without pasta. It is the family favourite standby, with a variety of sauces, mostly simple, some a bit more elegant, and these are the recipes you will find in this chapter. It grieves me that a dish like Lasagne has been so bastardized by the purveyors of the worst type of fast food. A true lasagne is a most delicious dish, and my version of the classic Beef Lasagne is in this chapter, along with several variations, including one or two (you can omit the crispy bacon topping from Leek and Cheese Lasagne) for non-meat eaters. I like to include bacon and chicken livers in the traditional meat sauce.

As a family we are also passionate rice eaters. Risotto has become almost a rival to pasta, not only in our family but generally. It is even possible to buy a choice of risotto rices on many supermarket shelves, where it would have meant a trip to a specialist Italian shop or a good delicatessen to find Arborio rice until as recently as four or five years ago. These days I have seen Carnaroli rice, the larger-grained risotto rice, for sale in three main supermarkets. The other chief risotto rice, Vialone Nonno, I can only buy in Valvona and Crolla, my most favourite of all food shops in Edinburgh.

When it comes to rice other than for risotto, I use Basmati rice. I love it for its flavour. I used to use brown rice, but I so much prefer Basmati that I haven't cooked brown rice now for years – but this is just a matter of my personal taste. At cooking demonstrations I find myself making the point repeatedly that taste is very individual, so if you prefer brown rice to Basmati, substitute it in all the recipes in this chapter where I recommend Basmati.

Apart from an accompanying salad, I think that all the recipes here are for one-dish main courses, whether hot or cold. And many of the recipes are eminently suitable for those who don't include meat in their diet.

Pasta with Asparagus, Cream and Crispy
Bacon Sauce

·

Pasta with Cheese and Crispy Bacon

·

Pasta with Creamy Mushroom and
Garlic Sauce

·

Pasta with Garlic, Olive Oil and Black Olives

·

Pasta with Stilton Cheese and Walnuts

·

Pasta with Smoked Cod or Haddock
and Cheese

·

Pasta with Smoked Haddock and Leeks

·

Pasta with Tunafish and Chives

·

Beef Lasagne

Chicken, Smoked Bacon and
Mushroom Lasagne

·

Leek and Cheese Lasagne with Crispy
Bacon Topping

·

Tomato, Spinach and Cheese Lasagne

·

Mushroom Risotto

·

Mushroom and Broccoli Risotto

·

Spinach and Mushroom Risotto

·

Kedgeree

·

Rice Salad

·

Peppered Smoked Mackerel and Rice Salad

Pasta with Asparagus, Cream and Crispy Bacon Sauce

This is one of those special occasion dishes which take about 5 minutes to prepare and another 5 minutes to put together. If you are making it for non-meat eaters you obviously won't want to include the bacon, so I suggest chopped cashew nuts which have been fried in a small amount of butter with a pinch or two of salt. This gives a good contrasting crunchy texture, as well as a complementary taste.

Which pasta you use depends on you. I like to make this dish using short pasta, that is, not spaghetti or tagliatelle, but shell shapes or bows. You only need a salad to go with it.

Serves 6

1 lb/450 g asparagus

About 18 oz/500 g pasta, preferably bow or shell shapes

¾ pint/420 ml single cream

Freshly ground black pepper (the bacon should add enough saltiness)

A grating of nutmeg

6 rashers of smoked streaky bacon, grilled till crisp, then broken into small bits

1–2 tbsp chopped parsley and snipped chives, mixed

Apart from the pasta, the other ingredients can be cooked or prepared in advance, so all you need to do before the meal is cook the pasta and add the ready prepared ingredients.

Prepare the asparagus by chopping off and throwing away the tough ends, and cutting it into pieces about 1 inch/2.5 cm long. Steam the pieces until just tender, but don't undercook it – I think that undercooked asparagus has a rather revolting taste.

Cook the pasta in plenty of boiling salted water or, better still, in vegetable or chicken stock. When it is just tender (stick a clean thumbnail into a piece to test it), drain it, return it to the pan, and add the steamed asparagus, single cream, pepper and nutmeg. Just before serving, stir in the chopped bacon, parsley and chives.

Serve immediately! If you like, have a bowl of freshly grated Parmesan cheese to hand around.

Pasta with Cheese and Crispy Bacon

This is a more interesting version of that old stand-by, macaroni cheese. A cheese sauce can be made very much more definite in its flavour by adding mustard to the roux, and balsamic vinegar to the sauce, neither of which will in any way be identifiable. The crispy bacon crumbled into the sauce at the last minute makes a good contrast in flavour and a crunch in texture. Serve with a mixed-leaf green salad.

Serves 6

2 oz/56 g butter

1 onion, skinned and finely chopped

2 oz/56 g flour less 2 tsp

2 tsp mustard powder

1¼ pint/710 ml milk

4 oz/112 g good Cheddar cheese, grated

2 tsp Balsamic vinegar

Salt and freshly ground black pepper

A grating of nutmeg

12 oz/340 g pasta – I often use pasta shells
    when making this (more if you are feeding
    teenagers with large appetites, say
    18 oz/500 g)

1 tbsp olive oil

6 rashers of streaky bacon, grilled till crisp,
    then broken into bits as small as you can

Melt the butter and sauté the chopped onion in it till it is very soft and just beginning to turn golden. Stir in the flour and mustard. Let this cook for a minute, then gradually add the milk, stirring all the time till the sauce boils. Draw the pan off the heat and stir in the cheese, balsamic vinegar, salt, pepper and nutmeg to your taste. Stir till the cheese melts. Cover closely with a dampened piece of baking parchment, to prevent a skin forming.

Meanwhile, cook the pasta in plenty of boiling salted water, till when you stick your – clean – thumbnail into a piece of pasta it feels tender. This is the stage known as al dente – overcooked pasta is slimy. Drain the pasta, then toss it in a tablespoon of olive oil, which will help prevent it from sticking together.

Serve as immediately as you can, stirring the crispy bacon through the sauce just before spooning it over each helping of pasta. Alternatively, you can toss the pasta and sauce together before serving it on to the plates. The hot pasta will reheat the sauce when it is stirred into it.

Pasta with Creamy Mushroom and Garlic Sauce

As our family would happily choose pasta (or rice) seven days a week, this sauce turns pasta into a dish fit for a special occasion. It is invariably chosen by one or other of our offspring for a birthday supper, and it's simplicity itself to make as well as tasting so good – all the tastes, I, too, love. All it needs to go with it is a good mixed green salad.

Serves 6

2 oz/56 g butter + 1 tbsp sunflower oil

1 lb/450 g mushrooms, wiped, stalks cut off
    level with the caps, and the mushrooms
    chopped

2 garlic cloves, skinned and finely chopped

6 rashers smoked bacon, grilled till just
    beginning to crisp, then chopped into bits
    (optional)

Salt and freshly ground black pepper

18 oz/500 g dried pasta per person

½ pint/285 ml single cream

2 tbsp finely chopped parsley

Heat the oil and melt the butter in a wide saucepan and cook the mushrooms and garlic together, stirring over a high heat, till the mushrooms are almost crisp. Stir the chopped cooked bacon in with the mushrooms if you are including it, and season with a pinch of salt and lots of freshly ground black pepper.

Meanwhile, cook the pasta in a pan with plenty of boiling salted water, cooking it till when you push a – clean – thumbnail into a bit it is just tender, no more. Drain it, and pour in the cream. Stir in the mushrooms and garlic (and bacon) and the chopped parsley, and serve immediately.

Pasta with Garlic, Olive Oil and Black Olives

Provided you have pasta in the store cupboard, and olive oil, olives and garlic, and some grated fresh Parmesan cheese in the freezer, this is a real store-cupboard lunch or supper which tastes delicious if you, like me, have distinctly Mediterranean tastes. The Parmesan will thaw during the time it takes for the water to boil to cook the pasta, and also during this time you can be chopping the garlic finely and stoning and cutting in half the olives. If you should happen to grow parsley, or have a bunch in the fridge, a few tablespoons of fairly coarsely chopped parsley adds even more taste, but if not, don't worry.

Serves 6

About 18 oz/500 g pasta – I like spaghetti best for this, for no real reason except that it is my preference

As much extra virgin olive oil as you like, but at least ¼ pint/140 ml

2–3 garlic cloves, skinned and very finely chopped

As many black olives as you like, preferably the best, stoned and cut in half or quarters

Finely chopped parsley, if you have some

Lots of freshly ground black pepper

Boil the pasta in plenty of salted water till it is just tender but with a slight bite to it – al dente.

Drain the cooked pasta well, then put it back into the pan in which it was cooked and immediately stir in the olive oil, chopped garlic, chopped olives and parsley – if you are using it – and grind in lots of black pepper. Stir all together well, and eat immediately, with a bowl of freshly grated Parmesan cheese.

Pasta with Stilton Cheese and Walnuts

This recipe is quick and simple to make for one person, and combines the creamy sharpness of the Stilton (you can substitute any other type of blue cheese with the exception of Danish Blue, which has all the sharpness but none of the creaminess and smells like a week-old nappy bucket) with the crunch of the walnuts.

It really is worthwhile dry-frying the chopped walnuts first, because it freshens up their taste no end. All nuts tend to become stale as they sit on our shelves, no matter how airtight their containers, but I think walnuts deteriorate much more noticeably than others. The sliced leeks are perfect, tastewise, with both the walnuts and the Stilton. Use any shape of pasta you choose, and I like to eat a green salad with this.

Serves 1

About 3 oz/84 g pasta, fresh or dried, boiled
  in plenty of salty water till you can push
  your – clean – thumbnail into a bit; beware
  of overcooking, which renders pasta slimy

1 tbsp olive oil

1 medium leek, washed, trimmed and thinly
  sliced

1 garlic clove, skinned and very finely
  chopped

2 oz/56 g walnuts, chopped, and dry-fried in a
  saucepan for about 5 minutes

Freshly ground black pepper

2–3 oz/56–84 g Stilton cheese, crumbled

Heat the oil and cook the sliced leek and
garlic till the leek is quite soft – about 3–4
minutes. Add the chopped walnuts and the
pepper. Mix this into the drained cooked
pasta with the crumbled Stilton and eat
immediately.

Pasta with Smoked Cod or Haddock and Cheese

*This is just a variation on a fish pie (one of
my favourite dishes) which came to mind
(and then to table) when our third
daughter, Meriel, went through a phase of
not liking potato-topped pies. It's rather
good, and very simple to make.*

*You can use either smoked cod or
smoked haddock, but I prefer to use cod
because of the large and juicy flakes of fish.
It's good with a tomato salad. I use pasta
shells or bows for this dish.*

Serves 6

2 lb/900 g smoked haddock or cod – feel for
  bones with your fingers, and cut them out of
  the fish before cooking

2 pints/1.1 litres milk

2 oz/56 g butter

1 onion, skinned and finely chopped

2 oz/56 g flour

2 pints/1.1 litres of the milk in which the fish
  cooked

6 oz/170 g Cheddar cheese, grated

Freshly ground black pepper

12 oz/340 g pasta

2 tbsp finely chopped parsley

Put the fish into a saucepan with the milk
and over a moderate heat, bring it to a
gentle simmer. Take the pan off the heat and
let the fish cool in the milk. Then strain the
milk into a jug and flake the fish, removing
all skin.

Melt the butter in a saucepan and cook
the finely chopped onion in the butter till the
onion is soft and transparent-looking. Stir in
the flour, cook for a minute, then gradually
stir in the strained fish milk, stirring all the
time till the sauce boils. Take the pan off the
heat, stir in about two-thirds of the grated
cheese, and season with black pepper. Stir in
the flaked fish.

Meanwhile, cook the pasta in plenty of
boiling salted water till soft – about 8
minutes. Drain, and mix into the smoked
fish and cheesy sauce. Pour into a buttered
pie dish and scatter the rest of the grated
cheese over the top. Grill till the cheese has
melted, then scatter the chopped parsley
over, and serve.

Pasta with Smoked Haddock and Leeks

Leeks and smoked fish go together awfully well. Bound together in a sauce made with milk in which the fish cooked, this makes a really good sauce for pasta. Use any small-shaped (as opposed to long, like spaghetti or fettuccine) pasta, such as shells or bows, for this dish. This is good served with a tomato and basil salad.

Serves 6

1 lb/450 g smoked haddock, the undyed version

1 pint/570 ml milk

2 oz/56 g butter

4 leeks, washed well, trimmed and sliced
   thinly

2 oz/56 g flour

Freshly ground black pepper and, if you like,
   a grating of nutmeg – the fish will have
   enough saltiness for most people's tastes

12 oz/340 g pasta (or more, depending on
   appetites)

Feel the fish all over and remove any bones. Cut it into smallish pieces and put it into a saucepan with the milk. Over a moderate heat, heat the milk till a skin forms, then take the pan off the heat and let the fish cool in the milk.

Meanwhile, in another saucepan melt the butter. Add the sliced leeks and cook till they are really soft. Then stir in the flour, let it cook for a minute, then gradually add the strained fish milk, stirring till the sauce boils. Draw the pan off the heat, season with pepper and nutmeg, and stir in the fish. Cover closely with dampened baking parchment, to prevent a skin forming.

Cook the pasta in plenty of boiling salted water till a piece of pasta feels just tender when you stick your – clean – thumbnail into it. Drain well and mix in the sauce. Serve as soon as you can, to avoid the pasta cooking further in the hot sauce.

Pasta with Tunafish and Chives

This is a quick and easy pasta sauce that tastes delicious. It can be made by child or adult – our children would eat tunafish with anything, so this is often made by them. If you can't lay your hands on chives, you can substitute snipped top ends of spring onions.

Serves 6

2 oz/56 g butter

1 tbsp flour

1½ pints/850 ml milk, or, if you like,
   1 pint/570 ml milk and ½ pint/285 ml single
   cream

Salt and freshly ground black pepper

Two 6½-oz/185-g tins tunafish, drained of oil
   or brine and flaked

3 oz/84 g Cheddar cheese, grated

2 tbsp snipped chives

18 oz/500 g pasta

2 tbsp sunflower oil, or olive oil

Melt the butter in a saucepan and stir in the flour. Cook for a minute, then gradually add the milk, a little at a time, stirring continuously. If you use a wire whisk to do this you will get a really smooth sauce without the danger of lumps forming. Once the sauce boils it is impossible to break down any lumps, so take care when stirring and adding the milk not to let this happen. Once all the milk is added let the sauce boil, still stirring, and then take the pan off the heat. Don't worry, the sauce will be runny. Season with salt and pepper, and stir in the flaked drained tunafish and the grated cheese. Stir in the chives.

Boil the pasta in a large saucepan with plenty of salted boiling water. Boil till you can stick the prongs of a fork into a bit of pasta. Then drain, put it back in its pan and toss it with a couple of tablespoons of either sunflower or olive oil.

Serve immediately, with a ladleful of sauce spooned on to each helping of pasta.

Beef Lasagne

Lasagne is a whole meal in one dish, completed by a green salad. It freezes beautifully.

Serves 6–8

1 lb/450 g pre-cooked lasagne

2 rounded tbsp grated Lancashire cheese

For the meat sauce:

6 tbsp olive or sunflower seed oil

1½ lb/675 g minced beef

8 oz/225 g chicken livers, picked over and
   roughly chopped

4 rashers unsmoked bacon, cut into thin
   slices

1 large onion, peeled and very finely chopped

1 or 2 (depends on your taste) garlic cloves,
   peeled and very finely chopped

2 carrots, peeled and finely diced

1 stick of celery, finely sliced (optional)

3 rounded tbsp tomato purée

Salt and freshly ground black pepper

½ rounded tsp dried basil

½ rounded tsp sugar

½ pint/285 ml red wine

½ pint/285 ml stock, or omit stock and use
   1 pint/570 ml wine

For the cheese sauce:

2 oz/56 g butter

2 oz/56 g plain flour

2 rounded tsp mustard powder

2 pints/1.1 litres milk

4 oz/112 g Lancashire cheese, grated

Salt and freshly ground black pepper

A little freshly grated nutmeg

To make the meat sauce, heat the oil in a saucepan and brown the minced beef, bit by bit, until it is all really well browned. Keep it warm in a separate dish. Put the chicken livers in the hot oil until they are sealed all over – about 2 minutes. Remove, and add them to the minced beef.

Lower the heat a bit and add the bacon, onion, garlic, carrots and celery, and cook gently for about 10 minutes, until the onion looks transparent. Stir in the tomato purée, salt and pepper, basil and sugar, the red wine and the stock. Replace the meat and chicken livers, and partially cover the pan with a lid. Cook, with the mixture barely simmering, for an hour or so. The sauce should then be thick, and smell delicious.

To make the cheese sauce, melt the butter in a saucepan and stir in the flour and mustard. Cook over gentle heat for 2–3 minutes, stirring, then gradually add the milk, stirring all the time until the sauce boils. Simmer for 1 minute then draw the saucepan off the heat and stir in three-quarters of the grated cheese, salt, pepper and nutmeg. Stir until the cheese is melted. The sauce should be fairly liquid: the pasta needs the liquid to absorb as it cooks.

In a large, shallow, ovenproof dish, layer the meat mixture, the pasta and the cheese sauce until all is used up, ending with a layer of cheese sauce. Sprinkle the top with the remaining grated cheese.

Bake in a moderate oven, 350°F/180°C/ Gas Mark 4, for 45 minutes, uncovered. Stick a knife into the centre – if it 'feels' soft, the lasagne is cooked.

Chicken, Smoked Bacon and Mushroom Lasagne

In this recipe I whiz the raw chicken with the streaky bacon in a food processor. This is best done a small amount at a time. It is made into a sauce with mushrooms and garlic, and it does seem to go down very well with children as well as adults.

It needs only a crunchy salad of shredded cabbage and grated carrots, or a plain green salad, to go with it.

Serves 6

8 chicken breasts

8 rashers of smoked streaky bacon

2 oz/56 g butter and 2 tbsp sunflower oil

1 onion, skinned and finely chopped

1–2 garlic cloves, skinned and finely chopped

½ lb/225 g mushrooms, wiped and chopped

2 oz/56 g flour

2 pints/1.1 litres milk

Salt and freshly ground black pepper

12 sheets of green pre-cooked lasagne (the green makes the result look more interesting)

3 oz/84 g Cheddar cheese, grated

Slice the chicken into bits, removing any skin and bone. Put the bits into the food processor with the bacon, cut into 1-inch/2.5-cm lengths. Whiz together briefly to just chop them, rather than to pulverize.

Heat the oil and melt the butter together in a wide saucepan – a sauté pan – and brown the chicken and bacon mixture, mashing it with a wooden spoon to break it up. As it browns, remove it to a dish to keep warm. Then cook the chopped onion and the garlic, till the onion is soft and just beginning to turn colour. Add the mushrooms, and almost immediately stir in the flour. Gradually add the milk, stirring all the time till the sauce boils. Take the pan off the heat, stir in the browned chicken and bacon mixture, and season with salt and pepper.

Spoon some of this sauce over the base of

Tomato, Avocado, Orange and ▶
Sunflower-Seed Salad, page 243

a buttered ovenproof dish. Cover with a layer of pasta, then cover this with more sauce. Continue layering up the pasta and sauce, ending with sauce. The sauce will be rather runny but don't worry – the pasta absorbs a lot of liquid as it cooks. Scatter the grated cheese over the surface.

Bake in a moderate oven, 350°F/ 180°C/Gas Mark 4, for about 30 minutes, till when you stick a fork in the middle the pasta feels soft. The cheese will be golden brown. Serve as soon as possible.

Leek and Cheese Lasagne with Crispy Bacon Topping

The leeks and cheese go together so well, and the crispy bacon is sprinkled over the surface doubling up both as a garnish and a different texture and also as a taste enhancer. Another meal in one dish, my ideal, and a dish which can be put together easily by a fairly competent child – by this I mean one that will wash up properly after the making is finished!

Serves 6

2 oz/56 g butter + 2 tbsp sunflower oil

12 medium to large leeks, each washed well and trimmed, and sliced neatly into ¼-inch/0.5-cm bits

1 garlic clove, skinned and finely chopped

2 oz/56 g flour

2 pints/1.1 litres milk

8 oz/225 g Cheddar cheese, grated – set aside about a third of this

Salt and freshly ground black pepper

A grating of nutmeg

About 12 sheets of lasagne – I like to use the green type for this

12 rashers of smoked streaky bacon, grilled till crisp, then broken up

Butter a shallow ovenproof dish. Melt the butter in a saucepan and add the sunflower oil. Cook the sliced leeks in this till they are really soft. This doesn't take very long if you use a fairly wide pan – a sauté pan is ideal. Then add the chopped garlic and stir in the flour. Cook for a minute, then gradually add the milk, stirring continuously till the sauce boils. The sauce will be quite runny, but it is meant to be – the pasta absorbs a lot of milk as it cooks.

When the sauce has boiled, take the pan off the heat, stir in two-thirds of the grated cheese, and season with salt, pepper and nutmeg. Spoon some of the sauce over the base of the dish. Layer up the pasta and sauce, ending with the sauce. Sprinkle the rest of the grated cheese over the surface, and bake in a moderate oven, 350°F/ 180°C/Gas Mark 4, for about 25–30 minutes, till the pasta feels soft when you stick a fork in it. The cheese on top should be golden brown.

Sprinkle the broken-up bacon evenly over the surface before serving.

◀ Roast Vegetable Salad
page 245

Tomato, Spinach and Cheese Lasagne

This is delicious, and it freezes well. The lasagne which doesn't need pre-boiling is such a boon, but you do have to remember not to make the sauces too thick, otherwise you end up with a very stodgy dish. The lasagne needs to be able to absorb a lot of liquid as it cooks.

Serves 8

12 oz/340 g green lasagne (the sort you do not
   need to pre-boil)

For the tomato sauce:

3 tbsp olive oil

1 onion, skinned and chopped finely

1 stick of celery, washed and sliced very finely

1 carrot, peeled and chopped finely

1 garlic clove, skinned and chopped finely

A 15-oz/420-g tin of tomatoes, liquidized

¼ pint/140 ml red wine

½ tsp sugar

Salt and freshly ground black pepper

For the spinach and cheese sauce:

3 oz/84 g butter

2 tbsp sunflower oil

1 onion, skinned and chopped finely

3 oz/84 g flour

1 rounded tsp mustard powder

2 pints/1.1 litres milk

8 oz/225 g grated Cheddar cheese

Salt and freshly ground black pepper

Freshly grated nutmeg

1 lb/450 g frozen spinach, thawed, well
   drained, and puréed in a food processor

Start by making the tomato sauce. Heat the olive oil in a saucepan and add the chopped onion, celery and carrot. Cook for 5–7 minutes, stirring occasionally to prevent the mixture burning. Add the finely chopped garlic, cook for a few minutes, then pour in the liquidized tomatoes and the red wine. Season with the sugar, salt and pepper. Simmer, with the pan uncovered, for 20–30 minutes.

Make the spinach and cheese sauce by melting the butter and heating the oil together in a saucepan and adding the finely chopped onion. Cook for about 5 minutes, then stir in the flour. Cook for a further couple of minutes before stirring in the mustard powder, and the milk, then stir continuously until the sauce boils. Take the pan off the heat, stir in the 6 oz/170 g of the grated cheese, and season to your taste with salt, pepper and nutmeg. Stir in the puréed spinach.

In an ovenproof dish put a layer of spinach and cheese sauce, a layer of tomato sauce, then a layer of pasta, and continue till the dish is filled, ending with a layer of either tomato or spinach and cheese sauce, not the pasta. Sprinkle the surface with the reserved grated cheese.

Bake in a moderate oven, 350°F/180°C/Gas Mark 4, for 45 minutes, till the sauce is bubbling and when you stick a knife into the centre it feels soft.

Mushroom Risotto

This is a top favourite meal with each one of the six of us – with other dishes there are invariably one or two of the family who are lukewarm in their enthusiasm, but for mushroom risotto and for most pasta recipes we are as one in our appreciation for them.

Good risotto needs good stock. You can use a cube and water but proper stock makes all the difference in the world. It is also so important to cook the rice for several minutes in the olive oil with the onions, garlic and mushrooms so that each grain becomes coated in oil, and then the stock and dry white wine must be added in small amounts, and the rice stirred slowly with a wooden spoon from time to time. The rice will absorb the liquid as it simmers gently.

If you, like us, pick your own wild mushrooms, you can chop those and use them instead of the cultivated mushrooms. Add the chopped parsley at the very last minute before serving.

Serves 6

4–5 tbsp extra virgin olive oil

2 onions, skinned and finely chopped

1–2 cloves of garlic, skinned and finely chopped

1 lb/450 g mushrooms, wiped and chopped

About 1 lb/450 g Arborio rice

¼ pint/140 ml dry white wine

2–2½ pints/1.1–1.4 litres good chicken or vegetable stock

Salt and plenty of freshly ground black pepper

2–3 tbsp finely chopped parsley

Freshly grated Parmesan cheese, to hand around with the risotto

Heat the oil in a wide sauté pan and add the chopped onions. Cook till they are soft and transparent, then add the garlic and mushrooms and cook them for a couple of minutes before stirring in the rice. Cook, stirring gently, for a couple of minutes, then pour in the wine. Simmer very gently, and when the wine is almost absorbed, add a small amount of the stock. Simmer gently and when the stock is almost absorbed, add more. Continue till the stock is used, and stir in the salt, pepper and parsley just before serving.

Mushroom and Broccoli Risotto

Mushroom risotto is my great stand-by when I am racking my brain about what to have for supper. I always keep a large supply of Arborio rice (the rice with which risotto is made and which has the ability to absorb quantities of liquid and yet retain the individual grain shape) in my store cupboard. If you have good chicken (or vegetable) stock to hand, with just a handful of vegetables you can make a delicious supper, needing only a salad as accompaniment. Mushrooms, I think, make the best risotto, but one day I had a head of broccoli and I used that with the mushrooms. It was voted a winning combination. Freshly grated Parmesan cheese is an essential, to be handed around for your supper eaters to help themselves.

Serves 6

4–5 tbsp olive oil
2 onions, skinned and finely chopped
1½ lb/675 g broccoli
About 1 lb/450 g Arborio rice
1–2 garlic cloves, skinned and finely chopped
1 lb/450 g mushrooms, wiped and chopped
3 pints/1.7 litres chicken stock
¼ pint/140 ml dry white wine
Salt and freshly ground black pepper
Freshly grated Parmesan cheese, to hand around with the risotto

Heat the oil in a large sauté pan and cook the onions till they are soft. Meanwhile, trim the broccoli into small florets, and slice the stems into neat matchsticks. Add the rice and garlic to the onions in the pan, and the mushrooms, and cook for about 4–5 minutes, stirring, so that each grain of rice is coated in oil. Then add the broccoli and, a small amount at a time, the stock and wine, stirring occasionally, and cooking over a low to moderate heat. Cook like this till all the stock is incorporated. Season with salt and black pepper, and serve – it shouldn't be stodgy, but fairly sloppy.

Spinach and Mushroom Risotto

This risotto, like the two previous recipes, is eminently suitable for those who don't eat meat or fish, providing that a good vegetable stock is substituted for the chicken stock of my choice. Any home-made stock is preferable to stock cubes and water, but if you do have to resort to cubes, those with no additives such as Kallo or Friggs are far superior to those which are heavily laced with monosodium glutamate, which gives a syrupy sameness to all the various flavoured cubes.

Serves 6–8

4–5 tbsp good olive oil (I use extra virgin, usually Berio, for cooking)
2 onions, skinned and neatly chopped
1–2 garlic cloves, skinned and finely chopped (optional)
1 lb/450 g mushrooms, wiped and chopped (you can use wild mushrooms; I use our chanterelles and horns of plenty when they are in season)
1 lb/450 g Arborio rice (or similar risotto rice)
¼ pint/140 ml dry white wine
2½–3 pints/1.4–1.7 litres chicken or vegetable stock
A couple of pinches of saffron threads (optional, but delicious)
Salt and freshly ground black pepper
3 oz/84 g baby spinach leaves, torn into bits
Freshly grated Parmesan cheese, to hand around with the risotto

Heat the oil in a wide-based and fairly deep sauté pan and cook the chopped onions for several minutes, till they are transparent. Stir in the chopped garlic and the mushrooms and the rice, all together, and mix well, so that pretty well each grain of rice has a coating of olive oil. This will take several minutes' stirring around. Then stir in the dry white wine, and after that, in stages, a small amount at a time, the stock, stirring from time to time as the risotto cooks very gently. When you first add the stock, add the saffron, too, if you are using it. Season with salt and pepper, and lastly stir in the torn up spinach which will wilt in the heat of the risotto.

In this country risotto tends to be too stiff; it is so much nicer slightly on the sloppy side, so watch out for this. Taste, and season with salt and pepper as you like it. Serve with the freshly grated Parmesan cheese handed round separately.

Kedgeree

Because this is a rice-based dish, it is a great favourite with our children as well as with Godfrey and me. If you think children tend not to like eating fish, it is usually not the taste as much as the fear of finding bones. You can assure them they won't find a bone, in all honesty, if you feel the raw fish with your fingertips before you cook it and cut out or pull out any bones you feel – they are much harder to remove once the fish is cooked, and very difficult to see.

I like kedgeree best when it is made with smoked haddock or cod – and I really prefer smoked cod, with the large juicy flakes of fish. I cook the rice in the milk-and-water liquid the fish cooked in. Proper kedgeree has sultanas in it – I leave them out, because two of our children dislike them so much. I do, on the other hand, cook a teaspoon of medium strength curry powder in the butter and oil when I sauté the chopped onions. This, and the chopped

parsley stirred through the kedgeree just before dishing up, really makes a delicious dish.

All you need is a salad of grated carrots or mixed salad leaves to accompany the buttery kedgeree.

Serves 6

1½ lb/675 g smoked haddock or cod
1 pint/570 ml milk + 1 pint/570 ml water
2 tbsp sunflower oil + 1 oz/28 g butter
2 medium onions, skinned and finely chopped
1 tsp medium strength curry powder
12 oz/340 g long grain rice
3 hardboiled eggs, shelled and chopped
3 oz/84 g butter, cut in bits
Lots of freshly ground black pepper
2 tbsp chopped parsley

Feel the fish with your fingertips and remove all bones. Put the fish into a saucepan with the milk and water, and heat gently till the liquid forms a skin and just begins to simmer. Take the pan off the heat and leave to cool completely. When cooled, strain the liquid into a jug, and flake the fish into a bowl, removing all skin.

Heat the oil and melt the butter together in a saucepan and add the finely chopped onions. Cook for several minutes till they are soft and transparent-looking, then stir in the curry powder. Stir in the rice, and cook for several minutes till the rice is coated on each grain with oil.

Pour in the strained fish-cooking liquid till it comes an inch/2.5 cm above the rice – you need to take the pan off the heat to do this, as the heat initially will create a lot of steam that makes it impossible to see the depth of liquid till the heat lowers. Don't stir once the liquid is added, but replace the pan on the heat, cover the pan with a folded teatowel, then with the lid off the pan cook gently on moderate heat for 5 minutes. Then take the pan off the heat and leave, covered, for 15 minutes. By this time the liquid should be completely absorbed by the rice.

Stir in the flaked fish – I use a fork to do this – and the chopped hardboiled eggs and the bits of butter. Season with black pepper – the fish will be sufficiently salty so there is no need to add salt. Just before serving, fork through the chopped parsley.

Rice Salad

Rice salad can be pallid stodge. This is the nicest rice salad I have ever come across: the almonds, raisins and rice are all contrasting textures, and the dressing makes all the difference not only to the taste but also to the texture of the rice.

It is particularly delicious with all mayonnaise or otherwise sauced cold chicken, meat or fish dishes, including the Smoked Chicken and Mango Salad with Curried Mayonnaise (see page 239).

Serves 6–8

8 oz/225 g white Basmati rice
Salt
2 oz/56 g flaked almonds
2 tbsp raisins
2 tbsp french dressing

Cook the rice in plenty of boiling salted water until just tender but not soft. Drain and run cold water through it until the rice is cold. Toast the flaked almonds lightly under the grill. Combine the rice, almonds, raisins and French dressing and serve.

Peppered Smoked Mackerel and Rice Salad

This is a perfect dish for a summer lunch. Fillets of smoked mackerel coated with crushed black peppercorns can be bought in most fish shops and good food departments. When flaked into a mixture of rice, chopped hardboiled eggs and plenty of chopped chives and parsley, and all mixed into a slightly mustardy yoghurt sauce which counteracts the richness of the mackerel, the result is superb.

Serves 6–8

2 tsp grainy mustard
2 tbsp mayonnaise
5 fl oz/140 ml natural yoghurt
8 oz/225 g Basmati rice, boiled until cooked but still with a slightly nutty crunch
6 fillets of peppered mackerel, flesh flaked and bones removed
3 hardboiled eggs, shelled and chopped
3 heaped tbsp chopped chives and parsley mixed
Tomatoes, quartered (optional)

Stir the mustard, mayonnaise and yoghurt together. Fold together the rice, the flaked mackerel and the hardboiled eggs, together with most of the chopped parsley and chives. Fold the mustardy sauce into the fish rice mixture and heap on to a flat serving dish.

Press wedges of tomato around the sides of the rice, if you like. Sprinkle the remaining chives and parsley over the top.

Barbecues and Picnics

Of all types of eating, I love barbecues and picnics the best. It must be because both types of food are eaten outdoors. Usually. I say that because living in Skye, where we are cursed with midges on warm, fine summer evenings, we tend to cook our barbecued foods outdoors but rush indoors to eat, away from the unwelcome attentions of the legions of midges.

I deplore the way that food writers seem to decry a barbecue. They imply that barbecued food is dry, and that chargrilled is too often charburnt. Well, I quite agree with them that cremated foods all taste the same, and acridly disgusting at that, but thankfully encounters with food like this are so rare that I simply can't remember when last I had such misfortune at a barbecue. Most people now know the importance of letting the charcoals burn down from a flame-leaping red heat to a glowing white heat, for the proper chargrilling.

There is an informality to a barbecue which appeals greatly to me. And both barbecues and picnics share the same range of occasion. By this I mean that either event can consist of family food, in the case of the barbecue simply grilled sausages and chicken, with ketchup unashamedly to the fore and inelegant rolls of kitchen paper, a bowl of salad and packets of potato crisps. Or, at the other end of the spectrum, a barbecue might include the kebabs of pork fillet, or the scallops wrapped in bacon and served with elegant salads (a wide range of which can be found in the salads chapter), and accompanied by warm breads (again, see the breads chapter in this book). Similarly, a picnic can include filling food, such as the delicious Bacon, Egg and Lettuce Rolls, or the slightly more elaborate but just as informal Apple and Pork Sausagemeat Puffed Roll, or it can take the form of altogether more elegant dishes such as the Watercress Roulade, with its smoked salmon filling, or the Chicken Terrine with Pistachios.

A picnic is not just a summer occasion. We often have winter picnics, and they are just as much fun as those in warmer weather. But the food for a cold-weather picnic is quite different. For a quick winter picnic it is hard to beat hot Heinz tomato soup in thermoses, with sausages grilled over a fire and eaten in pre-buttered buns. But in this chapter you will find our favourite recipes for winter picnics, such as Jugged Hare with Forcemeat Balls, or Pork or Venison Sausages with Braised Red Cabbage and baked potatoes – all easily transportable and all good and comforting food to be eaten outdoors in the winter months. I feel that appetites are definitely heightened when food is eaten outside. Mine is, certainly.

Barbecued Fillet of Beef with Horseradish
Mousse

•

Barbecued Marinated Chicken with Avocado
and Tomato Salsa

•

Homemade Hamburgers

•

Kidney and Mushroom Kebabs

•

Pork and Orange Kebabs

•

Barbecued Salmon with Tomato and Dill
Mayonnaise

•

Apple and Pork Sausagemeat Puffed Roll

•

Avocado, Bacon and Egg Salad

•

Bacon, Egg and Lettuce Rolls

•

Brie, Lettuce and Bacon Toast Sandwiches
with Mayonnaise

•

Chicken and Smoked Bacon Filo Pastry
Parcels

Chicken Terrine with Pistachios

•

Crab, Lime Mayonnaise and Cucumber Rolls

•

Frittata

•

Cold Baked Ham

•

Cold Ham, Parsley and Cheese Tart

•

Jugged Hare with Forcemeat Balls

•

Pitta Bread with Chicken and Roast Red
Pepper Mayonnaise

•

Pork or Venison Sausages with Braised Red
Cabbage and Baked Jacket Potatoes

•

Scotch Quails' Eggs in Sesame Seeds

•

Venison Pasty

•

Watercress and Smoked Salmon Roulade

•

Brown Sugar Meringues

Barbecued Fillet of Beef with Horseradish Mousse

Barbecued fillet of beef is, for me, the nicest, most delicious way to eat beef, and I prefer it cooked then cooled and served cold. Some time ago I was at a pre-confirmation lunch for Melanie Palmer whose parents John and Carol are great friends of ours. They live near Kirkmichael in a part of Perthshire which is high and remote and beautiful. We had a most delicious lunch and one of the two main courses was cold sliced barbecued fillets of beef – lucky me! Whether you serve the meat hot or cold, the horseradish mousse goes so well as an accompaniment and it can be made two days ahead and kept, covered, in the fridge.

An average-sized fillet of beef weighs about 2½ lb/1.125 kg and will serve five when hot from the barbecue, six if served cold. Trim the fillet of excess fat and gristle, and tuck the flat end under so that there is much the same thickness the length of the fillet, which prevents the thinner end from overcooking. It isn't necessary to marinate but if you like to do so, use the marinade below which I use for beef.

Serves 6

1 fillet of beef (see introduction above)

For the optional marinade:

6 tbsp olive oil

1 onion, skinned and quartered

1 garlic clove, skinned and halved

1 stick of celery, halved

A handful of parsley

1 tsp black peppercorns + 1 tsp rock salt

1 pint/570 ml red wine

For the horseradish mousse:

1 sachet of powdered gelatine (½ oz/14 g)

¼ pint/140 ml cold water

2 heaped tsp grated horseradish

Juice of half a lemon

1 rounded tbsp chopped parsley and chives mixed

½ pint/285 ml double cream, whipped

2 egg whites

For the marinade, heat the oil and add the onion, garlic, celery and parsley. Cook for a few minutes, then pour in the red wine, and add the peppercorns and salt. Simmer for 5 minutes then take off the heat and cool. Pour this cold marinade over the ready trimmed fillet in a dish. Leave for several hours, turning the fillet so that it marinates on each side.

Before barbecuing, take the fillet out of the marinade and pat it dry with kitchen paper. How long you grill it for depends on how rare you like your beef. Turn it regularly on the barbecue so that it cooks evenly, and for a rare result give it about 10 minutes' grilling each side.

To prepare the mousse, sprinkle the gelatine over the water, in a saucepan, then dissolve over gentle heat. Mix in the horse-radish, lemon juice, parsley and chives, and stir this into the whipped cream. Whisk the egg whites till stiff and, with a metal spoon, fold them into the horseradish cream. Put into a dish to set.

Serve a small spoonful at the side of each helping of beef.

Barbecued Marinated Chicken with Avocado and Tomato Salsa

When barbecuing pieces of chicken, it is wise to marinate them for 24 hours (or longer) in a simple mixture of olive oil, soya sauce and chopped garlic to avoid potential dryness as they cook.

Serves 6

6 pieces of chicken, with skin on
½ pint/285 ml olive oil
4 tbsp dark soya sauce
2 large garlic cloves, finely chopped

For the salsa:

8 tomatoes, skinned, halved, and de-seeded
1–2 garlic cloves (to taste)
Half a red onion, skinned and very finely diced
2 red peppers, halved, de-seeded, and skinned as described on page 277
1–2 fresh chillies (to taste), de-seeded and very finely chopped
2 sticks of celery, washed, trimmed, and sliced as thinly as possible
1 tbsp chopped coriander leaf
1 tbsp chopped flat-leaved (if possible) parsley
3 avocados, skinned, diced, and tossed in 2 tbsp lemon juice
Salt and freshly ground black pepper
4 tbsp olive oil
1 tsp balsamic vinegar

Mix together the marinade ingredients and pour over the chicken pieces. Leave to marinate for 24 hours or more, turning the pieces over whenever you remember.

For the salsa, chop half the tomatoes into chunks and put them in a food processor or blender, along with the garlic, red onion, 2 of the red pepper halves and the chillies. Whiz until well blended.

Cut the rest of the tomatoes and red peppers into small dice. Put the contents of the food processor into a bowl and stir in all the other ingredients, mixing well.

Barbecue the chicken for about 15 minutes – until the juices run clear – and serve with a spoonful of salsa beside each piece.

Homemade Hamburgers

I have a horror of bought hamburgers, because unless I know the butcher who made them, I don't know what has gone into them. I much prefer to make my own, by buying good meat and pulverizing it in my food processor. I like to make it quite chunky, rather than smooth. You do need a bit of fat to make the hamburgers juicy. I also like to add sautéed onions to the mixture, and an egg, and a dash of Worcestershire sauce. I find that children like to have a – clean – hand in making them and the hamburgers do taste good when cooked on a barbecue – I love the taste of charcoal-grilled food.

All that is needed to go with them is a lot of tomato ketchup, but only Heinz will do, buttered buns, salad and a bowl of potato crisps. And a lot of paper table napkins (or absorbent kitchen paper) to mop up.

Makes 12

| 2 lb/900 g fairly lean steak – I use rump |
| 2 onions, skinned and very finely chopped |
| 2 tbsp sunflower oil |
| 1 egg |
| 1 tbsp Worcestershire sauce |
| Freshly ground black pepper |

Trim any gristle from the meat, but try to leave some fat on. Cut the meat into bits and put it into the food processor. Cook the chopped onions in the sunflower oil till they are soft, then cool them. Add them to the meat, and whiz, taking care not to let the meat become too smooth. Add the egg, Worcestershire sauce and pepper to the contents of the processor and whiz briefly to amalgamate the lot.

Shape twelve hamburgers and put them on a tray lined with greaseproof paper, cover them with clingfilm and put them into the fridge till you are ready to barbecue them.

Kidney and Mushroom Kebabs

Kebabs are very versatile. You can make all sorts of delicious meat and vegetable combinations, stick them on a skewer and barbecue them. You can buy beautiful kebab skewers or use ordinary kitchen skewers – the proper kebab skewers are easier to handle than kitchen skewers as they have larger ends to hold on to, and their blades are broader and flatter, which holds the food in place better. Lambs' kidneys make delicious kebabs.

Serves 6

| 15 lambs' kidneys |
| 15 rashers streaky bacon, halved |
| 18 mushrooms |
| Sunflower oil |

Skin, halve and core the kidneys. Wrap each kidney half in streaky bacon, and push them on the skewers, alternating with a mushroom, until the skewers are evenly filled. Brush with oil and cook on the barbecue, turning during cooking, for 20–30 minutes.

These kebabs are good served with a mustardy mayonnaise.

Pork and Orange Kebabs

These make a more elegant main course for a barbecue party. I like to serve them with Rice Salad (see page 262), a perfect accompaniment.

Serves 6

| 3 pork fillets, about 8 oz/225 g each |
| 2 red peppers |
| 18 mushrooms |
| 2 medium onions, peeled |

For the marinade:

| 14 fl oz/400 ml sunflower seed oil |
| 7 fl oz/200 ml fresh (or diluted frozen) orange juice |
| 2 garlic cloves, peeled and chopped |
| A few strips of orange rind |
| A few sprigs of rosemary |
| Freshly ground black pepper |

Mix all the marinade ingredients together. Cut the pork fillets into 1-inch/2.5-cm chunks. You want about five pieces per person. Put them in the marinade, cover and refrigerate for at least 12 hours.

Cut the red peppers in half and scoop out the seeds. Cut each half in three. Cut the onions in quarters, then cut the quartered onions in half again. Put these large pieces of onion into a saucepan of cold water, bring to the boil, and simmer for 3 minutes. Add the pieces of red pepper, cook for 2 more minutes, then drain and cool.

Drain the pieces of pork from the marinade. Thread them on to six skewers, alternating with a piece of onion, a piece of red pepper, and a mushroom, until the skewers are evenly filled. Cook on the barbecue, turning the kebabs so that they cook evenly, for 20–30 minutes.

Barbecued Salmon with Tomato and Dill Mayonnaise

This is my all-time favourite main course. I get such satisfaction each time I give it to people because those for whom barbecued salmon is a first-time experience all say the same thing – that they just can't believe how perfect and delicious it is. I think that, being a rich fish, it is ideal barbecue material, and the flavour of charcoal just seems to be made for salmon more than anything else. The salmon has to be foil wrapped, with the foil slashed in several places to allow the charcoal to penetrate. I have often cooked whole fish this way, but it does take time.

A much quicker way is to have the salmon filleted, place it on butter-smeared foil, grind black pepper liberally over it, lay sprigs of parsley and slices of lemon on top, dot with more butter then seal it into a foil parcel. Slash the foil a few times, put the parcel on the barbecue and cook for several minutes each side depending on the thickness of the fillets of salmon: allow 3–5 minutes on one side, then turn it over and give it the same amount of time on the other side. Open the foil, test to see if it is cooked and give it a further couple of minutes if not.

Serve with the Tomato and Dill Mayonnaise on page 292.

Apple and Pork Sausagemeat Puffed Roll

This is made in a fat roulade shape and I slice it thickly. It is vital to use the best pork sausages you can find. The apples in the recipe aren't discernible as such, but they do complement the flavour of the sausagemeat so well, with the onions and thyme.

Serves 6–8

2 tbsp sunflower oil

1½ lb/675 g pork sausages, each slit down the centre with a sharp knife, and the skins peeled off

1 onion, skinned and finely chopped

1 garlic clove, skinned and finely chopped (optional)

3 good eating apples, e.g. Granny Smith's, peeled, cored and diced

A large pinch of dried thyme or the tiny leaves stripped from a sprig of fresh thyme

A pinch of salt and freshly ground black pepper

½ pint/285 ml dry cider

1½ lb/675 g puff pastry

Milk for glazing

Heat the oil in a sauté pan and cook the sausagemeat, mashing it with a wooden spoon to break it up from its sausage shape. When the sausagemeat is browned remove it, with a slotted spoon, to a warm dish. Add the onion, garlic and chopped apples to the sauté pan and cook till the onions are really soft – about 5 minutes. Replace the sausagemeat, and stir in the thyme, seasoning and cider. Let the mixture bubble gently till the liquid has reduced away. Then let the mixture cool.

To make the roll, roll out the puff pastry into two neat oblongs, each about 9 inches/ 23 cm long. Divide the sausage mixture between them, putting a line down the middle of each oblong, and leaving about an inch or so at either end. Brush the edges with milk, fold the short ends in, and pinch together the long ends in the centre of each roll. With two fish slices slip the rolls on to baking trays – no need to oil or butter the baking trays for puff pastry – and brush each roll with milk.

Bake in a hot oven, 425°F/220°C/Gas Mark 7, for 15–20 minutes, then lower the heat to 350°F/180°C/Gas Mark 4 and cook for a further 20–25 minutes, till well puffed up and deeply golden all over. Cool, then slice, before packing for the picnic. This is easiest transported on a tray or a rigid surface, wrapped in foil.

Avocado, Bacon and Egg Salad

This is delicious on a summer Sunday evening, served with warm Cheese, Mustard and Garlic Granary Bread (see page 369), or rolls. You can prepare all the salad in the morning with the exception of the avocados – try not to do them too far ahead as they tend to turn brownish.

Serves 8

For the salad:

1½ average-sized Iceberg lettuces, sliced and chopped

4 hardboiled eggs, chopped

3 avocado pears, skinned, and the flesh chopped in quite large chunks

8 rashers smoked streaky bacon, grilled till crisp, then broken in pieces

8 tomatoes, skinned, de-seeded and sliced in segments

A handful of chives, snipped

A handful of parsley, torn into small sprigs

For the dressing:

½ tsp salt

½ tsp sugar

A good grinding of black pepper

½ tsp mustard powder

1 tbsp wine vinegar

2–3 tbsp oil

1 tsp pesto (optional)

Mix together all the salad ingredients. Mix the dressing ingredients together well – you can keep it in a screw-topped jar. Dress the salad just before serving.

Bacon, Egg and Lettuce Rolls

These are the rolls I make for a picnic when I am stuck for an idea, because I know that they are the family favourite. It is generally recognized within our family that my mother makes the best egg and bacon rolls – she is a dab hand at many other things besides – but these come a close second to hers. Good rolls are essential, and I split them open – easiest with a serrated knife – trying to leave them joined at one section, and carefully pull out the dough from the top and bottom of each roll, to make room for more filling which, because of the cavity created by the dough removal, then won't squidge out of the roll on biting.

How many you allow per person depends entirely on the age and appetite (the two are directly connected) of the guests.

Fills 6 rolls

8 large eggs, hardboiled by simmering them for 5 minutes, then running cold water into the saucepan till the eggs are cold

4 oz/112 g softened butter

4 tbsp mayonnaise – preferably homemade

1 tsp mustard powder (or Dijon mustard, if you prefer)

A pinch of salt – the bacon will add saltiness – and lots of pepper

8 rashers smoked streaky bacon, grilled till crisp, then broken into small bits

Crisp lettuce leaves

Prepare the rolls as described in the introduction. Shell the eggs and put them into a deep bowl. With a sharp knife cut the eggs till they are chopped as fine as you like – I find it less messy to cut them in the bowl than chop them on a board – and then mash in the softened butter, mayonnaise, mustard powder, salt and pepper. Mash and mix all together well. Lastly, mix in the broken bits of bacon.

Line each roll with lettuce on one half, and divide the egg and bacon mixture between the rolls. Slice each in half with a serrated knife, for easier eating, and wrap in clingfilm.

Brie, Lettuce and Bacon Toast Sandwiches with Mayonnaise

These are not the sandwiches which are toasted when filled, but sandwiches made with toast instead of bread. The toast has to be made just before the sandwiches are to be eaten, but the fillings can be prepared well in advance, and toast sandwiches are utterly delicious. The most popular type is probably the classic bacon, lettuce and tomato, but this recipe is good, and you can put anything you choose inside the toast.

There are two ways to make sure that your toast sandwiches really are as good as they should be. One is to use good bread – my choice is for thick-sliced malted or granary bread. The other is to spread the hot toast with good mayonnaise instead of butter. In this case, mix a tablespoon of snipped chives into the mayonnaise before spreading the toast – it just adds more flavour to the other filling items.

Fills 4 sandwiches, generously

8 slices of thick granary bread

4 tbsp good mayonnaise – homemade if at all
   possible

1 tbsp snipped chives

Any lettuce leaves you choose – my
   preference is for rocket

1 lb/450 g Brie, rind left on and sliced as thinly
   as possible

8 rashers smoked streaky bacon, grilled till
   crisp, then broken up

Toast the bread. Spread each slice with the
mayonnaise mixed with the snipped chives.
Divide the lettuce leaves between four of the
slices, then divide up the slices of Brie and
put them on top of the lettuce. Press the bits
of bacon on to the other four mayonnaise-
spread slices of toast, and put these on top
of the other four. With a serrated knife cut
each sandwich into quarters, slicing
diagonally.

Chicken and Smoked Bacon Filo Pastry Parcels

*Apart from bread, pastry of whichever sort,
puff, short, or as in this case filo, is an
excellent way to encase a substantial filling
for a picnic. The smoked bacon in the
filling for these filo parcels is delicious and
adds a complementary flavour to the
chicken.*

   *Allow 3–4 parcels per person, depending
on age (which is an indication of appetite)
and whether this is the main part of the
picnic or one of two or three items.*

Makes 16 parcels

2 tbsp sunflower or olive oil

1 onion, skinned and finely chopped

6 rashers of the best smoked back bacon,
   sliced into fine dice – easy with a really
   sharp knife

8 oz/225 g cream cheese

4 cooked chicken breasts (either roast or
   poached), skin removed, the chicken meat
   cut into fine dice

A pinch – no more – of salt and plenty of
   freshly ground black pepper

8 sheets of filo pastry

Melted butter in a saucepan

Heat the oil in a saucepan or frying pan and
cook the finely chopped onion and bacon
together, stirring, till the onion is soft and
beginning to turn golden, and the bacon is
well cooked. Cool this mixture. In a bowl
beat the cream cheese till it is smooth and
creamy (you can do this in a food processor
but then scrape it into a bowl), and mix in
the finely diced chicken meat, the seasoning,
and the cooled onion and bacon mixture.

   Lay a sheet of filo on a table or work
surface and brush completely with melted
butter, using a pastry brush. Cover with a
second sheet of filo, and brush again with
melted butter. Cut the double sheets in half
widthways, then in half across. Put a spoonful of filling in the centre of each square and
fold the edges inwards, to form a parcel.
Brush each parcel with melted butter and
put them on a butter-brushed baking tray.

   You can do all this in advance, if you keep
the parcels, covered with clingfilm, in a cool
place till you are ready to bake them. To

cook them, bake in a hot oven, 425°F/ 220°C/Gas Mark 7, for 7–10 minutes, or till the pastry is golden and crisp. Cool them a bit before wrapping them in baking parchment, then in foil, to transport them. If you wrap them when they are too hot the danger is that they will become soggy. Failing the baking parchment, you can wrap them in a teatowel and then in foil.

Chicken Terrine with Pistachios

This tastes delicious, and is very portable. I would advise slicing it before packing it in with the other picnic contents.

Serves 6–8

For the terrine:

3 bay leaves

8 streaky bacon rashers

1½ lb/675 g white chicken meat, diced quite finely – you need a sharp knife

1 lb/450 g good pork sausages, each slit down the centre and the skin peeled off

2 oz/56 g pistachio kernels

For the marinade:

4 tbsp olive oil

¼ pint/140 ml port (you can use red wine instead, but port gives a richer flavour)

1 onion, skinned and chopped finely

Pared rind of 1 lemon (I use a potato peeler to avoid getting bitter white pith too)

½ tsp salt and plenty of freshly ground black pepper

A pinch of dried thyme

Line a 1½–2 lb/approximately 1 kg loaf or terrine tin with foil, then lay the bay leaves down the centre. With the blunt side of a knife, flatten the rashers of streaky bacon and lay them across the tin widthways – their ends will overhang at either side.

Put the marinade ingredients into a saucepan and bring to the boil, simmer for 3–5 minutes, then take off the heat and leave to cool completely before pouring over the diced chicken in a dish. Leave for several hours or overnight.

Discard the strips of lemon peel, and mix the chicken, marinade, sausagemeat and pistachio kernels together – the only way to do this job thoroughly is to use your hands. When thoroughly mixed, pack this into the bacon-lined tin. Fold the overhanging flaps of bacon over the meat surface, and fold over the foil to seal it, then put the loaf or terrine tin into a roasting tin with water coming halfway up the sides.

Cook in a moderate oven, 350°F/ 180°C/Gas Mark 4, for 2 hours, until when you stick a skewer into the middle of the terrine the juices run clear. If you are in any doubt give it a further 20 minutes' cooking time. Take the tin out of the roasting tin, put a weight on top – I use a couple of tins of tomatoes or something similar – and leave to get quite cold. When cold, keep the terrine in the fridge.

Crab, Lime Mayonnaise and Cucumber Rolls

This is a filling for rolls for a special occasion. The type of roll you choose to encase this filling is dependent on your preference – either soft white baps or crisper-crusted granary rolls. But as the filling tends to be rather moist, I suggest the rolls are split and buttered and the filling taken separately, in a bowl, with a spoon to fill each roll before eating.

It takes a matter of seconds to fill the rolls.

Fills 6 large rolls

1 whole egg + 1 egg yolk
1 tsp caster sugar
½ tsp salt and plenty of freshly ground black pepper
Grated rind of 1 lime
⅓ pint/200 ml mixed olive and sunflower oils
Juice of 2 limes
Half a cucumber
1 lb/450 g crabmeat; I prefer half white and half brown meat, mixed – I think the brown meat has more flavour

To make the mayonnaise, put the egg, yolk, sugar, salt, pepper and lime rind into a processor and whiz, gradually adding the oils – drop by drop initially, then, when you have an emulsion, in a thin trickle. Lastly, whiz in the lime juice. Adjust the seasoning by adding more salt and pepper if you like.

Peel the cucumber with a potato peeler and cut the flesh into chunks. Cut each chunk in half and scoop out the seeds, then dice the flesh. This prevents the cucumber making the filling watery.

Mix together the crabmeat, mayonnaise and diced cucumber. Put this into a Pyrex bowl (so much easier to wash afterwards than a solid plastic bowl) and store in the fridge till the moment of departure. Transport the crab filling in a cold box.

Frittata

A frittata is a thick Italian omelette, served at room temperature. It is ideal picnic food, because you can vary the flavourings to suit your tastes, it is easy to transport, and it only needs to be cut into wedges to serve. You can make it a day ahead, but it is much nicer made in the morning for a picnic lunch.

Frittata with goats' cheese and spinach

Don't be tempted to make this in a crêpe or omelette pan wider than 8 inches/20 cm, because the frittata should be about 1 inch/2.5 cm deep, rather than a thinner and therefore more leathery-textured cold omelette!

Makes 6 wedges

6 large eggs
Salt and plenty of freshly ground black pepper
1 tbsp olive oil + 1 oz/28 g butter
3 oz/84 g soft goats' cheese, crumbled into bits
2 oz/56 g baby spinach, torn into bits

Beat the eggs together well, seasoning them with salt and pepper.

Heat the oil and butter in an omelette or crêpe pan 8 inches/20 cm in diameter and, when the oil and melted butter are hot, pour in the egg mixture, adding the crumbled cheese and torn-up spinach, and stirring around the contents of the pan for a few seconds. Then stop stirring and leave the pan on a very low heat indeed, for about 10 minutes. The contents will be firm but the top will still be runny. Pre-heat the grill to halfway heat, then set the frittata – but do watch out not to brown it, or it will toughen.

When it is firm and set, slip the frittata from the pan on to several thicknesses of kitchen paper to cool. Wrap in foil for the picnic, having first cut the frittata into six wedges.

Frittata with red onions and peppers

This frittata needs a little more preparation in that the peppers, for maximum enjoyment, should be skinned, and the onions and skinned peppers are then gently sautéed together till the onions are really soft. Add as much garlic as you like.

Makes 6 wedges

3 red (or yellow) peppers

2 tbsp olive oil for cooking the onions and pepper

2 red onions, skinned and finely chopped

2 garlic cloves, skinned and chopped finely

1 tbsp olive oil + 1 oz/28 g butter for cooking the frittata

6 large eggs

Salt and plenty of freshly ground black pepper

Start by cutting the peppers in half, removing the seeds, and grilling under a red-hot grill till the peppers form great charred blisters. Then put the pepper halves into a polythene bag and leave for 10 minutes. The skins should then peel off easily. Chop the skinned peppers quite small.

Heat the 2 tablespoons of olive oil in a sauté pan and sauté the chopped red onions for 5 minutes over a moderate to gentle heat. Then stir in the chopped garlic and chopped peppers and continue to cook for a further 5 minutes. Let this mixture cool.

Heat the tablespoon of olive oil with the butter in a crêpe or omelette pan 8 inches/20 cm in diameter. Beat the eggs, seasoning them with salt and pepper, and, when the oil and melted butter are hot, pour in the eggs, mixing in the onion, garlic and pepper mixture, and stirring all together for a few seconds. Then turn the heat under the pan right down low, and leave the frittata to cook, without any more stirring, for 10 minutes. It should be firm, but still runny on top.

Pre-heat the grill to halfway heat – not red-hot by any means – and gently cook the top of the frittata under the grill, just till the top is firm – but not browned, which makes the frittata leathery in texture.

Slip the cooked frittata on to several thicknesses of kitchen paper to cool. When cold, cut into six wedges and wrap in foil.

Cold Baked Ham

Whether you get smoked or green ham is up to you, but it is much better to cook your own, because then you get a good ham stock to use for lentil soup at a later date.

Much as I prefer to buy and cook meat on the bone, it is undeniably easier to buy boned ham. Also, if ham is left on the bone, the part nearest the bone tends to get awfully dry after a few days.

A piece of boned ham weighing about 5 lb/2.25 kg
2 onions, each cut in half
2 sticks of celery, each broken in two
3 bay leaves
A few peppercorns
Whole cloves
4 tbsp thick honey
3 tbsp good quality (i.e. not very vinegary) grainy mustard

Put the ham into a large saucepan with the onions, celery, bay leaves and peppercorns and cover it all with water. Bring it to simmering point, then cover the pan with a lid and simmer very gently for about 1 hour and 10 minutes (20 minutes to the pound less 30 minutes). Let the ham cool in the stock.

When it is cold, take it out of the stock, cut off the skin, and then with a sharp knife cut diagonally across the fat going one way, then diagonally going in the other direction, and stick a clove in each diamond shape in the fat. Make a paste with the honey and mustard (dip the spoon in hot water between each spoonful when measuring out

the honey so that it slips off more easily) and spread it over the ham. Roast in a hot oven, 425°F/220°C/Gas Mark 7, for 35–40 minutes, basting it several times as the honey and mustard mixture will slip off the ham. Watch out that it doesn't burn. Put about 4 tablespoons of water into the roasting tin with the ham, to make the washing up easier.

When the ham is cooked, take it out of the tin, put it on a serving plate and leave it to cool. Cover it when cold. Slice it as thinly as you can. This ham is so good served with salads: if it is a knife-and-fork picnic *any* salad is delicious with it, but I like the potato salad and a tomato and basil salad.

Cold Ham, Parsley and Cheese Tart

This is so easy, but like all savoury tarts the filling is much nicer made with a higher quantity of egg yolk to whole eggs – it gives the custard a much softer texture.

Serves 6

For the pastry:

4 oz/112 g butter, hard from the fridge, cut into bits
6 oz/170 g plain flour + 1 tsp icing sugar
½ tsp each of salt and freshly ground black pepper

For the filling:

1 lb/450 g boiled or baked ham, trimmed of fat and gristle and cut into slivers
2 large eggs + the yolks of 2 large eggs

½ pint/285 ml milk – as creamy as possible

Freshly ground black pepper – the ham will be
salty enough for most tastes

2 tbsp chopped parsley and snipped chives,
mixed

3 oz/84 g grated Cheddar cheese

Put all the ingredients for the pastry into a
processor and whiz till the mixture resembles fine crumbs – or rub the butter into
the sieved seasoned flour using your fingertips. Pat this firmly around the sides and
base of a 9-inch/23-cm flan dish. Put the
dish into the fridge for an hour minimum,
then bake in a moderate oven,
350°F/180°C/Gas Mark 4, for 20–25
minutes, till the pastry is golden brown at
the edges.

Scatter the sliced ham over the base of the
cooked pastry. Beat together the eggs and
yolks with the milk, season with pepper, stir
in the chopped parsley and snipped chives,
and pour into the pastry case, over the ham.
Scatter the grated cheese over the top – most
will sink down into the liquid, but it doesn't
matter. Bake in the moderate oven, as for
the pastry, for 15–20 minutes, or till when
you gently shake the flan dish the filling
barely wobbles in the centre – the centre is
the last part to 'set'. Take it out of the oven
and leave to cool.

This is very portable picnic food. All you
need to accompany it is a salad.

Jugged Hare with Forcemeat Balls

*The best shooting lunch I ever ate was
jugged hare with forcemeat balls. Whether it
was the relief of coming into a barn and the
comfort of sitting on the hay bales, and that
anything would have tasted delicious on that
day, I don't know, but I don't think so – I
am sure it was the deliciousness of the
jugged hare! I don't usually reckon anything
gamey to be appropriate eating for a shoot
lunch, but jugged hare is the exception. This
transports as well as any other casserole or
stew – in a dish in a thermal bag (and I
think the best are to be found in Lakeland
Plastics) with the forcemeat balls just
wrapped in a double thickness of foil.*

*The hare should come from the butcher
with a carton of blood, which does help
make this stew even more rich and delicious
– but don't worry if you can't get it.*

Serves 6–8

1 large hare, cut into joints

Seasoned flour

2 oz/56 g butter + 2 tbsp sunflower oil

2 onions, skinned and stuck with a few cloves

3 carrots, peeled and chopped

2 sticks of celery, trimmed and sliced

1 garlic clove, skinned and chopped

2 pared strips of lemon rind + 2 of orange rind
(I use a potato peeler to do this, it avoids
the risk of getting the bitter pith too)

1 oz/28 g plain flour

2 pints/1.1 litres water

3 tbsp redcurrant jelly

¼ pint/140 ml port

As much blood from the hare as possible

Coat each piece of hare in flour seasoned with salt and pepper. Heat the oil and melt the butter together in a heavy casserole and brown the pieces of hare on each side. Remove them to a warm dish. Add the onions to the oil and brown. Stir in the chopped carrots and sliced celery, the chopped garlic, lemon and orange rinds, and the flour. Cook for a minute or two, stirring to prevent anything from sticking. Then gradually add the water and redcurrant jelly. Stir till the sauce simmers. Replace the joints of hare amongst the vegetables. Cover with a lid and cook in a moderate oven, 350°F/180°C/Gas Mark 4, for 1¾ hours.

Take the casserole out of the oven and cool enough to strip the meat from the bones. (You don't want to have to cope with bones at a lunch eaten out of doors.) Replace the hare meat in the casserole. Remove the onions and cloves. (You can do this a day in advance.)

On top of the cooker, carefully (not too fast) reheat the casserole till it is gently simmering. Stir in the port. Ladle a small amount of hot hare gravy into the bowl with the hare blood and mix well. Stir this back into the casserole, taking great care not to let it simmer again once the blood has been added, in case it curdles.

To transport it, put a layer of foil on the bottom of a thermal bag to sit the dish or casserole containing the jugged hare.

Forcemeat balls

These freeze beautifully, only needing to be reheated. I freeze them once I have fried them.

1 oz/28 g butter

1 onion, skinned and very finely chopped

4 oz/112 g day-old crumbs made from baked bread (as opposed to steamed sliced bread)

2 oz/56 g shredded suet

Grated rind of 1 lemon

Salt and freshly ground black pepper

Beaten egg and flour for coating

Sunflower oil for frying

Melt the butter in a small saucepan and sauté the chopped onion till it is really soft. Cool. Then mix it with the crumbs, suet, grated lemon rind and seasonings. Form into small balls, of even size, about the size of a ping-pong ball, and dip each in beaten egg, then in flour.

Heat the oil in a non-stick frying pan and sauté the forcemeat balls, turning them so that they brown evenly. Once browned, put them on a dish with a double thickness of kitchen paper to absorb excess grease. Cool.

Reheat in a low temperature oven for 20–25 minutes before wrapping them in foil to transport them.

Pitta Bread with Chicken and Roast Red Pepper Mayonnaise

This is such a good filling – I think, for my taste, anyway! The garlic content is mild and sweet in flavour due to its roasting along with the red peppers. You can pulverize the peppers and garlic in with the mayonnaise, but I prefer to chop them. It really does matter to dice the chicken finely, and this is easy provided you have a really sharp knife. I love the Kitchen Devil knives.

Filling for 6 pitta bread pockets

2 red (or yellow, but not green) peppers

2–3 garlic cloves, skinned and chopped

2 tbsp olive oil

3 chicken breasts, either roast or poached

1 whole egg + 1 egg yolk

½ tsp salt

½ tsp caster sugar

A good grinding of black pepper

½ tsp mustard powder

¼ pint/140 ml oil – I mix extra virgin olive oil with sunflower oil

3 tsp Balsamic vinegar, or 2 tbsp wine vinegar

6 pitta breads, opened into pockets

Start with the peppers. Cut each in half and scoop away the seeds. Put the peppers, skin side uppermost, under a red-hot grill, till their skins form great black blisters. Then put them into a polythene bag for 10 minutes, after which their skins should peel off easily. Chop them as neatly as you can, mix them with the chopped garlic and olive oil, and roast them in a hot oven for 10 minutes. Cool.

Slice each chicken breast across into thin strips, holding the breast with the flat of your hand, then slice it into thin strips down, then thinly slice it across again, which will give you finely diced chicken.

Put the egg, yolk, salt, sugar, pepper and mustard into a food processor and whiz, adding the oil drop by drop till it is all included. Lastly whiz in the vinegar.

Scrape the mayonnaise into a bowl. Fold in the cooled roast peppers and garlic, and the diced chicken. Divide the mixture evenly between the pitta breads.

Pork or Venison Sausages with Braised Red Cabbage and Baked Jacket Potatoes

This is a very portable picnic menu for a chilly day out.

Choose the type of sausage you like – for my taste it is pork, with the highest percentage of porkmeat that I can buy. But you can buy delicious venison sausages made by MacBeth's, the butcher's shop in Forres, who also do mail order. I grill the sausages to the degree of brownness I like, which is very well grilled, then I wrap them in foil.

The recipe for Braised Red Cabbage, with apples, onions and a hint of juniper, is on page 222. I transport this in a dish, in an insulated thermal bag.

Scrub the potatoes and stab each right through wth a knife – this helps them to cook rather more quickly, and also prevents them bursting during cooking, as occasionally happens. If you like, rub each potato with a very small amount of sunflower oil and roll each one in rock salt. This is purely optional.

The potatoes are best wrapped separately in foil. Don't forget to take butter to eat with them. I find it easiest to cut the butter into generous bits before I put it in with the picnic things.

together at the join. Press each sausage-encased egg in the sesame seeds and salt.

Shallow-fry, ideally in a non-stick frying pan, in a small amount of sunflower oil, turning the eggs over – I use two forks for this – till they are golden brown all over. As they cook, remove them to a plate lined with kitchen paper, to absorb excess oil. Pack them for the picnic either whole or cut in half, whichever you prefer.

Scotch Quails' Eggs in Sesame Seeds

These make ideal picnic food, being rather less dauntingly hefty than the more usual Scotch egg, made with hens' eggs. As with anything made with sausages, I think it is of paramount importance to use the best sausages you can find.

Makes 12

12 quails' eggs

1 lb/450 g best quality pork sausages

4 oz/112 g sesame seeds mixed with ½ tsp salt

Sunflower oil for frying

Cook the quails' eggs in simmering water for 3 minutes, then run cold water into the saucepan till the eggs feel cold. Shell them carefully – they have surprisingly hard shells compared to hens' eggs.

Slit each sausage skin with a sharp knife and peel off the skins. Divide each sausage in half and press out the sausagemeat. Wrap it around a shelled egg, pinching the meat

Venison Pasty

This is made with cold cooked venison – we always seem to have some left over from a roast haunch and it makes up into ideal picnic food as venison pasties.

Makes 8 pasties

1½ lb/675 g cold cooked and trimmed venison

3 tbsp sunflower oil + 2 oz/56 g butter (I realize this sounds rather a lot, but the minced venison is quite dry)

2 onions, skinned and finely chopped

2 carrots, peeled and very finely diced

3 tsp tomato purée + 2 tbsp Worcestershire sauce

½ pint/285 ml leftover gravy, or 2 tsp flour + ½ pint/285 ml lager

Salt and freshly ground black pepper

1½ lb/675 g shortcrust pastry

Cut the venison into bits and whiz in a food processor till the meat is just coarsely grated (or minced) in appearance – I don't pulverize it too finely.

Heat the oil and melt the butter together in a heavy-based sauté pan. Add the chopped onions and diced carrots and cook over a moderate heat for several minutes, until when you stick a fork into a bit of carrot it feels tender. Stir in the minced venison, mix well, and stir in the tomato purée, Worcestershire sauce and gravy or (if you have no gravy) flour with, after a minute, the lager. Simmer all together gently for 10 minutes, then cool. Season with salt and pepper.

Roll out the pastry and cut it into eight circles, each measuring about 6 inches/ 15 cm in diameter. Put a good spoonful of the venison mixture down the middle of each circle. Brush the edges of the circle with milk and pinch them together. Very lightly butter a baking tray and put the pasties on this. Bake in a hot oven, 425°F/220°C/Gas Mark 7, for 15–20 minutes, or till the pastry turns golden, then reduce the heat to moderate, 350°F/180°C/Gas Mark 4, and cook for a further 15–20 minutes.

These are delicious cold, providing they are baked the same day that they are to be eaten. Alternatively, you can serve them warm.

Watercress and Smoked Salmon Roulade

This pale green roulade looks beautiful with its pink-flecked cream filling. It also tastes very good! We make it here at Kinloch to serve as a first course for our guests, but it makes a perfect smart picnic main course too, accompanied by a mixed leaf salad and/or a tomato salad, and a good bread, such as the Lemon, Thyme and Garlic Bread (see page 370).

Serves 8

For the flavoured milk:

1 pint/570 ml milk

1 onion, skinned and halved

A stick of celery, washed and halved

A frond of fennel (optional)

A few black peppercorns

1 tsp rock salt

A handful of parsley

For the roulade:

2 handfuls of watercress

2 oz/56 g butter

2 oz/56 g plain flour

Salt and freshly ground black pepper

4 large eggs, separated, + 1 whole egg

For the filling:

¾ pint/420 ml double cream, whipped

Grated rind and juice of 1 lemon

Plenty of freshly ground black pepper

8 oz/225 g smoked salmon, cut into fairly fine shreds

Bring the milk to scalding point – when a skin starts to form – in a saucepan, together with the flavourings. Take the pan off the heat and leave it to stand for an hour, then strain the milk, throwing away the flavourings.

Line a baking tray measuring 10–12 inches x 12–14 inches (25–30 cm x 30–35 cm) with baking parchment. Liquidize the watercress with the flavoured milk. Melt the butter in a saucepan, stir in the flour and let it cook for a couple of minutes to make a roux. Add the watercress and milk mixture gradually to the roux, stirring continuously till the sauce boils. Season with salt and pepper, and take the pan off the heat. Beat in the whole egg and the 4 egg yolks. Whisk the 4 egg whites till they are very stiff then, with a large metal spoon, fold them quickly into the sauce.

Pour this into the paper-lined baking tray, and bake in a moderate oven – 350°F/180°C/Gas Mark 4 – for about 25 minutes, till it feels firm to the touch. Take it out of the oven, cover with a fresh piece of paper and a damp teatowel over that, and leave to cool.

To make the filling, whip the lemon juice and rind into the whipped cream, and season with black pepper. Fold the shredded smoked salmon into the cream.

To roll up the roulade, lay a piece of baking parchment on a table or work surface, uncover the roulade and, taking the short ends of its paper in either hand, flip it over on to the work surface. Carefully peel the paper off its back, in strips parallel to the roulade, which will prevent the roulade tearing with the paper. Cover the surface with the smoked salmon cream, and roll up.

Slip it on to a serving plate and slice it thickly (one less thing to do on the picnic site) before loosely wrapping the roulade and its plate in foil. Take a large palette knife or fish slice to serve the roulade from the serving dish to each plate.

Brown Sugar Meringues

This is a perfect pudding for a picnic when combined with lemon curd (see page 316) and whipped cream and strawberries.

Serves 6

4 oz/112 g granulated sugar

4 oz/112 g Demerara sugar

4 large egg whites

Mix together the two sugars. Line a baking tray with a piece of baking parchment. Whisk the egg whites till stiff then, whisking continuously, add the sugar a spoonful at a time. When the sugar is all incorporated, use a fluted nozzle to pipe the meringue on to the prepared baking tray in even-sized rounds – I aim for about 2–2½ inch/5–6 cm diameter.

Bake in a cool oven, 250°F/120°C/Gas Mark ½ for 2–2½ hours. Cool on a wire rack, and store the meringues in an airtight tin. Transport them in the tin to the picnic, and sandwich them together with whipped cream and lemon curd to serve.

Stocks, Salad Dressings and Savoury Butters

There is no real substitute for stock, the real thing, as opposed to the ubiquitous stock cube. It doesn't matter what you are making – if the recipe includes stock as one of its ingredients, the end result will be far better if you use homemade. Don't be put off, as I used to be, by the thought of making stock – it isn't an endless chore. It can be thrown together in two ticks, be it chicken, vegetable, fish, or game, and can be left simmering away quietly for a couple of hours.

The stocks I use most are chicken and vegetable. I find the faint smell of chicken stock cooking, permeating the kitchen, very comforting. I cook my chicken stock overnight in the top-right oven of my Aga. The result of this very long, slow cooking is a most mouthwatering-smelling stock, dense with flavour. But you don't have to have an Aga or a Raeburn to make good stock, of course. An electric stewpot is ideal, if you have one, and then vegetable and fish stocks can also be made, most successfully, in a microwave oven, because neither of these stocks is dependent on long cooking.

When cold, stock can be frozen in plastic mineral water bottles – so much handier than freezing the liquid in bowls.

The salad dressings in this chapter can act as both garnish and taste-enhancer to a variety of foods, not always salads. Barbecued salmon, for instance, is quite delicious served with Lime and Parsley Mayonnaise, or with Tomato and Cucumber Mayonnaise. There are some revolting bottled salad dressings and mayonnaises to be found on the supermarket shelves. Again, none is as good as homemade, and you will find that these recipes are all so simple, yet so very good. As with all cooking, taste is individual, so you should adjust seasonings to suit your own liking. I love peppery food, for example, so I am inclined to add more pepper than the recipe dictates. Seasonings given in a recipe are only meant to be guidelines.

Savoury butters are most convenient and can dress up a simple piece of baked chicken, or a grilled chop, a steak or a piece of fish. Because the butters have to be made in advance, they are convenient, too, in that they need only slicing and putting on top of the meat or fish. Garlic butter must be the best known of all savoury butters, and it is good on or in warm bread or rolls, as well as with a baked jacket potato. The Lime, Parsley and Chive Butter is really more suitable for fish, but it is good, too, with grilled or baked chicken. The Mustard and Chive Butter is excellent with all types of meat, and with robust fish like baked fillet of cod. The Red Pepper and the Tomato and Basil Butter are good with fish, chicken and meat alike.

Chicken Stock

·

Vegetable Stock

·

Fish Stock

·

Game Stock

·

French Dressing

·

Green Dressing

·

Mayonnaise

·

Curried Mayonnaise

·

Lime and Parsley Mayonnaise

Sorrel and Lettuce Mayonnaise

·

Tomato Mayonnaise

·

Tomato and Cucumber Mayonnaise

·

Tomato and Dill Mayonnaise

·

Garlic Butter

·

Lime, Parsley and Chive Butter

·

Mustard and Chive Butter

·

Red Pepper Butter

·

Tomato and Basil Butter

Chicken Stock

Make more than you need and freeze half the quantity. If you are going to use the stock for a light summery soup, skin the onions. Otherwise, leave the skins on, as they colour the stock a warm, rich brown.

Makes about 3 pints/1.7 litres

2 chicken carcasses

A small handful of black peppercorns

2 bay leaves

4 onions, quartered

3–4 carrots, halved

A handful of fresh parsley

Some celery leaves, or 2 celery stalks

1 tbsp salt

Put all the ingredients into a large saucepan and add 6 pints/3.4 litres of water. Bring to the boil, then half cover and leave to simmer for 2–3 hours. Cool. Strain the stock into a bowl, jug or polythene container and store in the fridge. If kept for more than a few days, boil for 15 minutes every other day.

Vegetable Stock

Vegetable stock is wonderfully tasty and can be substituted for any other stock. All vegetables are perfectly delicious in vegetable stock except potatoes and turnips. Somehow turnips make the stock taste bitter, and potatoes make it taste sour and go cloudy. The following recipe is only a guide – you can put in whatever you have to hand in the vegetable line.

Makes about 3 pints/1.7 litres

4 onions, quartered

4 large carrots, halved

2 large parsnips, halved

2 celery stalks

Half a cabbage, or the equivalent in outer leaves of Brussels sprouts

4 leeks, quartered

2 garlic cloves, halved

A small handful of black peppercorns

2 tsp salt

A handful of fresh parsley

2 bay leaves

Put all the ingredients into a large saucepan and add 6 pints/3.4 litres of water. Bring to the boil. Half cover the saucepan and simmer gently for 2 hours. Cool, strain the stock, and keep in the fridge or freezer.

Fish Stock

Fish stock is the quickest of all to make – you can have delicious fish stock an hour after you put it on to cook. If you buy your fish in a fishmonger's your fish will be sold to you ready filleted, so do remember to ask for the skin and bones as well. The bones and skin of turbot and skate have very gelatinous properties so the resulting stock from them, when cold, sets to quite a firm jelly – delicious!

Spinach and Mushroom Risotto ▶ page 260

Makes about 2½ pints/1.4 litres

Fish bones, skin and trimmings

1 pint/570 ml white wine

2 onions, sliced

A small handful of black peppercorns

A large handful of fresh parsley

A few celery leaves (optional)

Put all the ingredients into a saucepan and add 3 pints/1.7 litres of water. Bring the liquid to the boil. Cover the pan tightly and simmer for 45–60 minutes. Remove from the heat and leave to go cold, then strain the stock. Use the same day.

Game Stock

Game stock is the basis for one of the best of all soups – game soup. Up until a few years ago, game anything had rather elite connotations, as game was associated with the privileged few rather than the average household. This is not true now, with pheasants and hares being widely available, comparatively cheaply, and venison being farmed more and more. You can put any game you have to hand into game stock.

Makes about 3 pints/1.7 litres

2 pheasants, either whole if you have an
  abundance, or their carcasses, *and/or*

1 rabbit, or the legs, *and/or*

◀ Frittata with Red Onions and Peppers
page 277

1 or 2 old grouse *and/or*

1 or 2 pigeons

4 onions, quartered

2 celery stalks

4 carrots

Bacon rinds (optional)

12 juniper berries, crushed

A small handful of black peppercorns

2 tsp salt

2 bay leaves

Pared rind of 1 orange

Pared rind of 1 lemon

A handful of fresh parsley

Put all the ingredients into a large saucepan and add 6 pints/3.4 litres of water. Bring to the boil. Half cover the pan and simmer gently for 3–4 hours. Cool. Strain the stock and keep, covered, in the refrigerator. If you don't use it immediately, boil it up every other day.

French Dressing

Serves 6

1 tsp salt

1 rounded tsp caster sugar

About 15 grinds of black pepper

1 tsp mustard powder

¼ pint/140 ml oil (sunflower or olive)

2 tbsp wine vinegar – more, if you like a
  sharper flavour

Shake all the dressing ingredients together well, in a screw-topped jar. This dressing can be kept for up to a week in the fridge. Give the jar a good shake to mix up the ingredients before dressing the salad.

Green Dressing

Serves 6

2 avocados

2 tsp mustard powder

½ tsp sugar

½ tsp salt

Lots of freshly ground black pepper

¼ pint/140 ml olive oil (or sunflower)

3–4 tbsp lemon juice

Cut each avocado in half and flick out the stone. Scoop the flesh into a bowl or food processor and add the mustard powder, sugar, salt and pepper. Beat or blend until smooth. Then add the oil in a very slow trickle, continuing to beat or blend. Lastly add the lemon juice. Taste, and if it isn't sharp enough for you, add more lemon juice.

Mayonnaise

As with French dressing, seasoning mayonnaise is a matter of individual taste. I personally like sugar in mine, and I don't like making mayonnaise with all olive oil as I find the flavour of olive oil alone too obtrusive. This is how I make mayonnaise, but change the amounts of the ingredients to suit your own tastes.

Serves 6

2 egg yolks

1 tsp salt

1¼ tsp mustard powder

Freshly ground black pepper

1¼ tsp caster sugar

¼ pint/140 ml olive oil

¼ pint/140 ml sunflower oil

3 tbsp wine vinegar

Put the egg yolks, salt, mustard, pepper and sugar into a blender or food processor. Blend together. With the motor running, slowly add the oils, in a very thin trickle. As the mayonnaise thickens, add the oil in a slightly faster trickle, until it is all used up. Add 2 tbsp of the vinegar, then taste and add more if you like. Keep in a covered bowl in the fridge.

To this basic recipe you can add tomato purée, finely chopped garlic, finely chopped mixed fresh herbs, grated lemon or lime rind, or puréed avocado.

Curried Mayonnaise

This mayonnaise is delicious with the Smoked Chicken and Mango Salad on page 239.

Serves 6

1 whole egg + 1 egg yolk

1 tsp mustard powder

½ tsp salt

1 tsp honey or sugar

1 garlic clove, skinned and chopped

1 rounded tsp curry powder

Freshly ground black pepper

½ pint/285 ml oil (I use sunflower or a
   mixture of olive and sunflower)

3 tbsp wine vinegar

2 tbsp boiling water

Put the whole egg, egg yolk, mustard powder, salt, honey, garlic, curry powder and pepper into a food processor or blender and liquidize. With the motor running, gradually add the oil, a drop at a time to start with. When all the oil is incorporated, add the wine vinegar – use more or less to suit your taste. Finally blend in the boiling water, which makes the mayonnaise thinner and helps it to coat the salad.

Lime and Parsley Mayonnaise

This 'dresses up' so much plain grilled or barbecued food, whether chicken, meat or fish.

Serves 6

1 whole egg + 1 egg yolk

1½ tsp mustard powder

½ tsp salt

1½ tsp sugar

Freshly ground black pepper

½ pint/285 ml sunflower or olive oil, or a mixture of both

2 tbsp white wine vinegar

2 tbsp chopped fresh parsley

Grated rind and juice of 2 limes

Put the whole egg, egg yolk, mustard, salt, sugar and pepper into a blender or food processor and blend until smooth. With the motor running, add the oil drop by drop to start with. As the mixture begins to thicken, add the oil in a steady trickle until it is all incorporated. Blend in the vinegar. Add the parsley and the lime rind and juice. Transfer to a serving bowl.

Sorrel and Lettuce Mayonnaise

This sauce has a delicate flavour, and is a beautiful pale green colour. It can be made in advance.

Serves 6

4 oz/112 g Webb's Wonder or iceberg lettuce, shredded

4 oz/112 g small sorrel leaves, shredded

Salt and freshly ground black pepper

1 egg

½ tsp mustard powder

Lemon juice

½ pint/285 ml olive oil

Cook the lettuce and sorrel with 3 tbsp water for about 4 minutes until the sorrel has 'fallen'. The lettuce will remain quite crisp. Drain well, season and cool.

Blend the egg with the mustard powder and lemon juice in a blender or food processor. With the motor running, pour the oil in a slow steady stream. Transfer to a bowl and season. Fold in the sorrel and lettuce.

Tomato Mayonnaise

This mayonnaise is particularly good with fish of all types, whether hot or cold.

Serves 6

1 whole egg + 1 egg yolk

1 tbsp tomato purée

Salt and freshly ground black pepper

1½ tsp sugar

Half a garlic clove, skinned

½ pint/285 ml mixed sunflower and olive oil

3 tbsp white wine vinegar

A handful of fresh parsley, stalks removed

Put the whole egg, egg yolk, tomato purée, seasoning, sugar and garlic into a blender or food processor and blend briefly. Add the oil, drop by drop, still blending. When about half the oil has been added, the remainder may be added more quickly. Blend in the vinegar and parsley. Taste the mayonnaise and adjust the seasoning if necessary. Store the mayonnaise in a screw-topped jar in the fridge.

Tomato and Cucumber Mayonnaise

A delicious summery mayonnaise with a crunchy texture.

Serves 6

1 whole egg + 1 egg yolk

1 rounded tsp mustard powder

½ tsp salt

1 tsp caster sugar

Freshly ground black pepper

About ½ pint/285 ml oil (I use olive oil or a
   mixture of olive and sunflower)

About 3 tbsp wine vinegar (taste after adding
   2 tbsp, and add more if you like a sharper
   mayonnaise)

3 tomatoes, skinned, de-seeded and chopped

Half a cucumber, halved lengthways,
   de-seeded and finely diced

Put the whole egg and the yolk into a liquidizer or food processor, and add the mustard powder, salt, sugar and pepper. Blend until smooth. Continue blending and add the oil, drop by drop at first. When the mayonnaise is thick and smooth add the rest of the oil in a slow trickle, still blending. Lastly add the wine vinegar. If the mayonnaise is too thick, add 2 tablespoons of very hot water. Turn the mayonnaise into a serving bowl, and carefully fold into it the tomatoes and cucumber.

Tomato and Dill Mayonnaise

This is, to my taste, the ideal sauce for barbecued salmon. You can leave out the garlic if you prefer. Dill is one of my favourite flavours. (Garlic, basil, coffee, chocolate, lemon and vanilla are the others!)

Serves 6

1 whole egg + 1 egg yolk

1 rounded tsp caster sugar

½ tsp salt and lots of freshly ground black
   pepper

1 rounded tsp mustard powder

1 garlic clove, skinned and chopped

½ pint/285 ml sunflower oil

3–4 tbsp wine vinegar (depending on how
   sharp you like your mayonnaise)

2 tbsp chopped dill fronds

4 tomatoes, skinned, de-seeded and chopped

Put the mayonnaise ingredients – save for the oil, vinegar, dill and tomatoes – into a food processor and blend until smooth. Continue blending and add the oil, drop by drop at first. When the mayonnaise is thick and smooth add the rest of the oil in a slow trickle, still blending. Then add the wine vinegar and stir in the dill and chopped tomatoes to serve.

If you make this mayonnaise the day before, don't worry that the chopped tomatoes will make it watery. They won't, because their seeds have been removed and it is they that make for wateriness.

Garlic Butter

4 oz/112 g butter

2 garlic cloves, crushed

Salt and freshly ground black pepper

Beat the butter until it is very soft, add the garlic, and season to taste. Form the butter into a log shape in baking parchment and put it into the fridge. When firm and chilled, roll it into a cylinder and wrap it in clingfilm. Store in the fridge until needed.

Lime, Parsley and Chive Butter

This is good with any grilled chicken, fish, or chops.

8 oz/225 g slightly salted butter

Rind of 2 limes – the limes well scrubbed under running water to remove the preservative with which they are sprayed, then dried before grating finely

Juice of the limes

Salt and freshly ground black pepper

2 tbsp finely chopped parsley and snipped chives mixed

In a bowl beat the butter until it is soft, easiest done using a hand-held electric whisk, and beat in the lime rinds and, drip by drip, the lime juice. Lastly, beat in the salt and pepper and the parsley and chives.

Form the butter into a log shape in baking parchment and put it into the fridge. When it is firm and chilled, roll it into a cylinder and wrap it in clingfilm.

Slice it thickly, and serve one or two slices on top of the grilled food.

Mustard and Chive Butter

This butter is especially good with grilled meats.

8 oz/225 g slightly salted butter

2 tsp mustard powder

2 tsp Dijon mustard

2 tbsp snipped chives

In a bowl beat the butter until it is soft, then gradually beat in the dry mustard and the Dijon mustard. Mix in the snipped chives, and scoop the butter on to a piece of baking parchment. Form it into an oblong and put it in the fridge. When it is chilled and firm, roll it into a neat cylinder shape and wrap it in clingfilm or baking parchment. Put it back in the fridge till you are ready to serve it.

Slice it thickly, and put a slice on top of each grilled chop or steak.

Red Pepper Butter

This is especially good with grilled chicken or lamb chops, or with grilled or barbecued steaks.

2 red peppers

4 garlic cloves, in their skins

2 tbsp lemon juice

Salt and freshly ground black pepper

8 oz/225 g slightly salted butter

Cut each pepper in half, scoop away the seeds and put the pepper halves skin side uppermost under a red-hot grill. Grill the peppers till their skin forms great black blisters, then take them out and put them in a polythene bag for 10 minutes. Then skin them and chop their flesh. Meanwhile, simmer the garlic cloves for 2 minutes, drain, cut off the ends of each clove and squeeze them from their skins – they should pop out easily – into a food processor. Add the chopped peppers and whiz, adding the lemon juice gradually. Season with salt and pepper.

In a bowl beat the butter with electric beaters until it is soft, then gradually add the pepper and garlic purée, a small amount at a time, till the butter and purée are well combined. Wrap the butter in baking parchment, rolling it to an approximate log shape. Put this into the fridge, and when it is chilled, roll it firmly into a cylinder.

Slice it thickly and put a slice or two on each piece of chicken or chop or steak.

Tomato and Basil Butter

This is particularly good with grilled or baked salmon fillets or steaks.

8 oz/225 g slightly salted butter

2 tsp tomato purée

2 tbsp chopped basil

Salt and freshly ground black pepper

2 tomatoes, each skinned, de-seeded, and the tomato flesh cut into fine dice

I hate chopping basil with a knife, because metal tends to turn basil brown at the edges, but there is no alternative for this butter.

In a bowl beat the butter until it is soft, then gradually add the tomato purée and the chopped basil. Season with salt and pepper and mix in the diced tomatoes. Form the butter into a log shape wrapped in baking parchment. Put it into the fridge. When it is chilled and firm roll it into a neat cylinder shape, wrap it in clingfilm or baking parchment, and store it in the fridge.

To serve, slice it thickly and put one or two slices on top of each piece of grilled fish.

Sauces

Sauces have a double role in recipes as far as I'm concerned. They act as a complementary taste to whatever dish they are accompanying and are, in many cases, a garnish. I am not a great one for garnishes that take the form of, for example, radishes sculpted into roses, or tomato skins curled up to supposedly resemble a flower. Wherever possible I like a garnish to be an integral part of a dish and a sauce is so ideal for this purpose. A colour contrast is most desirable, as in a roast red pepper sauce, which enhances the appearance of a wide range of foods from grilled fish to a smooth pale mousse. Similarly, a sweet sauce such as Raspberry and Blackcurrant can enhance both the appearance and the taste of a Lemon Mousse, say, or a soufflé. You won't find any recipes for fruit or vegetable 'coulis' in this book. I like to call a sauce a sauce, and calling it something else is for me in the same category as sculpting radishes into roses.

In many cases sauces can be made in advance. One or two need last-minute attention – Hollandaise, for example. This classic sauce is simple and straightforward to make, keeps warm surprisingly well, and it should not be feared – I know that to some people the making of a Hollandaise sauce is fraught with potential disaster. These fears are completely unfounded. Also, Hollandaise is versatile: add chopped mint and it becomes Sauce Paloise, quite delicious with all lamb dishes from a plain grilled chop to a Herb Crust Roast Rack of Lamb (see page 161).

You will find cold dressings and mayonnaise recipes – and they are varied in their flavourings – on pages 288 to 294; in this section are hot savoury and sweet sauces, and cold sauces in both categories. Probably the best known and most widely used of all hot savoury sauces is the Tomato Sauce; versatile, low in fat, and a good contrast in colour to the many dishes with which it can be served, ranging from pasta to steamed broccoli to grilled fish or chicken.

A hot sweet sauce enables us to serve ice cream all the year round. For instance the Toasted Coconut Ice Cream on page 327 is delicious served with the Warm Brandy and Mincemeat Sauce, and many of the ice creams in that chapter are irresistible with a warm, dark and glossy chocolate sauce, or a fudge or caramel sauce. A fruit sauce, such as the Blackberry Sauce, spiked with lemon to enhance its flavour, is a delicious and healthy alternative to whipped or pouring cream with an apple pie, or a fruity crumble.

Hot Sauces

Apple and Thyme Sauce

•

Apricot and Lemon Sauce

•

Spiced Apricot Sauce

•

Barbecue Sauce

•

Sauce Bercy

•

Bread Sauce

•

Cream Cheese, Crispy Bacon and
Garlic Sauce

•

Dill Sauce

•

Hollandaise Sauce

•

Minty Hollandaise Sauce

•

Lemon and Caper Sauce

•

Lemon, Parsley and Horseradish Sauce

Mushroom and Madeira Sauce

•

Mushroom and White Wine Sauce

•

Orange Sauce (for barbecued food)

•

Prune and Red Wine Sauce

•

Saffron Sauce

•

Creamy Saffron and Lemon Sauce

•

Simple Tomato Sauce

•

Tomato Sauce with Basil

•

Tomato and Madeira Sauce

•

Vermouth and Tomato Sauce

•

White Sauce

Apple and Thyme Sauce

This sauce is delicious served with roast pork, or with grilled pork chops.

Serves 6

2 oz/56 g butter

1 onion, skinned and very finely chopped

4 cooking apples, peeled, quartered, cored
   and chopped

A good sprig of fresh thyme, tiny leaves
   stripped from the stalks, or 2 pinches of
   dried thyme (thyme, along with rosemary,
   dries passably well)

1 tsp sugar or honey

Salt and freshly ground black pepper

Melt the butter and cook the onion over a moderate heat for several minutes till it is really soft. Then add the chopped apples and cook until they fall into mush, which cooking apples do. Add the thyme and sugar or honey. Taste, and season with salt and pepper if you like. Strange as it may sound, the sautéed onion adds a certain amount of sweetness to this otherwise tart sauce.

Apricot and Lemon Sauce

This sauce is delicious with roast duck.

Serves 6

6 oz/170 g dried apricots

1 rounded tbsp granulated sugar

¼ pint/140 ml red wine vinegar

1 pint/570 ml chicken stock or stock made
   with the duck giblets and root vegetables,
   scrubbed and chopped

1 rounded tbsp cornflour

Grated rind and juice of 1 lemon

Salt and freshly ground black pepper

Chop the apricots. Put them in a saucepan, cover with water and simmer for 40–45 minutes, then drain.

Put the sugar and the wine vinegar into a saucepan over a gentle heat. When the sugar has dissolved completely, boil fast until you have a caramel-like syrup. Pour on the stock, and boil fast for another 5 minutes. Slake the cornflour with the lemon juice, and stir in a little of the hot liquid from the pan. Stir the lemony mixture back into the hot liquid, and continue stirring until the sauce boils.

Add the grated lemon rind and the plumped-up apricots. Season with salt and freshly ground black pepper to your taste, and reheat when you are ready to serve.

Spiced Apricot Sauce

This delicious sauce is equally good with hot and cold roast lamb. The spice in it is cumin seed, full of flavour but not at all hot in the fiery sense, so don't be put off by the word 'spiced'.

Serves 6

2 tbsp sunflower oil

1 medium onion, skinned and chopped

Half a garlic clove, skinned and chopped

1 tsp cumin seed (not ground, which
   has much less flavour than the whole
   seed)

6 oz/170 g dried apricots, snipped in half with scissors

½ pint/285 ml chicken or vegetable stock

Salt and freshly ground black pepper

Heat the oil in a saucepan and add the onions. Cook for about 5 minutes, stirring occasionally to prevent them sticking and to make sure that the onions cook evenly. Add the chopped garlic, cook for a minute or two, then add the cumin. Cook for a couple of minutes before adding the snipped dried apricots, and stir in the stock.

Simmer gently till the apricots are plumped up and soft – about 30–35 minutes – adding a little more liquid if they boil too fast and the liquid reduces so much that the apricots are in danger of sticking to the bottom of the saucepan.

When the apricots are cooked, take the pan off the heat, cool and liquidize the sauce, and add salt and pepper to your taste.

Barbecue Sauce

This sauce is good with all barbecued meats – especially chicken and sausages.

Serves 6

2 tbsp olive oil

3 onions, skinned and sliced thinly

1 tbsp soft dark brown sugar or molasses sugar

Two 15-oz/420-g tins chopped tomatoes

4 tbsp Heinz – no other – tomato ketchup

1 tbsp white wine vinegar

A dash of Worcester sauce

Salt and freshly ground black pepper

Heat the oil and sauté the sliced onions till soft – about 5–7 minutes. Then stir in all the other ingredients and simmer, uncovered, stirring occasionally, for 25–30 minutes.

Sauce Bercy

This delicious sauce can be liquidized if you prefer. It is good with all grilled fish, meat and chicken, or steamed vegetables.

Serves 6

1 onion, skinned and finely chopped

4 tbsp dry white wine

2 fl oz/56 ml chicken stock (if you are making the Jerusalem Artichokes Timbales on page 60 use the stock that the Jerusalem artichokes were cooked in)

2 oz/56 g butter, cut into pieces

Juice of half a lemon

1 tbsp finely chopped parsley

Put the onion into a saucepan together with the white wine and chicken stock. Bring to a gentle simmering point and simmer, with the saucepan uncovered, until the liquid has reduced by half and the onion is soft.

Whisk in the butter a piece at a time, then whisk in the lemon juice, making sure that the liquid doesn't boil at all after the butter is added. Just before serving, whisk in the finely chopped parsley.

Bread Sauce

This is bread sauce as we like it – if you prefer it without the flavouring of cloves, leave them out of the recipe. As with so many things, bread sauce is very much a matter of personal taste.

Serves 6

1 pint/570 ml milk

1 medium onion, skinned

About 12 cloves

½ lb/225 g white breadcrumbs, from a day-old loaf, weighed when crumbed

Salt and plenty of freshly ground black pepper

2 oz/56 g butter, cut in pieces

Put the milk into a saucepan with the onion, stuck with the cloves, and warm it over a gentle heat till it forms a skin. Take the pan off the heat, and leave for a couple of hours, to infuse the milk well and truly with the onion and clove flavours. Then remove and discard the onion, stir in the breadcrumbs, salt and pepper, and pieces of butter. The butter won't melt now, but don't worry, it will when the bread sauce is reheated to serve.

Butter an ovenproof dish well, and pour the bread sauce into it. Cover, label and freeze. Take the bread sauce out of the freezer the day before you want to eat it, and reheat it in its dish (all ready to serve, you see – minimum effort, that's what I like!) in a moderate oven, 350°F/180°C/Gas Mark 4, for 30 minutes. Stir it with a fork once or twice during reheating, to mix through the melting bits of butter.

Cream Cheese, Crispy Bacon and Garlic Sauce

This sauce is really best with all types of pasta. But it can also be served with plain boiled potatoes, new or old.

Serves 6

6 rashers of bacon, smoked or unsmoked (I prefer smoked myself)

¾ lb/340 g cream cheese

1 garlic clove, skinned and chopped

2½ fl oz/70 ml milk

1 flat dssp chopped parsley

Cook the bacon till crisp, then drain and cool it on kitchen paper, and break it into small bits.

Put the cream cheese into a food processor or liquidizer with the chopped garlic and whiz till smooth, gradually adding the milk till you have a thick cream. Whiz in the broken-up bacon and chopped parsley, then put the cream cheese and bacon mixture into a serving bowl. You can make this sauce two days in advance provided you cover the bowl and keep it in the fridge.

Dill Sauce

This is a warm mayonnaise-type sauce, well flavoured with dill, a herb which I love to combine with all fish as well as the salmon with which it is more usually associated.

Serves 6

1 small egg + 1 egg yolk

¼ tsp salt

½ rounded tsp mustard powder

Freshly ground black pepper

½ tsp caster sugar

¼ pint/140 ml oil (I use sunflower oil)

2 tbsp wine vinegar, more if you like

2½ fl oz/70 ml near-boiling water

1½ tbsp fresh dill

Put the egg and extra yolk into a food processor or liquidizer with the salt, mustard powder, freshly ground black pepper and caster sugar and whiz, gradually adding the oil – drop by drop at first, then in a very thin trickle. The mayonnaise should be very thick. Whiz in the wine vinegar and the dill, and lastly, with the machine still running, the hot water. This will thin down the sauce so that you can more easily mix it with the fish you are serving in it.

Hollandaise Sauce

A rich warm hollandaise sauce turns even simple vegetables, such as asparagus, into a special dish.

Serves 6

¼ pint/140 ml white wine vinegar

1 bay leaf

A blade of mace (optional)

6–8 black peppercorns

A few fresh parsley stems

4 egg yolks

8 oz/225 g butter, cut into 6 equal pieces

Put the vinegar, bay leaf, mace, peppercorns and parsley stalks into a small saucepan and bring to the boil. Simmer until the liquid has reduced by about half.

Put the egg yolks into a bowl, and beat with a wire whisk. Whisk in the strained seasoned vinegar. Put the bowl over a saucepan half full of hot water and place over medium heat. Add the pieces of butter one at a time, whisking each well before adding the next. When all the butter has been incorporated, the sauce will be thick and golden.

Leave over the saucepan of hot water, off the heat, whisking from time to time, until you are ready to serve. If the sauce separates, whisk frantically, adding a small ladleful of hot water from the saucepan and the sauce will come together again – disaster averted! Try not to keep the sauce warm for much more than 20–25 minutes.

Minty Hollandaise Sauce

Serves 6

¼ pint/140 ml white wine vinegar

6 peppercorns

A slice of onion

1 bay leaf

4 egg yolks (from large eggs)

8 oz/225 g butter, cut in small pieces

A couple of pinches of salt

2 tbsp chopped mint, preferably applemint

Make this as you would the classic hollandaise sauce in the previous recipe, stirring in the chopped mint and salt to taste when all the butter has been added. Serve, in a sauceboat or bowl. This sauce is delicious with roast lamb or lamb chops.

Lemon and Caper Sauce

One of the classic British dishes is leg of lamb with caper sauce. The sauce is made from some of the strained liquid from the lamb joint, thickened with a small amount of flour, egg yolks and cream, and flavoured with lemon. For the caper content it is worthwhile seeking out the very best capers you can find – they are a world apart from the run-of-the-mill capers tasting of nothing but the harsh brine in which they are preserved. They are usually salted, the better quality capers, and so need to be rinsed under cold water.

Serves 6

2 oz/56 g butter

2 oz/56 g flour

1 pint/570 ml strained stock from around the cooked lamb

3 oz/84 g butter, cut into bits

Grated rind of 1 lemon and its juice

¼ pint/140 ml double cream

Freshly ground black pepper – taste to see if salt is needed and add it as you like

4 tsp of the best capers you can buy – a good delicatessen should stock salted capers

Melt the butter in a saucepan and stir in the flour. Let it cook for a minute then, stirring continuously – I find a small balloon whisk ideal for this and all sauce-making – add the stock.

Stir till the sauce boils. Take the pan off the heat and whisk in the bits of butter, a piece at a time. Whisk in the lemon rind and juice and lastly, the cream. Season with pepper, add the capers and mix them well into the sauce, then check to see if you think it is sufficiently salty. Keep the sauce warm while you carve the lamb.

Lemon, Parsley and Horseradish Sauce

This sauce is tangy and delicious, so good with both chicken and grilled fish.

Serves 6

¼ pint/140 ml single cream

¼ pint/140 ml milk

1 tbsp grated horseradish

1 tsp flour

2 oz/56 g butter

2 egg yolks

Salt and freshly ground black pepper

Grated rind of 2 lemons and juice of 1 lemon

2 rounded tbsp finely chopped parsley

Put all the ingredients except the lemon juice and parsley into a liquidizer or food processor, and blend until smooth. Pour into a heatproof bowl.

Stand the bowl in a large saucepan with water coming halfway up the sides of the bowl. Cook, with the water just about simmering, stirring from time to time with a wire whisk, for about 20–25 minutes.

When the sauce has thickened, stir in the lemon juice and, just before serving, the finely chopped parsley. If you add the parsley too soon, so that it has to sit in the hot sauce, it will lose its bright fresh colour. Serve separately in a bowl or sauceboat.

Mushroom and Madeira Sauce

This is a good sauce to serve with a roast fillet of beef.

Serves 6

½ pint/285 ml Madeira

1 onion, skinned and chopped very finely

½ tbsp beef dripping

½ lb/450 g mushrooms, wiped, de-stalked, and sliced thinly

½ oz/14 g flour

½ pint/285 ml good beef stock – or, as a short cut, use good (Crosse & Blackwell) beef consommé

Salt and freshly ground black pepper

Put the Madeira and finely chopped onion in a saucepan and, over a moderate heat, simmer the Madeira till it has reduced down to approximately 2½ fl oz/70 ml of syrupy liquid. The onion will be soft and well cooked.

In another saucepan, melt the dripping, and add the thinly sliced mushrooms. Cook over a high heat for several minutes, stirring occasionally, so that the mushrooms really

brown. Then stir in the flour and cook for a further couple of minutes before pouring in the beef stock, stirring till the sauce boils.

Stir in the Madeira and onion mixture, season to taste with salt and pepper and served with the sliced roast beef fillet.

Mushroom and White Wine Sauce

This is good with all fish, chicken and pork, whether grilled or baked. As with so many sauces, it 'dresses up' the main course.

Serves 6

1 pint/570 ml dry white wine

2 medium onions, skinned and finely chopped

2 oz/56 g butter

8 oz/225 g mushrooms, wiped and sliced

2 rounded tbsp flour

1 pint/570 ml milk

Salt and freshly ground black pepper

Freshly grated nutmeg

Finely chopped parsley to garnish

Put the wine and onions into a saucepan over a moderate heat, and simmer, un-covered, until the wine has reduced by about three-quarters and the onions are very soft.

Melt the butter in another saucepan and add the sliced mushrooms. Stir in the flour and cook for a couple of minutes. Gradually add the milk, stirring continuously until the sauce boils.

Stir in the salt, pepper and nutmeg, and the onion and wine liquid, reheat and, just before serving, stir in chopped parsley to taste.

Orange Sauce (for barbecued food)

This thin orange sauce has snipped chives stirred through it, for both colour and taste. It is very good with barbecued pork fillets.

Serves 6

¾ pint/420 ml orange juice, fresh if possible

2 sprigs of rosemary

½ pint/285 ml chicken or vegetable stock

1 tbsp arrowroot slaked with 2–3 tbsp water

Salt and freshly ground black pepper

1 heaped tbsp snipped chives

Put the orange juice, rosemary and stock in a saucepan and bring to simmering point. Simmer for 5 minutes, then stir some of the hot liquid into the slaked arrowroot, pour this back into the saucepan, season and stir till the sauce boils. Take it off the heat, cool, take out and throw away the rosemary, and stir in the snipped chives.

Serve this sauce either warm or cold.

Prune and Red Wine Sauce

This sauce doesn't take a minute to make, and its sharpness and sweetness go so very well with roast pork.

Serves 6

Fat and juices from roasting the pork

1 medium onion, skinned and finely chopped

1 rounded tbsp flour

½ pint/285 ml red wine

½ pint/285 ml vegetable stock

Salt and freshly ground black pepper

1 tbsp lemon juice

About 8 cooked prunes, stoned and quartered

Drain some of the fat and juices from the pork into a saucepan while the pork is cooking (there is no need to wait until the last minute to make this sauce). Add the onion to the saucepan. Cook over a moderate heat for 5–7 minutes, stirring occasionally, then stir in the flour. Cook for a further couple of minutes, then gradually add the red wine and vegetable stock, stirring continuously until the sauce boils. Season with salt and pepper and stir in the lemon juice. Finally add the prunes.

Keep warm until you are ready to serve and then pour into a bowl or sauceboat.

Saffron Sauce

This is an exceptionally useful and delicious sauce. Don't be tempted to substitute powdered saffron for the strands, though.

Serves 6

1 large or 2 small or medium onions, skinned and very neatly chopped

3 tbsp olive oil

½ tsp saffron strands

1 pint/570 ml good chicken stock

5 oz/140 ml double cream

Salt and freshly ground black pepper

Make this sauce in a sauté pan for speed. Heat the oil and cook the finely chopped onion for several minutes till well softened and turning golden. Soak the saffron in the stock and then pour this into the onions. Let it simmer and reduce by about half in quantity. Pour in the cream and let the sauce bubble for a couple of minutes. Season with salt and pepper.

This is good with chicken or fish.

Creamy Saffron and Lemon Sauce

This simple sauce is a delicious accompaniment to roast chicken – simple it is, but indulgent in its components.

Serves 6

2 oz/56 g butter
1 onion, skinned and very finely chopped
½ pint/285 ml good chicken stock
2 good pinches of saffron strands
Grated rind and juice of 1 lemon
½ pint/285 ml double cream
Salt and freshly ground black pepper

Melt the butter in a sauté pan and cook the very finely chopped onion over a moderate heat till it is really soft. Add the chicken stock and saffron and simmer till the stock has reduced by more than half. Add the lemon rind and juice and reduce for a further couple of minutes' cooking.

Pour in the cream – it must be double, the danger with single cream is that it can curdle, or split. Double won't. Let the sauce bubble till it has the texture of thick cream. Season with salt and pepper. The sauce will be a golden colour, from the saffron. Don't be tempted to substitute saffron powder, which is generally adultered. Only the strands will do!

Simple Tomato Sauce

Serves 6

3 tbsp olive oil
2 onions, skinned and chopped
1 stick of celery, trimmed and sliced
1–2 garlic cloves, skinned and finely chopped
Three 15 oz/420 g cans chopped tomatoes
Salt, pepper and a pinch of sugar

Heat the oil and gently sauté the chopped onions and sliced celery till the onion is soft and just beginning to turn golden brown. Then add the chopped garlic (for a more pronounced garlic taste – if you prefer a milder taste add the garlic at the beginning of the onions' cooking time) and sauté for a few seconds. Stir in the contents of the cans of tomatoes, and season with salt, pepper and sugar. With the lid off the pan, simmer this sauce gently for 20 minutes. Then cool and liquidize the sauce – check the seasoning and add more salt and pepper if you think it needs it.

Tomato Sauce with Basil

This sauce is one of the most valuable of all sauces to have in your repertoire. It is so versatile – delicious with vegetables or fish, or in pizzas – and has the added bonus of being low in calories, too. If making the sauce in summer, when fresh basil is available, add the basil when you purée the sauce. I think that fresh basil loses its pungency in cooking.

Serves 6

5 tbsp olive oil

2 onions, chopped

1 celery stalk, cut into 1 inch/2.5 cm chunks (optional)

1 red pepper, cored, de-seeded and chopped

Two 15-oz/420-g cans of tomatoes, or 1½ lb/675 g fresh tomatoes, skinned, halved and de-seeded

½ tsp sugar

1 large garlic clove, chopped

Salt and freshly ground black pepper

A small handful of fresh basil leaves, or 1 tsp dried basil

Heat the oil in a saucepan, add the onions and cook for 5 minutes, stirring occasionally. Add the celery and red pepper. Cook for a further 2–3 minutes, then add the tomatoes, sugar, garlic and seasoning, and the basil if you are using dried. Let the sauce simmer, uncovered, for 25–30 minutes.

Allow to cool slightly, then pour into a blender or food processor. Add the fresh basil, if using, and blend until smooth.

This sauce freezes beautifully, and will keep very well in the fridge for 2–3 days.

Tomato and Madeira Sauce

The idea for this sauce came from Brigadier Ley, a neighbour of my parents and a great cook and gourmet. The onion and tomatoes in the sauce are my embellishment, but it is the Madeira that makes it so special. It can be made a day in advance and reheated to serve.

Serves 6

1 medium onion, skinned and very finely chopped

¾ pint/420 ml Madeira

2 oz/56 g butter

2 oz/56 g flour

1 pint/570 ml milk

4 tomatoes, skinned, de-seeded and chopped

A very little salt and freshly ground black pepper

Freshly grated nutmeg

1 tbsp finely chopped parsley

Simmer the onion and Madeira together in a saucepan, until the Madeira has reduced by about three-quarters and the onion is cooked.

Melt the butter in another saucepan and stir in the flour. Cook for a couple of minutes, then gradually add the milk, stirring all the time, until the sauce boils. Stir in the onion and Madeira mixture, the tomatoes, and the salt, pepper and nutmeg.

Just before serving, stir the parsley through the sauce. By adding it at the last minute you keep the bright colour of the parsley – if it sits too long in the hot sauce it will go dull and brownish.

Vermouth and Tomato Sauce

This sauce is perfect served with roast pork.

Serves 6

½ pint/285 ml red vermouth

2 medium onions, skinned and chopped very
   finely

2 oz/56 g butter

2 oz/56 g flour

1 pint/570 ml milk

Freshly ground black pepper

A grating of nutmeg

3 tomatoes, skinned, de-seeded, and chopped

1 tbsp chopped parsley

Put the vermouth and finely chopped onions into a saucepan and simmer gently till the onions are very soft and the vermouth is reduced almost to nothing. Melt the butter in another saucepan, and stir in the flour, let it cook for a minute or two, then stir in the milk, stirring all the time till the sauce boils. Simmer for a minute, then take the pan off the heat, and season to taste with pepper and nutmeg.

You can prepare the sauce this far in the morning for dinner that evening, but cover the surface of the sauce with a piece of greaseproof paper wrung out in water to prevent a skin forming.

Prepare the tomatoes and chop the parsley, and stir these into the sauce when you have reheated it ready to serve. Also, if you are roasting pork, stir in some of the juices from the roasting pan. Serve in a sauce tureen.

White Sauce

A well made white sauce, with a glossy sheen to it, is the basis of so many other sauces and dishes. With cheese and mustard added to it, it becomes a sauce delicious with cauliflower, leeks and grilled fish. It is the basis of many hot soufflés, and simply flavoured with a few spoonfuls of finely chopped fresh parsley or mixed herbs it becomes the perfect companion for all vegetables (particularly broad beans), fish and ham. There is no shortcut to this method of making a good white sauce.

Serves 6

2 oz/56 g butter

2 oz/56 g plain flour

1 pint/570 ml milk

Freshly grated nutmeg

Salt and pepper, white or freshly ground
   black, whichever you prefer

Melt the butter in a saucepan. Add the flour and stir it in well, then cook for a couple of minutes. Gradually add the milk, stirring continuously until the sauce boils. Simmer for a couple of minutes, stirring all the time, until thickened and smooth. Remove the pan from the heat and add nutmeg and seasoning to taste.

Cold Sauces

Avocado Sauce
·
Cumberland Jelly
·
Horseradish Sauce
·
Horseradish, Apple and Crème Fraîche Sauce
·
Pink Peppercorn Sauce
·
Tapenade
·
Tartare Sauce

Avocado Sauce

This smooth, pale green sauce can be also used as a delicious dip for crudités.

Serves 6

1 whole egg + 1 egg yolk

1 rounded tsp mustard powder

1 tsp sugar

½ tsp salt (use more if you like a saltier taste)

Freshly ground black pepper (about 15 grinds will do)

½ pint/285 ml oil (I like to use a mixture of olive and sunflower)

3 tbsp wine vinegar

2 tbsp lemon juice

1 medium avocado (if it is very small, use 2; I prefer the smaller, knobbly black ones)

Put the egg, egg yolk, mustard, sugar, salt and pepper into a liquidizer or food processor and blend. While the machine is still blending, very slowly add the oil a drop at a time, until it is all used up and you have a thick mayonnaise.

Blend in the wine vinegar and lemon juice, taste, and add more lemon or vinegar if necessary.

Cut the avocado in half, flick out the stone, scoop out the flesh into a food processor or bowl, and blend by machine or hand until it is well mixed and smooth. Finally, fold in the mayonnaise.

Cumberland Jelly

This is very good served with a terrine, or with any cold meat or game for that matter.

Makes 1 lb/450 g pot – enough for 6–8

8 oz/225 g redcurrant jelly

1 tbsp Dijon mustard

¼ pint/140 ml port

2 tsp powdered gelatine

Grated rind and juice of 1 lemon

Grated rind and juice of 1 orange

Put all the ingredients into a saucepan and heat gently till the jelly has dissolved. Pour into a warmed jar, seal and store in a cool place.

Horseradish Sauce

You can buy a wide variety of horseradish sauces and relishes, but if you can, buy a jar of dried, grated horseradish. This isn't easy to find, but you do occasionally come across them in good delicatessens. Otherwise buy fresh, peel it and grate it – beware, it is ferociously fiery in its raw state – and use it sparingly.

Serves 6

4 tbsp dried horseradish or 1 tsp fresh

½ pint/285 ml crème fraîche

1 tsp sugar

1 tbsp lemon juice

1 tsp wine vinegar

Mix all the ingredients together well, and serve.

Horseradish, Apple and Crème Fraîche Sauce

This is a good accompaniment for smoked trout mousse, hot-smoked salmon, or for cold or hot roast pork.

Serves 6

3 good eating apples, peeled and grated
  coarsely

2 tbsp lemon juice

½ pint/285 ml crème fraîche

4 tsp good horseradish dressing, home-made
  or a good bought one, such as Moniack

Mix all the ingredients together very well, and serve.

Pink Peppercorn Sauce

This is so simple and so good with roast beef – or with steaks.

Serves 6

Half a jar of pink peppercorns, drained of their
  brine

1 tub of crème fraîche (7 fl oz/200 ml)

Mix the ingredients together and serve in a bowl to accompany roast beef.

Tapenade

How many this serves does depend on the appetites of those consuming it! This amount is enough, however, to serve with Roast Red Pepper Mousses, on page 56.

Serves 6

6 oz/175 g black olives, weighed when stoned

1 egg yolk

1 garlic clove, skinned and chopped

A squeeze of anchovy paste

Juice of half a juicy lemon

¼ pint/140 ml olive oil

Freshly ground black pepper

Put the stoned black olives into a food processor and whiz. Add the egg yolk and the garlic, and the anchovy paste, and whiz again. Still whizzing, add the oil, a drip at a time to begin with, then in a steady trickle, till it is all incorporated. Whiz in the lemon juice, and season to taste with black pepper.

Tapenade will keep in a covered bowl in the fridge for up to 5 days.

Tartare Sauce

Tartare sauce is such a delicious sauce, and simple to make, and it can be made up to 2 days ahead and kept, covered, in the fridge.

Serves 6

1 large whole egg + 1 egg yolk

1 tsp sugar

½ tsp salt

Several good grindings of black pepper

1 tsp French mustard

1 garlic clove, skinned and chopped

½ pint/285 ml oil (sunflower or olive, or a
  mixture of both)

2–3 tbsp white wine vinegar

1 tbsp chopped parsley

1 tsp chopped capers

2 hardboiled eggs, chopped finely

6–8 black olives, stoned and chopped

About a 6-inch/15-cm piece cucumber,
  skinned, de-seeded and diced finely

Whiz the first six ingredients – the egg, egg yolk and flavourings – together, in a liquidizer or food processor. Then slowly add, drop by drop at first, then in a steady trickle, the sunflower or olive oil or mixture of both. When all is incorporated, whiz in the white wine vinegar – taste, and add more if you like, but remember that the capers and black olives will add a certain amount of sharpness. Transfer to a bowl and stir in the rest of the ingredients.

Cover and keep in the fridge until required.

Sweet Sauces

Blackberry Sauce

•

Brandy and Mincemeat Sauce

•

Orange-Flavoured Brandy Butter

•

Caramel Sauce

•

Cherry Jam and Brandy Sauce

•

Chocolate Sauce

•

Dark Chocolate Sauce

•

Coffee Cream Sauce

•

Vanilla Custard or Crème Anglaise

•

Fudge Sauce

•

Lemon Curd

•

Pecan or Walnut Caramel Sauce

•

Raspberry and Blackcurrant Sauce

•

Rhubarb and Ginger Sauce

Blackberry Sauce

This sauce is the very essence of Autumn and goes wonderfully with an apple pie. Make it 2 or 3 days in advance and store it in the fridge.

Serves 6

1½ lb/675 g blackberries, thawed if frozen

6 oz/170 g sugar

Put the blackberries into a saucepan with the sugar. Cover and cook gently until the blackberries are very soft, about 20 minutes.

Sieve the blackberries, and their juice, through a nylon sieve to make a purée. Add a little more sugar to sweeten, if necessary. Pour the sauce into a jug and serve hot or cold.

Brandy and Mincemeat Sauce

This sauce is delicious with many flavours of ice cream.

Serves 6

8 oz/225 g mincemeat

Grated rind of 1 orange

3 tbsp brandy

Put all the ingredients together in a saucepan and stir over a gentle heat. Don't let it boil. Serve the sauce hot, with the ice cream.

Orange-Flavoured Brandy Butter

This keeps very well in the fridge for 3–4 weeks, so you can make it well in advance, but do keep it in a covered container.

Serves 6

4 oz/112 g softened butter

4 oz/112 g icing sugar, sieved

Grated rind of half an orange

2½ tbsp brandy

Put the butter into a bowl and beat it well – I find a hand-held electric beater ideal for doing this. Gradually beat in the sieved icing sugar, and the grated orange rind. Then, still beating, add the brandy half a spoonful at a time. (If you add the brandy all at once, you are in danger of curdling the brandy butter.)

Scoop into a bowl, cover, and store in the fridge.

Caramel Sauce

Serves 6

½ pint/285 ml water

6 oz/170 g granulated sugar

2 oz/56 g Demerara sugar

4 oz/112 g butter cut into bits

¼ pint/140 ml double cream

A few drops of vanilla extract, or

½ tsp essence

Put the water and sugars into a fairly large and heavy-based saucepan, over a moderate heat. Shake the pan gently till the sugars dissolve completely. Be sure that they are dissolved before you let the liquid come to the boil. Boil for 10 minutes. Then take the pan off the heat and whisk in the butter, bit by bit. Lastly, stir in the cream and the vanilla.

Cool, and store in a screw-top jar. Reheat to serve – you will find that the sauce separates in the jar, with the fudgy top and the sugar syrup base. It all comes together on stirring and remains together on reheating. Before serving, boil the sauce for 2 minutes.

Cherry Jam and Brandy Sauce

This sauce is embarrassingly easy to make. But it is delicious, and much enjoyed by all who eat it. I serve it with plain homemade vanilla ice cream. If you use cherry brandy, you get a sweeter sauce than if you use plain brandy. Any left over can be stored in a covered jar. Sometimes I double the brandy for an extra boozy sauce.

Serves 6

1 lb/450 g cherry jam

4 tbsp either cherry brandy or plain brandy

Put the two ingredients together in a saucepan and warm through gently, until the jam melts. Try not to let the sauce boil, as then the alcohol will evaporate. Serve the sauce hot, with good vanilla ice cream.

Chocolate Sauce

I am such a chocolate addict and how I wish I wasn't, but it is just one of those things you have to learn to live with! This sauce fills my best expectations of all that a chocolate sauce should be.

Serves 6

8 oz/225 g soft dark brown sugar

3½ tbsp cocoa powder, sifted

3 oz/86 g butter

2 tsp coffee powder

1 tsp vanilla essence or a few drops of extract

3 tbsp golden syrup

½ pint/285 ml boiling water

Put all the ingredients into a saucepan and heat until smooth, then bring to the boil. Simmer gently, stirring occasionally, for 5 minutes.

This sauce keeps well in a jar in the fridge, but it becomes thick and fudgy when cold. To reheat, stand the jar in a warm place and then pour the sauce into a saucepan.

Dark Chocolate Sauce

This is an invaluable sauce to have stored away in a screw-topped jar in the fridge, ready to be heated up and served with all sorts of different puddings, or with ice creams, or fruit, especially pears or bananas. Chocolate sauces vary so much. The ones I abhor are those which are too milky or, worse still, watery, tasting insufficiently of chocolate, and thin and dreary in texture. You can't say that about this one!

Serves 6

6 oz/170 g caster sugar

1 tsp vanilla essence or a few drops of extract

3 tbsp golden syrup

6 tbsp cocoa powde

7 fl oz/200 ml boiling water

Put all the ingredients together into a saucepan, and heat gently until the sugar is dissolved and the syrup is melted. Stir until smooth. Boil fast, for about 5 minutes. The more you boil this sauce, the fudgier it becomes.

Coffee Cream Sauce

This delicious sauce enhances any chocolate pudding.

Serves 6

½ pint/285 ml single cream

1 tbsp instant coffee granules

3 egg yolks

3 oz/84 g caster sugar

1 tsp cornflour

Put the single cream and instant coffee granules together in a saucepan and heat gently. Meanwhile beat the egg yolks in a bowl, gradually adding the sugar. Sieve in the cornflour and beat all well together. Pour in a little of the coffee-flavoured cream, mix well, then pour the contents of the bowl into the saucepan. Over a gentle to moderate heat, stir until the sauce thickens to the consistency of pouring cream. Allow to cool.

Serve cold or warm, but not hot.

Vanilla Custard or Crème Anglaise

This is one of my favourite of all sauces. But it is very much nicer made using vanilla extract than essence.

Serves 6

4 large egg yolks

3 oz/84 g caster sugar

1 tsp cornflour, sieved

½ tsp vanilla essence, or a few drops of extract

1 pint/570 ml milk or, better still, single cream

Beat together the yolks, sugar, cornflour and vanilla, then gradually mix in the milk (or cream). Cook by stirring, in a heavy-based saucepan, over a gentle heat till the custard thickens – this is a lengthy process and can't be hurried for fear of curdling the custard. Or, if you have a microwave, put the bowl into the microwave on a halfway heat setting for 2 minutes. Take out and whisk the custard, then replace it in the microwave for a further 2 minutes on halfway heat. Whisk, and repeat the cooking – it will take between 6 and 8 minutes' cooking altogether to thicken.

Serve warm.

Fudge Sauce

This sauce is delicious with vanilla ice cream and also with pears. And you can see how simple it is!

This recipe was my grandmother's cook's (Mrs Day's) recipe.

Serves 6

4 oz/112 g butter

6 oz/170 g soft brown sugar, dark or light

7 fl oz/200 ml double cream

Put the butter, sugar and cream together in a saucepan; heat gently, stirring, until the butter is melted and the sugar completely dissolved. Then boil gently over a steady heat, for a good 5 minutes. This sauce keeps well in a screw-top jar in the fridge for several days.

Lemon Curd

This is quite sharp in taste. If it is too sharp, just increase the amount of sugar by an ounce or two. Use Seville oranges instead of lemons, when they are in season.

Makes approximately 2 lb/900 g

Grated rind and juice of 3 lemons

3 oz/84 g butter

3 oz/84 g caster sugar

2 whole eggs

2 egg yolks

Put the grated lemon rinds and juice, butter and sugar together either in a double saucepan over simmering water, or in a heavy-bottomed saucepan over a gentle heat. Stir the mixture occasionally, until the sugar has completely dissolved.

Beat together the eggs and the yolks until well mixed, then pour a little of the hot lemon mixture on to the eggs. Mix well and pour the egg mixture into the pan with the rest of the lemon, sugar and butter mixture. Over a gentle heat, and stirring continuously, cook until the mixture thickens. Do not let it boil.

Remove from the heat, and put into jars – this quantity will fill two 1 lb/450 g jars or rather less.

Pecan or Walnut Caramel Sauce

This takes about 10 minutes to make and, although good with vanilla ice cream, is especially delicious with coffee ice cream.

Serves 6

4 oz/112 g butter

4 oz/112 g granulated sugar

1 tbsp golden syrup

3 tbsp milk

A few drops of vanilla essence

4 oz/112 g pecans or walnuts, chopped

Put all the ingredients into a saucepan and stir them over a gentle heat till the butter has melted and the sugar dissolved. Stir in the nuts and boil the sauce for 5 minutes, still stirring. This sauce keeps warm indefinitely.

Rhubarb and Ginger Sauce

This sauce is particularly delicious with cream-filled meringues.

Serves 6

2 lb/900 g rhubarb cut in chunks about
1 inch/2.5 cm long

4 oz/112 g sugar

2 rounded tsp ground ginger

6 pieces of ginger preserved in syrup, drained
(optional)

Put the chunks of rhubarb into a saucepan, together with the sugar and ginger, and put a lid on. Put the pan on a gentle to moderate heat. As it heats, the juice will seep from the rhubarb, and this makes for a much better end result than starting the rhubarb off with water. As the juice flows, turn up the heat a bit, and cook until the rhubarb is starting to fall apart – about 30 minutes. Remove the saucepan from the heat and cool.

Liquidize in a blender, then sieve the purée. This may sound unnecessary (I loathe washing sieves), but it is worth it to get an absolutely velvety sauce. Taste, and add more sugar if you like, and a bit more ginger if you think it needs it. If you are using the preserved ginger, cut it into little slivers and stir them through the sauce.

Raspberry and Blackcurrant Sauce

This is so good either with vanilla ice cream or with raspberry or blackcurrant ice cream or sorbets.

Serves 6

1 lb/450 g each raspberries and blackcurrants
– there is no need to strip the currants from
their stems, as the sauce will be liquidized
and sieved

4 oz/112 g granulated sugar

Icing sugar (optional)

Put the raspberries and blackcurrants together in a saucepan with the sugar. Over gentle heat, cook till the juices run and the currants are soft. Take them off the heat, cool, liquidize and sieve. If you would like a sweeter sauce, add some sieved icing sugar.

Puddings

This chapter is divided into four sections: Frozen Puddings, Light Puddings, Substantial Puddings and Gateaux. I must declare my hand before I go any further – I *love* puddings. When I plan the menus here at Kinloch for our hotel guests, I start with the puddings and work backwards up the page. We have a choice of two puds, one usually rich and chocolatey, the other a lighter (supposedly!) and fruit-based alternative.

Puddings are seasonal, as with all other dishes. Any fruit puds involving fresh raspberries, strawberries or blackberries or gooseberries are best eaten in these fruits' natural season to this country. I deplore fruit such as strawberries being imported throughout the year – people forget just how delicious a strawberry grown in Britain tastes. Some soft fruit freezes well – blackcurrants, for instance, and blackberries (or brambles, call them what you will) and raspberries – and this preserves them for winter use in suitable puddings such as the Baked Lemon and Raspberry Pudding, a light and delicious cold-weather pud. You see, it isn't just the fruit content that makes puddings seasonal, it is also the type of pudding. A frozen pudding such as the Lime and Mango Sorbet wouldn't appeal to me for winter eating, but that doesn't mean that I never eat ice cream in the winter. I frequently put an ice on the menu here, and, if it is cold outside, accompany it by a warm sauce. The Frozen Honey and Whisky Creams, for example, make a perfect accompaniment to the Hot Fresh Fruit Salad with Honey, Ginger and Cardamom. A good dark and glossy chocolate sauce with the Coffee and Chipped Dark Chocolate Ice Cream, or with a good plain vanilla ice cream, is delicious all year round, whatever the temperature outside.

Pies, tarts and cheesecakes fall into the same category of being either for summer eating only, as in the Tarte aux Fruits, or, as in the Baked Dark Chocolate Cheesecake (one of my favourites), for all-year-round eating. The recipes in the Gateaux section of this chapter are really all-year-round dishes, too. Sadly, they are calorifically laden, every single one of them, but I feel strongly that whereas we are all very conscious of what we eat, and rightly so, balance is the all-important point to bear in mind. A splurge occasionally is fine. There is nothing so boring as a calorie fanatic, or someone who is anti-fat and takes theory to an extreme.

Watercress and Smoked Salmon Roulade ▶
page 283

None of us these days is likely to indulge in a pudding every day (sadly!), as in the pre-war days, but I feel that if we did it wouldn't be as bad for us as might be thought, providing that we all took more exercise.

Puddings are the most convenient of all the courses in that, for the most part, they can be made several hours, if not a day, in advance. There are few people indeed who don't love a pudding, and in this chapter you will find any number of choices to indulge yourself, your family and your friends.

This chapter has also given me the oppor- tunity to include several recipes from my mourned-for Chocolate book, now sadly out of print. But since I wrote that book many other new chocolate ideas for recipes have occurred in our repertoire here at Kinloch, and they, too, make an appearance in this chapter.

The joy of my life and its almost total involvement with food means that I am con- tinually experimenting, and, as ever, I start experimenting with puddings, combining flavours and textures. I hope that those of you who love both making and eating puddings of all descriptions find inspiration in this chapter.

◀ Lemon Mousse with Raspberry Sauce
page 333

Frozen Puddings

Blackcurrant and Blackcurrant Leaf Water Ice
·
Lime and Mango Sorbet with Mango and
Lime Salad
·
Brown Bread Ice Cream
·
Chocolate and Ginger Meringue Bombe
·
Chocolate and Marrons Glacés Ice Cream
·
Chocolate and Peppermint Crisp Ice Cream
·
Rich Chocolate, Raisin and Rum Ice Cream
·
Cinnamon Ice Cream with Raspberries
·
Toasted Coconut Ice Cream
·
Coffee and Chipped Dark Chocolate Ice Cream
·
Raspberry Ice Cream
·
Vanilla Ice Cream
·
Frozen Honey and Whisky Creams
·
Frozen Plum, Cinnamon and Port Parfait

Blackcurrant and Blackcurrant Leaf Water Ice

Adding the blackcurrant leaves to the syrup of this water ice enhances the flavour.

Serves 6–8

1 pint/570 ml water
8 oz/225 g granulated sugar
Rind and juice of 2 lemons
A handful of blackcurrant leaves
8 oz/225 g blackcurrants

Put the water, 6 oz/170 g of the sugar and the lemon rind together in a saucepan over a gentle heat, and stir until the sugar has dissolved completely. Then boil fast for 5 minutes. Remove from the heat, and stir in the lemon juice and the blackcurrant leaves. Leave until cold.

Put the blackcurrants, the remaining sugar and 4 tablespoons of water together in a saucepan – don't bother to top and tail the blackcurrants, they will be puréed and sieved later. Cook over a gentle heat until the currants are soft. Cool, purée in a blender and sieve, to give a really smooth purée. Strain the cold lemon and black-currant leaf syrup, and stir it into the black-currant purée.

Put the mixture into a plastic container and freeze for 2–3 hours, until it is setting round the edges and mushy in the middle. Beat it with a rotary whisk or electric hand-beater, or better still, put it into a food processor and whiz. Return the purée to the plastic container, re-freeze, and after a couple of hours repeat the beating. Do this three or four times, and you will have a smooth water ice which is easy to spoon out of the container straight from the deep freeze.

Lime and Mango Sorbet with Mango and Lime Salad

Mangoes are so easy to buy these days. I even found some perfectly ripe ones in the Co-op in Broadford, our local town here on Skye. They make a delicious sorbet, refreshing yet with more substance to it than lemon sorbet, for instance. Accompany the sorbet by chopped mangoes (it is pretty well impossible to slice a mango neatly without wasting at least half of the fruit) with lime juice squeezed over them which just sharpens up the taste of the whole.

Serves 6–8

1 pint/570 ml water
6 oz/170 g granulated sugar
Pared rind and juice of 2 limes
2 mangoes, pared of their skin and flesh chopped from the stones

For the salad:

4 mangoes, skin pared off and the flesh chopped as neatly as possible
Juice of 2 limes

Put the water and sugar into a saucepan with the pared lime rinds. Over a moderate heat shake the pan or stir from time to time, till the grains of sugar have completely dis-solved. Then, and only then, let the liquid come to the boil. Boil for 5 minutes, then draw the pan off the heat and stir in the lime juice. Let this cool. When it is cold, fish out the strips of lime rind and whiz with the mango flesh in a liquidizer or food processor. If you have an ice cream making machine, freeze and churn the mixture in it till it is a soft, smooth and thick frozen sorbet. Freeze it in a solid container.

If you don't have a machine, freeze the purée in a shallow container. When you remember, chip the frozen sorbet (which will have the texture of ice lollies) into a food processor and whiz. Refreeze this slush. Repeat this three more times. If you are making this over a period of days don't worry about refreezing the semi-thawed ices – it has no dairy produce in it. By whizzing the sorbet in the processor like this you improve the texture so much that you will be able, after four whizzings, to spoon the sorbet from the freezer.

For the accompanying salad, just put the chopped mango flesh into a pretty dish and pour over the lime juice.

Brown Bread Ice Cream

This is an exquisitely flavoured and textured ice cream. The recipe was given to me originally by Jean Lindsay – since she gave it to me I've come across many recipes for brown bread ice cream and none of them is a patch on this one. It is very easy to make, and draws audible cries of glee and surprise from the dining-room at Kinloch when it is on the menu!

Serves 6

3 oz/84 g wholewheat or other brown breadcrumbs – we use crumbs made from the granary bread we make each day at Kinloch

2 oz/56 g granulated sugar

3 tbsp water

¾ pint/420 ml double cream

3 oz/84 g icing sugar, sieved

½ tsp vanilla essence or a few drops of extract

Toast the breadcrumbs until they are evenly golden brown all over. Put the sugar into a heavy saucepan, add the water and heat gently until the sugar has dissolved completely – shake the pan, don't stir with a spoon. Then boil fast for 2 minutes. Stir the toasted crumbs into the hot syrup and stir until the syrup cools – the crumbs will become sugar encrusted. Any that form a hard lump can be bashed into smaller bits.

Whip the cream with the icing sugar and vanilla essence or extract and stir in the cooled, sugar-crusted crumbs. Pour the mixture into a polythene container and freeze. Remove the ice cream from the deep freeze as you start dinner, and put it in the fridge. Take it out of the fridge and leave at room temperature as you begin to serve the main course.

Chocolate and Ginger Meringue Bombe

Chocolate and ginger go together so very well. Because of the meringue content this bombe is easily sliced. I like to make it in a clingfilm-lined loaf tin or terrine tin, but if you prefer you could put it to freeze in a pudding bowl lined with clingfilm. If you really want to 'gild the lily' – as I do – accompany it with Dark Chocolate Sauce.

Serves 6–8

3 large egg whites

6 oz/170 g caster sugar

A few drops of vanilla extract

½ pint/285 ml whipped cream

4 oz/112 g best dark chocolate, grated

6–8 pieces of stem ginger, drained of their
preserving syrup, and chopped quite finely

Line a baking tray with a sheet of baking parchment. In a clean bowl whisk the whites till they are stiff, then, whisking all the time, gradually sprinkle in the sugar, a spoonful at a time and whisking well between each spoonful. When it is all incorporated, briefly whisk in the vanilla. With a metal spoon, put even-sized dollops of meringue on to the prepared baking tray and bake in a cool oven, 250°F/125°C/Gas Mark ½, for 2½–3 hours – the meringues should lift off the paper when they are cooked. Cool them, then scrunch them in your hand.

Line a loaf or terrine tin (or a bowl) with clingfilm. Fold together the crushed meringues, whipped cream, grated dark chocolate and ginger. Pack this stiff mixture into the lined tin and freeze. When frozen,

cover with clingfilm and put it back in the freezer.

Before serving, take the tin into room temperature for 10 minutes. Dip the tin briefly in very hot water, turn it on to a serving plate and peel off the clingfilm. Slice to serve.

Chocolate and Marrons Glacés Ice Cream

This is one of my favourite chocolatey ice creams. The contrast in texture between the smooth, rich ice cream and the pieces of marron glacé is quite delicious.

Serves 6–8

3 oz/84 g caster sugar

6 tbsp water

6 oz/170 g dark chocolate

4 large egg yolks

½ pint/285 ml double cream, whipped

8 marrons glacés cut in pieces

Put the sugar and water into a saucepan and heat gently without letting the liquid boil until the sugar has dissolved completely, then boil fast for 3 minutes.

Meanwhile, break the chocolate into a blender or food processor. Pour the hot sugar syrup straight on to the chocolate, put the lid on and whiz – the noise will be horrendous but the chocolate soon melts in the heat of the syrup. Still whizzing, add the egg yolks. Leave to cool, then fold into the whipped cream. Fold the marrons glacés through, then freeze.

Leave for 20 minutes at room temperature to soften slightly before serving.

Chocolate and Peppermint Crisp Ice Cream

Use top-quality peppermint crisp choco-lates for the finest result – Elizabeth Shaw or Bendicks Crisps are ideal.

Serves 8

4 large eggs, separated
4 oz/112 g icing sugar, sieved
½ pint/285 ml double cream
2 tsp cocoa powder
8 oz/225 g dark chocolate peppermint crisps

Whisk the egg whites until they are stiff, then, still whisking continuously, add the icing sugar, a spoonful at a time, until you have a thick meringue. Next, whip the cream. Whisk the egg yolks in another bowl until they are pale and slightly thickened and whisk in the cocoa. Fold the cocoa and egg yolk mixture into the cream. Fold this into the meringue mixture.

Very finely chop the chocolate pepper-mint crisps in a blender or food processor, a few at a time, and fold them through the mixture. Pour into a container, cover and freeze.

Leave the ice cream at room temperature for 30 minutes before serving.

Rich Chocolate, Raisin and Rum Ice Cream

This basic chocolate ice cream recipe is the best I know but I can't claim credit for it because it is the invention of Katie Stewart who very kindly let me include it in my book Sweet Things. *I have to say that the raisins and the booze were my ideas.*

Serves 6–8

3 oz/84 g raisins
6 tbsp white or dark rum
8 oz/225 g dark chocolate
6 tbsp water
3 oz/84 g caster sugar
4 large egg yolks
½ pint/285 ml double cream

Soak the raisins in the rum for as long as possible – overnight is best, in a bowl covered with clingfilm. When you take off the clingfilm the fumes will knock you out for a second or two!

Break the chocolate into a blender or food processor. Put the water and sugar into a saucepan. Over a gentle heat, dissolve the sugar, then boil fast for 3 minutes. Pour the hot sugar syrup on to the chocolate, cover the lid of the blender or processor with a teatowel, and whiz for several seconds.

When the mixture is quite smooth, add the yolks, one by one, and whiz until they are smoothly incorporated. Leave the choco-late mixture to cool.

Meanwhile, whip the cream until it just holds its shape, whipping in any un-soaked-up rum from the raisins. Fold the raisins into the cream, then fold together the cream and raisins mixture and the cooled chocolate mixture. Pour into a polythene container, cover and freeze.

Take the ice cream out of the freezer about 30 minutes before serving, and leave it at room temperature.

Pick over the raspberries, pile into a dish and dust with caster or icing sugar. Take the cinnamon-flavoured ice cream out of the deep freeze 20 minutes before serving. Scoop dollops of the ice cream into individual plates or dishes and spoon the raspberries over the top.

Cinnamon Ice Cream with Raspberries

I have noticed in the past few years how trendy cinnamon has become as a spice with soft fruit. I have been making this ice cream for years now, and it is delicious with raspberries and all other soft fruits, such as black or redcurrants, baked plums, blackberries and strawberries.

Serves 6–8

4 eggs, separated

4 oz/112 g icing sugar, sieved

1 rounded tbsp ground cinnamon

½ pint/285 ml double cream, whipped

1½ lb/675 g raspberries

Caster or icing sugar for the raspberries

Beat the egg yolks with 1 oz/28 g of the sieved icing sugar until pale and thick, then beat in the ground cinnamon. Stir this mixture into the whipped cream.

Whisk the egg whites until fairly stiff, then whisk in gradually the remaining sieved icing sugar. Fold this meringue into the cinnamon cream, and pour into a plastic container. Cover and freeze.

Toasted Coconut Ice Cream

This is a lovely pud for a winter's evening. Serve with Brandy and Mincemeat Sauce (see page 313).

Serves 8

4 eggs, separated

4 oz/112 g icing sugar, sieved

½ pint/285 ml double cream, whipped

3 rounded tbsp desiccated coconut, toasted until golden brown, then cooled

Whisk the egg whites until they are quite stiff, then add the sieved icing sugar, spoonful by spoonful, whisking all the time. In a separate bowl, beat the yolks until smooth then fold them into the whipped cream. Fold the cream and yolk mixture into the egg white mixture, alternately with the cooled, toasted coconut. Put the ice cream mixture into a polythene container with a lid, and freeze.

You do not need to beat this ice cream as it freezes, but take it out of the deep freeze 20 minutes before you want to eat it.

Coffee and Chipped Dark Chocolate Ice Cream

The inspiration for this ice cream came when I was indulging in a visit to Häagen Dazs, in Heathrow Airport. I ate the most delicious and decadent combination of tastes in one ice cream: it was called Cappuccino Commotion, and consisted of coffee ice cream with bits of chocolate, toasted almond and caramel chips. Well, I combined three of those four most complementary tastes in this ice cream.

Serves 6–8

4 oz/112 g dark chocolate

3 large eggs, separated

3 oz/84 g sieved icing sugar

2 tbsp very strong black coffee – use
   1 rounded tsp instant coffee granules
   dissolved in 2 tbsp boiling water, then let it
   cool

½ pint/285 ml double cream, whipped

Melt the chocolate in a bowl over a pan of barely simmering water, and pour it on to a sheet of baking parchment on a baking tray. Cool, then break this into bits. It doesn't matter if the bits of chocolate are different sizes.

Whisk the whites till fairly stiff, then, still whisking, gradually add the sieved icing sugar, holding back about 1 tablespoon. When you have a stiff meringue-like mixture, and using the same unwashed whisks, whisk the yolks till thick and pale, with the remaining tablespoon of icing sugar. Whisk the coffee into the yolks.

With a large metal spoon fold the yolks

mixture into the whipped cream, and then the meringue mixture and the chipped chocolate.

Pour into a solid container and freeze.

Raspberry Ice Cream

You can make this ice using thawed frozen raspberry purée. Unlike the other ice cream recipes here, this needs to be beaten during freezing to prevent the fruit purée crystallizing.

Serves 8

3 eggs, separated

3 oz/84 g icing sugar, sieved

½ pint/285 ml double cream

2 lb/900 g raspberries

Purée the raspberries by cooking them just until their juices run, then liquidizing and sieving them.

Whisk the egg whites, gradually adding nearly all the sieved icing sugar and whisking until the meringue is stiff and peaky. Whisk the yolks with the remaining sugar, until quite pale.

Fold the yolks, meringue and raspberry purée together, and taste. If you think this isn't sweet enough, sieve a little more icing sugar into the whipped cream before folding the cream into the raspberry mixture. Pour it into a polythene container and freeze.

Take the container out of the freezer after a couple of hours, and beat the mixture well. Return it to the freezer, then beat again after another 1½–2 hours. If you have an ice cream machine, put the prepared raspberry cream into it, and churn-freeze for 25 minutes, then put the resulting ice cream into a polythene container and freeze.

Remove from the freezer and leave at room temperature for about 30 minutes before serving.

Vanilla Ice Cream

This is the recipe I like best. It tastes good, has an excellent texture, and doesn't need beating at half frozen.

Serves 6–8

4 large eggs, separated

4 oz/112 g sieved icing sugar

A few drops of vanilla extract, or ½ tsp essence

½ pint/285 ml double cream, whipped, but not too stiffly

Whisk the egg whites till they are fairly stiff, then, whisking continuously, gradually add all but about 1 tablespoon of the sieved icing sugar, whisking till you have a stiff meringue. There is no need to wash the whisks, go straight on and whisk the yolks, adding the remainder of the icing sugar, and whisking till you have a thick and pale mixture. Whisk in the vanilla.

With a large metal spoon, fold the yolks into the cream, then fold in the meringue mixture. Freeze this in a solid container.

Take the container out of the freezer and into room temperature for 20 minutes before serving.

Frozen Honey and Whisky Creams

This is a real 'Taste of Scotland' recipe, what with the whisky and the honey. It is extremely easy and quick to make. The recipe was given to me by Margaret Clark, in Edinburgh, and the recipe was given to her with brandy as the alcohol content. Whilst browsing through one of John Tovey's books recently I came across the same recipe with the brandy, so I'm sure his was the original source of inspiration. I asked him whether he minded my including it in this book, and in his usual generous way he not only gave me his blessing to use it, but almost made me feel that the idea had been originally my own! Because of the alcohol in this recipe, the cream never freezes rock hard and so doesn't need to be removed from the deep freeze until just before it is to be served.

Serves 8

½ pint/285 ml double cream

4 tbsp whisky

3–4 tbsp thick honey

4 egg yolks (use the whites to make vanilla ice cream or meringues)

Whip the cream, gradually adding the whisky, until fairly thick. Warm the honey in a saucepan until hot and runny. Put the yolks into a bowl and, using a hand-held electric whisk, whisk them, gradually pouring on the hot honey. Whisk until the mixture is thick and pale. This mixture and the whipped cream and whisky should have about the same consistency. Fold both together, and divide between eight ramekins. Freeze, and when firm on the surface, cover each one with a piece of clingfilm.

Frozen Plum, Cinnamon and Port Parfait

This is more of a frozen mousse than an ice cream. The cinnamon and port, whilst scarcely detectable in themselves, combine with the plums to make a really exquisite flavour. Don't make it with Victoria plums, which are so good to eat. They are a dessert fruit and when cooked seem to lose their attraction and become bland tasting. Any of the other yellow or dark red, rather sharp-tasting plums are ideal.

Serves 8

1 lb/450 g plums

2 wine glasses port

1 rounded tbsp granulated sugar

1 rounded dssp ground cinnamon

3 eggs, separated

3 oz/84 g caster sugar

½ pint/285 ml double cream

Put the plums into a heavy saucepan, pour on half the port, add the granulated sugar, and cover the pan with a lid. Put the pan on a moderate heat, and cook until the plums are soft. Remove from the heat and remove the stones. Then, using a slotted spoon, put the plums together with the cinnamon in a liquidizer and blend to a purée. (If the plums have made a lot of juice, don't add it all to the liquidizer, because the purée will be too runny.) Leave to get cold.

Whisk the egg yolks and gradually add the caster sugar, whisking until they are very pale and thick. Fold the cooled purée into them. Whip the cream and remaining port together, not too stiffly, and fold this mixture into the purée. Then whisk the egg whites stiffly and fold them in, using a metal spoon. Pour into a polythene container and freeze.

Remove from the freezer and leave at room temperature for 30 minutes before serving.

Light Puddings

Cream and Yoghurt Pudding with
Demerara Sugar
•
Rhubarb and Ginger Syllabub
•
Chocolate Amaretto Macaroon Mousse
•
Lemon Mousse with Raspberry Sauce
•
Raspberry and Lemon Parfait
•
Lemon and Vanilla Soufflés
•
Dark Chocolate Soufflés
•
Coffee and Tia Maria Jelly with Chocolate
Chantilly Cream
•
Chocolate Meringues with Rum-
Whipped Cream
•
Walnut and Brown Sugar Meringues

Cinnamon Pavlova with Blackcurrant Cream
•
Vanilla and Chocolate Cream Pavlova
•
Crème Brulée
•
Dark Chocolate Terrine with Coffee
Cream Sauce
•
Orange, Grape and Ginger Terrine
•
Chocolate Roulade
•
Chocolate Roulade with Prune and
Armagnac Cream
•
Lemon Roulade with Raspberry Cream
•
Hot Fresh Fruit Salad with Honey,
Ginger and Cardomom
•
Poached Pears with Ginger Crème Anglaise

Cream and Yoghurt Pudding with Demerara Sugar

This is so easy it's unbelievable. My mother first introduced me to it about fifteen years ago, and it has become much in demand. It is good served on its own, but also makes a delicious accompaniment to stewed fruit or fresh fruit salad.

Serves 6–8

½ pint/285 ml double cream

¼ pint/140 ml natural yoghurt

Demerara sugar

Whip the cream fairly stiffly and then stir in the yoghurt. Pour this into a bowl and cover the top with a layer of demerara sugar – as thick or as thin as you like. Leave for several hours or, better still, overnight.

Rhubarb and Ginger Syllabub

This is for those who love ginger.

Serves 6–8

1½ lb/685 g rhubarb, cut in small chunks

3 oz/84 g sugar

1 pint/570 ml double cream

5 fl oz/200 ml ginger wine

8 pieces of stem ginger preserved in syrup, drained

Put the rhubarb in a saucepan with the sugar. Cover the pan with a lid, put it on a gentle heat, and cook slowly for about 30 minutes, until the rhubarb is cooked and soft. Cool, then purée in a blender.

Whip the cream and the ginger wine together. Cut the ginger into slivers, and stir them into the whipped cream. Fold together the ginger cream and the rhubarb purée, and divide it between glasses.

Chocolate Amaretto Macaroon Mousse

Amaretto biscuits are widely available from good delicatessens. They can enhance many a pud, but especially this mousse, the crunch of the crushed amaretti punctuating its smooth creaminess. And I love the taste of Amaretto liqueur.

Serves 6–8

5 oz/140 g dark chocolate, broken up

4 oz/112 g amaretto biscuits

3 tbsp Amaretto liqueur

4 large eggs, separated

5 oz/140 g caster sugar

¼ pint/140 ml double cream

Put the chocolate into a heatproof bowl over a saucepan of gently simmering water. Break up the amaretti by crunching them in your hands, and put them into the bottom of a serving bowl. Sprinkle the Amaretto liqueur over the broken-up biscuits.

Whisk the egg yolks, gradually adding the caster sugar, and continue whisking until the mixture is pale and thick. Fold in the melted chocolate and leave until the mixture is quite cold, then fold in the cream whipped until it just holds its shape. Lastly, whisk the whites until they are very stiff and, using a large metal spoon, fold them quickly and thoroughly through the chocolate mousse. Pour the mixture on top of the amaretti in the serving bowl.

As your guests help themselves to this mousse, remember to ask them to dig down with the spoon so that they get some of the delicious almondy biscuits at the bottom!

Lemon Mousse with Raspberry Sauce

Lemon and raspberries seem made for each other, so well do their flavours complement each other. A really lemony lemon mousse is still the favourite way to end a dinner party for many people. This mousse can be made a day or two in advance and kept, covered, in the fridge – but do remember to take it out of the fridge when your guests sit down to dinner, then it will be at room temperature by the time it is ready to be served. Serve the raspberry sauce in a bowl to go with the mousse.

Serves 6

For the mousse:

4 large eggs, separated

4 oz/112 g caster sugar

Finely grated rind of 2 lemons

Juice of 1½ lemons

Scant ½ oz/10 g powdered gelatine

7 fl oz/200 ml double cream, whipped

For the sauce:

¾ lb/420 g raspberries

2 oz/56 g icing sugar – more if you like a less sharp sauce

Whisk the egg yolks, gradually adding the caster sugar and whisking till the mixture is very thick and pale in colour.

Put the finely grated lemon rind and juice into a saucepan and sprinkle over it the gelatine. Over a gentle heat, dissolve the gelatine granules completely in the lemon juice, then heat it to just before boiling point and, still whisking, pour it steadily but slowly on to the yolks. Whisk well, and when cold, fold the whipped cream into the lemon mixture.

When the mixture is thick enough to coat the back of a metal spoon thickly, whisk the egg whites until very stiff and, with a metal spoon, fold them quickly and thoroughly into the creamy lemon mixture. Pour this into a glass or china serving dish, cover, and put the bowl in the fridge.

To make the sauce, liquidize together the raspberries and icing sugar, then sieve the purée, which is the only way to get rid of the woody pips. Serve in a bowl, to accompany the lemon mousse.

Raspberry and Lemon Parfait

Much as I loathe the word, a parfait seems to be a cream-less mousse, and therefore a very useful part of our menu. After a fairly rich lunch, it is something of a relief to have a dessert without one rich ingredient, and this parfait has a light texture and an intense flavour of raspberries enhanced by lemon.

Serves 6–8

2 lb/900 g raspberries (fresh or frozen)

Pared rind of 2 small lemons (I use a potato peeler to avoid any pith)

Scant ½ oz/14 g gelatine

Juice of 1 lemon

6 large eggs, separated

6 oz/170 g caster sugar

Fresh raspberries, to garnish

To start with, put the raspberries and pared lemon rinds into a saucepan and cover with a lid. Heat till the juices run from the raspberries. Meanwhile, sprinkle the gelatine over the lemon juice in a small pan, leave to sponge up, then heat gently until the gelatine dissolves completely. Take the pan off the heat; leave to cool. Liquidize the raspberries and lemon rind together with the dissolved gelatine and lemon juice. Sieve the purée – this is the only way to get rid of the woody pips.

Whisk the egg yolks, gradually adding the sugar, and continue whisking till the mixture is very thick and pale. Fold in the raspberry and lemon purée. When it has set enough to coat thickly the back of a spoon, whisk the egg whites till very stiff, and, with a large metal spoon, fold them thoroughly through the raspberry mixture. Pour into glass or china serving bowls and decorate with fresh raspberries.

Lemon and Vanilla Soufflés

I love the combined flavours of lemon and vanilla. These soufflés make delicious eating for a special lunch- or dinner-time pudding. They are convenient to prepare because you can make them in their entirety, including folding in the whisked whites, then cover the whole lot with cling-film, get washed up, and leave the soufflés for a couple of hours. Whip off the cling-film before putting them into the oven to cook. But, as with all soufflés, they must then be eaten immediately – dust with icing sugar, which you have all ready with the spoon and sieve!

Fills 6 large ramekins

5 large eggs, separated

5 oz/140 g caster sugar

Grated rind of 2 well washed and dried lemons

Juice of 1 lemon

A few drops of vanilla extract, or ½ tsp essence

2 oz/56 g ground almonds, sieved

Icing sugar, to serve

Butter the ramekins and dust them out with icing sugar.

Whisk the egg yolks, gradually adding the sugar and whisking till the mousse-like mixture is very pale and thick. Whisk in the lemon rinds and juice, the vanilla and the ground almonds. In a separate bowl, with clean whisks, whisk the whites till they are stiff. With a large metal spoon fold them quickly and thoroughly through the lemon mixture. Divide evenly between the prepared ramekins. Bake in a moderate oven, 350°F/180°C/Gas Mark 4, for 25 minutes.

Dust each with icing sugar and serve immediately, with a bowl of whipped cream, or with a sieved raspberry purée if you prefer (see page 333). Or with both.

Dark Chocolate Soufflés

This is one of my favourite of all puddings, provided the chocolate is the best. We buy a Belgian chocolate called Callebaut, and I like it the best of all the very many chocolates I have tasted. These are simple to make, but they must be eaten as soon as they emerge from the oven. That is why I have discovered that they cook perfectly in a moderate oven for 25 minutes, which allows you to put them into the oven as you serve the main course – 25 minutes seems the right time from then till pudding! Serve them with plain whipped cream, cold from the fridge.

Serves 8

8 oz/225 g of the best dark chocolate, broken into bits

½ pint/285 ml single cream

A few drops of vanilla extract, or ½ tsp vanilla essence

2 tsp caster sugar

5 large eggs, separated

Icing sugar, to serve

Butter eight ramekins and dust each one with caster sugar. Put them into a baking tray with an inch/2.5 cm of water in the tray.

Melt the chocolate in the cream in a saucepan and leave till quite cold. Don't worry if it looks as though it's curdling as it melts – as you stir, all will come smoothly together.

Beat in the vanilla, sugar and the egg yolks, one by one and beating well. In a clean bowl whisk the whites till stiff and, with a large metal spoon, fold them quickly and thoroughly through the chocolate mixture. Divide this between the prepared ramekins and put the tray into a moderate oven, 350°F/180°C/Gas Mark 4, for 25 minutes.

Dust each soufflé with sieved icing sugar before serving them, accompanied by a bowl of whipped cream. Have the sieve, icing sugar and a spoon ready, as well as small plates on which to sit the ramekins once the soufflés' cooking time is up, so as to take as little time as possible getting them to the table and your guests.

Coffee and Tia Maria Jelly with Chocolate Chantilly Cream

The coffee jelly can be made a day or two in advance, and the dark chocolate for the cream grated and kept in a covered bowl in the fridge, so all that remains to do before dinner is to turn out the jelly, whip the chantilly cream and fold in the grated chocolate. Heap this in the centre of the jelly ring. Simple!

I serve this with the Chocolate Oatmeal Crisp Biscuits on page 386.

Serves 8

For the coffee jelly:

¼ pint/140 ml Tia Maria and water mixed
  (mostly Tia Maria!)

2 sachets powdered gelatine (approx.
  1 oz/28 g)

1¼ pints/710 ml very good strong hot Italian-
  roast coffee (good decaffeinated is fine),
  freshly made

For the chocolate chantilly cream:

½ pint/285 ml double cream

1 large egg white

2 oz/56 g caster sugar

½ tsp vanilla essence or a few drops of extract

4 oz/112 g good dark chocolate, grated (this is
  easiest done in the grater of a food
  processor)

Put the Tia Maria and water mixture into a saucepan, sprinkle over the gelatine, then heat gently till the gelatine dissolves – you will need to stir it, because in the thick liqueur it tends to sit on the bottom. When it is dissolved, stir it into the hot coffee (which I like to make in a cafetière). Pour into a ring mould and leave to set in the fridge.

Whip the cream together with the egg white. Whip in the caster sugar and vanilla essence, and fold in the grated chocolate. Pile into the centre of the turned-out coffee and Tia Maria jelly ring.

Chocolate Meringues with Rum-Whipped Cream

These meringues are foolproof – they are 'cooked' as they are made, by whisking the egg whites and the icing sugar together over the heat. The cocoa powder is then folded into the thick meringue. Don't be tempted to whisk the cocoa into the egg whites together with the icing sugar, or the meringue simply will not thicken. These meringues can be stored in an airtight container for several days, and sandwiched together with the rum-flavoured whipped cream two or three hours before serving.

Serves 6

4 large egg whites

8 oz/225 g icing sugar, sieved

1 oz/28 g cocoa powder

½ tsp vanilla essence or a few drops of extract

½ pint/285 ml double cream

4 tbsp white or dark rum

4 oz/112 g dark chocolate

Put the egg whites into a heatproof bowl over a saucepan of simmering water. Add the icing sugar and whisk for several minutes until the mixture becomes very thick. Then take the bowl off the heat, sieve the cocoa powder over the meringue in the bowl, and fold this and the vanilla essence through the meringue, using a large metal spoon.

Line a large baking tray with non-stick baking parchment and pipe even-sized meringues on to it. To serve six people you need 12 meringues, so aim to pipe meringues about 2 inches/5 cm in diameter. For an especially pretty result, use a large star-shaped nozzle.

Bake the meringues in the oven preheated to 225°F/110°C/Gas Mark ¼, for about 3 hours. Take the meringues out of the oven, lift them off the paper and cool completely on a wire rack. When they are completely cold, store them in an airtight container.

Two or three hours before serving, whip the cream until stiff, gradually adding the rum. Coarsely grate the chocolate, then fold it into the cream. Use this to sandwich the meringues together. I think they look decorative served piled up on a small cake-stand.

ful at a time and whisking till you have a stiff meringue and all the sugar is incorporated. With a large metal spoon fold the chopped walnuts quickly and thoroughly through the meringue.

Divide the meringue between the two marked circles and smooth evenly. Bake in a cool oven, 250°F/130°C/Gas Mark ½, for 2–2½ hours. Take the meringues out of the oven and cool them.

Put one meringue on a serving plate, spread it with lemon curd, then spread with the whipped cream. Put the other meringue on top and dust with icing sugar.

Walnut and Brown Sugar Meringues

Serves 6

3 large egg whites

3 oz/84 g granulated sugar and
   3 oz/84 g demerara sugar mixed together

2 oz/56 g walnuts, broken into small bits and
   dry toasted to refresh their flavour, then
   cooled completely

Lemon Curd (see page 316)

½ pint/285 ml double cream, whipped

1 tbsp icing sugar, sieved, for decoration

Line one large or two smaller baking trays with baking parchment and mark out two circles, pencilling around a plate about 8 inches/20 cm in diameter. Put the whites into a bowl and whisk till stiff, then gradually whisk in the combined sugars, a spoon-

Cinnamon Pavlova with Blackcurrant Cream

This cinnamon-flavoured marshmallow-textured pavlova goes so well with the blackcurrants and whipped cream on top. If you really don't like blackcurrants, you could substitute raspberries, whose flavour are also well complemented by cinnamon.

Serves 8

For the pavlova:

4 large egg whites

8 oz/225 g caster sugar

1 tsp wine vinegar

2 rounded tsp powdered cinnamon

For the blackcurrant cream:

1 lb/450 g blackcurrants, stripped of their
   stalks

4 oz/112 g sugar

Pared rind of 1 small lemon

½ pint/285 ml double cream, fairly stiffly
whipped

Line a baking tray with baking parchment and mark on it a large circle, about 9 inches/ 23 cm in diameter.

Whisk the egg whites till stiff then, still whisking, gradually add the caster sugar, a spoonful at a time. When the sugar has all been whisked in, fold in the wine vinegar and powdered cinnamon. Spoon the cinnamon meringue on to the marked circle, smoothing it even.

Bake in a moderate oven, 350°F/180°C/ Gas Mark 4, for 5 minutes, then 225°F/ 110°C/Gas Mark ¼ for a further 45 minutes. Take it out of the oven and cool it on its baking parchment on a wire cooling rack. Then carefully peel off the paper and put the pavlova on to a serving plate.

For the blackcurrant cream, first cook the fruit gently with the sugar and pared lemon rind till the currants are soft. With a slotted spoon, spoon the currants from their juices, throwing out the lemon rind and draining off as much juice as you can. Fold the currants into the whipped cream and spoon this mixture on to the pavlova. It needs no further decoration.

Vanilla and Chocolate Cream Pavlova

A favourite combination of soft vanilla meringue, whipped cream and dark chocolate.

Serves 8

4 large egg whites

8 oz/225 g caster sugar

1 tsp cornflour, sieved

1 tsp white wine vinegar

1 tsp vanilla essence or a few drops of extract

For the decoration:

½ pint/285 ml double cream

6 oz/170 g dark chocolate, coarsely grated

Line a baking tray with non-stick baking parchment. Mark a large circle or a square or rectangle if you prefer.

Whisk the egg whites until they are stiff, then, still whisking, add the caster sugar a spoonful at a time, until all the sugar is incorporated and you have a stiff meringue. Using a large metal spoon, fold in the cornflour, vinegar and vanilla essence. Smooth the meringue into the desired shape on the prepared baking tray, and bake in the oven preheated to 350°F/180°C/Gas Mark 4, for 5 minutes, then 225°F/110°C/Gas Mark ¼ for a further 45 minutes. Take the meringue out of the oven and leave it to cool completely on the baking parchment.

When the pavlova is quite cold, carefully peel off the paper and put it on a serving plate or tray. Cover with cream, whipped until fairly stiff. Then sprinkle with the grated chocolate.

Crème Brulée

My favourite of all puddings – and my father's too. It must be the richest and most extravagant of all but it is worth every single calorie. When we have it on the menu in the hotel I always hope to have the will-power not to touch any that happens to be left over, but I never do! Tastes vary, with regard to the sugar used for the top of this dream pud, but personally I prefer caster sugar – I find Demerara gives too obtrusive a flavour, and anything which might mask the subtle flavour of vanilla is a sacrilege.

Serves 6

| 1 pint/570 ml double cream |
| A vanilla pod or a few drops of vanilla extract |
| 6 egg yolks |
| 1 rounded tbsp caster sugar |
| More caster sugar for the top |

Put the cream into a very thick-bottomed saucepan, or a double boiler, and put the vanilla pod into the cream. Heat until it begins to form a skin. Meanwhile, beat the egg yolks and tablespoon of sugar together, then pour the scalded cream on to the egg yolks, and beat well. Return to the saucepan.

Over a very gentle heat, cook, stirring all the time, until the cream coats the back of a wooden spoon. This takes quite a time, about 7–10 minutes, but it can't be hurried. If the heat is turned up the eggs will curdle, and that is enough to make me weep! So be patient, it will thicken, and when it does coat the back of the spoon, pour it through a sieve into a shallow ovenproof dish.

Leave it in a cool place for several hours (or overnight). A skin will form on top. Sprinkle caster sugar on the surface, not very deep but enough to give an even white covering. Preheat a grill to red-hot and put the dish under it. Watch it carefully as the sugar dissolves. When it is just golden and liquid, remove from the heat and leave in a cool place until you are ready to eat it. The sugar will harden and form a glass-like surface which has to be cracked with the back of the spoon.

Dark Chocolate Terrine with Coffee Cream Sauce

This is irresistible for those who, like me, are complete chocolate addicts. This is very densely chocolatey, and the slightly bitter coffee cream sauce goes well with it – much nicer than whipped cream.

Serves 6

| 1 sachet gelatine (approx. ½ oz/14 g) |
| ½ pint/285 ml water and Tia Maria or Kahlua, mixed half and half |
| 2 lb/900 g good dark chocolate |
| 1½ pint/850 ml single cream |
| 8 egg yolks |
| Coffee Cream Sauce (see page 315) |

Sprinkle the gelatine over the mixed water and coffee liqueur in a saucepan, then warm gently till the gelatine dissolves. Set aside.

Line the base and narrow ends of a 1–1½ lb/450–675 g terrine or loaf tin with a strip of baking parchment.

Break the dark chocolate into the bowl of a food processor, and put the single cream into a saucepan. Heat the cream to scalding point, and pour it on to the chocolate. Put the lid back on the processor, cover the lid with a teatowel, and whiz till the chocolate and cream form a smooth mixture. Whiz in the egg yolks, one by one, and the dissolved gelatine and water/liqueur mixture. Pour the chocolate into the lined terrine or loaf tin and leave to set.

To turn out, dip the terrine for a count of barely ten in a bowl of warm water, slip a knife dampened in warm water down the long sides, and turn on to a serving plate. Remove the tin, and peel off the paper.

Serve with Coffee Cream Sauce.

Orange, Grape and Ginger Terrine

This is one of my favourite puddings at any time of the year. Many supermarkets stock fresh orange juice in convenient pint-sized bottles for using when you can't be bothered to squeeze your own. This is a perfect pud to end an otherwise rather heavy and/or rich lunch or dinner.

Serves 8

½ pint/285 ml orange liqueur (such as Cointreau) and water mixed – I leave the ratio up to you!

Juice of half a lemon

2 oz/56 g caster sugar

2 sachets of powdered gelatine (1 oz/28 g) or 8 leaves of gelatine

1 pint/570 ml fresh orange juice

¾ lb/340 g grapes, green or black, cut in half and seeds removed

6–8 pieces of preserved stem ginger, drained of their syrup and chopped neatly

Line a 2 lb/900 g loaf tin with clingfilm.

Put the orange liqueur and water, the lemon juice and the caster sugar into a saucepan over a moderate heat and stir till the sugar has dissolved. Then either sprinkle in the gelatine or feed in the gelatine leaves, whichever you are using – the leaves are the best to use. Stir till the gelatine is dissolved but don't let the liquid boil.

Take the pan off the heat and cool. Then stir the contents into the fresh orange juice. Stir the halved de-seeded grapes into the liquid, along with the chopped ginger, and pour it into the lined loaf tin. Leave to set in the fridge, forking through the contents of the loaf tin as it sets to make sure that the grapes don't sink to the bottom but are distributed as evenly as possible.

Turn it out by dipping the tin briefly in hot water – not too hot as otherwise it melts the jelly – turn it upside down on to a serving plate, peel off the clingfilm, dip a knife in a jug of hot water and slice to serve.

Chocolate Roulade

There are lots of versions of this roulade which is simple and quick to make and freezes beautifully. If you don't freeze it you can add sliced bananas and bits of preserved ginger to the whipped cream filling instead of the orange flavouring.

Serves 8–10

For the roulade:

6 oz/170 g dark chocolate

4 tbsp black coffee or water

6 eggs, separated

6 oz/170 g caster sugar

Icing sugar for finishing

For the filling:

½ pint/285 ml double cream, whipped

Grated rind of 1 orange

1–2 tbsp orange liqueur, e.g. Cointreau

1 tbsp caster sugar

Line a Swiss roll tin about 10 x 8 inches/25 x 20 cm with a sheet of baking parchment.

Melt the chocolate in the coffee or water in a bowl over a saucepan of simmering water. Whisk together the egg yolks, gradually adding the caster sugar, and whisking until they are thick and pale. Stir the melted chocolate into the yolk and sugar mixture. Whisk the whites stiffly, and using a metal spoon fold them into the yolk and chocolate mixture. Pour this into the lined tin and smooth it evenly into each corner. Bake in a moderate oven, 350°F/180°C/Gas Mark 4, for about 15 minutes or until firm to touch. Remove from the oven and cover the roulade with a dampened teatowel. Leave for several hours until completely cold.

Put a fresh piece of baking parchment on a table or working surface and cover it with sieved icing sugar. Remove the teatowel from the roulade and, gripping both your courage and each of the shorter sides of the roulade paper, turn it over, chocolate side down, on to the sugared paper. Carefully peel off the paper sticking to the roulade, in small strips. Instead of peeling the strips off vertically, peel them backwards parallel to the surface of the roulade – you will then have no trouble at all. This all sounds rather daunting, and something of a major operation, but please don't be put off because when you are actually doing it, it is dead easy.

Flavour the whipped cream with the grated orange rind, orange liqueur and caster sugar. Cover the surface of the roulade with the flavoured cream, taking it right to the edges. Roll the roulade up lengthways, then slip it on to a flat plate or serving dish. It will inevitably split a bit down both sides, but this doesn't matter. Cover and freeze at this point if you wish.

Thaw for about 3 hours if you have frozen the roulade, and sprinkle with more sieved icing sugar before serving. Serve in slices, cutting with a serrated knife.

Chocolate Roulade with Prune and Armagnac Cream

This unusual roulade has a luxurious filling of cream, well-flavoured with Armagnac and dotted with chopped prunes.

Serves 8

For the roulade:

6 oz/170 g dark chocolate

6 large eggs, separated

6 oz/170 g caster sugar

Sieved icing sugar, to finish

For the filling:

½ pint/285 ml double cream

4 tbsp Armagnac

8–10 large prunes, soaked, simmered until
  plump in China tea, then well-drained,
  stoned and chopped

Line a baking tray about 14 x 16 inches/35 x 40 cm with non-stick baking parchment.

Break the chocolate into a heatproof bowl, set over a saucepan of gently simmering water. Heat gently until the chocolate has melted, then take the bowl off the heat. Stir just until mixed.

Meanwhile, whisk the egg yolks in a bowl, gradually adding the sugar, and whisk until the mixture is very pale and thick. Stir in the chocolate.

Whisk the egg whites until they are very stiff, and, using a large metal spoon, carefully and thoroughly fold the whites through the chocolate mixture. Pour on to the prepared baking tray and spread out evenly.

Bake in a moderate oven, 350°F/180°C/Gas Mark 4, for 20–25 minutes or until the mixture springs back when pressed lightly with a finger. Remove the roulade from the oven, cover with a damp teatowel and leave for several hours, or overnight.

Put a sheet of non-stick baking parchment on a work surface and sieve a spoonful of icing sugar over it. Take the teatowel off the roulade, and taking the shorter ends of the paper under the roulade in either hand, tip it face down on to the icing sugar. Carefully peel off the lining paper, tearing the paper in strips horizontal to the roulade – that way you won't tear it.

Whip the cream for the filling with the liqueur, until it just holds its shape. Spread the liqueur-flavoured whipped cream over the surface of the roulade, taking it right to the edges. Scatter the prunes over. Roll up lengthways, then slip the roulade on to a serving plate or tray. Dust with icing sugar and serve in slices about 1½ inches/4 cm thick.

Lemon Roulade with Raspberry Cream

This is a convenient pudding in that the roulade has to be made in advance. You can substitute blackcurrants, blackberries, or sliced strawberries for the raspberries in the recipe. We sometimes spread it with lemon curd, or, in season, with lemon and elderflower curd. In the early months of the year I make it with Seville oranges, instead of lemons. It is really a versatile, useful, but above all delicious pud. It is perfect for a summer lunch or dinner party.

Serves 6–8

For the roulade:

5 large eggs, separated

5 oz/140 g caster sugar

Grated rind of 2 washed and dried lemons

Juice of 1 lemon

2 oz/56 g sieved ground almonds

Sieved icing sugar for dusting finished
    roulade

For the filling:

1 lb/450 g raspberries

2 oz/56 g caster sugar

½ pint/285 ml double cream, whipped

Line a baking tray about 12 x 14 inches/30 x 35 cm with baking parchment.

Whisk the egg yolks with the sugar till the mixture is pale and very thick. Whisk in the lemon juice and the grated rind, and the sieved ground almonds. In a bowl, whisk the whites till they are very stiff, then, using a large metal spoon, fold the whites quickly and thoroughly into the lemon mixture. Pour this into the lined tin and smooth even.

Bake in a moderate oven, 350°F/180°C/ Gas Mark 4, till firm to the touch, about 25 minutes. Take the roulade out of the oven, cover with a damp teatowel and leave for several hours.

To fill, fold the raspberries and sugar into the whipped cream. Put a fresh sheet of baking parchment on to a work surface and sieve a little icing sugar over it. Tip the roulade face down on to the paper and care- fully peel the paper off the back of the roulade. Spoon the raspberry cream over the roulade, as evenly as possible, and roll it up away from you, slipping it from the paper on to a serving plate.

Dust with sieved icing sugar before serving, cut into slices. The cutting is easiest done with a serrated knife.

Hot Fresh Fruit Salad with Honey, Ginger and Cardamom

This is one of the nicest ways to eat fruit at any time of the day, and it makes a delicious course for a winter lunch. If you don't like the taste of honey – and it is surprising just how many people don't – use maple syrup instead.

Serves 6–8

Half a 1-lb/450-g pot of thick honey

3 good eating apples, e.g. Cox's, peeled,
    cored and sliced

4 cardamom pods, crushed, and the tiny
    black seeds removed to use

1 medium pineapple, skin cut off and the flesh
    cut into chunks

½ lb/225 g grapes, black or green, whichever is
    best, cut in half and pips removed

4–6 pieces of preserved stem ginger, drained
    of their syrup and chopped

3 pink grapefruit, skin and pith cut off and the
    flesh cut into segments, cutting inside the
    pith

Melt the honey in a wide sauté pan and gently cook the sliced apples in it for a few minutes. Stir in the cardamom seeds, pine- apple, grapes, ginger and grapefruit. Heat them all together gently – the only possible casualty might be the grapefruit, which tend to break up a bit in the heat. Keep the fruit salad warm till you are ready to serve.

Poached Pears with Ginger Crème Anglaise

Crème anglaise is really just custard in French, but it is so much nicer than the word 'custard' implies. Crème anglaise is made with, in this case, single cream and egg yolks. It is so quick and easy to make, especially if you have a microwave oven. In this pudding, the peeled pears – this, too, is very easy if you use a potato peeler – are poached, then served with the creamy ginger custard poured over them. Ginger and pears go together so well, and the third thing which complements both extremely well is dark chocolate, which you can grate over the surface.

Serves 6

6 good pears, each peeled, quartered and cored; slice each quarter into half, giving you 8 pieces to each pear, and cover closely with clingfilm

For the poaching syrup:

2 pints/1.1 litres of water

12 oz/340 g granulated sugar

The pared rind of 1 lemon

For the crème anglaise:

4 large egg yolks

2 oz/56 g caster sugar + 1 level tsp cornflour, sieved

1 pint/570 ml single cream

½ tsp vanilla essence or a few drops of extract

6 pieces of preserved stem ginger, drained of their syrup and chopped finely

Dark chocolate

Put the water, sugar and lemon rind into a fairly large saucepan. Over a moderate heat shake the pan slightly till all the granules of sugar have completely dissolved, then boil the syrup fast for 5 minutes. Then poach the pears gently in the syrup for a further 5 minutes. With a slotted spoon, carefully scoop out the pieces of pear, and put them in a shallow serving dish. Mop up, with absorbent kitchen paper, any syrup which accompanies the pears into the dish.

Beat together the yolks, sugar and cornflour, then beat in the cream. Put the bowl into a microwave oven for 2 minutes on a halfway heat. Then whisk the mixture. Re-cook for 2 minutes, then whisk again. Re-cook for a third lot of 2 minutes, and whisk again. You will probably have to give it another minute's cooking – how long exactly the crème anglaise takes to cook depends what material the bowl is made from. It should be as thick as good double cream. Cool.

If you do not have a microwave, heat the yolks, sugar and cornflour and cream in a heatproof bowl over a pan of simmering water until it thickens, about 30 minutes.

Stir in the vanilla and the chopped ginger. Pour it over the pears in the serving dish. Grate dark chocolate over the surface – hold the chocolate wrapped in a double thickness of foil, to prevent the warmth from your hand melting the chocolate, and use a potato peeler to get thin curls of chocolate.

Substantial Puddings

Profiteroles with Chocolate and Coffee Icing

•

Cinnamon Crêpes with Calvados Butter
and Spiced Apple Filling

•

Cinnamon Crêpes with Chocolate Cream

•

Chocolate Pecan Pie

•

Rich Lemon Tart

•

Pear and Almond Glazed Tarts

•

Rhubarb Meringue Pie

•

Tarte aux Fruits with Crème Pâtissière

•

Bread and Butter Pudding with Cream
and Nutmeg

•

Steamed Bramble and Lemon Suet Pudding

•

Baked Lemon and Raspberry Pudding

•

Lemon and Syrup Sponge

•

Upside-Down Pear and Walnut
Gingerbread Pudding

•

Mrs Hill's Christmas Pudding

Profiteroles with Chocolate and Coffee Icing

These profiteroles can be made several weeks in advance and frozen, then heated in a moderate oven for 3–5 minutes to refresh them, before they are iced and filled with whipped cream.

Makes about 20

1 pint/570 ml water

8 oz/225 g butter, cut in small pieces

10 oz/285 g plain flour, sieved twice

5 large eggs, beaten

¾ pint/420 ml double cream

For the chocolate and coffee icings:

2 oz/56 g butter

6 oz/170 g granulated sugar

½ pint/285 ml water

4 oz/112 g icing sugar, sieved with a rounded
   tbsp cocoa – not drinking chocolate

4 oz/112 g icing sugar, sieved

2 tsps instant coffee granules dissolved in
   1 tbsp boiling water

Put the water and cut-up butter into a saucepan over a gentle-to-moderate heat, and melt the butter in the water, taking care not to let the water boil before the butter has melted. As soon as the first rolling bubbles appear in the butter-and-water mixture, whoosh in the twice-sieved flour all at once and, with a wooden spoon, beat like mad till the mixture comes away from the sides of the saucepan. Then let the mixture cool for about 10 minutes, before adding the beaten eggs a little at a time, beating really well between each addition.

When all the eggs are added, rinse two baking trays with cold water – this is so that, as the profiteroles cook, the steam which rises from the dampened baking trays helps them to rise too. Pipe small profiteroles the size of a 50-pence piece evenly on to the baking trays. Or, if you prefer, using a plain piping nozzle, pipe 2-inch/5-cm long éclair shapes, cutting the choux mixture off at the required length with scissors dipped in water to prevent it from sticking to the scissor blades. With a damp finger, gently press the surface of the éclair down if there should be any points sticking up from where you cut it.

Bake the profiteroles or éclairs in a hot oven, 425°F/220°C/Gas Mark 7, for 20–25 minutes, till they are golden and quite firm – swap the trays around half way through the cooking. Ease them off the baking trays with a palette knife, and cool them on wire cooling racks.

Whip the cream until stiff and fill the profiteroles.

To make the icings, put the butter, granulated sugar and water into a saucepan and heat gently, stirring, over a moderate heat until the sugar has dissolved completely. Then let it boil for 2 minutes.

Beat half this syrup into the chocolate and icing sugar mixture, and beat the other half together with the plain icing sugar and dissolved coffee granules. Beat well until you have glossy icings. Before serving, ice the profiteroles with the chocolate and coffee icing.

If you like, you can freeze the unfilled and uniced profiteroles, in which case pack them carefully into tins to protect them in the freezer.

Cinnamon Crêpes with Calvados Butter and Spiced Apple Filling

This recipe may sound a fiddle to make, but it really isn't. It is also quite delicious, and most convenient because the whole dish freezes very well, only needing a couple of hours of thawing at room temperature before the crêpes are reheated for 20 minutes in a moderate oven, then flamed with Calvados to serve.

Serves 8

For the crêpes:

4 oz/112 g plain flour

1 tsp ground cinnamon

1 oz/28 g caster sugar

1 oz/28 g butter, melted

2 large eggs

½ pint/285 ml milk and water mixed

Butter to cook the crêpes

For the Calvados butter:

4 oz/112 g softened butter

4 oz/112 g sieved icing sugar

4 tbsp Calvados

For the spiced apple filling:

8 apples – Cox's if possible

1 tbsp lemon juice

2 oz/56 g butter

1 tsp ground cinnamon

A grating of nutmeg

2 oz/56 g soft brown sugar

To finish:

4 tbsp Calvados and icing sugar

Mix together all the ingredients for the crêpe batter, beating really well in a food processor or by hand, then leave the batter for an hour at least (you can make it up and leave it in the fridge overnight, but give it a good stir before using) before making it up into crêpes. Making crêpes is so much easier (and less boring!) a job to do if you have two crêpe pans and, if you make a lot of them, it is well worthwhile investing in a second one.

Melt a small knob of butter in the pan till foaming, then swirling the pan with your left hand (if you are right-handed) pour in a small amount of batter to cover the bottom of the pan thinly and evenly. Cook for a minute or so, then, using a small palette knife and your fingers, turn the crêpe over and cook on the other side. Continue till the batter is all used up, and as they are made stack them on a plate, with a piece of baking parchment between each. This amount of batter makes about 16 crêpes.

Next make the Calvados butter. Put the butter for this into a bowl and, with a handheld electric whisk, beat it very well, gradually adding the sieved icing sugar. Beat in the Calvados, a spoonful at a time, beating really well.

To make the filling, first peel, core and chop the apples and toss them in the lemon juice. Melt the butter in a pan and add the chopped apples, the spices and the soft brown sugar. Cook over a moderate heat for about 20 minutes, or until the apples are soft when pressed against the sides of the pan with the back of your wooden spoon.

To assemble the dish, spread each crêpe with some Calvados butter, put a rounded teaspoonful of apple mixture in the middle of each, and fold into a fat parcel. Butter a shallow ovenproof dish, and arrange the stuffed crêpes in it. Cover with clingfilm and freeze. Thaw at room temperature for a couple of hours, then reheat for 20 minutes in a moderate oven – 350°F/180°C/Gas Mark 4. Sieve a spoonful of icing sugar over the crêpes, and warm 4 tbsp of Calvados in a saucepan. Ignite it and pour the flaming Calvados over the crêpes before serving them.

Cinnamon Crêpes with Chocolate Cream

The crêpes can be made up a day or two in advance and kept in the refrigerator in a sealed polythene bag, with a disc of non-stick parchment between each one. Fill and roll them up several hours before serving.

Serves 8

For the crêpes:

4 oz/112 g plain flour

1 tsp ground cinnamon

1 oz/28 g caster sugar

1 oz/28 g butter, melted

2 large eggs

½ pint/285 ml milk and water mixed

Butter to cook the crêpes

For the filling:

½ pint/285 ml double cream

4 oz/112 g dark chocolate, grated

To finish:

1 tbsp icing sugar, sieved

First make the batter. In a blender or food processor, whiz together all the batter ingredients until smooth, or beat them very well together by hand. Let the mixture stand for about 1 hour, then make into crêpes, as thin as possible.

Put a small piece of butter – about ½ oz/14 g – into a crêpe pan, and melt over a fairly high heat. Pour in a small amount of batter, swirling it round so that it coats the base of the pan as thinly as possible. After a minute or so, turn the crêpe over with the help of a small palette knife. Let it cook for about a minute on the other side. As they cook, cool the crêpes individually on a board. When cool, stack with a strip of baking parchment between each crêpe.

To make the filling, fold together the cream, whipped until it holds its shape, and the chocolate. Divide the chocolate cream among the crêpes, allowing two crêpes per person. Fold the crêpes into rectangular parcels, tucking the ends under. Put them into a wide ovenproof dish. Just before serving, heat the grill until it is red-hot. Dust the top of the crêpes with the icing sugar and pop the dish under the grill for just long enough to caramelize the sugar – count to thirty! – and serve.

Chocolate Pecan Pie

This yummy pie has a hint of coffee in the flavouring, which combines so well with the chocolate and the pecans. Pecans are widely available now in good grocer's shops and delicatessens. They are not always in the freshest condition, though, and I always put them in a saucepan over a moderate heat, shaking them from time to time to prevent them from burning, for 5–7 minutes, then cool them, and this freshens them up. If you can't find pecans, substitute walnuts and give them the same freshening-up treatment.

Serves 6–8

For the pastry:

4 oz/112 g butter, chilled
5 oz/140 g plain flour
1 oz/28 g icing sugar
A few drops of vanilla essence

For the filling:

4 oz/112 g butter, diced
4 oz/112 g soft light brown sugar
2 oz/56 g dark chocolate
1 tsp instant coffee
3 large eggs, beaten
6 oz/170 g shelled pecans

To make the pastry, cut the butter into bits in a food processor and add the flour, icing sugar and vanilla. Whiz for a few seconds, until the mixture resembles breadcrumbs. Or grate the butter into the sieved flour, rub in with the fingertips until the mixture resembles breadcrumbs, then stir in the icing sugar and vanilla essence. Knead lightly together, then press the mixture round the base and sides of a 9-inch/23-cm flan dish.

Chill in the fridge for at least 30 minutes, then bake in an oven preheated to 350°F/180°C/Gas Mark 4 for 20–25 minutes, until the pastry is golden. Remove from the oven and leave to cool.

To make the filling, put the butter into a heatproof bowl with the sugar, chocolate and coffee granules. Set the bowl over a saucepan of gently simmering water until the butter has melted and the sugar dissolved.

When the butter mixture has melted, remove the bowl from the heat and stir in the beaten eggs. Strew the pecans over the cooled baked pie crust, then pour in the chocolate mixture. Put the pie carefully into the oven preheated to 350°F/180°C/Gas Mark 4, for 20–25 minutes, until the filling is just firm to the touch.

I like to serve this pie warm with whipped cream – it is nicest eaten soon after it is baked, rather than being made and reheated.

Rich Lemon Tart

This is a most satisfying tart to end a lunch or dinner. The lemon is sufficiently sharp in flavour – I think that a bland lemony pud is a disappointment. This one isn't!

Serves 6–8

For the pastry:

4 oz/112 g butter, chilled
5 oz/140 g plain flour
1 oz/28 g icing sugar
½ tsp vanilla essence or a few drops extract

For the filling:

5 oz/140 g butter
8 oz/225 g caster sugar
Grated rind and juice of 3 lemons
5 large eggs, well beaten together

To make the pastry, cut the butter into bits in a food processor and add the flour, icing sugar and vanilla. Whiz for a few seconds, until the mixture resembles breadcrumbs. Or grate the butter into the sieved flour, rub in with the fingertips until the mixture resembles breadcrumbs, then stir in the icing sugar and vanilla essence. Knead lightly together, then press the mixture round the base and sides of a 9-inch/23-cm flan dish.

Chill in the fridge for at least 30 minutes, then bake in an oven preheated to 350°F/180°C/Gas Mark 4 for 20–25 minutes, until the pastry is golden. If the sides of the pastry case should slip down the sides of the flan dish, just press them back up using a metal spoon and bake for a further few minutes.

While the pastry cooks, make the filling. Cut the butter into bits and put into a Pyrex or similarly heatproof bowl with the caster sugar, grated lemon rind (but *not* – yet – the juice) and the beaten and sieved eggs. Put the bowl over a pan containing simmering water and stir occasionally as the butter melts and the sugar dissolves. Then take the bowl off the heat and stir in the lemon juice. Carefully pour this into the still warm baked pastry case, and, very carefully so as not to spill the contents, put into a moderate oven, 350°F/180°C/Gas Mark 4. Bake till the filling is just set, about 15 minutes. Try not to let it change colour, it looks so attractive if it retains its fresh colour.

Garnish, if you like, with dried or crystalized lemon slices, or if you prefer, you could sprinkle the surface with icing sugar (sieved) and caramelize, using a blow-torch (or under a hot grill), to give you the thinnest crisp golden layer. Small, hand-held blow-torches are obtainable from ironmongers and are perfect for this. Hold the flame ¾ inch/2 cm above the icing sugar layer until it turns pale golden. Hold the torch steady – don't wiggle it about, because that slows down the process considerably. When the melted sugar has cooled, it will form a crisp layer. Delicious.

Pear and Almond Glazed Tarts

You can prepare this pud well in advance – you can even bake the tarts and reheat them, but they are nicest baked then eaten. However, you can do all the messy work and get everything washed up in advance, so I don't see much point pre-baking the individual tarts anyway. It is such a help being able to buy ready rolled-out puff pastry. This is an ideal pud to make in the autumn, when pears are in their natural season. You need firm pears, not too ripe.

Serves 6

Ready rolled-out puff pastry, cut into 6 oblong shapes approx. 3 x 2 inches/7.5 x 5 cm
3 good-sized pears, round rather than the elongated shape of Conference pears
4 oz/112 g ground almonds
1 oz/28 g caster sugar
Grated rind of 1 washed and dried lemon

Juice of half a lemon

A very few drops of almond extract – not, if at
all possible, essence

2 oz/56 g butter, melted

3 tbsp caster sugar

Put the pastry oblongs on to a baking tray –
no need to butter the baking tray. With a
potato peeler, peel the pears, cut each in half
and scoop out the core. In a bowl mix
together the ground almonds, sugar, grated
lemon rind and juice and the almond extract
and, using your hand, mix together. The
warmth of your hand and the lemon juice
will combine to bind together the mixture
into an almond paste. Divide this almond
paste between each pastry oblong and put a
pear half on top. Brush each oblong of
pastry and pear half all over with melted
butter, then sprinkle each with caster sugar.

Cover closely with clingfilm till you are
ready to pop the tray into the oven. Bake in
a hot oven, 400°F/200°C/Gas Mark 6, till
the pastry is puffed and golden and the pear
is just turning golden.

Serve warm, with Vanilla Custard (see
page 315).

Rhubarb Meringue Pie

*Fruity meringue pies I love. I wish I didn't
like sweet things so much. This is delicious
served with crème fraîche, or with vanilla
ice cream, which is especially good if you
serve the pie warm.*

Serves 8

For the pastry:

5 oz/140 g butter, chilled and cut into little bits

6 oz/170 g plain flour

2 oz/56 g icing sugar

1 rounded dssp ground ginger

For the filling:

1½ lb/675 g rhubarb, trimmed and cut in
1-inch/2.5-cm pieces

Grated rind and juice of 1 orange

3 oz/84 g sugar

For the meringue:

4 egg whites

8 oz/225 g caster sugar

Put the butter, flour, icing sugar and ginger
in a food processor and whiz until the
mixture resembles breadcrumbs. Press
lightly over the sides and bottom of a flan
dish about 9 inches/23 cm in diameter. If
you do not have a food processor, rub the
butter into the dry ingredients, using your
fingertips, until the mixture looks like
breadcrumbs. Put the dish into the fridge for
at least 30 minutes, then bake in a hot oven,
400°F/200°C/Gas Mark 6, for 30 minutes,
or until the pastry is pale golden and
cooked. Remove from the oven to cool.

Put the rhubarb, orange rind and juice
and sugar together in a saucepan, cover with
a lid, and cook gently until the rhubarb is
just tender, but not mushy. Cool, then spoon
over the cooked pastry, using a slotted
spoon so that just the rhubarb goes on to the
flan, and as little of the juice as possible.

Whisk the whites fairly stiff, then whisk

in the caster sugar gradually, until the meringue is stiff and standing in peaks. Spoon over the rhubarb, covering the surface of both rhubarb and pastry entirely with meringue. Bake in a cool oven, 250°F/130°C/Gas Mark ½, for 20–30 minutes.

Serve warm or cold.

Tarte aux Fruits with Crème Pâtissière

You can vary the fruits you use according to what you can get! This is a most attractive pie – and it is delicious. I love the contrast between the textures of the crisp pastry, the smooth cream and the fruit.

Serves 6

For the pastry:

3 oz/84 g butter, chilled and cut into bits

5 oz/140 g plain flour

1 tbsp icing sugar

½ tsp vanilla essence, or a few drops of vanilla extract

For the crème pâtissière:

¾ pint/420 ml single cream

4 egg yolks – from large eggs

3 oz/84 g caster sugar

½ tsp vanilla essence, or a few drops of vanilla extract

1 tsp cornflour

For the fruit and glaze:

A selection of fruit – halved strawberries, sliced peaches or nectarines, halved green or black grapes, whole raspberries, halved apricots are all suitable

Good apricot jam, warmed and sieved, to brush over the entire surface

Put the ingredients for the pastry into a food processor and whiz till the mixture resembles fine breadcrumbs. Pat this firmly around the sides and base of a flan dish measuring approximately 9 inches/23 cm in diameter or a rectangular oven tray measuring approximately 11 x 7½ inches/28 x 19 cm.

Put the dish in the fridge for at least one hour, then bake in a moderate oven, 350°F/180°C/Gas Mark 4, till the pastry is pale golden brown – if the pastry shows signs of slipping down the sides as it cooks, press it back up with the back of a metal spoon. The cooking time will be about 20–25 minutes.

Make the crème pâtissière by beating together all the ingredients well. Cook over a very low temperature in a thick-bottomed pan, stirring constantly till the cream thickens – this takes some time. Alternatively, put the bowl in a microwave oven on a medium heat setting for 2 minutes. Take out, whisk well and repeat three times, giving in total 8 minutes' cooking time. The cream should be thickened beautifully. If you are in any doubt, give it another minute's cooking.

Leave the cream to cool in the bowl, then

Orange, Grape and Ginger Terrine ▶
page 340

spoon it over the base of the baked pastry case. Arrange the sliced fruit in circles and brush the entire surface with the sieved apricot jam – I mean even the sides of the pastry.

Bake in a moderate oven, 350°F/180°C/Gas Mark 4, for about 20 minutes, or until the nutmeg custard is just set. Serve warm.

Bread and Butter Pudding with Cream and Nutmeg

This is a ritzy version of the old nursery favourite – of some. But this version, I have found, appeals to just about everyone. The bread is rich, and there are no hard chunks of peel because any peel is soft within the bread. Yet there is a distinct but subtle citrus flavour with the grated orange and lemon rinds. It is soft and creamy in texture.

Serves 6–8

12 slices of malt loaf (the sort with peel and raisins in it), buttered and cut in half

¾ pint/420 ml single cream

1 whole egg + 2 large egg yolks

2 oz/56 g caster sugar

A good grating of nutmeg

Grated rind of ½ lemon and ½ orange

1 rounded tbsp demerara sugar

Butter an ovenproof dish. Arrange the sliced buttered bits of malt bread in the dish. Beat together the cream, egg and yolks, caster sugar, nutmeg and lemon and orange rinds. Pour this over the malt bread, and sprinkle the surface evenly with demerara sugar.

◀ Tarte aux Fruits with Crème Patissière
page 352

Steamed Bramble and Lemon Suet Pudding

To many people, suet puddings are still redolent of institutions. This is really sad, because a good steamed pudding, as long as it has a generous and flavour-packed filling, really beats fruit pie. It is easy to make, too. This is real Sunday lunch stuff, and is always greatly appreciated. Lemon and blackberries go together extremely well, and in this pudding there is also butter and brown sugar – the combined flavours are heavenly. I use this quantity of suet pastry to line a pudding bowl with a capacity of about 3 pints/1.7 litres.

Serves 6–8

For the pastry:

8 oz/225 g plain flour

½ tsp baking powder

4 oz/112 g shredded suet

For the filling:

1½ lb/675 g blackberries

6 oz/170 g soft brown sugar

Grated rind of 3 lemons

3 oz/84 g butter, cut in bits

Mix all the pastry ingredients together with enough cold water to make a dough, and knead for a bit. Cut about one-quarter of the pastry off and set aside (this is for the lid). Roll the remaining pastry out. Lightly butter the inside of a 3-pint/1.7-litre pudding basin – or a plastic bowl with a snap-on lid. Line the buttered bowl with the pastry.

Mix all the filling ingredients together and pack into the pastry-lined bowl. Roll out the remaining piece of pastry and put on top. Scrunch the edges together to seal. Cut a circle of baking parchment to go over the top of the pastry and snap on the lid of the pudding bowl. Or tie on a pudding cloth or piece of foil.

Put the bowl into a sufficiently large saucepan to hold it comfortably, and pour water into the pan to come about halfway up the sides of the bowl. Cover the saucepan with a lid, and put on the heat. Bring to a gentle simmer, and cook for 2½ hours, topping up the water from time to time.

Serve piping hot, straight from the basin.

Baked Lemon and Raspberry Pudding

This lovely pudding separates whilst cooking to form a very light sponge-like top with a thick raspberry-lemon sauce underneath. I like it best served warm. It doesn't take long to make, once all the ingredients are collected together, and if you have a food processor all except the whisking of the whites can be done in that.

Another wonderful thing about this delicious pud is that it freezes perfectly. I discovered this quite by chance, when I had a whole pud left after dinner in the hotel one evening and, as is my wont with left-overs, I tucked it into the deep freeze for the family to eat up at a later date. It emerged from the freezer for Sunday lunch two or three weeks later. I warmed it up, and I don't think I could have told in any way that it had been frozen.

Serves 8

1½ lb/675 g raspberries
3 oz/84 g butter
8 oz/225 g caster sugar
Grated rind of 3 lemons
Juice of 2 lemons
6 eggs
2 oz/56 g plain flour
½ pint/285 ml milk

Put the raspberries into an ovenproof dish – I use a large soufflé dish. Put the butter into a bowl and cream it, gradually adding the caster sugar. Beat the butter and sugar together until they are pale and fluffy. Beat in the grated lemon rinds then gradually add the lemon juice. Separate the eggs, and beat in the yolks one by one. If the mixture curdles, don't worry, it doesn't affect the end result. Beat in the sieved flour, and lastly the milk.

Whisk the egg whites until stiff and, using a large metal spoon, fold them into the butter and lemon mixture. Pour this on top of the raspberries, and put the dish into a roasting tin. Pour about 2 inches/5 cm hot water into the tin, and put it all into a moderate oven, 350°F/180°C/Gas Mark 4. Bake for 40–45 minutes until golden and firm on top.

Serve warm or cold, whichever you prefer.

Lemon and Syrup Sponge

There is nothing to beat a hot pudding on a chilly day. But puddings such as this steamed lemon and syrup sponge are so much better eaten at lunch-time than in the evening for dinner or supper, when they can lie rather heavily on the tum – I prefer to give lighter puddings in the evening. Some people tend to think that steamed puddings are laborious to make and rather complicated – nothing could be farther from the truth. The lemon in this recipe tends to taste like lemon marmalade after the length of cooking, but that is the taste I love.

Serves 6

4 generous tbsp golden syrup – if you dip the spoon in very hot water before each spoonful, the syrup will slip easily off the spoon
Finely grated rind of 3 lemons – wash them well first, and dry them
8 oz/225 g self-raising flour
1 tsp bicarbonate of soda
A pinch of salt
4 oz/112 g grated or shredded suet – use vegetarian suet if you prefer
3 oz/84 g soft light brown sugar
1 large egg
¼ pint/140 ml milk
1 tsp vanilla essence, or a few drops of vanilla extract

You will need a 3–4 pint/1.7–2.3 litre boilable plastic pudding bowl with a snap-on lid. There is no need to grease or butter this, but you will need to if you are using any other type of bowl to steam your pud in.

Start by spooning the syrup into the bottom of the pudding bowl, and mix about a quarter of the grated lemon rind in with the syrup. Sieve the flour, bicarbonate of soda and salt into a bowl. Stir in the suet, sugar, egg, milk, vanilla and the rest of the grated lemon rind, mixing all together very well. Spoon and scrape this on top of the syrup.

Cut a disc of baking parchment to cover the top of the pudding, but make a pleat in the centre of the paper to allow for the pudding to rise up slightly as it cooks. Put this paper over the surface of the pudding. Snap on the lid of the pudding bowl, and put the bowl into a large saucepan with water coming halfway up the sides of the bowl. Simmer the water around the pudding bowl for 2½–3 hours, with the lid on the pan. Check the level of the water from time to time, so that it runs no risk of simmering dry. Top it up when necessary.

Before serving, if you like, turn the pudding out on to a warmed plate, otherwise just spoon it straight from the bowl. Serve with the Vanilla Custard on page 315 if you like – I do!

Upside-Down Pear and Walnut Gingerbread Pudding

This freezes beautifully. It is a most delicious and comforting pud on a cold day.

Serves 5–6

4 oz/112 g self-raising flour
½ tsp bicarbonate of soda
2 tsp ground cinnamon
1 tsp ground ginger
A pinch of ground cloves and a grating of nutmeg
1 large egg
4 oz/112 g soft light or dark brown sugar
3 oz/84 g treacle
4 fl oz/112 ml milk
2 oz/56 g butter, melted

For the topping:

2 oz/56 g butter
4 oz/112 g soft brown sugar
1 tin of pears, drained
A few walnuts

Make the topping first. Melt the butter and sugar together and stir for 1–2 minutes over a gentle heat. Pour into an ovenproof dish and arrange the pears and walnuts over it.

Sieve the flour and the dry ingredients into a bowl. Add the egg, sugar, treacle, milk and melted butter and mix well. Spoon the mixture over the pears and walnuts and bake in a moderate oven, 350°F/180°C/Gas Mark 4, for 40–50 minutes.

Serve warm, with either Crème Anglaise (see page 315), or whipped cream mixed with natural yoghurt, or crème fraîche, or a good vanilla ice cream.

Mrs Hill's Christmas Pudding

This recipe is unique because it contains no flour or breadcrumbs whatever, and I have never seen another recipe for Christmas pudding which contains neither. Mrs Hill was the wife of the vicar in my home village of Tunstall, in Lancashire, many, many years ago. We have made it every Christmas since she gave my mother the recipe. This amount makes one large pudding, or two smaller ones.

12 oz/340 g raisins
12 oz/340 g sultanas
6 oz/170 g currants
12 oz/340 g shredded suet, beef or vegetarian
6 oz/170 g chopped crystallized peel
3–4 oz/84–112 g flaked almonds, toasted
Grated rind of 1 lemon
About ½ tsp freshly grated nutmeg
6 large eggs, beaten
¼ pint/140 ml brandy
7 fl oz/200 ml milk
6 oz/170 g brown sugar (optional)

Mix all the ingredients together very well, then put the mixture into a buttered 3-pint/ 1.7-litre pudding bowl – I use the boilable plastic ones with the snap-on lids. Put a pleated disc of baking parchment over the top of the mixture before snapping on the lid. Cook the pudding by steaming it in a saucepan with simmering water coming halfway up the sides of the pudding bowl, and with the lid on the saucepan. Steam for 5–6 hours, but do keep an eye on the level of the water in the pan – it will need regular topping up. Boiling a pudding dry is a thing you only do once!

After it has cooked, keep it in a cool place – ideally a larder – and reheat before serving by steaming again for 1½–2 hours.

To serve, turn the pudding on to a warmed serving plate – it will turn out easily. Warm some brandy, whisky, or rum in a small saucepan – take care, though, not to let it boil. Ignite the alcohol in the saucepan, then pour it over the pudding. This is much easier to do than pouring alcohol over and then trying to ignite it. Stick a sprig of holly on top of the pudding, and bring it to the table. Accompany with Orange-Flavoured Brandy Butter (see page 313) and/or Vanilla Custard (see page 315).

Gâteaux

Cherry and Chocolate Meringue Gâteau

•

Chocolate and Almond Cake

•

Chocolate Brandy Cake

•

Hot Baked Chocolate Cheesecake

•

Chocolate Mousse Cake

•

Dark Chocolate Truffle Cake

•

Coffee, Chocolate and Almond
Meringue Gâteau

Cherry and Chocolate Meringue Gâteau

This is one of those meringue puddings that freezes very successfully, complete, filled with the whipped cream and cherries. It is a particularly stable form of meringue, but don't *be tempted to whisk the cocoa in with the whites and icing sugar; it won't work, and has to be folded in once the meringue has really thickened, over heat.*

Serves 6–8

4 large egg whites

8 oz/225 g icing sugar, sieved

1 oz/28 g cocoa powder

For the filling:

½ pint/285 ml double cream

2 tbsp Kirsch (optional)

A 15-oz/420-g can stoned black cherries, well drained, or 8 oz/225 g fresh cherries, stoned

2 oz/56 g dark chocolate, grated

1 tbsp icing sugar, sieved

¼ pint/140 ml extra double cream (optional)

To make the meringue, put the egg whites and the icing sugar in a heatproof bowl over a saucepan of gently simmering water, and whisk for several minutes until the meringue is very thick. Take the bowl off the heat and fold in the sieved cocoa powder.

Line two baking trays with non-stick baking parchment and mark a circle about 9 inches/23 cm in diameter on each – I use a plate to draw round. Divide the chocolate meringue mixture between the rounds, and smooth it out evenly. Bake in an oven preheated to 225°F/110°C/Gas Mark ¼ for

2½–3 hours, then remove the meringues from the oven and leave to cool.

Fold together the cream, whipped until fairly stiff, and Kirsch, if used, the drained cherries and grated chocolate, and spread over the top of one of the meringue rounds. Cover with the other round and dust with icing sugar. If you like, use the extra cream, whipped stiffly, to pipe rosettes round the edge of the gâteau.

To serve, have a serrated knife dipped in a jug of very hot water to hand – it makes for a much easier job when cutting this delicious gâteau. If you are going to freeze the gâteau, cover it carefully and freeze, without the dusting of icing sugar. Add this just before serving. To thaw, allow 3–4 hours at room temperature.

Chocolate and Almond Cake

This very simple, very rich cake makes a delicious pudding. I like to serve it with cream, whipped until it holds its shape and flavoured with vanilla, or with the Vanilla Ice Cream on page 329. Unlike most cake recipes, where you are told to test when the cake is cooked by whether a skewer stuck in the centre comes out clean, in this one the cake is ready when the skewer comes out with some of the cake sticking to it, as it should be slightly gooey and moist.

Serves 8–10

8 oz/225 g butter

8 oz/225 g soft light brown sugar

8 oz/225 g dark chocolate, melted

1 tsp vanilla essence, or a few drops extract

6 large eggs

8 oz/225 g ground almonds, sieved

1 tbsp icing sugar, sieved

Butter a 9-inch/23-cm springform cake tin and line the base with non-stick baking parchment.

In a mixing bowl, cream the butter, gradually adding the sugar. Beat until the mixture is soft and fluffy. Beat in the cooled melted chocolate, vanilla essence, and the eggs, one by one, beating well after each addition. Lastly, fold in the ground almonds.

Pour the cake mixture into the prepared tin. Bake in an oven preheated to 350°F/180°C/Gas Mark 4 for 35–40 minutes.

Remove the cake from the oven and allow to cool completely in its tin. Turn it out, when cold, on to a serving plate, and dust with icing sugar. Hand round a bowl of whipped vanilla-flavoured cream or a dish of Vanilla Ice Cream to serve with slices of the dark, moist cake.

Chocolate Brandy Cake

This cake is extremely rich, and can be used as a dinner party pudding. It can be made up to 5 days in advance – it keeps in the fridge and it also freezes well. One of my father's favourites – and as he is an extreme chocolate fanatic, you can't say more for this cake.

Serves 8–10

8 oz/225 g butter

8 oz/225 g dark chocolate

3 tbsp brandy

8 oz/225 g digestive biscuits, crushed into crumbs

3 oz/84 g walnuts, broken into bits

3 oz/84 g glacé cherries, roughly chopped

2 large eggs

3 oz/84 g caster sugar

Melt the butter and chocolate together in a saucepan over a gentle heat. Stir until well mixed, then cool. Add the brandy, the crushed biscuits, broken walnuts and chopped cherries. Whisk the eggs and sugar until really thick and pale and fold into the chocolate brandy mixture.

Line a 2-pint/1.1-litre loaf tin with baking parchment as neatly as possible – the more tidily you cut the paper to line the tin, the neater the end product will be. Pour the chocolate brandy mixture into the prepared tin, cover with clingfilm, and put into the fridge to set.

When it is really hard, run a palette knife down the sides between the paper and the tin, turn the cake on to a plate, and peel off the paper. I like to lay walnut halves and halves of glacé cherries in rows on top.

Hot Baked Chocolate Cheesecake

You can eat this cheesecake cold, but it is much nicer hot – it keeps warm very satisfactorily for 20 minutes or so in a low oven. It is nicer slightly undercooked – you don't taste the cream cheese. It is a heavenly pie and, as you can see, extremely quick to put together.

Serves 6

For the base:

4 oz/112 g chilled butter

5 oz/140 g plain flour

1 oz/28 g icing sugar

A few drops of vanilla essence

For the filling:

8 oz/225 g cream cheese

8 oz/225 g soft light brown sugar

A few drops of vanilla essence

2 oz/56 g cocoa

4 large eggs

Sieved icing sugar, to finish

To make the base, whiz all the ingredients for the base together in a food processor until the mixture resembles breadcrumbs. Alternatively, cut the butter into the flour and icing sugar with a knife, then rub in with your fingers until it reaches the bread-crumb stage. Press this mixture round the base of a 9-inch/23-cm flan dish.

Chill the flan in the fridge for 30 minutes, then bake in an oven preheated to 350°F/180°C/Gas Mark 4 for 20–25 minutes, until the pastry is pale golden brown. Remove from the oven, and leave to cool while you make the filling.

Put the cream cheese into a blender or food processor and whiz, gradually adding sugar, then the vanilla essence, cocoa, 2 whole eggs and 2 egg yolks. Blend until smooth. Alternatively, mix all the ingredients very thoroughly in a bowl. Whisk the remaining 2 egg whites until they are stiff, and, using a large metal spoon, fold them quickly and thoroughly through the chocolate mixture.

Pour into the cooked pastry shell, and bake in an oven preheated to 350°F/180°C/Gas Mark 4 for 35–40 minutes, until set. Dust with icing sugar to serve.

Chocolate Mousse Cake

This is a delicious combination of rich, squidgy chocolate cake with a soft, creamy chocolate mousse on top. It is made in a springform tin, carefully unmoulded on to a serving plate, and served cut in wedges. If you like, you can decorate the surface of the mousse cake with a little grated choco-late, or you can leave the cake plain – it's perfectly delicious! The layer of mousse isn't very deep, so the overall result is not overwhelmingly rich.

Serves 8–10

For the cake:

6 oz/170 g dark chocolate

5 large eggs, separated

5 oz/140 g caster sugar

2 tbsp orange liqueur, such as Cointreau

For the mousse:

1 tsp powdered gelatine

Juice of 1 orange

6 oz/170 g dark chocolate

2 tbsp orange liqueur, such as Cointreau

4 eggs, separated

¼ pint/140 ml double cream

For the decoration:

A little grated dark chocolate (optional)

Butter a 10-inch/25-cm springform cake tin and line the base with a disc of non-stick baking parchment.

Break the chocolate into a heatproof bowl set over a saucepan of gently simmering water (take care not to let the bottom of the bowl touch the water). Heat gently until the chocolate has melted, then take the bowl off the heat.

In another bowl beat the egg yolks, gradually adding the caster sugar and the liqueur. Beat until the mixture is thick and pale. Stir in the cooled melted chocolate. Whisk the egg whites until they are stiff, and, using a large metal spoon, fold them quickly and thoroughly through the chocolate mixture. Pour this into the prepared tin and bake in an oven preheated to 350°F/180°C/Gas Mark 4 for 35 minutes, until a skewer inserted into the centre of the cake comes out clean. Remove the cake from the oven and leave to cool in the tin (about 1 hour).

To make the mousse, sprinkle the gelatine over the orange juice in a small saucepan, then heat through very gently until the gelatine granules have dissolved completely. Break the chocolate into a heatproof bowl set over a saucepan of gently simmering water. Heat gently until the chocolate has melted. Take the bowl off the heat and stir in the liqueur and the liquid gelatine. Beat the egg yolks into the chocolate mixture, one by one, and leave them to cool for 5 minutes, then fold in the cream, whipped until it just holds its shape. Whisk the egg whites until they are very stiff, and, using a large metal spoon, fold them quickly and thoroughly into the chocolate mousse.

With your fingertips, press down the sugary crust on top of the cooled cake – this will have formed during baking. Pour the mousse on the top of the cake in the tin and leave for several hours to set.

To serve, dip a palette knife in hot water and run it round the inside of the tin. Undo the spring sides of the tin, and, using a fish slice, carefully ease the cake on to a serving plate. Decorate, if you like, with grated chocolate sprinkled over the surface of the mousse.

Dark Chocolate Truffle Cake

This recipe is John Tovey's. Being the generous and kind friend that he is, he didn't – appear to! – hesitate when I asked him for permission to use this recipe in this book. It is quite simply the best recipe for the most satisfying, densely chocolatey truffle-textured pudding I have ever come across, and I am a complete chocolate addict. As with all chocolate recipes, it is vital to use the best chocolate you can lay your hands on. Don't for a moment consider using stuff like Cakebrand or Scotchoc chocolate flavouring in any cooking. In a rich pudding like this it would be a total waste of your other ingredients.

John calls this pudding Chocolate Orange Gâteau, but when we put it on the menu for our guests here at Kinloch we leave out the orange and call it Dark Chocolate Truffle Cake. It is, needless to say, one of Godfrey's most favourite of all the puddings we make.

---

3 fl oz/84 ml liquid glucose

5 tbsp water

3 oz/84 g caster sugar

1 lb/450 g good dark chocolate, broken into
  pieces

2 tsp instant coffee granules dissolved in
  8 tbsp boiling water

¾ pint/420 ml double cream

1 egg white

Sieved cocoa powder to finish

Lightly grease a loose-bottomed, springform cake tin about 10 inches/25 cm in diameter. Line the base with baking parchment.

Heat the glucose, water and caster sugar together gently, to melt the sugar. When the sugar has melted, bring the liquid to the boil. Melt the broken-up chocolate in the coffee in a bowl over a pan of barely simmering water – take care not to let the water touch the bottom of the bowl. Mix the glucose mixture into the melted chocolate and leave to cool for 10 minutes or so.

Whip the double cream till it forms soft peaks and fold this into the chocolate mixture. Whisk the egg white till it is very

stiff and, with a metal spoon, fold this quickly and thoroughly into the creamy chocolate mixture. Put this into the prepared loose-bottomed springform tin. Leave in a cool place for several hours.

Turn on to a serving plate, peel off the disc of paper from the top of the cake, and dust with sieved cocoa powder. I personally think it needs no further embellishment, but for Godfrey's fiftieth we stuck a candle in the middle – a large one, rather than fifty smaller ones.

Coffee, Chocolate and Almond Meringue Gâteau

This is probably the richest recipe in this book – a yummy concoction combining coffee-flavoured meringue with a rich coffee- and chocolate-flavoured butter-cream filling and covering. It is covered with toasted flaked almonds, which provide a delicious combination of flavours as well as a good contrasting crunch. It has the added bonus of being much better made the day before it is to be eaten.

Serves 8

For the meringue:

4 large egg whites

8 oz/225 g caster sugar

2 tsp instant coffee dissolved in 2 tbsp boiling
  water, then cooled

For the filling:

8 oz/225 g unsalted butter

8 oz/225 g icing sugar, sieved

4 egg yolks

**4 oz/112 g dark chocolate, melted in a
heatproof bowl over simmering water with
2 tsp instant coffee dissolved in 2 tbsp hot
water**

**3 oz/84 g flaked almonds, toasted until golden
brown**

To make the meringue, first line two baking trays with non-stick baking parchment. Mark out a circle about 9 inches/23 cm in diameter on each tray – I use a plate to draw round.

Put the egg whites into a clean bowl and whisk until stiff, then, still whisking, gradually add the caster sugar a spoonful at a time. Whisk until all the sugar is incorporated and you have a stiff meringue. Using a large metal spoon, quickly fold in the cold coffee liquid, then divide the meringue between the two circles. Smooth into rounds and bake in an oven preheated to 225°F/110°C/Gas Mark ¼ for 2½–3 hours, then cool.

To make the filling, beat the butter, gradually adding the icing sugar a spoonful at a time and beating until the mixture is pale and soft. Beat in the egg yolks one at a time, alternating with the cooled melted chocolate and coffee mixture.

Sandwich the meringue rounds together with about half of this buttercream, then spread the top and sides of the gâteau with the remaining buttercream. Cover the surface with the toasted flaked almonds, and leave the gâteau in a cool place overnight, until you are ready to serve it. To help slice it evenly, a serrated knife dipped into a jug of very hot water is invaluable.

Breads, Scones, Cakes and Biscuits

This small chapter contains many of my most favourite recipes. I think that if I could choose one meal above all others to eat each day, it would be tea-time food. For a week or two, at any rate! I would be so happy on dark -wintry afternoons, with the curtains drawn against the gathering dusk, to sit beside a fire and eat Apple Drop Scones with Cinnamon Butter, a recipe you will find in the first section of this chapter. It would be good to have Lemon and Cinnamon Fruit Bread the following day, and warm Oven Scones, with butter and good homemade (it goes without saying) jam or lemon curd. And for breakfast nothing – to me – could be nicer than Spicy Raisin Buns, served warm with butter and marmalade.

The bread recipes I've included here are all so good, and so varied in their interestig flavourings. You just can never buy bread with enough taste, but you can make bread with such ease, and at the same time add as much of the flavourings as you like. For instance, you can put as much garlic, black olives and sun-dried tomatoes into the bread in the first recipe as appeals to you. And that bread, along with the Pinhead Oatmeal and Garlic Bread, and the Cheese, Mustard and Garlic Granary Bread, is quite delicious with any of the soups in the First Courses chapter, and with most of the salads in the relevant chapter as well.

As for cakes – well, I declared my hand at the start of this introduction! Show me a cake, and all thoughts of diets seem to disappear. My favourite among the cakes in this section must be the Chocolate Cake with Chocolate Fudge Icing. It is a winner. But then I love the Coffee and Praline Cake too, and the Hazelnut and Apple Chocolate Cake, and the Vanilla Sponge with Vanilla Buttercream and Raspberry Jam. And the Christmas Cake recipe is the best I have ever come across.

I have included all my firm favourites in the biscuits section, but if I had to choose one from amongst the recipes it would be the Sultana Biscuits. They are so simple, yet quite irresistible. Tucked in at the end of the biscuits section is a recipe for Dark Chocolate Truffles with Angostura Bitters. I feel its lone inclusion needs a bit of explanation! They are just the best truffles, made so by the bitters as an ingredient. And I must give credit to Godfrey for this invaluable bit of information. Our first Christmas, 28 years ago, he told me that if I put Angostura bitters in the truffles I was making, they would be exceptionally good. He was right, they were, and I've been making them ever since, but I wish he could remember how he discovered this invaluable tip!

Breads and Scones

**Black Olive, Sun-Dried Tomato and
Garlic Bread**

•

Granary Bread

•

Cheese, Mustard and Garlic Granary Bread

•

Lemon, Thyme and Garlic Bread

•

Pinhead Oatmeal and Garlic Bread

•

Cinnamon Coffee Bread

•

Lemon and Cinnamon Fruit Bread

•

Apple Drop Scones with Cinnamon Butter

•

Fresh Herb Scones

•

Hot Cheesy Scones with Poppy Seeds

•

Oven Scones

•

Spicy Raisin Buns

Black Olive, Sun-Dried Tomato and Garlic Bread

I realize that you can buy this type of flavoured bread in many shops, but none is as good as the bread you make yourself. It matters very much to use the best black olives – not those awful ones uniformly pitted and packed in bitter brine, but the juicy olives with their stones in, packed in herbs and the minimum of the best brine. The garlic amount may sound rather lavish, but bread seems to absorb the flavour of garlic, and I love a pronounced garlic taste. This bread is so good on its own, but it embellishes any soup, or it can be eaten with the best Brie – which, for me, is the one made by the Curtis's called Bonchester Brie – and salad, for the most perfect lunch.

Makes 1 large or 2 smaller loaves

1 tsp sugar
2 tsp dried yeast
½ pint/285 ml hand-hot water
1 lb/450 g double 0 white flour (00)
½ tsp salt
3 garlic cloves, skinned and chopped finely
About 6 pieces of sun-dried tomato, chopped
About 14–18 best black olives, chopped, stones thrown away
2 tbsp olive oil

Lightly oil a baking tray with olive oil.

Stir the sugar and yeast into the water and stand it in a warm place till a head of froth has formed the same size as the amount of liquid. Sieve the flour and salt into a bowl and stir in the garlic, chopped sun-dried tomatoes and chopped olives. Stir in the yeast liquid and mix very well. Stir in the olive oil.

Turn the dough on to a floured surface and knead till the dough is no longer sticky. Divide in two, if you want two smaller loaves, and knead a bit longer. Shape into oblongs and put on to the oiled tray. Leave in a warm place till the dough has just about doubled in size, then bake in a hot oven, 425°F/220°C/Gas Mark 7 for 20 minutes – the bread should sound hollow when tapped on the base. Cool on a wire rack.

Granary Bread

This is the bread we make each day for our guests at Kinloch. Not an elegant bread, but it is my favourite of all breads.

Makes three 1-lb/450-g loaves

2 oz/56 g dried yeast, such as Allinson's
½ pint/285 ml hand-hot water
2 tsp sugar
1 tbsp salt
2 tbsp demerara sugar
1¼ pints/710 ml hot water
3 lb/1.35 kg granary flour
4 tbsp oil (I use sunflower)

Stir the dried yeast into the water and sugar and leave in a warm place until it trebles in volume.

Stir the salt and demerara sugar into the hot water. Leave the flour in a large mixing bowl in a warm place while the yeast grows – the secret of good breadmaking lies in keeping everything warm.

Mix the yeast-and-sugar water into the flour, pour in the salt-and-sugar water, and measure in the oil. Mix all together, then turn the dough on to a well-floured surface and knead well (I knead and count to 200), then divide the dough into three pieces, and knead each to a further count of 50. Put each piece of dough into an oiled 1 lb/450 g loaf tin, and leave all three tins in a warm place, covered with a teatowel, to double in size – about 20–25 minutes.

Bake in a hot oven, 425°F/220°C/Gas Mark 7, for 20–25 minutes – try not to over-cook the loaves as this toughens the dough. They are cooked when they sound hollow when tapped on their base. Cool on a wire rack in a warm place – if they cool in a draught or a cold place that toughens the dough, too. Slice thickly, and toast if you like.

Cheese, Mustard and Garlic Granary Bread

We make granary bread each day here at Kinloch for our guests. Several years ago I was having a lovely conversation with one of the guests, who was telling me the sort of things about his stay here with us that is pure pleasure to hear, and make you wish you had the entire staff beside you to hear as well, because the impact of compliments seems to lose much in the passing on! But we were discussing bread, and he was telling me what a keen baker he is, and had I ever made cheese bread? He so enthused

me that I went straight back to the kitchen and made some. Since then I have embellished it with garlic, dry mustard and a dash of Tabasco sauce as well as so much grated cheese that initially you wonder whether the dough can absorb that much. Don't worry, it can – and still rises, too! It is quite delicious, but even more so when sliced thickly and toasted. It is an ideal accompaniment for soups, and is very good served with grilled tomatoes. It freezes as well as other bread does.

Makes three 1-lb/450-g loaves

½ pint/285 ml warm water
2 tsp sugar
2 oz/56 g dried yeast
1¼ pints/710 ml hot water
1 tbsp salt
2 tbsp demerara sugar
3 lb/1.35 kg granary flour
2 tsp mustard powder
A good dash of Tabasco sauce
10 oz/285 g strong white Cheddar cheese, grated
1–2 large garlic cloves, chopped finely

Stir together the ½ pint/285 ml warm water with the 2 teaspoons of sugar and the dried yeast, and leave it in a warm place until it has trebled in volume.

Stir the salt and demerara sugar into the hot water.

Measure out the flour into a bowl, add the mustard and a dash of Tabasco and leave it in a warm place – the secret of good breadmaking is to keep everything warm.

When the yeast mixture has trebled in frothy volume, stir it and the water, sugar and salt mixture into the flour. Mix well, then turn the dough on to a well-floured surface. Spread it out and spread over its surface the grated cheese and finely chopped garlic. Roll up and knead well until the dough feels less sticky and more elastic – anyone who makes bread regularly will know just what I mean! I knead the whole and count slowly to 200, then divide it in three, and knead each piece to a further count of 50. Put each kneaded loaf-to-be into an oiled 1-lb/450-g loaf tin, and leave the tins in a warm place, covered with a teatowel. How quickly they rise depends on how warm the place is – 15 minutes on an Aga, out of any cold draughts. I find it is better to bake the loaves as they are still 'proving', because they rise a bit more in the cooking.

Bake in a hot oven, 425°F/220°C/Gas Mark 7, for 25 minutes. Turn out of their tins and cool on a wire rack in a warm place. Cooling the loaves in the warmth prevents them from becoming tough. To slice a loaf warm from the oven, turn it upside-down first.

Lemon, Thyme and Garlic Bread

This bread is so good with chilled soups in the summer, and, too, with all salads.

Makes 1 large or 2 smaller loaves

2 tsp dried yeast

1 tsp sugar

½ tsp salt

½ pint/285 ml hand-hot water

1 lb/450 g strong plain white flour

2 cloves of garlic, peeled and chopped very finely

A small sprig of fresh thyme, tiny leaves plucked from the stalks, or a good pinch of dried thyme

Grated rind of 1 lemon

2 tbsp extra virgin olive oil

First, stir the yeast, sugar and salt into the hand-hot water and leave in a warm place till a head of froth has formed on top of the liquid; the mixture should have doubled in volume.

Add the yeast mixture to the flour, along with the chopped garlic, thyme leaves and grated lemon rind and olive oil. Mix all together well, then tip the dough onto a floured work surface and knead till the dough is no longer sticky, but is pliant.

Lightly oil a baking tray, shape the dough into a rough sausage shape and put it on the baking tray. Leave, uncovered, till the dough has doubled in size.

Bake in a very hot oven, 425°F/220°C/ Gas Mark 7 for about 20 minutes – the loaf should sound hollow when you tap its bottom – and cool on a wire rack in a warm place (a cold place or draught will cause the dough to toughen).

Pinhead Oatmeal and Garlic Bread

This bread is delicious, and only takes about 45 minutes to make. You can freeze the extra loaves.

Makes 3 loaves

½ pint/285 ml hand-hot water with 1 tbsp sugar dissolved in it and 2 tbsp dried yeast, e.g. Allinson's, stirred in well

2½ lb/1.125 kg wholemeal flour

½ lb/225 g pinhead oatmeal dry-toasted with 2 tsp salt

2 garlic cloves, skinned and very finely chopped

1 pint/570 ml hot water with 2 tsp salt and 1 tbsp molasses sugar stirred in

Leave the yeast liquid in a warm place till it forms a head of froth equal in size to the water beneath it. Then stir this into the flour, oatmeal and chopped garlic and stir in the sugar-and-salt water. Mix well, then turn the dough on to a floured surface and knead – I knead to a count of 200. Divide the dough into three equal-sized pieces, knead each one, and put them into three oiled tins (roughly 1 lb/450 g capacity). Cover with a teatowel and leave in a warm place till the dough has doubled in size in the tins.

Bake in a hot oven, 425°F/220°C/Gas Mark 7, for 15–20 minutes, till the loaves turn out of their tins and sound hollow when you tap them on the base. Cool on a wire rack, but not in a draught, which would toughen the cooling bread.

This bread is good toasted as well as untoasted, and goes wonderfully well with the Avocado and Bacon Salad on page 237.

Cinnamon Coffee Bread

I do love the sweet cakey breads the Americans eat at breakfast-time, and this recipe is an adaptation of my own from a couple of recipes given to me by friends from the United States. It can be made and frozen, but warm it up to serve.

For the bread:

6 oz/170 g butter

6 oz/170 g soft brown sugar

10 oz/285 g plain flour

1 tsp bicarbonate of soda

1 tsp baking powder

3 large eggs, beaten

½ tsp vanilla essence, or a few drops extract

For the covering:

4 oz/112 g demerara sugar

2 tsp ground cinnamon

3 oz/84 g chopped pecan nuts (you can substitute walnuts, but pecans are widely available now and much nicer)

2 oz/56 g butter, melted

For the bread dough, beat together the butter and soft brown sugar really well till the mixture is light and fluffy. Sieve in the flour, bicarbonate of soda and baking powder alternately with the beaten eggs, mixing all well into the mixture. Stir in the vanilla essence.

Grease a baking tin or a small roasting tin measuring about 8–10 x 12 inches/20–25 x 30 cm and line it with baking parchment. Pour the mixture into the lined tin. Mix together the ingredients to cover the bread dough, and sprinkle this as evenly as you can over the surface. Bake the bread at 375°F/190°C/Gas Mark 5 for 30 minutes. Take it out of the oven and let it cool a little in the tin.

Mark it into squares, and serve it warm.

Lemon and Cinnamon Fruit Bread

This bread can be made and frozen two to three weeks before Christmas and then served as the most perfect bread for Christmas Day breakfast. I like to serve it warm, but the icing tends to dissolve into the bread – this really doesn't matter though, because it tastes so good! All European countries have a traditional yeast fruity bread at Christmas time – Stollen in Germany, panettone in Italy – and I thought we should follow their good example.

Makes 2 bread circles

For the fruit bread:

2 tsp sugar

½ pint/285 ml hand-hot water

2 oz/56 g dried yeast

2 lb/900 g wholewheat flour

4 rounded tsp ground cinnamon

6 oz/170 g raisins

3 oz/84 g chopped mixed peel

3 oz/84 g caster sugar

Grated rind of 2 lemons

¼ pint/140 ml warm water

2 oz/56 g butter, melted

2 large eggs, beaten

For the icing:

Juice of 1 lemon

4 heaped tbsp icing sugar, sieved

1 rounded tsp ground cinnamon

Sprinkle the sugar into the hand-hot water. Stir in the dried yeast, and leave this yeast mixture in a warm place until it has frothed up and nearly trebled in size.

Mix together the flour, cinnamon, raisins, chopped mixed peel, caster sugar and lemon rind in a bowl and put this in a warm place. When the yeast has all frothed up, mix it into the flour etc., along with the warm water, the melted butter and the beaten eggs. Mix well, then turn on to a floured surface and knead very well – I count to 200 – till the dough feels pliable.

Divide the dough in two pieces, and knead each for a further count of 100, or about 2 minutes. Form each piece of dough into a ring on a greased baking tray, and leave in a warm place, covered with a teatowel, till the dough has doubled in size – 20–25 minutes if it is a draught-free really warm place, longer if not.

Bake in a hot oven, 425°F/220°C/Gas Mark 7, for 20–25 minutes, then take it out of the oven and cool it on a wire rack in a warm place (if you cool it too quickly in a cold place the dough toughens, I find).

When the fruit bread is quite cold, ice it with the lemon and cinnamon icing. To make this, warm the lemon juice and mix it into the icing sugar and cinnamon. Pour over the top of each ring, and let the icing trickle down the sides. When the icing has set, cover with clingfilm and freeze.

Thaw for a couple of hours at room temperature, or, much more convenient, thaw overnight.

Apple Drop Scones with Cinnamon Butter

Prepare the cinnamon butter two or three days in advance and keep it, covered, in the fridge. The batter may be made the evening before you wish to serve the scones. Stir the batter and add the grated apple just before cooking the scones.

Makes 8–10 scones

4 oz/112 g plain flour
Pinch of salt
1½ tsp baking powder
1 oz/28 g demerara sugar
1 oz/28 g unsalted butter, melted
1 egg, beaten
4½ fl oz/125 ml milk
1 tsp lemon juice
1 small crisp dessert apple, peeled

For the cinnamon butter:

4 oz/112 g unsalted butter
2 oz/56 g caster sugar
2 oz/56 g demerara sugar
4 tsp ground cinnamon

To make the cinnamon butter, beat all the ingredients together. Spoon into pots, level the surface, cover with clingfilm and put in the fridge. Remove from the fridge at least 30 minutes before serving.

Mix the flour, salt, baking powder and sugar together in a bowl. Make a well in the centre. Mix the butter, egg, milk and lemon juice together and pour into the well in all the dry ingredients. Gradually draw the dry ingredients into the liquid to make a smooth thick batter. Grate in the apple.

Butter a griddle, electric hotplate, or large heavy-bottomed, preferably non-stick frying pan. Place over a moderate heat. Drop 3 or 4 small spoonfuls of the batter on to the griddle, hotplate, or frying pan, keeping the blobs well spaced apart, and spread each one out slightly with the back of the spoon. Cook for 2–3 minutes until bubbles appear on the surface, then turn each one over with a palette knife and cook the other side for about 2 minutes. Keep the scones warm between two teatowels whilst cooking the remaining scones in the same way.

Serve warm, with the cinnamon butter.

Fresh Herb Scones

Use any fresh herbs or just lots of finely chopped parsley, flat-leafed if possible for maximum flavour.

Serves 6

12 oz/340 g self-raising flour
½ rounded tsp salt
1 rounded tsp baking powder
1 egg, beaten
1 tbsp sunflower seed oil
Just less than ½ pint/285 ml milk
3 rounded tbsp finely chopped herbs, e.g. parsley, chives and fennel

Sieve the dry ingredients into a bowl and stir in the egg, oil, milk and herbs. Knead together well – it will be quite a sticky dough.

Pat the mixture out on a well-floured surface, to a thickness of about 1 inch/2.5 cm. Cut the scones into 2½-inch/6-cm circles, and put them on a baking tray.

Bake in a hot oven, 425°F/220°C/Gas Mark 7, for 10–15 minutes, until they are well risen and golden brown. Serve warm.

Hot Cheesy Scones with Poppy Seeds

These are most useful to serve with summery soups, or with any salad first course.

Makes 9

12 oz/340 g self-raising flour
½ rounded tsp salt
1 rounded tsp baking powder
2 rounded tsp mustard powder
1 egg, beaten with 1 tbsp sunflower oil
Just less than ½ pint/285 ml milk
4 oz/112 g strong Cheddar cheese, grated
1 rounded tbsp poppy seeds

Sieve the dry ingredients into a bowl and stir in the egg, sunflower oil and milk. Add the cheese and knead all the ingredients together well – it will be a rather sticky mixture.

Pat the mixture out on a well-floured surface to a thickness of about 1 inch/2.5 cm. Using a floured 2½-inch/6-cm cutter, cut the scones into circles and put them on a baking

tray, sprinkling the surface of each with poppy seeds.

Bake in a hot oven, 425°F/220°C/Gas Mark 7 for 10–15 minutes, until they are risen and golden brown.

Serve the scones warm. You can mix all the dry ingredients in advance, if you like, ready to add the egg and milk and pop them into the oven at the last minute.

Oven Scones

This recipe is used by Peter Macpherson, who makes the scones freshly each morning at the hotel, for breakfast.

Makes 20–25

1½ lb/675 g self-raising flour
1 rounded tsp salt
2 rounded tsp sugar (optional)
2 rounded tsp baking powder
2 eggs
2 tbsp sunflower oil
About ¾ pint/420 ml milk

Sieve the dry ingredients together into a mixing bowl. Beat together the eggs and oil in a measuring jug and make up to 1 pint/ 570 ml with milk. Stir the egg, oil and milk mixture into the dry ingredients. Knead (it will be fairly sticky), then pat the mixture out on a floured surface until it is about 1 inch/2.5 cm thick. Cut out the scones with a 2½-inch/6-cm cutter.

Bake in a hot oven, 425°F/220°C/Gas Mark 7, for 10–15 minutes.

These are best made and eaten the same

day, but they freeze well. You can add some grated cheese to the basic recipe – to this quantity I would add 4 tablespoons of grated cheese. Warm, buttery cheese scones are delicious and go surprisingly well with jam, particularly strawberry, raspberry or blackberry.

Spicy Raisin Buns

You can cut a cross on top of these, just before baking, using a razor blade or a very sharp knife, to turn them into hot cross buns for Easter eating. They haven't got any mixed peel in them, which seems to be the part that more people dislike than like, and yet you get the citrus flavour via the grated lemon and orange rinds. As with all bread food, these freeze very well.

1 lb/450 g wholemeal or strong plain white flour – I like to use double 0 (00 on the packet) flour from an Italian delicatessen

2 tsp ground cinnamon and a good grating of nutmeg

Black pepper, about 12 grinds of the peppermill

1 scant tbsp dried yeast – I use Allinson's

½ pint/285 ml hand-hot water with 2 tsp sugar stirred in

1 large egg, beaten

2 oz/56 g butter, softened

4 oz/112 g sultanas or raisins

Grated rinds of 1 lemon and 1 orange

Put the flour and spices into a large mixing bowl. Stir the yeast into the sugared water and leave in a warm place – but not on direct heat – till a head of froth forms equal in size to the liquid underneath. Mix this into the flour with the egg and soft butter and stir in the raisins and grated orange and lemon rinds. Mix well, then turn the sticky dough on to a floured surface and knead till it is not sticky. Cut the dough in half, then cut each half in half again, and continue to divide the dough like this till you have 12 or 16 bits of dough. Roll each into a bun shape and put on to a lightly oiled baking tray.

Leave in a warm place till they are twice their original size, then bake in a very hot oven, 425°F/220°C/Gas Mark 7, for 12–15 minutes – when a bun sounds hollow if tapped on the base it is cooked. Cool on a wire rack.

I like these buns best served warm, with butter and marmalade.

Cakes

Chocolate Cake with Chocolate Fudge Icing

•

Chocolate Fudge Brownies

•

Chocolate and Orange Cake

•

Christmas Cake

•

Toasted Coconut and Chocolate Cream Cake

•

Coffee and Praline Cake

•

Hazelnut and Apple Chocolate Cake

•

Orange Cake

•

Vanilla Sponge with Vanilla Buttercream and
Raspberry Jam

Chocolate Cake with Chocolate Fudge Icing

No good tea-table is complete without a chocolate cake. This recipe exactly fills my bill for everything that a chocolate cake should be. It is very gooey, and very chocolatey. It keeps extremely well, and it is a most adaptable cake, because you can juggle around with the ingredients. If you would prefer an even stickier and rather fudgy cake, use dark brown soft sugar or, better still, muscovado sugar instead of caster sugar; and if you would prefer a less gooey and slightly less rich cake, use less drinking chocolate powder and more flour. It has the advantage of being very quick and easy to make, using only one bowl.

Serves 6–8

For the cake:

6 oz/170 g butter

6 oz/170 g caster, dark brown, or muscovado sugar

4 large eggs

8 oz/225 g drinking chocolate powder

2 oz/56 g plain flour

A few drops of vanilla essence

For the buttercream:

3 oz/84 g butter

3 oz/84 g icing sugar, sieved

A few drops of vanilla essence

For the chocolate fudge icing:

2 oz/56 g butter

2 oz/56 g granulated or caster sugar

6 tbsp water

6 oz/170 g icing sugar

2 rounded tbsp cocoa powder

Cream the butter and sugar well together, until they are light and fluffy. Add the eggs, one by one, beating really thoroughly in between. Sieve the flour and drinking chocolate together and add to the butter, sugar and egg mixture, and stir in a few drops of vanilla essence. The mixture will be fairly runny.

Grease and flour two sandwich cake tins, about 8–9 inches/20–23 cm in diameter, and divide the mixture between them. Bake in a moderate oven, 350°F/180°C/Gas Mark 4, for about 30 minutes, or until a skewer pushed into a cake comes out clean. Take them out of the oven, and leave to cool in the tins for a few minutes, then turn out on to a cooling rack to cool completely.

To make the buttercream, beat together the butter and icing sugar until pale and flavour with a few drops of vanilla essence. Sandwich the cakes together with this vanilla buttercream.

Finally, make the icing. Put the butter, sugar and water in a small saucepan. Heat gently until the butter is melted and the sugar dissolved, then boil for 5 minutes. Sieve the icing sugar and cocoa powder together, pour on some of the liquid from the saucepan, and beat the icing really well, adding more liquid as you need it. As it cools, it becomes glossy. When it coats the back of the wooden spoon without running off, coat the cake with it.

To turn this cake into more of a gâteau, which can be served as a pud for dinner, decorate with walnut halves, or crystallized rose or violet petals, or with piped blobs of chocolate buttercream.

Chocolate Fudge Brownies

It is vital that these yummy brownies be served with Vanilla Ice Cream (see page 329). They are very chocolatey and very good. They actually keep quite well in a tin, but the opportunity does not usually arise, because people don't stop eating them! They need to be undercooked, so test by sticking a knife or a skewer in the middle: it should come out with mixture clinging to it. If you don't like walnuts, just leave them out of the recipe. And do try making them with pecans instead of walnuts – they are even more delicious then!

Makes about 16

4 oz/112 g butter, diced
4 oz/112 g dark chocolate
10 oz/285 g soft light brown sugar
4 large eggs, beaten
8 oz/225 g plain flour
1½ oz/42 g cocoa powder
3 oz/84 g walnuts, chopped

Butter and flour a baking tin about 12 x 14 inches/30 x 35 cm.

Put the butter and chocolate, broken into bits, into a saucepan and melt together over a gentle heat. Add all the remaining ingredients and mix together very well. Pour this mixture into the prepared tin and bake in an oven preheated to 350°F/180°C/Gas Mark 4 for about 15 minutes, until still sticky in the middle. Remove from the oven and cool in the tin.

When cold, cut into small squares or rectangles and store in an airtight container. Serve warm, with Vanilla Ice Cream.

Chocolate and Orange Cake

This is a really fudgy-textured cake, flavoured with orange, and with a chocolate fudge icing. It is very simple to make, but so good!

Serves 8

For the cake:

6 oz/170 g butter
6 oz/170 g soft light brown sugar
2 oz/56 g self-raising flour
8 oz/225 g drinking chocolate powder
4 large eggs
Grated rind and juice of 1 orange

For the filling:

4 oz/112 g butter, softened
4 oz/112 g icing sugar, sieved
Grated rind of 1 orange

For the icing:

2 oz/56 g butter
2 oz/56 g granulated sugar
Juice of 1 orange
2 tbsp water
6 oz/170 g icing sugar
1 oz/28 g cocoa powder

Butter and flour two 8-inch/20-cm sandwich tins and line the base of each with a disc of non-stick baking parchment.

Cream the butter in a bowl, gradually adding the sugar. Beat really well until the mixture is soft and fluffy, then sieve together the flour and the drinking chocolate powder. Beat the eggs into the creamed mixture, alternately with spoonfuls of the sieved flour and drinking chocolate mixture. When it is all incorporated, beat in the orange rind and juice.

Pour the mixture into the two prepared tins and bake in an oven preheated to 350°F/180°C/Gas Mark 4 for 30 minutes. Remove the cakes from the oven and leave to cool in their tins for a few minutes before turning them on to wire racks. Leave until completely cold, then peel off the lining paper.

Meanwhile, make the orange buttercream for the filling. Cream the butter in a bowl, gradually adding the icing sugar and the orange rind. Beat until light and fluffy.

To make the icing, put the butter, granulated sugar, orange juice and water into a saucepan. Heat gently until the butter has melted and the sugar completely dissolved, then boil fast for 5 minutes. Sieve the icing sugar and cocoa together in a bowl, and beat in the boiled orange syrup. Beat from time to time until cool, thick and glossy.

To assemble the cake, put one of the cake halves on a serving plate and spread the buttercream evenly over the top. Put the remaining cake half on top. Cover the top and sides of the cake with icing. If you like, arrange pieces of crystallized orange peel around the edge of the top of the cake, either in a continuous circle, or in evenly spaced clusters.

Christmas Cake

This quantity makes a cake about 10 inches/25 cm in diameter.

6 oz/170 g chopped candied peel
6 oz/170 g glacé cherries, chopped
6 oz/170 g flaked almonds, toasted
1 lb/450 g sultanas
1 lb/450 g raisins
12 oz/340 g currants
6 oz/170 g dried apricots, snipped with scissors
10 oz/285 g plain flour, sieved
10 oz/285 g butter
10 oz/285 g soft brown sugar, light or dark, or muscovado
Grated rind of 2 lemons and 1 orange
3 tbsp black treacle (if you heat the spoon in very hot water or over a flame the treacle will slither off it easily)
6 eggs, beaten
1 rounded tsp ground mixed spice
1 rounded tsp freshly grated nutmeg
2 rounded tsp ground cinnamon
5 fl oz/200 ml brandy, sherry, or whisky

Prepare a 10-inch/25-cm round cake tin, by buttering it, then lining it with a double layer of baking parchment. Either tie a double thickness of brown paper round the outside of the tin, or, if you have one handy, put the tin in a small cardboard box. (This reduces the heat around the sides of the cake while baking.) Finally, cut two circles of baking parchment to go on top of the cake during cooking.

Prepare all the fruit. Chop the cherries, toast the almonds (if you like, I love the flavour which comes from them through the cake) and put all the fruit and the almonds together in a bowl, with 2 rounded table-spoons of the flour. Using your hands, mix all together thoroughly, so that the fruit is evenly coated with flour.

Beat together the butter and the sugar, beating until they are fluffy, and paler in colour. Beat in the grated orange and lemon rinds and the black treacle. Beating all the time, add the eggs, a little at a time, adding some of the flour at the same time to prevent the mixture from curdling. Then mix in the rest of the flour, the spices and the brandy, sherry or whisky. Lastly, stir in the mixed fruit.

Put the cake mixture into the prepared tin, hollowing down the middle with the back of the wooden spoon. Put the 2 circles of baking parchment on top of the cake, and put the cake into a moderate oven, 350°F/180°C/Gas Mark 4, for 20–30 minutes, then lower the heat to 275°F/ 140°C/Gas Mark 1 and bake for 3 more hours. Test to see if the cake is cooked by pushing a skewer into the centre. If it comes out clean, the cake is cooked. Remove from the oven, and cool in the tin.

Have ready a double thickness of foil, big enough to wrap completely round the cake. When the cake is cold, turn it out onto this foil. Before you wrap it up, stick a skewer into the cake all over, from top to bottom, and trickle some more brandy, sherry or whisky all over the cake. This part of the operation is purely optional, but it's what I do! Then wrap the cake up tightly and store it in a cool larder until you are ready to marzipan and ice it.

Toasted Coconut and Chocolate Cream Cake

This light, vanilla-flavoured sponge cake is filled and covered with whipped cream and toasted coconut, with a layer of grated dark chocolate in the filling and on top of the cake. The combination of the flavours of toasted coconut and dark chocolate is sublime.

Serves 8

For the cake:

3 large eggs

3 oz/84 g caster sugar

3 oz/84 g self-raising flour

1 tsp vanilla essence, or a few drops extract

For the filling and covering:

¾ pint/420 ml double cream

4 oz/112 g desiccated coconut, toasted until golden, then cooled completely

8 oz/225 g dark chocolate, grated

Butter two 8-inch/20-cm sandwich cake tins and line the base of each with a disc of non-stick baking parchment.

Whisk the eggs into a bowl, gradually adding the sugar. Continue whisking until the mixture is so thick that a trail from the end of the whisk holds its shape on the surface of the mixture. This takes about 7–10 minutes, using a hand-held electric whisk.

Sieve the flour and fold it with the vanilla essence thoroughly through the egg mixture, using a large metal spoon. Divide the mixture between the two prepared tins and smooth the tops. Bake in an oven preheated to 350°F/180°C/Gas Mark 4 for 20–25 minutes, or until the sides of the cakes are just beginning to shrink away from the sides of the tins. Remove the cakes from the oven, leave to cool for a couple of minutes in their tins, then turn them on to wire racks and leave to cool completely. When they are cold, peel off the lining paper.

To make the coconut cream for the filling and covering, whip the cream – not too stiffly – and fold in the coconut.

To assemble the cake, put one of the cakes on a serving dish and spread with some of the coconut cream. Sprinkle over some of the grated chocolate. Put the remaining cake on top. Cover the top and sides of the cake with the remaining coconut cream. Sprinkle the remaining grated chocolate over the top of the cake. Keep the cake in a cool place until you are ready to serve it. Use a serrated knife to cut the cake.

Coffee and Praline Cake

This is a delicious mixture of fudgy coffee icing, creamy filling, light sponge cake, and slightly crunchy praline. It really should be made the day it is to be eaten, but it could, at a pinch, be made the day before, because any leftovers seem to taste very good the next day!

Serves 8

For the praline:

2 oz/56 g granulated sugar

1 oz/28 g almonds, whole or flaked

For the cake:

3 large eggs

3 oz/84 g caster sugar

3 oz/84 g self-raising flour

1 level tbsp instant coffee powder

For the buttercream:

4 oz/112 g butter, softened

3 oz/84 g icing sugar, sieved

1 level dssp instant coffee powder

For the icing:

¼ pt/140 ml water

1 oz/28 g granulated sugar

2 oz/56 g butter

8 oz/225 g icing sugar, sieved

1 level dssp instant coffee powder

To make the praline, put the sugar and almonds together in a saucepan over a moderate to high heat, and shake the saucepan as the sugar begins to dissolve. When the sugar has dissolved completely and there is a golden syrup in the pan, pour on to a well-greased baking sheet and leave to cool and harden. When it is quite cold, cover the praline with a piece of greaseproof paper and bash it with a rolling pin into large crumb-sized bits. This praline keeps well in a screw-topped jar.

Line an 8-inch/20-cm cake tin with baking parchment. Put the eggs in a large bowl and whisk them until they are just beginning to thicken. Gradually add the caster sugar, whisking all together until the mixture is so thick that you can trace a squiggle off the end of the whisk which remains on top of the mixture. This takes about 7–10 minutes with a hand-held electric whisk.

Sieve the flour and coffee powder on to a plate or into a bowl and sieve it again on to the cake mixture – folding it in with a large metal spoon as quickly as possible. Pour the cake mixture into the prepared tin and bake in a moderate oven, 350°F/180°C/Gas Mark 4, for 25–30 minutes, until the cake is beginning to come away from the sides of the tin. Cool in the tin for 2–3 minutes, then turn on to a cooling rack and leave until quite cold. Using a serrated knife, cut the cake horizontally in half, and put the bottom half on a serving plate.

For the buttercream, beat the butter, gradually adding the sieved icing sugar and the coffee powder, and beating all together until light and fluffy. Spread this evenly over the bottom half of the cake, and put the other half on top.

Finally, make the fudge icing. Put the water, granulated sugar and butter together in a small saucepan. Place over a gentle heat until the sugar has dissolved and the butter melted, then turn up the heat and boil fast for about 5 minutes. Sieve the icing sugar into a bowl with the coffee powder. Stir in the boiled sugar and butter syrup, and beat from time to time as it cools. If it gets too stiff as it cools, add a very little boiling water. Spread this fudgy icing over the top and sides of the cake, and sprinkle the praline over the surface.

We sometimes make twice the amount of buttercream and, using a large star nozzle, pipe large rosettes round the top of the cake. If you want to make it a real showpiece, pipe rosettes round the bottom of the cake too – by now the cake will serve ten people!

Hazelnut and Apple Chocolate Cake

This is a very moist apple and hazelnut cake, with a covering of chocolate buttercream.

Serves 6–8

For the cake:

1 lb/450 g dessert apples

6 oz/170 g soft light brown sugar

¼ pint/140 ml sunflower oil

3 large eggs

6 oz/170 g self-raising flour

1 tsp bicarbonate of soda

3 oz/84 g hazelnuts, whizzed in a blender or processor to large crumb size, then toasted until pale golden, and cooled

2 tsp ground cinnamon

For the buttercream:

8 oz/225 g butter, softened

8 oz/225 g icing sugar

4 oz/112 g dark chocolate

1 tbsp water

½ tsp vanilla essence, or a few drops extract

To decorate:

3 oz/84 g dark chocolate, pared into curls using a potato peeler

To make the apple purée, chop but do not peel or core the apples and cook in a very little water until soft. Rub through a sieve and leave to cool.

Butter two 9-inch/23-cm sandwich cake tins, and line the base of each with non-stick baking parchment.

Mix together the apple purée and the sugar, then stir in the oil. Beat in the eggs, one at a time. Stir in the flour sieved with the soda, and the hazelnuts and cinnamon. Mix all together well.

Divide the mixture between the two prepared tins, smooth the tops and bake in an oven preheated to 350°F/180°C/Gas Mark 4 for 25–30 minutes, until a skewer stuck in the centre of the cake comes out clean. Remove the cakes from the oven and leave to cool in their tins for 5 minutes, then turn them on to wire racks and leave them to cool completely. Peel off the lining paper.

To make the buttercream, cream the butter, gradually adding the icing sugar, and beat until the mixture is fluffy. Break the chocolate into a small bowl and add the water. Stand the bowl over a pan of simmering water and heat gently, stirring occasionally, until the chocolate is melted. Cool slightly, then beat into the buttercream with the vanilla.

Put one of the cakes on a serving plate and spread with some of the buttercream. Put the remaining cake on top and cover the top and sides of the cake with the rest of the buttercream. Sprinkle with chocolate curls. Leave the cake in a cool place until set.

Orange Cake

This is another great favourite at home.

Serves 6

For the cake:

6 oz/170 g butter

6 oz/170 g caster sugar

3 medium eggs, separated

6 oz/170 g self-raising flour, sieved

Grated rind of 2 oranges

Juice of 1 orange

For the buttercream:

3 oz/84 g butter, softened

3 oz/84 g icing sugar, sieved

Grated rind of 1 orange

For the icing:

6 oz/170 g icing sugar, sieved

Juice of 1 orange, plus a few drops of
near-boiling water if needed

Grease and flour two 8-inch/20-cm sandwich cake tins.

Cream the butter and sugar together until they are light and fluffy. Beat the egg yolks, one by one, into the creamed mixture, then fold in the sieved flour and grated orange rind, and stir in the orange juice. Lastly, whisk the egg whites till they are stiff and fold them into the mixture.

Divide the mixture between the two tins and bake in an oven preheated to 350°F/180°C/Gas Mark 4 for 20–30 minutes. The cakes are cooked when a skewer inserted into the middle comes out clean. Take them out of the oven and leave to cool for a few minutes in the tins, then turn them on to a cooling rack to cool completely.

Make the buttercream by beating the butter, icing sugar and orange rind together, and use it to sandwich the cakes. Make the icing by mixing together the icing sugar and orange juice. Loosen with a little near-boiling water if necessary to make it spreadable. Cover the top of the cake with the orange-flavoured icing. It doesn't matter if the icing trickles down the sides.

Vanilla Sponge with Vanilla Buttercream and Raspberry Jam

This is one of the favourite cakes which appears on our tea-table. The lightest sponge cake is filled with a fluffy vanilla-flavoured buttercream and raspberry jam and the top of the cake is dusted with icing sugar. An alternative is to flavour the cake with the grated rind of a lemon, and to fill it with homemade lemon curd and whipped cream. The cake will freeze very well if cooled quickly and frozen immediately. You can fill it two or three hours before serving.

Serves 6

For the cake:

3 large eggs

3 oz/84 g caster sugar

A few drops of vanilla essence

3 oz/84 g self-raising flour, sieved twice

8 oz/225 g raspberry jam

Sieved icing sugar, to dredge

For the buttercream:

4 oz/112 g butter, softened

4 oz/112 g icing sugar, sieved

A few drops of vanilla essence

Butter two 8-inch/20-cm sandwich cake tins and line the base of each tin with baking parchment.

Break the eggs into a large mixing bowl, and whisk with an electric beater. Gradually add the sugar and vanilla essence, whisking until the mixture is very thick, almost white in colour and mousse-like in texture. This will take about 7 minutes. To test if the mixture is thick enough, stop whisking and lift the whisk out, trailing a squiggle of the mixture over the surface. If it sits on top, the mixture is thick enough; if it vanishes into the mixture, continue whisking! Sieve the flour over the mixture. Using a metal spoon, fold the flour quickly and thoroughly into the egg mixture.

Divide the mixture between the prepared cake tins, and bake in an oven preheated to 350°F/180°C/Gas Mark 4 for about 20 minutes, until the cakes are golden brown on top and just beginning to shrink from the sides of the tin. Cool on wire racks.

To make the buttercream, beat the butter until creamy and gradually add the icing sugar, beating until the buttercream is pale and fluffy. Beat in the vanilla essence.

Put one cake layer on a serving plate and spread it with the buttercream. Cover the buttercream with the raspberry jam, then put the second cake layer on top. Dredge icing sugar over the surface of the cake. This cake is easier to cut with a serrated knife.

Chocolate Mousse Cake ▶
page 361

Biscuits

Chocolate Oatmeal Crisp Biscuits
·
Flapjack Fingers
·
Crisp Ginger Biscuits
·
Sultana Biscuits
·
Walnut Toffee Squares
·
Dark Chocolate Truffles with Angostura Bitters

◀ Coffee, Chocolate and Almond
Meringue Gâteau, page 363

Chocolate Oatmeal Crisp Biscuits

These chocolatey biscuits have an extra crunch provided by the oatmeal. They seem to vanish as soon as they are made.

Makes 18–20

4 oz/112 g butter	
3 oz/84 g caster sugar	
4 oz/112 g plain flour	
1 oz/28 g cocoa powder	
A few drops of vanilla essence	
1 oz/28 g medium oatmeal	

Put the butter in a bowl and beat until smooth, then beat in the caster sugar, until well creamed. Sieve the flour and cocoa and stir into the creamed mixture with the vanilla and oatmeal, mixing thoroughly. You will have a stiffish dough.

Roll out on a floured work surface to a thickness of about ¼ inch/6 mm, and cut into circles about 2 inches/5 cm in diameter. Put the circles on a greased baking sheet. Bake in a preheated moderate oven, 350°F/180°C/Gas Mark 4, for 10–12 minutes.

Remove them from the oven and leave on the baking sheet for a minute, then carefully lift them on to a cooling rack. When they are quite cold store them in an airtight tin.

Flapjack Fingers

This recipe was given to me by Araminta Dallmeyer. When I arrive at the Dallmeyers' house around tea-time, I always make a bee-line for the biscuit tin in the hope of finding flapjacks within.

Makes 12

4 oz/112 g butter	
1 tbsp golden syrup	
4 oz/112 g caster sugar	
2 oz/56 g rolled oats	
2 oz/56 g self-raising flour	
3 oz/84 g cornflakes or Rice Krispies	

Melt the butter and golden syrup together in a saucepan, then stir in the remaining ingredients.

Spread the mixture about ½ inch/1 cm thick on to a greased baking tray, and bake for 15 minutes in a preheated hot oven, 400°F/200°C/Gas Mark 6.

Transfer to a rack to cool and cut into fingers before completely cold.

Crisp Ginger Biscuits

These don't take a minute to mix, and are very good. They keep very well in an air-tight tin.

Makes 12–16

4 oz/125 g butter	
4 oz/125 g caster sugar	
4 oz/125 g self-raising flour	
2½ tsp ground ginger	

Beat the butter until creamy and gradually beat in the caster sugar. When the mixture is light and fluffy, sieve in the flour and ginger and beat well. Roll the mixture into walnut-sized balls and put them on a baking sheet.

Bake at 300°F/150°C/Gas Mark 2 for 45–50 minutes, until golden brown. Leave to cool for a couple of minutes on the baking sheet, then gently lift the biscuits off on to a wire rack to cool completely.

Sultana Biscuits

These biscuits don't sound particularly exciting, but they are among the most delicious ones I know. They keep very well for two to three days in an airtight tin.

Makes 12–16

4 oz/112 g butter

4 oz/112 g caster sugar

1 tbsp golden syrup

6 oz/170 g self-raising flour, sieved

½ tsp bicarbonate of soda

2 oz/56 g sultanas

Beat the butter with the caster sugar and golden syrup until fluffy, then beat in the flour and bicarbonate of soda. Mix in the sultanas. Roll the dough into walnut-sized balls and arrange them on greased baking sheets.

Bake at 350°F/190°C/Gas Mark 5 for 15 minutes. Let set for a few minutes, then lift off the baking sheets with a palette knife and cool on a wire rack.

Walnut Toffee Squares

These are very easy to make, and quite delicious if you like nuts. You can do the whole recipe in a food processor, if you have one, or a mixer using a dough hook.

Makes 12

For the base:

4 oz/112 g butter, straight from the fridge

6 oz/170 g plain flour

2 oz/56 g brown sugar

For the top:

2 large eggs

2 rounded tsp ground cinnamon

3 oz/84 g desiccated coconut

4 oz/112 g broken walnuts

½ tsp vanilla essence, or a few drops extract

6 oz/170 g brown sugar

½ tsp baking powder

A pinch of salt

Put the base ingredients in the food processor and blend until the mixture is like crumbs. Then press it into a lightly greased 8-inch/20-cm tin. Bake in a moderate oven, 350°F/180°C/Gas Mark 4, for 15 minutes. Next mix together the remaining ingredients and spread on the top of the pastry. Cook for a further 15 minutes at the same temperature. Cool in the tin, and cut into squares.

Dark Chocolate Truffles with Angostura Bitters

These are delicious. Most people associate rum or brandy with truffles, but the Angostura bitters work really well.

Makes about 24–30

12 oz/340 g dark chocolate

2 tsp instant coffee dissolved in 2 tbsp boiling water

6 oz/170 g unsalted butter, diced

About ½ tsp Angostura bitters

Cocoa powder to finish

Break the chocolate into a heatproof bowl, and add the coffee liquid. Put the bowl over a saucepan of hot water, and heat very gently until the chocolate has melted. Remove the bowl from the pan and beat in the butter, bit by bit. Beat in the Angostura bitters and leave the mixture in a cool place until quite firm.

Sieve the cocoa powder over a work surface and rub some between the palms of your hands. Take a teaspoonful of the chocolate mixture and roll it into a ball between your hands. Roll it in cocoa and put it on a tray. Continue in the same way until all the chocolate mixture is used up.

Put the finished truffles in the fridge to firm up, then pack them into containers, with a layer of greaseproof paper between each layer of truffles.

Seasonal Availability of Foodstuffs in Britain

We are in danger of forgetting when foodstuffs are actually in their natural season in this country, because so much is flown to us out of season from around the world. As a result, a generation is growing up under the impression that strawberries are available twelve months of the year.

Unfortunately, imported fruit and vegetables just don't taste the same as home-grown produce. I was horrified recently to see raspberries on sale in March, flown in from Peru. They cost a fortune, and didn't even smell of raspberry, so what they tasted of I can't imagine.

I hope this table of seasonal availability will be of both interest and use to readers of this book.

Fruit and Nuts

Apples, cooking

Bramley's Seedling	Oct – July
Early Victory	Jul – Aug
Grenadier	Aug – Sept
Lord Derby	Oct onwards
Newton Wonder	Dec – Mar

Apples, eating (English)

Cox's Orange Pippin	Sept – May
Egremont Russet	Oct – Dec
George Cave	Jul – Sept
James Grieve	Aug – Sept
Laxton's Fortune	Sept – Oct
Scarlet Pimpernel	July
Worcester Pearmain	Sept – Nov

Apples, eating (imported)

Granny Smith	Mar – Aug
Red Delicious	Apr – Sept

Apricots	May – Aug
Bilberries	July – Aug
Blackberries	July – Oct
Blackcurrants	July – Aug
Blueberries	July – Sept
Cherries (English)	Jun – Jul
Cherries (imported)	Apr – Aug
Chestnuts	Oct – Dec
Crab apples	Sept – Oct
Cranberries	Oct – Feb
Figs	Aug – Dec
Gooseberries	end Apr – Sept
Hazelnuts	throughout autumn

Loganberries	July – Aug
Nectarines	July – Sept
Peaches (English, hot-house)	May – Oct
Peaches (imported)	Mar – Dec

Pears, dessert (English)

Comice	Oct – Dec
Conference	Sept – Feb
Packham's Triumph	Oct – Nov
William's	Aug
Winter Nelis	Nov – Jan

Pears, cooking (English)

Pitmaston Duchess	Oct – Dec

Pears, dessert (imported)

Comice	Mar – June
Packham's Triumph	Feb – June
William's	Nov – Mar
Winter Nelis	Feb – July

Plums and damsons, dessert

Czar	Aug
Kirk's Blue	Aug – Sept
Pershore	Aug
Victoria	Aug – Sept
Warwickshire Drooper	Sept

Quinces	Oct – Nov
Raspberries	July – Aug
Redcurrants	July – Aug

Rhubarb

forced	Dec – Apr
natural	Mar – Jun

Strawberries	May – Aug
Whitecurrants	July – Aug

Vegetables

Artichokes	
globe	late summer
Jerusalem	Oct – Mar
Asparagus (homegrown)	May – June
Aubergine	all year
Avocados	all year
Beetroot	all year
Beans	
broad	Apr – Sept
French	all year
kidney	June – Nov
runner	July – Oct
Broccoli	all year
Brussels sprouts	Aug – Mar
Cabbage	
spring	Apr – May
spring greens	Nov – Apr
summer & autumn	June – Oct
winter	Aug – Mar
white	Oct – Feb
savoy	Aug – May
red	Aug – Jan
Calabrese	July – Dec
Carrots	all year
Cauliflower	all year
Celeriac	Oct – Mar
Celery	most of year
Chicory	most of year
Courgettes	all year
Cucumber	best late summer
Endive	late autumn – winter

Fennel	all year
Garlic	all year
Horseradish	Sept – Mar
Kale	Nov – May
Kohl rabi	July – Apr
Leeks	Aug – May
Lettuce	all year
Marrow	July – Oct
Mushrooms	all year
Okra	Dec – June
Onions (homegrown)	Sept – Mar
Parsnips	Sept – Apr
Peas (homegrown)	May – Oct
Peppers	all year
Salsify	Oct – May
Sea kale	Aug – Mar
Shallots	Sept – Mar
Spinach	all year, best Mar – Apr
Spring onions	Mar – May
Sweetcorn (homegrown)	July – Nov
Sweet potato	winter
Tomatoes (homegrown)	Mar – Nov
Turnips	Aug – Mar
Watercress	all year

Fish

White fish

Bass	May – Aug
Bream	June – Dec
Brill	Jan – Apr
Catfish	Sept – Feb
Cod	Oct – April
Cod roe	Jan – Feb
Coley	all year
Dab	Apr – Jan
Dogfish (Huss)	Sept – May
Dover sole	all year, best May – Feb
Flounder	Sept – Feb
Haddock	all year, best Nov – Feb
Hake	July – Mar
Halibut	Aug – Apr
Lemon sole	Dec – Mar
Monkfish	all year, best Jan – Mar
Plaice	all year, best Jan – Apr
Skate	Oct – Apr
Turbot	all year, best Apr – July
Whiting	all year

Oily fish

Carp	June – Mar
Eel	
common	autumn/early winter
conger	Mar – Oct
Herring	all year, best June – Mar
Mackerel	all year, best winter/spring
Mullet	
grey	July – Feb
red	May – Sept
Perch	*Season:* 16 June – 14 Mar
Pike	*Season:* 16 June – 14 Mar
Salmon	
farmed	all year
wild	best May – July
Sardine	Mar – Sept
Smelt	Jan – Mar
Sprat	autumn/winter
Trout	
rainbow, farmed	all year
rainbow, river	Mar – Sept
sea, farmed	all year
sea, wild	Mar – July
Whitebait	Feb – July

Shellfish

Clam	all year, best autumn	**Mussels**	all year, best Sept – Mar
Cockles	all year, best Sept – Apr	**Oysters**	Sept – Apr
		Prawns	all year
Crab	all year, best May – Oct	**Scallops**	all year, best Sept – Mar
Crayfish	Apr – Sept	**Shrimps**	all year
Dublin Bay prawns	all year, best May – Nov	**Whelks**	all year, best Sept – Feb
Lobster	all year, best Apr – Aug	**Winkles**	all year, best Oct – May

Game

Grouse	*Season:* 12 Aug – 10 Dec, best Aug – Oct	**Quail**	all year
		Rabbit	all year
Hare	*Season:* 1 Aug – 31 Mar, best Oct onwards	**Snipe**	*Season:* 12 Aug – 31 Jan, best Nov
Mallard	*Season:* 1 Sept – 28 Feb, best Nov/Dec	**Teal**	*Season:* 1 Sept – 28 Feb, best Dec
Partridge	*Season:* 1 Sept – 31 Jan, best Oct /Nov	**Venison**	*Season:* June – Jan
Pheasant	*Season:* 1 Oct – 31 Jan, best Nov/Dec	**Wild goose**	*Season:* Oct – end Dec
Pigeon	all year, best Aug – Oct	**Woodcock**	*Season:* 1 Oct – 31 Jan, best Nov/Dec

Suggestions for Seasonal Menus

You will find here three menus for each of our seasons – spring, summer, autumn and winter. These menus consist of suggestions for recipes using not only foods in their relevant seasons, but also the type of dish I feel inclined towards in the varying seasons. Cheese Beignets with Tomato Sauce make an ideal first course in cold winter months, for instance, whereas a cool Watercress and Lime Mousse with a Roast Red Pepper Sauce is perfect for a warm summer's day. And Cinnamon Crêpes with Apple and Calvados Brandy Butter are delicious and autumnal, whereas walnut and brown sugar meringues with Rhubarb and Ginger Sauce are a perfect pudding for springtime.

However, as I am so fond of saying, taste is a very personal thing. These are only my suggestions, of combinations of dishes I like. The choice in the end, obviously, is yours!

Spring

1

Jerusalem Artichoke Timbales
with Sauce Bercy

•

Lamb Cutlets Braised in Red Wine and Redcurrant Jelly

•

Brown Sugar Meringues with Rhubarb
and Ginger Sauce

2

Warm Chicken Liver Salad

•

Fish Cakes with Creamy Saffron and Lemon Sauce

•

Hot Baked Chocolate Cheesecake

3

Chicken and Smoked Bacon Filo Pastry Parcels
with Chive Cream Sauce*

•

Mixed Fish Mayonnaise

•

Lemon and Vanilla Soufflés

* Simmer together ½ pint double cream, small bunch
snipped chives, salt and pepper
for two minutes – then serve.

Summer

1

*Marinated Cod with Sweet Pepper
and Garlic Sauce*

•

Asparagus Puff Pastry Parcels with Hollandaise Sauce

•

*Blackcurrant and Blackcurrant Leaf
Water Ice*

2

Herb Crêpes with Smoked Salmon and Cucumber

•

*Chicken Breasts with Aubergines,
Tomatoes and Garlic*

•

Tarte aux Fruits with Crème Pâtissière

3

Watercress and Lime Mousse with Red Pepper Sauce

•

*Monkfish with Tomatoes, Garlic and
Black Olives*

•

Cinnamon Pavlova with Blackcurrant Cream

Autumn

1

Fish and Vegetable Chowder

•

Collops of Pork Fillet with Cream,
Brandy and Apple Sauce

•

Brown Bread Ice Cream with Blackberry Sauce

2

Game Soup

•

Mushroom and Garlic Roulade

•

Frozen Plum, Cinnamon and Port Parfait

3

Crab Mousse

•

Silverside of Beef with Root Vegetables,
Dumplings and Horseradish Dressing

•

Cinnamon Crêpes with Calvados Butter
and Spiced Apple Filling

Winter

1

Cheese Beignets with Tomato Sauce

•

Winter Navarin of Lamb

•

*Toasted Coconut Ice Cream with
Brandy and Mincemeat Sauce*

2

Deep-fried Mushrooms with Tartare Sauce

•

*Baked Glazed Ham with Tomato and
Madeira Sauce*

•

*Mrs Hill's Christmas Pudding with
Orange-Flavoured Brandy Butter*

3

Pipérade with Garlic Croûtes

•

*Peppered Fillet Steak with Stilton Cheese
and Chive Butter*

•

*Hot Fresh Fruit Salad with Honey,
Ginger and Cardomom, with Frozen
Honey and Whisky Creams*

Index